FRANK MOYA PONS

THE
DOMINICAN REPUBLIC

A NATIONAL HISTORY

HISPANIOLA BOOKS
New Rochelle, N.Y.
1995

HISPANIOLA BOOKS CORPORATION
171 Sutton Manor, New Rochelle, NY 10801

This edition is published by Hispaniola Books Corporation
for the Dominican Studies Institute
of The City University of New York (CUNY)
at The City College of New York.

The CUNY Dominican Studies Institute gratefully acknowledges
the financial support of the Aaron Diamond Foundation
and the Honorable John Brian Murtaugh of the
New York State Assembly for the publication of this book.

Library of Congress Cataloging-in-Publication Data
Moya Pons, Frank
The Dominican Republic: A National History
Frank Moya Pons
544 p. Bibliography Index Maps
ISBN 1-885509-00-6 (Hardcover)
ISBN 1-885509-01-6 (Paperback)
1. Dominican Republic-History
2. Dominican Republic-Economic conditions
3. Dominican Republic-Politics and government
4. Dominican Republic-Foreign relations

Library of Congress Catalog Card Number: 94-76411

9 8 7 6 5 4 3 2 1 0
Printed in the United States on acid-free paper
Text and graphics composed by Lourdes Saleme y Asociados

Contents

Introduction

The Dominican Republic is one of the least studied countries in Latin America and the Caribbean despite the fact that it is the longest European-inhabited territory in the hemisphere. This book is an attempt to fill this academic gap by providing a modern historical narrative of the economic, social, and political evolution of Dominican society from pre-Columbian times to the present.

In contrast to their West Indian neighbors, Dominicans consider themselves more Latin American than Caribbean, a fact that often strikes scholars and travelers who approach the country for the first time. Readers of this book will see how in their early evolution as a nation, Dominicans diverged from their West Indian counterparts without losing their character as a Caribbean society.

Before becoming an independent nation, Dominicans experienced the political domination of Spain, France, Great Britain, and Haiti. The long colonial past produced a complex heritage out of Arawak, Spanish, African and French traditions that influenced the formation of many features of present-day Dominican society, but not all.

The Dominican Republic attained political independence before slavery was abolished in the Spanish Caribbean and over a century before decolonization became effective in the rest of the Caribbean. Both Haiti and the Dominican Republic stand out as examples of early national communities whose autonomous political history set them apart from the colonial societies of the surrounding islands.

Historically, the Dominican Republic has always maintained very close ties with the United States. After independence, and during the U.S. Civil War, the Dominican elite relinquished political autonomy and annexed the country to Spain. A bloody war convinced Spain that it could no longer rule its ancient colony, and had to evacuate it shortly afterwards.

Almost immediately, the Dominican leaders sought to annex the country to the United States and negotiated an annexation treaty that was barely defeated in the U.S. Senate in 1871. Had the U.S. Senate approved that treaty, the Dominican Republic would have entered the Union much before Utah, Oregon, Alaska, and Hawai, and would have opened the way for the annexation of Cuba and Puerto Rico.

The Dominican Republic fell under U.S. military rule in 1916, as a corollary of previous interventions in Panamá, Mexico, Nicaragua, and Haiti. The U.S. military government accelerated the modernization of Dominican society between 1916 and 1924. This book studies the economic and political continuities between the U.S. military government and subsequent regimes including the infamous Trujillo dictatorship that ruled the country from 1930 to 1961.

The text also covers the contemporary political scenario, focusing on the intense drama of a national community that incessantly struggles to built a democracy against the will of a corrupt and authoritarian political elite that clings to power at all costs.

This volume is based on my *Manual de Historia Dominicana*, which is now into its updated 9th edition. Yet, this is an entirely new book with a different structure. It is the only complete Dominican history available in English. Shortly after publication, the *Manual* became a standard text and reference book for universities and secondary schools across the Dominican Republic and abroad.

Given its ample acceptance, many scholars and friends urged me to prepare an English version intended for the U.S. and British markets. Though reluctant at first, I eventually realized that their enthusiasm was quite resonable, particularly after I had spent two years teaching Latin American History at Columbia University, and two more years teaching Caribbean History at the University of Florida. Then I was able to detect a very pressing need for a complete history of the Dominican Republic in English.

There are thousands of students in U.S. colleges and universities who must take courses in Latin American and Caribbean history, and need to understand how the Dominican Republic became a separate entity within its Caribbean neighbors. There are also thousands of tourists, travelers, business people, and diplomats who want to know more about the Dominican Republic's history. To all of them I dedicate this edition.

I have prepared this book with the help of many friends who have always believed in its value as a basic history text. I wish to express my gratitude to them for their permanent support, and I start with Rosa María Vicioso de Mayol, who many years ago persuaded the directors of the Gulf & Western Foundation in La Romana, Dominican Republic, to allocate a grant to pay for a draft translation.

As I edited the translation, I requested the advise of several friends who read it carefully and helped me to rewrite and improve the text. Among them, I gratefully acknowledge Pilar Soto de Rainieri, Jeannette Canals, Sarah Uribe, Humberto García Muñiz, Renée Merwin, Carol Bernard, Peter Frazer, Patricia Sharp, Robert Hurtwitch, Julie Franks, Raymond Rifenburg and Virginia Moore. Needless to say, none of them is responsible for my historical interpretations or for any errors this book may still contain.

I am equally grateful to Dr. Silvio Torres-Saillant, Director of the City University of New York Dominican Studies Institute at City College, and to his colleague at CUNY's LaGuardia Community College Professor Ramona Hernández. The Institute provided me the opportunity to work in the final preparation of the manuscript by inviting me to become a Visiting Research Professor at City College during the academic year 1993-94. Thanks to the CUNY Dominican Studies Institute this book circulates today in the United States. I hope it will serve to highten the cultural awareness of the thousands of Dominicans who live in the United States.

Frank Moya Pons

1.
Geography and the aboriginal population

GEOGRAPHY

Located between Cuba and Puerto Rico, the island of Hispaniola is the second largest in the Antilles. It is the only Caribbean island divided between two nations, Haiti and the Dominican Republic. Geologically, it is also the most complex. It is formed by the conjunction of several underwater ridges that originate in Central America and connect with the volcanic chains of the Lesser Antilles that link with the northern fringes of South America. The trade winds and the rugged topography are responsible for extreme ecological variations within the island. Rains normally fall on the windward northeastern slopes of the mountains leaving behind them a warm, humid, tropical environment with hundreds of rivers and streams. The leeward southwestern slopes are normally dry, and the land is covered by cacti and desert-like vegetation.

Three mountain chains extend across the island from east to west. Between them lie several long and narrow valleys and plains which have long been the main centers of population and agricultural production. The most important of these plains is the Cibao Valley. It stretches from the Bahía de Samaná, in the east, to the Plain du Nord, in northern Haiti. The Cibao Valley has four distinctive ecological regions. First, the eastern wetlands and swamps of the Yuna river basin, which remained almost depopulated until they were drained and developed in recent decades. Second, the fertile alluvial plains of the Central Cibao Valley, where most of the rural population originally settled. Third, the dry, semi-desert lands of the Yaque river basin, which remained almost depopulated until the introduction of irrigation in the 20th century. Fourth, the humid fertile Plaine du Nord in present-day Haiti, which receives a fair amount of rain and has been continually settled and cultivated since the mid-17th century. (See map No. 1)

Separating the north from the south, the island is crossed by the Cordillera Central, called Massif Central in Haiti, with elevations rising quickly to more than 10,000 feet. Given the complexity of this formation, there is considerable variation in temperature and rainfall according to the altitude of its regions. Ecological differences are sharp within several dozen miles, and the traveler easily passes from the very humid to the very dry lands, or from very hot lowlands to cool highlands in a drive of less than one hour. The Cordillera Central contains extensive pine forests, and some small alpine valleys that have been settled and developed in the 20th century. Enclosed in the western section of the cordillera lies the San Juan Valley which becomes the Plaine Centrale in Haiti. This is a low-altitude valley with extensive savannas suitable for cattle grazing.

The Cordillera de Baoruco dominates the southwestern section of the island. This mountain range is called Massif du Sud in Haiti. Some parts of it are still covered by pine forests, but most of it has been eroded through centuries of overcultivation and overgrazing. This is a common problem to most areas of the western side of the island. The trade winds discharge their rains in the eastern side presently occupied by the Dominican Republic, leaving the Haitian territory with little rainfall for productive agriculture. There are some small plains between the Massif Central and the Massif du Sud that have been intensively exploited since colonial times with the help of irrigation. Though most Haitian plains and valleys are small and dry, the Dominican Republic contains extensive valleys that are flat, fertile, humid, and well drained. The most important eastern flatlands are the Llanos del Este, a region bigger than Puerto Rico, that has been associated with cattle grazing since colonial times, and with sugar cane cultivation from the late 19th century on.

As in the rest of the Caribbean, the climate of Hispaniola is fairly even, with an average yearly temperature of 82 degrees Fahrenheit. The mountains are high enough to produce two distinct rainy seasons for both the north and the south. The north is rainy, cool, and humid during the winter months when the island is under the influence of the northern cold fronts. Because most of the humidity is retained in the northeastern slopes of the cordilleras, the south remains fairly dry, with calm seas, and fresh breezes from December to April. This pattern reverts in May. Then, the southern rainy season starts, while the northern lands start drying up. During the summer months, the south becomes more humid and hot, with heavy showers and thunderstorms becoming more frequent as the hurricane season approaches. Hurricanes are a common occurrence, and are intimately connected with the economic history of the southern region, particularly the city of Santo Domingo, which has been hit and devastated on numerous occasions.

Another common occurrence with important consequences in colonial and early republican times are the earthquakes, some of which destroyed entire cities that had to be moved to other sites or entirely rebuilt. A major earthquake completely destroyed Santiago and La Vega in 1562. Another one seriously damaged most of Santo Domingo in 1666. Azua was entirely devastated in 1751 by another earthquake that seriously damaged Santo Domingo. In 1842 another one completely razed Cap Haitien and Santiago. A more recent one produced severe damages in Nagua, La Vega, and Santiago in 1946. As construction techniques have improved, massive destruction has been avoided in recent decades, but the island is still subjected to frequent and often intense tremors, some reaching a level of 6 on the Richter scale. The aboriginal population feared hurricanes more than earthquakes. They called these tropical storms *huracán*, and held them to be powerful gods.

Despite these occasional disasters, the island enjoys a gentle climate and favorable temperatures as the tropical heat is moderated by a constant breeze created by the trade winds. Despite deforestation, the island remains pleasantly green due to its very fertile soils. Its skies are normally dotted with cottonwool clouds that discharge sporadic showers refreshing the hot summer days.

In prehistoric times, most of the land was covered with dense tropical forests inhabited by a varied fauna of birds, reptiles, spiders, and insects. The early Spanish chroniclers pointed out that none of these animals was poisonous enough to kill a human being. The island's complex landscape composed of multiple valleys and hills, swamps and savannas, and lakes and ponds, contains numerous ecological niches that were eventually settled by prehistoric migrants from South America. These early settlers still inhabited the island when the first Europeans arrived in 1492.

3,000 YEARS OF MIGRATION

Among the peoples who inhabited the Antilles prior to 1492, the aborigines of Hispaniola achieved the highest level of development. The theory of a South American origin, which is now undisputed, is supported by the similarities in language, their use of tobacco, their housing construction techniques, the cultivation of maize and manioc, their use of the hammock, the construction of canoes and, above all, by their ceramic styles. Archaeologists have unearthed and studied thousands of objects that reveal a society comparable to some of the early neolithic societies of ancient Europe. These artifacts, and the records left by some Spanish chroniclers show that at some point in their social evolution these peoples started developing cultural characteristics that eventually distinguished them from the jungle peoples of the Orinoco and Amazon river basins, from which they originated. This is revealed by many objects not found in South American cultures, such as the carved three-cornered stones that were used in ceremonies and rites for the fertilization of the earth.

It is not clear what prompted the first native groups to migrate from the tropical forests of South America to the Caribbean islands more than 3,000 years BC. The process was slow and sporadic, covering four clearly different migratory waves. The first migrants were nomadic people who made their homes in natural shelters, such as caves and overhangs on the banks of rivers, swamps, inlets, and coves, where they fished or collected their food. These people were neither farmers nor potters. Originally, the archaeologists called them Ciboneys, using the name discovered by chronicler Bartolomé de Las Casas in the 16th century, when there were still a few of these Indians living on the far west side of Cuba, at Punta Guanahacabibes, and at Punta Tiburón on the west side of Hispaniola. Today they are now known as "preceramist archaic groups."

The second group, traditionally known as the Igneri, were excellent ceramicists. They came from the great Arawak stock who still live in the tropical forests of South America. Today archeaologists call them "Saladoids," deriving the name from sites found in Saladero, Venezuela. These Indians eventually spread throughout most of the Lesser Antilles and various parts of Puerto Rico and Hispaniola, displacing or absorbing the Ciboney populations.

The third period covered a long migratory wave of Arawak groups from Venezuela and the Guianas, who, in spreading out, virtually absorbed or eliminated some of the Igneris and any remaining Ciboneys, and contributed to a more uniform population of the islands. This movement began just prior to the Christian era and lasted some 1,000 years. During this period independent cultural traditions evolved, and the Taíno culture and society appeared. By 700 AD this culture had well-defined characteristics. The Taínos inhabited and controlled most of the Greater Antilles when the Europeans arrived in 1492.

The fourth and last period began some time around the 11th century, with new migrant groups also belonging to the Arawak stock, but possessing different cultural characteristics from the earlier Taíno settlers. They were the Caribes: great navigators, well trained in the use of the bow and arrow, and eaters of human flesh, who wasted no time in assimilating the remaining Igneri of Trinidad and the Lesser Antilles. The Caribes hunted and ate the Taíno men and enslaved their women who served them as cooks, weavers, and potters. By the time Christopher Columbus reached America, the Caribes had spread throughout the Lesser Antilles, making frequent incursions into Puerto Rico and the eastern part of Hispaniola, and attacking the Taíno settlers.

ABORIGINAL LIFESTYLE

The Taínos became farmers without losing their fishing and hunting skills, thus holding on to the cultural traits that had proven useful in adapting to the environment of the Antilles. Their main legacy to Dominican society was the introduction of a number of plants that they evidently brought from South America during early migrations. The most important was the *yucca* (manioc) from which they made cassava bread using a complicated procedure similar to that still used today on the island. The Spaniards called cassava the "bread of the Indies," as the lack of wheat flour forced them to eat it in a variety of ways. Another important crop was *maíz* (corn). This word made its way to the continent, where the Spaniards adopted it. Other staple vegetables in the Taínos' diet were the *batata* (sweet potatoes), the *maní* (peanuts), some yams and tubers, and three types of chili peppers.

Most of the protein consumed by the Indians came from what they hunted and fished. At the time of the Spaniards' arrival there was still an abundance of small rodents and guinea pigs whose meat was prized by the Taínos. They also hunted iguanas and snakes, which they ate with pleasure. Bird hunting was normally left to the youngsters, who climbed trees to catch parrots, doves, and other birds. Fish, both salt and freshwater, were abundant. The Taínos used elaborate nets and made hooks out of fish bones to catch shrimp, crabs, and fish. The Taínos and Caribes also liked to eat worms, snails, sea conch, bats, spiders, and insects. They used harpoons to hunt the manatee that abounded in the shallow waters off the island's coasts.

In addition to farming, hunting, and fishing, Taíno men spent a great deal of time building their homes, which they called *buhíos*. There were two types: The most common was the circular style with a cone-shaped roof. The roof and walls were made from vines and palm leaves. The other style, made out of the same materials, was rectangular and generally larger, and was usually made for caciques or Indian chiefs.

The women made objects out of clay, such as pots, plates, bread pans, jugs, vats, and other cooking utensils. Large numbers of these objects have been found in archaeological sites. Basket weaving was also widely practiced, and they even made small idols out of cotton. All ceramic and woven goods were made without a wheel or loom, as these tools were unknown to the Taínos. They also made vases, spoons, and glasses using gourds from the common calabash tree that they planted specifically for this purpose. Canoes were built from a single tree trunk, usually from mahogany and *ceiba* trees The construction of clubs for combat and war was men's work, as was the making of stone hatchets which had various uses, including military ones. Fire was generally saved, but when it did go out it was started again by rubbing a smooth twig against two splinters from the light-wood *guázima* tree.

FAMILY AND SOCIAL STRUCTURE

Most of the Taínos were monogamous, although polygamy was common among caciques and other leaders. This suggests a social stratification based on economic wealth and political power. Both the commoners and the leaders were organized in large extended families, and many couples and their children lived under the same roof. Central authority was in the hands of the father, and the family structure appears to have been predominantly patriarchal.

Inheritance and succession, however, were matrilineal: in important families, when the father or cacique died, inheritance went to the oldest son, but if there was no son it went to the oldest son or daughter of the dead man's sister, because that bloodline could be accurately traced. Clans were also organized matrilineally, as far as succession of power and inheritance of goods were concerned. The Taínos were exogamous and horrified at incest, which they viewed as a portent of "bad death." Social punishment for incest was ostracism, the worst stigma that could befall an individual belonging to a society that strongly stressed community life.

The number of children in each nuclear family varied from three to five. They lived with their parents, apparently in the home of the paternal grandparents, and were educated by their parents and clan elders, education being both a family and community responsibility. Mothers were expected to nurture and raise their children, while fathers taught them hunting and farming skills. Boys were instructed in farming and other techniques, and girls learned tasks needed in the home. Thus, children learned to live according to a division of labor based on sexual differentiation. This division placed more work on women than men: in addition to weaving hammocks, women were expected to cook, prepare the cassava bread, and handcraft all of the domestic tools.

Men took care of planting, fishing, and hunting, as well as the construction of huts, which sometimes had to be large enough to house ten couples and their children. In their free time, men traded spare homemade goods at fairs held in the central plaza of the villages, known as the *batey*. Sixteenth-century chronicler Bartolomé de Las Casas wrote that trading went on at great length and that the actual value of the items bartered was not always equal. The Taínos used no currency, unlike the Incas, who used coca leaves as money, and the Aztecs, who used cocoa beans.

One of the most notable features of the Taíno society was its high degree of social solidarity, especially among clan members. The Spaniards noted that there were rarely quarrels within clans. The social structure itself encouraged tribal unity. Being a matrilineal organization with a tradition of patrilocal residence, ties between clans, groups, and tribes increased and theoretically strengthened as families grew and exogamous marriages increased. Marriage took place via a ceremony apparently equivalent to the buying of the bride. Gifts, usually necklaces made from pebbles and bones, were bestowed on members of the bride's family. The violation of an engagement agreement was cause for serious —and sometimes armed— conflict between the two clans. Fighting could also be prompted by territorial raids, thus the Taínos were careful not to hunt or fish in territories belonging to other tribes.

POLITICAL ORGANIZATION

The Taínos were united in a common front against the Caribes, who were their greatest threat of extinction. The Caribes periodically invaded the bigger islands in hopes of capturing and eating Taíno men and enslaving the women to use them as breeders of children who would then be castrated, fattened, and eaten. All of the Taínos on the big islands were well aware of the danger posed by the Caribes. On his first voyage, Columbus was warned in both Cuba and the Bahamas about the Caribes' cannibalism and fierceness. This common threat apparently served as a catalyst in the banding together of the various tribes of the island. A formal confederation of tribes seems to have been on the verge of formation in 1492, but it was interrupted by the Spaniards' arrival. There were intertribal marriages between rulers of at least two confederate Taíno tribes, suggesting that the tendency was toward establishing dynastic links that would eventually lead to the island's political unity.

There were five confederate Indian tribes on the island. They were headed by caciques Guarionex, Caonabo, Behechío, Goacanagarix, and Cayacoa. Spanish chronicler Oviedo describes them and their caciques in clear terms: Guarionex governed the flatlands and ruled more than 70 leagues in the center of the island. Behechío had the western part of the land. Goacanagarix ruled the northern part. Cayacoa held the eastern part. His people were considered to be the bravest because of their proximity to the Caribes. Caonabo, who had his kingdom in the mountains, had been a Caribe cacique. He married Anacaona, sister of Behechío.

Caonabo's marriage shows that some Caribes had already been accepted by the Taínos, possibly in exchange for having given up cannibalism. On the northeastern part of the island, where the Ciguayo lived, the bow and arrow were used, indicating that the Ciguayos may have been the result of mixing between Caribes and Taínos. According to Las Casas, many Ciguayos had forgotten their own language and spoke that of the Taínos, or a mixture of the two. Las Casas wrote that in the Ciguayo province of Macorix Arriba, the natives "spoke a strange language, almost barbaric." Although they used bows and arrows, they had lost the Caribe custom of poisoning the darts with the caustic latex of the *guao* plant. But they had kept the Caribe tradition of letting their hair grow long and painting their bodies black and red to appear more fearsome in battle. The Ciguayos were the Indians who attacked Columbus during his first stop on the island, at a place he called "Gulf of Arrows."

Political power was exercised with little or no democracy. Decisions to go to war were made by the leaders, without popular participation. Prominent among these leaders was the *behique*, a sort of witch-doctor who wielded considerable power over all members of the tribe, not only because he acted as intermediary between the men and their gods, but also because of his position as a medicine man. Without his approval, the Taínos would not undertake any important activity. *Behiques* were chosen for their skills as interpreters of dreams and for the accuracy of their predictions.

The government was headed by the caciques and their assistants, known as *nitaínos*, who composed the noble class within the Taíno social structure. They seem to have been the caciques' closest maternal relatives, or important clan chiefs who because of their influence over tribe members formed the necessary link between the caciques and the people. To exercise power, the caciques were assisted by a council of elderly *nitaíno* chiefs from confederate tribes. The cacique's legitimacy must have been determined through his acceptance by clan chiefs.

The *nitaíno* class and the caciques were served by a large servant class called the *naborías*. Today no one knows where or how the *naborías* originated. They seem to have been the remnants of the Igneri population assimilated and dominated by the Taínos. The existence of the *naborías* helps to explain the perplexing testimony of the early chroniclers who pointed out that all land was owned in common in a sort of primitive communism. It was worked by all tribe members without the commoners being burdened with taxes or contributions to sustain their rulers. The *naborías*, as an isolated layer specifically dedicated to the support of the caciques and their families, allowed the bulk of the populace to share goods and services collectively rather than work to pay tribute to support their rulers.

MYTHS AND RELIGIOUS EXPRESSION

The Taínos all spoke a common language and shared a common religious creed. Their South American origin was so remote that it was forgotten, and they considered themselves the original inhabitants of the islands. This is evident in their myths about creation, which also reflect their deep identification with their environment. Some of these myths were compiled by Fray Ramón Pané, at the request of Columbus, who wanted to learn more about the Indians' religious beliefs.

Pané's sources told him that the sun and the moon had come out of a cave called Jovovava. At that time there was no sea, and the human race lived in two mountains called Cacibajagua and Amayauna. From Cacibajagua "emerged most of the people who inhabited the island. When they lived in that cave, they kept watch at night, and put in charge someone called Macocael" with the job of watching over those leaving the cave in order to

divide them over the land. One day, Macocael was late in returning to the cave, and he was caught by the sun's rays and
turned into stone near the door. Legend has it that others were
likewise caught by the sun: one was turned into a nightingale
while gathering herbs at sunrise and others were turned into
trees called *jobos*.

Because of these events, one Indian named Guaguyona became angry and decided to leave the cave. He convinced all the
women to abandon their husbands and go with him. Their children were deserted near a stream, where they cried out in hunger and turned into frogs. The women were also eventually abandoned "and in that manner, all the men were left without wom-
en." The men's yearning for women made them go out in search
of footprints on rainy days, but to no avail.

One day, when they went to the river to wash, they saw "a
type of person, neither male nor female, man nor woman" moving through the branches of certain trees. They tried to catch
these beings, but they "slipped away as if they were eels." The
cacique sent for victims of a disease called *caracaracol*, similar to
mange, so that they could catch the strange creatures with their
rough hands. "After they had trapped them, they met to discuss
how they could turn them into women, as they had neither male
nor female sex." They bound their hands and feet and placed
woodpeckers on their bodies. "The birds, thinking they were trees
pecked away at the spot where the female sex organs usually are.
This is how the Indians obtained women, according to the old
people." From that moment on, and with the sun's permission,
men and women were able to move about in broad daylight.

Another myth, reminiscent of Asian and Yucatecan myths
about the universal deluge, tells of the creation of the sea. According to the Taínos, there was a man named Yaya who had a
son named Yayael. The son wished to kill his father, but the
father disowned him first and later killed him, placing his bones
in a gourd, which he hung from the ceiling of his house. One day

Yaya wanted to see his son, so he and his wife opened the gourd, finding that the bones had turned into fish, which they ate. On another day, when Yaya and his wife were away, the four children of a woman who had died giving birth to quadruplets came to the house, and one of them took down the gourd and started to eat the fish. Suddenly they heard Yaya returning, and in scrambling to hang up the gourd, it fell to the ground and broke. So much water poured from the gourd that it covered the earth, and fish came forth too, and that was the origin of the sea.

These myths were transmitted orally from one generation to the next by the most respected elders of the family, clan, or tribe. They formed part of a body of beliefs preserved in measured verses that were always sung in exactly the same way at festive gatherings called *areítos*. These were celebrations of past events in the life of the tribe that were considered important enough to be remembered. They were primarily didactic and tended to reinforce tribal unity, creating a feeling of identity with, and participation in, a common history.

More practical aspects of the Taínos' religion were carried out by the *behiques*, who made ample use of magic in healing the sick. These medicine men were great herbalists and knew the medicinal properties of many trees, plants, and herbs. Because they healed many people with this art, they were objects of great veneration and respect. Each witch-doctor had his own idols that were believed to have curative properties. There seems to have been a religious hierarchy among the Taíno idols. Some were used in rituals relating to rain, planting, harvesting, while others were used in private and familial ceremonies.

The Taínos' animism and spiritualism led them to assign religious significance and representation to many objects they made for daily use. These they decorated with symbolic designs. Similar designs appear in caves and bathing places. Paintings and engravings of birds, alligators, and crustaceans that formed part of their diet are frequent, alternating with other, more abstract, drawings related to religious life. In all the Caribbean islands the Taínos left many pictures and petroglyphs with common religious allegories and naturalistic themes. This suggests that most inhabitants of the Antilles shared a common body of religious beliefs.

The Taínos' artistic and religious imagination is best captured in their stone and ceramic work. More durable than wood, cloth or fiber, it has remained as a testimony of their ability to express their views of their surrounding world. Several themes are repeated in Taíno art: sex, illness, bats, turtles, frogs, birds, human heads with big eyes and bared teeth, female breasts, and occasionally dogs and monkeys. Typical of Taíno art, and a readily distinguishing factor among various prehistoric art styles, is the balanced geometric design of lines ending in rounded points, alternating with anthropomorphic and zoomorphic figures.

Nowhere else in the Antilles did Taíno art achieve the abstract complexity and figurative richness developed by the artisans of the island that Columbus baptized as Española. The similarity of styles and the profusion of pieces with similar finishes, decoration, and materials point to the existence of specialists in the production of idols, amulets, ceremonial chairs, body ornaments, and ceramics.

Yet, this society was bound for rapid extinction as soon as it was contacted by Europeans. Recent demographic studies show that the population of Española must have numbered 400,000 in 1492. This reflects a relatively low density and favorable man-to-land ratio. Hence, the Taínos could obtain an abundance of food from their environment with minimal effort, as is depicted in the Spanish chronicles. But forced labor and sudden exposure to European germs and diseases, combined with abortions and mass suicides carried out to escape slavery, caused a rapid drop in the population. In the following chapter we will examine the process of extinction of the Taíno society in the first 20 years of the 16th century.

2.
The early
Spanish rule
(1492-1606)

GOLD AND ENCOMIENDAS

When Christopher Columbus arrived at Española in December 1492, he encountered a society entirely different from the ones described by Marco Polo for Asia and India. During the previous weeks, Columbus had been sailing through the Bahamas and Cuba, and had already discovered that the natives of these regions went about naked, did not know the wheel or use any metal tools, practiced agriculture and fishing, possessed a complex social structure, and had an elaborate system of religious beliefs. These "Indians" called themselves Taínos, to signify that they were peaceful, although they defended themselves well from their neighboring enemies, the Caribes, who inhabited the Lesser Antilles.

Columbus soon realized that Española had some gold deposits, for he observed some Indians wearing ornaments made of this metal. Therefore, he decided to settle there, but first he returned to Spain carrying the news of his discoveries. Before departing the island, Columbus built a wooden fort with the remnants of one of his ships that wrecked on a coral reef on Christmas Eve 1492. He left 39 men in charge of the fort, which he baptized La Navidad. Columbus returned to La Navidad in December 1493, and found that the 39 men had been killed by the Indians after the Spaniards had abused their women.

Nevertheless, he went on with his plans of establishing a commercial outpost or *factoría* in Española to exploit the new lands. To honor the Spanish queen, Columbus named the *factoría* La Isabela and proceeded to build a new town 70 miles west of La Navidad. Columbus had learned about the factoría system when he sailed with the Portuguese in Africa several years earlier. In these enterprises, two or more partners would divide the profits derived from trading with the natives. They employed white artisans and craftsmen under a fixed wage system.

Despite Columbus's planning, La Isabela was beset with problems from the beginning. Adaptation to the new environment led to illness and death for many of Columbus's men, while the survivors lacked food and medicine. At first, neither Columbus nor the Spanish crown seemed aware that the *factoría* system was not compatible with the Castilian tradition of the Reconquista. During the Reconquista, the Spanish people became accustomed to occupying the newly conquered lands while forcing the defeated Moorish population to work for them as serfs.

Facing an unexpected shortage of laborers, Columbus ordered everyone to work without distinction of social rank. This provoked a serious rift between Columbus and some Spaniards who had joined the expedition. Some of these men were *hidalgos*, members of the Spanish lesser nobility, who had come to Española in search of fortune and considered manual labor unfit to their social position. Columbus soon discovered a conspiracy and crushed it by executing one of the ringleaders. This action also led to the desertion of several *hidalgos* who stole one of the ships and fled to Spain where they complained of their mistreatment by Columbus.

Fearful of an Indian rebellion, Columbus unleashed two violent military campaigns throughout the center of the island during 1494 and 1495. These campaigns were ostensibly designed to submit the Indians to the vassalage of the Catholic Monarchs, but Columbus discovered that he could save money if he gave his men Indians as slaves in lieu of monthly wages. He also hoped to obtain from the conquered Indians the gold that he had promised to the monarchs and the much needed food for the *factoría*. The Indians were forced to cultivate large cassava plantations to feed the Spaniards, but the military campaigns terrorized them and many abandoned the fields and fled to the mountains, thus depriving the Spaniards of fresh foodstuffs.

By early 1496, food was very scarce. Yet, in the middle of this crisis, Columbus decided to return to Spain to give the monarchs an account of his new discoveries in Cuba and Jamaica. Taking advantage of Columbus's absence, the workers of La Isabela revolted against his brothers Bartolomé and Diego, who had been left in charge of the *factoría's* government. The leader of the rebellion was Francisco Roldán, one of Columbus's servants. Roldán was very careful to declare that his rebellion was only against the Columbus family and not against the crown.

The rebellion lasted for two years, the length of time Columbus spent in Spain trying to organize a new expedition to populate Española with laborers, miners, and soldiers since more than half the population that had arrived in 1493 had died. La Isabela became completely depopulated. The rebels went to live in other regions of the island where food and Indian labor were more readily available. At the same time, Bartolomé Columbus and his followers moved to the south of the island, where gold mines had recently been discovered. There, he founded the city of Santo Domingo.

When Columbus returned in August 1498, he found his brother's authority greatly deteriorated. Most of the workers had gone to live in the western areas of Española. To them, the *factoría* meant oppression, lack of property, and lack of benefits. They demanded the granting of lands and Indian servants.

To pacify the island, Columbus gave in to the demands of the rebels. Roldán was appointed *alcalde mayor* of the entire island, while Columbus agreed to pay the full salaries of all the workers for the previous two years.

The rebellion served as a catalyst for important changes in the social and political life of Española. The rebels, who until then had belonged to the lower strata of Spanish society, became owners of the best lands and masters of great numbers of Indians. They were also given effective participation, through their chief Roldán, in the governing of the island. Roldán's rebellion also served to convince the Crown that Christopher Columbus should not continue managing an enterprise that went beyond the discovery of new lands.

In 1500, the Spanish monarchs sent a provisional governor to Santo Domingo to replace Columbus. This governor, Francisco de Bobadilla, was an experienced administrator of reconquered lands on the Spanish frontier and accepted the distribution of Indian slaves initiated by Columbus. By strengthening the power of Roldán and his followers, Bobadilla kept the island pacified until the arrival of a new permanent governor.

This new governor, Nicolás de Ovando, was appointed in September 1501. Ovando was also an experienced *comendador* in the Spanish borderlands, who learned how to deal with the Moorish infidels during the last years of the Reconquista. The instructions that Ovando received from the Crown were very precise. He should impose law and order and keep under his authority the 2,500 persons who accompanied him to Santo Domingo and the 360 individuals whom Bobadilla and Roldán ruled. Ovando also had instructions concerning proper treatment of the Indians.

Ovando arrived at Española in July 1502, and immediately sent Roldán and his closest followers to Spain, thus depriving the former rebel group of its main leaders as all were drowned in a shipwreck shortly after leaving Santo Domingo. Soon afterward, Ovando designed a scheme to break the power of the remainder of Roldán's group. He forced many of them to marry the Indian women with whom they were living. This gave the governor a pretext for depriving them of their land and serfs as punishment for having assimilated themselves into the inferior status of the natives.

In spite of these measures, Ovando could not bring everyone under his control. He had to proceed slowly for the old settlers were the ones who knew the island and its resources. Thus, Ovando continued the Indian *repartimientos* initiated by Columbus. To enslave Indians who had not already been appropriated by the older colonists, Ovando launched two new military campaigns in the unconquered regions of Higüey, in the east, and Xaraguá, in the west. There, Ovando coldly executed the Indian chieftains and proceeded to entrust their communities to his own men. With this practice, Ovando quickly created a new class of property owners of some noble extraction politically linked to him. With this new class, Ovando tried to introduce some political balance in the colony.

The captured Indians were put to work in the gold mines where they were grossly overworked, mistreated, and underfed. In 1501 the Crown had declared that the Indians were free and should be treated as such, but no one obeyed these orders. In 1503, Ovando convinced the Queen that if the Indians were not forced to work in the mines, the Spaniards would leave the island and the whole colony would be lost. Pressed by a dire need for gold to pay expenses in Europe, the Crown legalized the system of distributing the Indians among the Spaniards to work the mines. The only condition was that the recipients of Indians teach them the Catholic faith. This system of *encomiendas* was legally sanctioned by the Crown on December 20, 1503.

Once the Indians entered the mines, hunger and disease literally wiped them out. Those who did manage to survive for 8 to 12 months in the mines became so desperate that many eventually committed suicide in collective ceremonies. Pregnant women systematically aborted or killed their own children to prevent them from becoming slaves. The volume of deaths was such that a 1508 census revealed that there were only 60,000 Indians left out of an original population of around 400,000.

This census indicated the imminence of a serious labor shortage. To solve it, Ovando authorized the organization of slave hunting expeditions to the Lesser Antilles, Cuba, and the Bahamas. The rationale behind these expeditions was that those were "useless" islands containing no gold, whose Indians would never be Christianized because the Spaniards would never settle there. Although 40,000 Indians were captured from those islands between 1508 and 1513, the decline of Española's aboriginal population continued. A new census in 1510 revealed only 40,000 Indians. Another census taken in 1511 showed that the Indian population had decreased to 33,523 individuals.

The colonists' primary interest was to enrich themselves and return to Spain emancipated from manual labor. When Christopher Columbus's son, Diego, replaced Ovando as governor in 1509, the populace was mainly concerned with how to remain on good terms with the governor. Ovando had already demonstrated no reluctance in dispossessing those who obstructed his government, and had created a system of punishment and rewards based on the removal and granting of *encomiendas*.

Diego Columbus did not have Ovando's political abilities. Expecting that Diego, like his father, would act more in line with his own interests than with those of the Crown, the king had named a trusted Catalan bureaucrat, Miguel de Pasamonte, as treasurer general of the Indies to serve as an element of control in the administration of Española. As expected by the king, Diego soon entered into serious conflicts with both the Crown and the colonists. His maneuvers to appropriate for himself Indians formerly granted to other colonists put Diego at odds with many of the most powerful men in the colony.

The quarrels between Diego and Pasamonte about the possession, appropriation, and allocation of the Indians, eventually convinced the king that Diego was acting more as a private
encomendero than as an official at the service of the Crown. To
correct this tendency, the king created a royal court of appeals
in 1511, so that Diego's decisions would not be absolute and so
the aggrieved parties could have another recourse to revise his
decisions. This appellate court, or Real Audiencia, proved to be
an effective instrument to control the power of Diego. By 1512,
the two political factions led by Diego and Pasamonte fought
openly for the appropriation of the Indians.

To end this conflict, the king canceled Diego's privilege to
distribute Indians in 1513, and sent Rodrigo de Alburquerque
to Española in 1514 to make a new *repartimiento* of the Indians. Alburquerque was to take away the Indians remaining in
the hands of Roldán's group and confiscate most of the Indians
that Diego had granted to his followers. Those Indians were then
to be given to men that the king and Pasamonte deemed worthy.
With the *repartimiento* of Alburquerque, the Crown intended to
put all economic and political power in the hands of a small but
powerful colonial aristocracy developed under Ovando.

The importance of this new *repartimiento* can not be overstated, for it showed how severely the aboriginal population
had declined in only 20 years. The Indian society was on the
verge of extinction by 1514 for only 26,334 Indians remained
alive in the whole island. Of these, 12,663 were concentrated in
the four mining towns of Concepción, Santiago, Santo Domingo, and Buenaventura. *(See map No. 2)*

During this new *repartimiento*, a small colonial elite of 82
persons, representing only 11 percent of the *encomenderos*,
managed to appropriate 44 per cent of the Indians distributed.
This group comprised all royal and municipal officials. Apart
from the elite, only 646 colonists received Indians. The rest of
the population, which consisted of several thousand persons,

was left without Indians and with very limited possibilities to earn a living except by working with their own hands, an idea repugnant to those accustomed to Indian serfs performing most physical labor.

The *repartimiento* of 1514 closed the door for social and economic advancement in Española. A majority of the colonists blamed Alburquerque and mobilized for rebellion. A popular uprising was prevented only by the rapid intervention of the king who prohibited public discussion of the *repartimiento*. Those who lost their Indians decided to leave the island in search of new riches in Cuba, Darién, and Venezuela. Emigration, which was already quite intense by 1512, accelerated in 1515 due to the crisis provoked by the *repartimiento*.

This crisis was aggravated by the fact that the mines were becoming exhausted. Colonists who stayed on the island, especially the official elite, grew alarmed and began a frantic search for new sources of wealth to substitute for gold. Great effort was made by all those who had something to lose. They tried to redirect the island's economy toward agriculture by importing Spanish laborers and by experimenting with European and Asian seeds and plants. A consensus was reached regarding the convenience of developing a sugar cane industry with the capital accumulated by the *encomenderos*.

While the colonial elite was seeking new economic resources, an important political change took place in Spain. In February 1516, King Ferdinand died. Cardinal Francisco Jiménez de Cisneros was named regent until the heir, Prince Charles, came of age. The king's death occurred while a group of Dominican friars in Spain were actively advocating the total abolition of the *encomienda* system. One of the friars, Bartolomé de Las Casas, who had been an *encomendero* in Cuba before taking his religious vows in 1510, made several appeals to the Cardinal extolling the virtues of the Indians and denouncing the cruelties of the *encomenderos*.

Cisneros was deeply impressed by the friars' preaching. He accepted their plan to remove all Indians from the hands of the *encomenderos* and to place them in villages under the control of their own caciques to live in peace and multiply. The construction of these villages was entrusted to three Jeronymite fathers who were sent as governors to Española at the end of 1516. This "plan for the salvation of the Indies" failed completely. Just as the friars were beginning to move the remaining 11,000 Indians to the new villages a smallpox epidemic broke out, killing more than 8,000 Indians in one month. By February 1519, the already small native population was reduced to less than 3,000.

When the smallpox epidemic struck, it was already too late to save the Indians. Nothing could stop the disintegration of the aboriginal society. The Jeronymite fathers accepted the tragedy as a providencial design and reversed their policy of abolishing the *encomienda* system to entice the Spaniards to stay in the colony. The fathers then dedicated themselves to furnishing loans to those *encomenderos* who wished to build sugar mills. The new sugar mill builders were authorized to use the remaining Indians in the plantations and import African slaves to satisfy their labor needs. Both the gold economy and the Indian population became extinct at the same time. Only a small group of 500 Indians survived by fleeing to the mountains in 1519 under the direction of the cacique Enriquillo.

SUGAR AND SLAVES

The depletion of the gold mines and the extinction of the Indian population produced a radical socioeconomic transformation in Española. Cattle raising and sugar production replaced gold mining as the main economic activities. These new enterprises were dominated almost exclusively by the bureaucratic elite of Santo Domingo since many of the colonists decided to emigrate after learning that in Mexico there were new lands containing an abundance of silver and many Indians. Emigration was so intense that by 1528, seven Spanish towns had completely disappeared and those remaining held a combined population of only 1,000 Spaniards. A royal decree in 1526 prohibited the colonists from leaving the island under penalty of death, but emigration continued despite this law.

Both sugar production and the livestock business offered good profits. There was an increasing demand for cowhides in Europe during the entire 16th century. As the interior of Española was being depopulated, the remaining inhabitants became herders and hunters of the hundreds of thousands of cattle and hogs that roamed wild in the plains and mountains. Those herds were descendants of the animals imported by Ovando in 1502. The island's climate favored the reproduction of livestock. Many colonists made a living hunting cattle and selling hides, lard, and salted meat, while others profited from raising domesticated hogs or hunting wild ones to produce bacon for sale to the neighboring islands, to ships on exploring expeditions, and to the new settlements in the Continent.

Unlike the livestock industry, the development of the sugar industry was a major undertaking that required both technical skills and heavy investment. Sugar estates included not only the plantation area but also mills to grind the cane and manufacture the sugar. By 1527 there were 25 mills functioning at full capacity on the island. Of those, 23 were located in the vicinity of Santo Domingo which was the only city with enough wealthy residents to invest in the construction of sugar mills or *ingenios*.

Santo Domingo was also the seat of government and finance, and there investors could obtain government loans with relative ease. Loans were only given by the Crown to those individuals who belonged to the colonial elite. Thus, the sugar industry served as the economic basis supporting the continuity of power among the greatest *encomenderos* who quickly transferred their fortunes from the mines to the *ingenios*.

The crown firmly supported the development of the sugar industry. The *señores de ingenios* were exempt from customs duties on the importation of copper and machinery for their mills and from payment of church tithes. After 1529, *ingenios* could not be seized nor liquidated for their owners' debts. *Ingenio* owners enjoyed the right of patronage over church clerics and chapels on their plantations. They also enjoyed the privilege of primogeniture so the plantations could pass from father to son intact and without inheritance disputes.

As the island became depopulated, the *ingenios* became the most important centers of population containing not only large numbers of slaves but also Spanish overseers and foreign technicians called *maestros de azúcar* who managed the mills. The sugar masters were generally from the Canary Islands, Sicily, or Portugal, where there was a long tradition of sugar production.

The self-sufficiency and relative isolation of the plantations brought about a noticeable decentralization of political power. The *ingenios* gradually became the centers of authority in their regions. This process, together with the absence of a stable government from 1523 to 1528, consolidated the political power of the mill owners. The administration of the colony was left in the hands of the judges of the Real Audiencia who were also *señores de ingenios*. Thanks to the sugar industry, Santo Domingo remained a thriving port and the residence of the colonial elite.

Cattle raising constituted an important source of income for city residents as well as the mill owners. The city's ranchers possessed large herds of livestock that were sacrificed mainly for their hides since the population was insufficient to consume all the meat. The great wealth generated by the sugar and livestock industries gave Santo Domingo a lively and cosmopolitan flavor.

At the peak of the sugar age, in the middle of the 16th century, Santo Domingo had a strong nucleus of wealthy merchants connected to the great commercial houses of Seville, Antwerp, Genoa, and Lisbon. Wealthy men dressed in expensive clothes imported from Europe. In their homes, high-priced imported foods and drinks were consumed daily. Few bothered with activities other than sugar production, cattle raising, and collecting *campeche* wood and *cassia fistula* fruit. These were the main export items providing income to import European goods. *Campeche* was used for curing hides in the tanneries of Europe, while *cassia fistula* was widely used as a purgative.

Although the old wealthy class of *encomenderos* was to retain its economic power by becoming the owners of *ingenios* and cattle ranches, an important change took place in the colony. The advent of the sugar industry permanently altered the demographic composition of the island. The Jeronymite fathers accepted the suggestion of the colonists to import African slaves. The first *ingenios* to go into operation in 1520 were manned by a few hundred of the remaining Indians and several hundred newly arrived African slaves. As time went on, the plantations became populated mainly by African slaves.

There was a natural increase among the black population. In 1526, the crown decreed that one-third of the slaves to be imported into Española must be females. Since the cost of each slave fluctuated, the owners paid attention to their welfare so as not to lose their investment. In 1546, there were already some 12,000 slaves compared to the white population of less than 5,000. By 1568, the number of slaves had increased to around 20,000. The abundance of slaves led some *señores de ingenios* to export their surplus to Honduras and Venezuela.

The demographic difference between the white and black population had a decisive effect on the life of the colony. It was difficult for the small Spanish population to maintain strict control over the workers, and from the very beginning, the slaves continually rebelled or escaped. During the Indian war, between 1519 and 1533, Indians periodically came down from the mountains to attack Spanish settlements in the south of the island. The Indians, led by the rebel cacique Enriquillo, liberated slaves from the plantations. When Enriquillo finally made peace with the Spaniards in 1533, there were several hundred runaway slaves, or *cimarrones*, living in the southwestern mountains of Baoruco. Many remained in the area for years and attracted other slaves away from their masters.

In 1542, the authorities believed that there were from 2,000 to 3,000 black fugitives in the island. Girolamo Benzoni, an Italian traveler who spent several months in Española in the same year, believed that the number of runaway slaves reached 7,000. Once free, the *cimarrones* sought to regroup themselves with others who spoke the same language and belonged to their own or related tribes. These groups lived in organized communities with their own social and economic structure and a fiscal system that permitted them to maintain their leaders. They tried to reconstruct their native familial and religious organization.

Due to the numerical superiority of the blacks, the Spaniards knew that eventually their authority would be challenged. To prevent this, in 1543, the Crown appointed an experienced soldier, Alonso de Cerrato, as governor and president of the Real Audiencia ordering him to eliminate the threat. Cerrato found the island in a state of fear. The white population never left their farms in groups of less than 15 to 20 armed men since the *cimarrones* had lances and other weapons stolen from the Spaniards. For three years, Cerrato's squadrons fought a bloody war against the *cimarrones*, killing most of the black leaders. Captured slaves were punished, tortured, or killed. There was much fear among the rebels, many asked for pardon, and some leaders offered their services to capture their former companions in exchange for their lives.

By June 1546, the island was nearly pacified. The threat posed by the runaway slaves did not decisively affect the economy of the island. The merchants and planters of Santo Domingo continued exporting sugar to Spain. Between 1536 and 1565, approximately 800 ships passed through the port of Santo Domingo and other ports of the island bringing merchandise and manufactured goods and returning to Spain with sugar, hides, and other island products.

CATTLE AND CONTRABAND

The runaways were not the only danger in the middle of the 16th century. Corsairs also threatened the island. During most of the 16th century, Spain was at war with France and England, and both French and English corsairs were used by their governments to harm Spanish trade in the Indies. Corsairs confiscated ships with full cargoes, raided and burned plantations, and in general inspired fear on the island. These acts had a decisive impact on Española. The colonial authorities were forced to construct a wall to enclose and protect the city of Santo Domingo. In 1541, the Crown gave permission to increase taxes and use slaves in constructing the wall. These taxes were added to the others already imposed on meat and other merchandise, and their immediate effect was to increase the already high cost of living.

Given the proliferation of corsairs roaming the Spanish Main, in 1543 the Spanish Crown ordered that most ships travel together in well-guarded fleets. These fleets were to leave annually from Seville to arrive at the ports of Veracruz, Mexico, and Nombre de Dios on the Isthmus of Panama. After 1543, Havana became the most important port for the rendezvous of fleets, while Santo Domingo was left on the sidelines. This new system of fleets greatly altered navigation in the Caribbean and resulted in isolating Santo Domingo from the Spanish navigation routes. Ships to Santo Domingo could sail from Spain only with the fleet, but upon entering Caribbean waters, they would have to sail alone through corsair-infested waters as the fleet continued on to other ports.

Navigation to Española became more expensive with freight and insurance rates increasing as the international situation deteriorated. The isolation of Española was a serious blow to the island's economy and compounded the problems already posed by the Spanish monopoly in America.

This monopoly was established in 1503, and made Santo Domingo the only port authorized by the Spanish Crown to trade with Seville. But in the middle of the 16th century, as the ships became less frequent, European manufactured goods became more scarce. On many occasions, the colonists requested the abolition of the monopoly so they could sell their products to other nationals or to other merchants at other Spanish ports. In all instances the crown rejected these petitions. As the availability of imported goods decreased, the colonists resorted to contraband.

As the 16th century progressed, contraband trade was welcomed by the residents and cattle owners of the interior who were doubly harmed by the royal monopoly. While the cattlemen living in the south near the sugar ingenios could count on a market for their goods, the remainder had to transport their livestock to Santo Domingo from distant regions without roads. During this process many head of cattle were lost, slaves who accompanied them ran away, and the numerous bands of *cimarrones* continually assaulted the Spaniards.

Transportation facilities were almost nonexistent on the northern and western coasts of Española since Spanish ships increasingly used Havana as their main port. In early years, the residents of these areas sold their hides and other products to Spanish ships. But as the arrival of ships became less frequent, colonists gradually turned to French, English, and Portuguese smugglers. Fugitive slaves aided the development of contraband since the lack of safe travel impeded colonial authorities from effectively controlling all the regions of the island. The *cimarrones* learned that they, too, could trade products stolen form the Spaniards in exchange for imported goods.

Contraband offered all the inhabitants of the island distinct advantages over the official Spanish trade. Smugglers sold their goods at cheaper prices than the Seville merchants, and offered higher prices for sugar, hides, and other products of the colony. At first, the colonists preferred trading with the Portuguese since they spoke a similar language, they were smugglers not corsairs, and had inexpensive African slaves for sale. But since Portugal possessed little industry, most of the manufactured goods in demand were produced in England and France and proved to be cheaper when obtained without Portuguese intermediaries. The English and French were aware of the Spanish colonists' need for manufactured goods and were anxious to obtain raw materials from the island without passing through Seville.

The willingness of the residents of Española to trade with the smugglers was intolerable to the crown. Dozens of cédulas, royal orders, and laws were sent to the authorities in Santo Domingo commanding an end to the contraband. Merchants of Seville continually sent representatives to Santo Domingo to apply pressure on the authorities. Sometimes the pressure was successful, but in most cases contraband continued without hindrance. By 1577, smuggling was the basis of the economy of the northern and western regions of the island.

Contraband was practiced on a wide scale according to well-defined rules. Once the foreigners arrived at ports used for contraband, they fired two cannon shots to announce their presence. Local people quickly transmitted the news from ranch to ranch. Those who had not previously deposited their goods at warehouses near the coast did so at once. After landing, they proceeded to exchange hides for slaves, cloth, or wine. Both foreigners and natives, profited from these transactions. Control of the situation was impossible because everyone, including local officials, was involved.

As time passed, smuggling disrupted the economy of the city of Santo Domingo. Many local cattle owners took their animals to other regions where contraband trade was regularly conducted, since the Dutch, French, and English paid more per hide than Spain did. This trade became so intense that in 1598 the authorities estimated that nearly 80,000 hides were being smuggled every year. Meat became extremely scarce and expensive in Santo Domingo, while the city's exports severely declined because of the scarcity of hides and tallow. That decrease in official commerce resulted in a reduction of revenues for the royal treasury.

Smuggling was particularly irritating to the merchants of Santo Domingo and their associates in Seville since the volume of sugar, the island's other main export item, was also declining. A series of epidemics after 1586 had halved the slave population, leaving a manpower shortage on the sugar ingenios. The decline of sugar production was further exacerbated by increasing competition from Brazilian sugar and by the development of ginger farming in 1581, which offered higher profits than sugar. The cultivation of ginger, like sugar, required a large slave labor force. Many slaves were moved from the sugar plantations to the new ginger farms.

THE "DEVASTACIONES"

Contraband trade was also associated with an ideological problem that affected the roots of Spanish power and sovereignty over the colony. Contraband began to be viewed as more than just a violation of Spanish trade. It meant the penetration of religious ideas and political loyalties alien to the Spanish crown and people, especially those of Protestant England and Holland with whom Spain had been at war for almost 60 years. By 1588, the authorities referred to the foreign smugglers as heretics and enemies. In 1594, the archbishop of Santo Domingo warned the king that if a remedy were not found, the island would soon be lost to the Protestants. The archbishop denounced the growing tendency of the inhabitants of the north and west of Española to establish ties and obligations with Protestant sailors and merchants. For him, the most alarming fact was that many colonists were starting to baptize their children in Protestant rites and were choosing foreign godparents.

The situation was fully described in 1598 by Baltazar López de Castro, a local bureaucrat, who wrote to the Crown warning of the need to take measures to avoid the continuation of these practices. He stated that the only way to deal with the problem was to move all the residents and their cattle from the island's northern and western regions to the surrounding areas of Santo Domingo. According to him, this measure would prevent the foreigners from ilegally trading with the colonists, and would also provide Santo Domingo with an abundance of livestock and dairy products. Royal revenues would increase since the hides would be exported directly through the harbor of Santo Domingo. The Church would enjoy the additional advantage of increased tithes.

Since no other solutions were at hand, the Consejo de Indias adopted López de Castro's plan in January 1603. The Consejo recommended to the Spanish king that the towns of Puerto Plata, Bayajá, in the north, and La Yaguana, in the west, be depopulated. In August 1604, López de Castro returned to Santo Domingo from Seville with a set of royal *cédulas* ordering Governor Antonio de Osorio to proceed with the depopulation of the smuggling centers. With the population being drawn into Santo Domingo, the smugglers and heretics would be deprived of their prey. *(See map No. 3)*

The majority of the population adamantly protested this process. In Santo Domingo, an anonymous diatribe circulated against the authorities responsible for the proposed depopulation. Formal protests were prepared by the *cabildos* of Santo Domingo and La Yaguana. According to these *cabildos*, the depopulation should be postponed at least temporarily for a variety of reasons. They argued that it would be impossible to remove all the cattle since many were wild. Furthermore, the available labor force was insufficient to move the domestic herds. The inhabitants of those regions included many small proprietors who would be ruined by the move. They feared that runaway slaves would incite their slaves to escape, eventually allowing the *cimarrones* to control the contraband business.

The protests were completely ineffective. In the middle of February 1605, Governor Osorio went to the north to carry out his orders. A general pardon was proclaimed for all those that had been involved in smuggling. Once Osorio arrived at the designated towns, he ordered the people to gather their personal belongings, livestock, and slaves and to move to the designated areas near Santo Domingo where they would construct new settlements. As expected, there was great resistance from the inhabitants who were forced to leave their homes within 24 hours. The governor then burned the houses, ranches, churches, and crops to prevent the residents from remaining in those sites.

Governor Osorio was assisted by 150 soldiers from the garrison of Puerto Rico who had been dispatched for this purpose. As a result, Puerto Plata, Montecristi, La Yaguana, and Bayajá were depopulated. In Bayajá, the residents rose up in arms against Osorio. This was a true popular rebellion of common people who saw in the depopulation the beginning of their ruin. Although more than seventy persons were hanged for having dealt with the enemies after the new law, the rebel leaders were never captured. Sixteen Dutch ships anchored in the Bay of Gonaïves sought to take advantage of the confusion and offered the rebels military aid and political support on condition that they reject their loyalty to the king of Spain and renounce the Catholic faith. With this aid, some residents of La Yaguana put up great resistance, but were eventually defeated. Others preferred to flee to Cuba.

Governor Osorio concentrated most of the inhabitants of Montecristi, Puerto Plata, Bayajá, and La Yaguana in two settlements to the north of Santo Domingo. These settlements were called San Antonio de Monte Plata, to signify the merge of Puerto Plata and Montecristi, and San Juan Bautista de Bayaguana, which meant the merge of Bayajá and La Yaguana. The residents of the western regions of Neiba and San Juan de la Maguana were moved to the areas surrounding the abandoned mining village of Buenaventura.

The ill effects of these *devastaciones* were perceived almost immediately. As had been predicted by the *cabildos* of Santo Domingo and La Yaguana, it was impossible to remove even 10 percent of the animals from the northern and western areas. Of the estimated 110,000 domesticated livestock, only 8,000 arrived at the new locations and all but 2,000 died because of poor pasturage in the new area. For the inhabitants of the new towns of Monte Plata and Bayaguana the situation was particularly critical. Having lost most of their cattle and many of their slaves who had run away, most families in Monte Plata were financially ruined.

The situation in Bayaguana was equally desperate. More than one-third of the population died from hunger and disease between 1606 and 1609. Many youths of the town fled to eke out a living in the port of Santo Domingo despite an official prohibition. The plight of the residents reached a climax in May 1609, when a fire destroyed the majority of their shacks leaving many homeless. To alleviate the tragedy somewhat, Governor Osorio conceded licenses to various persons to return to the north and the west to bring back more livestock, but the cattle were too dispersed, the regions too far away, and the number of men too few for these patrols to succeed.

In 1606-07, there was a sharp increase in the number of hides shipped to Spain but this was caused by the massive and indiscriminate slaughter of livestock around Santo Domingo by cattle ranchers who feared the loss of their animals. This massive slaughter of cattle produced an acute scarcity of meat in 1608. Despite the immediate increase of hide exports, the other colonial exports did not grow. The amount of ginger being produced and exported from the island was unlikely to increase in the long run because 6,742 of the island's 9,648 slaves were already working on the ginger farms. The rest were used in the sugar industry or as domestic servants.

The *devastaciones* dramatically impoverished the colony. When a new governor arrived in Santo Domingo in 1608 to replace Antonio de Osorio, very few residents went out to receive him for lack of adequate clothing. Poverty worsened in the following years, and those with sufficient means began emigrating to other parts of the Indies despite official prohibitions. The general poverty of the island influenced the crown to lower export duties on the island's products and to assign a subsidy to the colony from the royal treasury of Mexico. This subsidy, called *situado*, was to pay for the general expenses of the government, including the salaries of the royal bureaucracy, the church, and the soldiers. Although it was meant as a temporary measure, the *situado* was to become a permanent feature of Española's economic life.

When considering the international situation, there seemed no urgent reasons for the *devastaciones* other than defense of the interests of Seville's merchants. When the decision was made in 1603, Spain was in the process of making peace with its European enemies. In 1598, Philip II had signed the Treaty of Vervins with France and consequently the number of French corsairs and smugglers in the Caribbean rapidly dwindled. In

1604, England was also partially neutralized through the second Treaty of Vervins so that in 1605 and 1606, when Osorio was carrying out the depopulations, only Holland was still at war with Spain. Although the Dutch had many ships in the Antilles and were carrying on piracy and contraband on a massive scale, Spain was too exhausted to continue with this struggle and sought peace with Holland in 1606. A truce was finally signed in April, 1609, only three years after the *devastaciones* had been completed.

As a measure to keep Spain's enemies away, the *devastaciones* were a total failure. The lands emptied by the *devastaciones* offered excellent ground for settlement to the same Europeans who Spain had tried to keep away from the island. Moreover, the island never recuperated from the *devastaciones*. Although livestock production increased sufficiently to provide meat for the city of Santo Domingo, hide exports never reached previous levels.

Santo Domingo, which had been left aside of the main navigation routes, suffered further due to the threats posed by the Dutch privateers during the Thirty Years War. Once this war started, the constant presence of pirates in the Caribbean made travel to and from Santo Domingo extremely hazardous. Few sailors cared to venture to the island to seek products that could be found elsewhere at a lesser risk. The permanent lack of shipping facilities discouraged production as exporting became nearly impossible. The sugar mills gradually stopped producing and the ginger farms were abandoned. The slave population declined rapidly as imports of slaves had ceased long before the *devastaciones*. By 1630, the slave population was insignificant since most slaves had either died or fled to the mountains.

3.
The island divided (1607-1697)

THE LOSS OF THE WESTERN LANDS

The Dutch took advantage of the truce with Spain to expand their possessions at the expense of the Portuguese colonies in Asia and Africa. Since Portugal and Spain had been united under the Castilian monarch since 1580, the Dutch eventually decided to move against Spanish possessions in the Antilles. Following the scheme of the Dutch East Indies Company that operated against the Portuguese in Asia and Africa, a group of Dutch capitalists formed the West India Company in 1621. The goals of this new commercial, maritime, and military organization were to promote war against Spain, and to practice piracy on a grand scale in the Atlantic.

When hostilities broke out between Spain and Holland in 1621, the French and English aligned with the Dutch. Both France and England had already shown an inclination to encourage small groups of colonizers working through private companies, and this activity was greatly stepped up during the war. As a result, between 1625 and 1635, Spain lost many territories in the Antilles including Barbados, San Cristóbal, Curaçao, Guadeloupe, and Martinique. Spain reacted by reorganizing the military in its

Caribbean possessions to reinforce strategic points hoping to prevent further territorial encroachment by its enemies.

Spain and Portugal could not prevent the Dutch from occupying Bahia, in Brazil, in 1624, nor could they halt the activities of French and English adventurers who roamed the Caribbean searching for suitable places to settle. In 1622, an English group established itself on the island of San Cristóbal and proceeded to plant tobacco with the support of metropolitan investors who furnished financing in exchange for future crops. San Cristóbal became the first permanent English settlement in the Caribbean and was quickly converted into the center of operations for London firms interested in the tobacco business.

Fleeing Spanish persecution in Jamaica, a group of French adventurers arrived in San Cristóbal and aided the English in waging a campaign of annihilation against the island's native population. In exchange for this assistance, the English agreed to divide the island with the French. When the Dutch captured the entire Mexican fleet in Cuban waters in 1628, the Spanish government reacted by organizing the Armada of Barlovento, ordering its commander to evict the French and English from San Cristóbal. This was accomplished with ease since dissension between both groups had weakened their defense. After a violent attack, the survivors were forced to leave the island. The Spanish troops leveled and burned their tobacco plantations.

Attracted by the tranquility of the abandoned northwestern coasts of Española, the English and French survivors moved from San Cristóbal to the island of Tortuga. The fertile grasslands on the southern coast of Tortuga proved excellent for the cultivation of tobacco. The abundance of wild cattle on nearby Española promised a high production of hides. The settlement prospered by selling tobacco, hides, meat, and dyewood to passing Dutch and English ships. The original population group of over 300 increased as residents from other islands came to live as tobacco farmers, cattle hunters, or pirates.

These activities did not go unnoticed by the Spanish authorities. Alarmed by the close proximity of the enemy, they launched a surprise assault on Tortuga killing 195 people, taking 39 prisoners, and capturing more than 30 slaves. The triumph, however, was shortlived. When the Spaniards left Tortuga, those who had escaped soon returned and resettled there. By 1636, some 80 Englishmen with 150 black slaves resided on the island hunting livestock and raising tobacco. In 1638, the Spanish navy attacked Tortuga again killing all enemies found there. Only those who fled to the northern coast of Española survived. After the Spanish ships departed the survivors again returned to Tortuga.

In 1639, 300 English adventurers settled in Tortuga and took control of it. Conflicts with the French settlers began immediately because the English Company of Providence wanted to monopolize the island's trade in direct competition with the Compagnie des Isles de l'Amerique, recently founded to foster French expansion in the Caribbean. The center of operations for the French company was established in San Cristóbal, which was repopulated under the company's patronage. Like its Dutch and English counterparts, the French company was financed by bourgeois groups and was sponsored by the Crown.

In response to complaints from the French on Tortuga regarding the English administration, the French governor of San Cristóbal sent an invasion under the command of an adventurer named Levasseur, in August 1640, to depose the English. The invasion was completely successful, enabling Levasseur to maintain absolute control over Tortuga for more that 12 years acting on behalf of the Compagnie.

The inhabitants of Tortuga were grouped into three distinct categories: filibusters, buccaneers, and tobacco cultivators. The filibusters were seafaring adventurers from many nations who used the fortifications of Tortuga to deposit, barter, or sell the booty obtained in their expeditions against Spanish ships and cities in Central America and the Antilles. The buccaneers lived on Española where they hunted the wild livestock that grazed on the depopulated grasslands of the island. The staple dietary item was smoked meat prepared on a spit called boucan from which they derived their name.

After a hunting season of several months, the buccaneers crossed the strait to Tortuga where they sold hides and restocked their stores with powder, munitions, and clothing. Once excess income was spent in taverns, which abounded on Tortuga, they returned to Española to begin a new cycle of hunting. The buccaneers also provided dry meat and tallow to the cultivators who grew tobacco and cotton, generally along the coastal areas of Española. They sold and bartered their produce to the French company in Tortuga.

The lives of these three groups were filled with danger and the constant threat of a new Spanish attack. The precariousness of their existence was increased by Levasseur, who imposed high duties on all business transactions. Failure to pay the tributes was a punishable offense. Levasseur's absolutism aroused hatred among the population. In 1652, his assassination at the hands of two adventurers solved the problem. Levasseur's death eased tensions among the population and led to a new period of growth and prosperity under a new governor who promoted French penetration into the northwestern lands of Española.

Alarmed at the increased activity of the French intruders, Spanish authorities in Santo Domingo launched a violent attack against Tortuga in January 1654. The campaign ended in a complete victory for the Spaniards, who burned all the buildings and crops, including a sugar mill built by the French. The island's population of 330 men, 170 women, and several children, was forced to leave on their ships, while the Spaniards left 150 well-armed men to prevent the return of the French.

The Spaniards had little time to enjoy their victory, for the taking of La Tortuga coincided with the preparation of an English expedition to conquer Española. This plan had been in the making for several years, but had been stopped short by the signing of the Peace of Westphalia in 1648 that put an end to the Thirty Years' War. The plan was also postponed several times due to England's internal disorders which ended with the beheading of Charles I. The new English government, under Oliver Cromwell, showed renewed interest and revived the scheme in August 1654. Cromwell named a commission to organize a powerful fleet to attack Santo Domingo and other Spanish possessions in the Indies, and on January 1, 1655, the English fleet of 34 warships and 10,000 men set sail. After delaying in Barbados where 3,000 more mercenary infantry troops were recruited, the fleet arrived at Española's coast on April 23, 1655.

The arrival of the English fleet was expected by the residents of Santo Domingo who had been informed by the Spanish government. The Spanish authorities recruited 200 soldiers and obtained munitions and weapons from Spain. They also recruited more than 1,300 lancers from the interior of the island to add to the city's garrison of 700 soldiers. Thus, by April 1655, the city was prepared to defend itself.

The numerical superiority of the invaders was offset by serious flaws in the expedition. From the beginning, the two English supreme commanders were unable to agree on many issues. These disagreements produced riots among the sailors and soldiers and threatened to ruin the expedition before arriving at Española. These problems were further enhanced by a tactical error by the English who landed in Nizao, 50 miles west of Santo Domingo, requiring a two-day march over rough terrain before reaching Haina, where the general headquarters was established.

On Sunday, April 25, the English attacked the city with more than 6,000 soldiers, and 120 cavalry units. During the initial

assault English losses were so high that the troops became disorganized and immediately retreated. While the English commanders were preparing their second attack, the Spanish
lanceros who had been hiding in the rearguard of the English
mounted their attack. The ambush, undertaken with skill, speed,
and great violence, killed more than 600 English soldiers. The
remaining English troops retreated in chaos.

On returning to their headquarters, the English commanders were uncertain about mounting another attack after such a
disastrous experience. The dead and wounded numbered over
1,600 and the remaining troops did not want to continue the
battle. The English decided to depart and one week later they
left their camp humiliated, divided among themselves, and accusing one another of cowardice. They went to Jamaica, which
was less populated and poorly defended. During the following
weeks, Jamaica was successfully attacked and became a permanent English colony.

The English attack left Española with the persistent worry
that the enemies of Spain, whether English or French, would
eventually return to Santo Domingo. This concern motivated the
colonial authorities to order the return of troops that had been
left in Tortuga a year and a half earlier. The rapid abandonment
of Tortuga was accomplished in September 1655, and once again,
when the French discovered that Tortuga was defenseless and
depopulated they began to return. By December 1656, Tortuga
was occupied and tobacco production was again underway. In
the same month, the French king granted Tortuga to Nombre Du
Rausset and appointed him governor. Du Rausset remained governor until November 15, 1664, when the French West Indies
Company forced him to sell his property rights. In June 1665,
Bertrand D'Ogeron, a long-time employee of the company, arrived in Tortuga to take possession as governor.

At that time, Tortuga was inhabited by 250 to 300 adventurers. On the northern coast of Española there were 800 French

buccaneers and settlers steadily expanding into the mountains and valleys of Española. This expansion was due to the growing scarcity of livestock on the northern and western coasts caused by the indiscriminate slaughter of animals by the buccaneers in earlier years. The scarcity was so widespread that in 1664 the buccaneers themselves suggested the number of hunters be limited to 200. By 1669, the French territories were completely devoid of livestock. *(See map No. 4)*

D'Ogeron's most ambitious plan was to attack and capture the city of Santo Domingo, which he believed to be poorly defended. His goal was to appropriate the entire island for the French company and thereby remove the Spanish military menace and open the whole island to French exploitation. With this objective in mind, the French governor sent numerous communications to the company proposing various invasion plans. In 1667, while a new war was being waged between Spain and France in Europe, the buccaneers and filibusters, organized under D'Ogeron, marched to the center of the island where they successfully attacked and pillaged Santiago de los Caballeros, the main Spanish city in the interior of the island.

In view of this success, D'Ogeron asked the company for more resources to attack Santo Domingo and make himself master of the entire island. As these plans required the backing of the company as well as the French government, in 1668 D'Ogeron set out for France. During his absence serious problems arose among the French colonists. The company prohibited trade with other countries and imposed such heavy duties that it was impossible for the settlers to enrich themselves. While the company received net profits, the majority of the colonists lived in poverty. When D'Ogeron returned in August 1670, he was attacked by disgruntled settlers who protested because they could not trade with Dutch ships anchored nearby.

By 1671 he still had not been able to subjugate the planters and buccaneers in the west. To resolve this problem, D'Ogeron decided to return to France, leaving the government of Tortuga and the western part of Española under the care of his nephew, M. De Pouançay. In January 1676, while in France, D'Ogeron died suddenly. As governor, De Pouançay continued with the plans initiated by D'Ogeron. De Pouançay organized the buccaneers and filibusters under his command, promoted the cultivation of tobacco, and further extended and fortified the settlements. In addition to La Tortuga, in 1677 there were 11 French villages in Española with more than 4,000 settlers, indentured workers, and slaves whose main occupation was the production of tobacco.

MISERY AND DECADENCE IN SANTO DOMINGO

The French settlers' situation was not much better than that of the population of the Santo Domingo. Española had never recuperated from the *devastaciones*. The reason was simple: Santo Domingo had been set aside from the main navigation routes, and ships avoided going there due to threats posed by the Dutch privateers during the Thirty Years' War. The permanent lack of shipping facilities discouraged production. As exports decreased, the merchants of Seville lost interest in Santo Domingo. The sugar mills gradually stopped producing, and ginger farms were gradually abandoned. By 1630, the slave population was insignificant since most slaves had either died or fled to the mountains.

The Thirty Years' War produced the militarization of Española and brought about radical changes in the life of the colony. Throughout this period, the *cabildos* lost their independence and became subjected to the dictates of the governor and captain-general who was always the president of the Real Audiencia. Despite royal checks, the power of the governors was nearly absolute. Although military power was resented by the creole elite, the more perceptive came to realize they would have to accept and accommodate to the military dictum if they wanted to survive.

The formation of a military elite began under Governor Chávez de Osorio (1628-36), who amassed a personal fortune by monopolizing important defense-related industries. The governor encouraged the construction of several fortifications and in 1633 promoted the construction of ten galleons using indigenous wood. The construction of the ships was never completed, but a great deal of money passed through the governor's hands during that period.

The succeeding governor, Juan Bitrián de Biamonte (1636-44), also enriched himself and his small group of followers. He controlled the granting of the export licenses upon which the colony's commerce depended, and sold clothing to the soldiers at exorbitant prices. Much of the governor's absolute power came from his ability to take advantage of the divisions and conflicts within the old colonial elite. He played one group against the other to enhance his position. During his administration many assassinations went unpunished since the murderers were men close to the governor.

Bitrián was also held responsible for bringing 250 Portuguese soldiers into the colony. Since Portugal had separated from Spain in 1640, these soldiers were perceived as foreigners. Thus, the common people and the creole elite found themselves at the mercy of a small military oligarchy of high-ranking officers and some 300 soldiers which Spain deemed necessary to defend the city's garrison. The terrified population could do nothing to fight the tyranny of Bitrián, his armed thugs, and corrupt bureaucrats.

Shortly before the Thirty Years' War ended in 1648, some residents of Santo Domingo began to develop cacao plantations. At the time it seemed that cacao would be the salvation of the colony's economy. Many enthusiastic landowners attempted to import slaves to replace those who died during a smallpox epidemic in 1651. In 1653, the *cabildo* of Santo Domingo sent a procurador to the court to request permission to import slaves, but this permission was delayed for several years.

In 1662, residents again requested from the Crown a license to import slaves for the cacao plantations. The Crown responded that slaves would be available because a contract had just been signed to introduce 3,500 Africans into the Indies annually. Since the colonists were in great need of laborers, they asked the governor to subdue the runaway blacks who had been living as *cimarrones* in the Sierra del Maniel for more than 30 years. After a short military campaign in mid-1665, 70 fugitives were taken prisoner and returned to their former masters or sold in Santo Domingo. However, these few slaves could do little to reinvigorate the stagnant economy of Española.

In 1666 a series of natural disasters struck the island. A new smallpox epidemic killed the majority of the slaves. The cacao plantations were struck by a blight. In 1667 the French, who were expanding more and more into Spanish territories, attacked Santiago. The Spaniards were incapable of either opposition or retaliation. In 1668, a hurricane tore through the Spanish colony leveling forests, crops, and buildings. Another smallpox epidemic killed approximately 1,500 people in 1669.

In 1669, a ship with 400 blacks for sale finally arrived in Santo Domingo, but by then money was so scarce that the residents could not purchase more than 140 slaves. The lack of money was due not only to the recent calamities, but also to the fact that the *situado* was three years in arrears, and that in the previous eight years only three *situados* had arrived. When the *situado* finally did arrive, all the money promptly flowed to local merchants and money lenders who had provided credit or loans to nearly everyone. Actually, very little money circulated in the colony.

In May 1671, the Real Audiencia reported to the Crown that

the city was still suffering the effects of a great hurricane that hit the island in 1668, and that none of the cacao plants had produced fruit since. The authorities also reported the lack of ships entering the port of Santo Domingo due to French pirate attacks. The French were also attacking the Spaniards' settlements in the island's interior, stealing cattle and slaves. Because of all this, the Audiencia stated, the city was suffering from a severe shortage of meat. Due to the new delay of the *situado*, many soldiers deserted from the military, further debilitating Spanish defenses on Española.

According to the Audiencia, in 1672 the economic activity of the entire colony had been reduced to subsistence farming due to the ruin of the cacao plants and lack of transportation for the export of cattle hides. People dedicated themselves to making cassava bread, cultivating vegetables, hunting, and raising livestock. Poverty was so overwhelming that members of the Real Audiencia requested that the crown move the institution to Venezuela. As the natural calamities continued, the population plunged into deeper misery. In September 1672, another hurricane destroyed the cassava and plantain plantations. An earthquake, in May 1673, destroyed many buildings in Santo Domingo.

Luckily, in 1674 there were no more disasters, and the population's mood became more positive in 1675. The new attitude was brought about by the belief that all the difficulties had been the product of astronomical influences that had been operating during a seven-year cycle that started in the ill-fated year of 1666. As this cycle came to a close, many residents chose to imitate the French who had made tobacco the main crop on the western part of the island, and had greatly increased their tobacco exports. Thus, many began to cultivate tobacco in addition to their traditional occupation of hunting and raising livestock.

Despite efforts to revive the economy, there were few possibilities to promote exports: shipowners avoided the island since it was well known that the inhabitants of Española did not have money. On August 18, 1678, the Real Audiencia wrote a report describing the poverty and hopelessness of the colony that produced only tobacco and hides for export. According to the Audiencia, there were only three ways to sell the colonial products: the first was foreign trade that was prohibited; the second was trade with other Spanish colonies, but this was unlikely since those colonies needed manufactured goods, not raw materials; the third, trade with Spain, was also impossible because merchant ships arrived only once every three years or so.

Poverty became so universal and so extreme that many families moved from the city of Santo Domingo to the countryside. There, they practiced subsistence farming and cattle herding, and killed boredom wachting cockfights. Most impoverished families who formerly possessed slaves were forced to sell them. Many left the island, despite the laws prohibiting their departure, allowing the French to penetrate further into the Spanish portion of the island. The Audiencia's report in 1678 concluded with a request for more frequent visits by merchant ships from Spain to provide a regular outlet for the island's products.

As evidenced by the report, the authorities of Española had come to the conclusion that their misery was a direct result of the Spanish commercial system, particularly the marginalization of Santo Domingo from the trade routes. Having lost its economic importance, Santo Domingo was replaced by Cuba and Puerto Rico as the key points of Spanish defense in the Caribbean. Spain itself was economically spent and deeply involved in European affairs and could offer little aid beyond granting the *situado*, the arrival of which was highly irregular.

The entire population was tied to a long chain of debts in which the last creditors formed a small commercial oligarchy. This group controlled the export of the few colonial products and the importation and sale of the very few manufactured goods that arrived in Santo Domingo. The largest debtor in the colony was the colonial government. It had to meet the current expenditures of the bureaucracy, make payment to the military and ، the church, and cover any extraordinary expenses for the defense of the colony.

The delays in the arrival of the *situado* and the inability of the colonial government to cover its expenses were so serious that in 1684 no one in Santo Domingo would lend money to the soldiers. When the *situado* finally arrived in 1687, the money barely defrayed the current expenses of the government and allowed only for partial payment of its debt to the money lenders. The government continued on arrears because it could not collect taxes due to the scarcity of trade. As the economic malaise affected everyone, moneylenders became more reluctant to finance public expenditures, making it more difficult for the government to pay the salaries of the military.

Within this atmosphere of scarcity, each sought the most convenient way to survive. Soldiers were forced to hire themselves out as dayworkers. Convents dedicated themselves to presenting bullfights and requesting alms with which to maintain their devotions. Because there were many religious orders in Santo Domingo, and because each one dedicated eight continuous days to bullfights, the population was away from work a good deal of the time. The city's population had little incentive to work as there was no assurance that what they produced would find a market either within the island or abroad. Thus, while the urban population lived an unpromising life in ruined and decayed buildings, the inhabitants of the interior lived almost completely isolated, practicing subsistence farming and cattle herding, and holding daily cockfights to kill boredom.

CONCTACTS WITH THE FRENCH

Things started to change in 1679, when news arrived in Santo Domingo saying that France and Spain had made peace in the previous year. The Spanish authorities sent a message to the French governor De Pouançay announcing the signing of the Treaty of Nimwegen and promoting the idea of peaceful relations. De Pouançay was very interested in promoting trade with the Spanish colonists. He knew the Spanish lacked the merchandise being brought to Tortuga on French ships. He also knew of his own colony's need for the livestock abundant in the Spanish territories. Thus, in 1681, despite mutual fear and suspicion between both groups, the Spaniards began selling horses, salted meat, and cowhides to the French in exchange for European merchandise. At the same time, farmers in Santiago began to cultivate tobacco according to French specifications to be exported to France.

The greatest problem with commercial relations was the tendency of the French to continually occupy greater areas of land on the Spanish part of the island. The Spanish authorities made great efforts to force the French governor to prohibit his subjects from advancing, but those efforts were to no avail. Spaniards were forced to seek other measures to halt the French advance. The most effective was the use of mobile military units to make surprise attacks on French settlements located in the north and west of the island. The patrols were comprised of about 30 men each, although the Spaniards and French called them *cincuentenas*, as if they were composed of 50 soldiers. The Spanish had few illusions about the capacity of these troops. They only served to obstruct the advance of the land occupations, not to protect them from an eventual massive French attack.

The colony's poverty and the presence of the French also involved the slaves and former slaves. In 1677, 12 slaves fled from the French possessions and sought refuge in Santo Domingo where the authorities accepted them and granted them freedom. This policy was based on the belief that by liberating the blacks who had run away from the French, the Spanish authorities could encourage more slaves to desert, thus harming the enemy. In a short time there were 50 refugee blacks settled on unused lands on the eastern side of the Ozama River, in an area which became known as San Lorenzo de los Mina, since most of the runaway slaves were from Mina, in Angola. This policy of sheltering blacks fleeing from the French and treating them kindly was endorsed by the Crown, and a special patrol was organized to search for them and bring them to San Lorenzo de los Mina.

The Spanish inhabitants were well aware of their own numerical inferiority. In 1681, the Spanish colony had fewer than 1,500 families spread throughout the country in small defenseless towns. Only by repopulating the island with Spanish subjects could the French penetration be resisted and the French eventually expelled. The authorities of Santo Domingo came to the conclusion that the Crown should encourage emigration of poor families from the Canary Islands to Española where they would be given better lands than they had in the Canaries. The Consejo de Indias welcomed this suggestion since the Canary Islands had become another problem area for the Spanish government. Extreme poverty in the Canary Islands resulted from demographic pressures, obsolete agricultural technology, and impoverished soils due to overcultivation and erosion.

In 1684, the first group of Canarians arrived in Santo Domingo. This group of 100 families was sent to the area of Santiago where they were to cultivate tobacco. A second group of 108 families was dispersed throughout different parts of the colony, with the largest group settling on the eastern banks of the Ozama River. Shortly after its arrival, this group suffered fevers and other illnesses, and was struck by a smallpox epidemic. In 1686, it was necessary to move the survivors to the hills on the outskirts of Santo Domingo where they founded the town of San Carlos.

In 1687, another 97 families arrived and were settled in various locations near the French areas. The most important site came to be the town of Bánica. The authorities intended to use the *canarios* as a living frontier. By defending their recently acquired land, the *canarios* would at the same time defend the colony against the French. In 1690, the authorities in Santo Domingo wrote to the Crown and requested more families. Only two-thirds of the recent arrivals had survived. This time the authorities asked for 100 families, 50 for Santiago, where protection was needed to prevent a new French attack, and the rest for Azua and San Juan de la Maguana, in the frontier areas of the south. The following year, the first 18 families, totaling 94 people, arrived and were immediately sent to Santiago.

The importance of these frontier settlements cannot be overstated. Since 1680, the French had requested that the Spaniards negotiate a boundary agreement between the two territories establishing the border at San Cristóbal only 20 miles from Santo Domingo, the capital city. While such proposals were adamantly refused by Spanish authorities, they clearly demonstrated the French intentions to enlarge their own colony.

Despite the Spanish authorities' refusal to officially sanction relations between the two colonies, trade continued in those zones nearest the French settlements, especially in Santiago. In 1687, the Spanish governor stated that because of the canarios immigration and the vigilance of the militia units, the French were contained within their territory. The Spanish residents in those zones had become so accustomed to the French that they received them on their ranches to sell them livestock.

The French frequently ventured as far as Santiago. The whole population of Santiago, including colonial officials and the clergy, reaped the maximum benefits from trading with the French. The livestock business was so prosperous that the

French demanded animals to start their own ranches. Some-times the flow of livestock from the Spanish to the French col-ony was so large that meat became scarce in Santiago. Such excesses alarmed the authorities in Santo Domingo, but those sent to investigate found a population that refused to cooperate with their investigations.

There was very little that the authorities could do to deter these relations that, although illegal, were rewarding for al-most everyone except the commercial elite of Santo Domingo. Commerce with the French was a natural response to the Span-ish monopoly. The authorities felt justified in permitting this illegal trade because it had been almost three years since a *navío de registro* had stopped in Santo Domingo. The popula-tion had been deprived of clothing and other necessities for many years and now had the opportunity to acquire them from the French.

In contrast with Santiago, the city of Santo Domingo suf-fered the rigors of the Spanish monopoly. The lack of legal trade with Spain kept the 11 shops of Santo Domingo completely depleted of merchandise. Poverty became so widespread in San-to Domingo that it affected everyone, including the soldiers. Since there were too few public works to occupy them as day-workers, the government allocated each soldier to a local fami-ly who would provide food and other basic necessities.

Other towns of the interior were similarly poor. According to a survey in 1690, Cotuí, a community of 70 households, had only 20 huts, while La Vega, comprised of 100 households, did not have more than 60 huts. This town was almost depopulated because most of the residents lived with their families on their farms, as did those of Cotuí. Only Santiago, which had ap-proximately 800 households, was in a somewhat better posi-tion since trade with the French had permitted some residents to obtain the means to build better homes. Santiago had about 200 huts, 30 stone houses, 5 churches, 2 chapels, and 1 convent. The people of Santiago had learned to make the most of their trade with the French. The entire population, including the colonial officials and the clergy, benefited from the trade in livestock.

CONFLICTS WITH THE FRENCH

The stability of the French colony during the Peace of Nimwegen attracted filibusters who preferred to settle and plant tobacco. A census taken in the French colony in May 1681 reported the population to be 7,848. Of those, there were 4,000 free French planters, 1,565 indentured workers, and 1,063 slaves, most of them involved in tobacco cultivation. A surplus of tobacco in the French market, due to imports from the Chesapeake Bay, led to a decline in prices. Many disenchanted settlers in Española abandoned tobacco cultivation and began experimenting with other crops including sugar cane, cotton, cacao, and indigo.

Following the death of De Pouançay in mid 1683, the new French governor, Tarin de Cussy, sought to maintain commercial relations with the Spaniards. De Cussy frequently wrote to the governor of Santo Domingo requesting that attacks by Spanish patrols on French settlements be discontinued. He also wanted to obtain official recognition for trade and establishment of clear boundaries to define the jurisdiction of both governments. There was little de Cussy could do since the Spanish authorities consistently refused to enter into boundary negotiations.

De Cussy worked hard at the internal reorganization of the French colony, which he divided into four large jurisdictions: Leoganne, Petit Goave, Le Cap, and Port de Paix, each to have its own courts of justice to reconcile disputes among the inhabitants. Concerned by the lack of white women and the practice of concubinage between the white masters and their female slaves, he arranged the importation of white indentured female workers but they were too few and concubinage with black or mulatto women became the norm in the French colony.

While the truce continued, the governors of both colonies continued discussing the French usurpation of Spanish lands. The governor of Santo Domingo continually warned that he would not permit the French to advance further to the east, while the French governor claimed those lands belonged to the French in accordance with the right of conquest. He insisted that he was to observe peace only as long as the Spaniards did not attack the French. He reiterated that if relations between the two colonies were broken, it would be because of Spanish hostility.

He held firm to his word and proved his intentions some time later. In August 1687, a Spanish brigantine sailing from Cuba attacked the population of Petit Goave in the southwest, forcing the French to flee. Another incident occurred in May 1688 when a ship from Santo Domingo attacked two French boats and captured their crew. De Cussy demanded the return of the prisoners, but the Spanish governor refused arguing that they had been captured in the act of pillaging Spanish territories.

De Cussy also received news that the Spanish authorities in Santo Domingo were making preparations for war. Hearing this news, he decided to respond by attacking first. During the final months of 1688 and all of 1689, De Cussy made plans to capture Santo Domingo and take the entire island from the Spanish. However, after surveying all his options, he decided to send his men only against the city of Santiago de los Caballeros.

To De Cussy's satisfaction, his plans coincided with the arrival of news that Spain was again at war with France. On July 6, 1690, De Cussy and 1,400 men entered Santiago de los Caballeros, destroyed the weak Spanish defenses, and ordered the city burned. While leaving the churches untouched, the French burned nearly 160 homes. The authorities in Santo Domingo immediately planned a campaign of retaliation.

The new Spanish governor, Ignacio Pérez Caro, moved to Santiago to reorganize the city and prepare the forces for a retaliatory attack. He requested from the Crown auxiliary naval forces to aid in dislodging the French from the island. By coincidence, on November 9, 1690, the Armada of Barlovento arrived in Santo Domingo with the *situado*. The commander was under orders to support the governor in whatever operations he intended against the French. With this aid, in two months the Spanish were ready to attack Cap Français, the main French settlement on the island.

On January 21, 1691, the Spaniards attacked the French troops who had been expecting them on the savanna of Guarico, in the north of the island. The encounter was violent and quick. Governor De Cussy, several of his lieutenants, and 400 other Frenchmen lost their lives. The Spanish casualties included 47 dead and 130 wounded. The next day, Spanish troops advanced and fell on Cap Français with the support of the Armada of Barlovento. After sacking the city, the Spaniards reduced it to ashes.

The destruction of Cap Français and the other French establishments in the Guarico left the region completely disorganized. However, as the attack had been directed only against this area, the rest of the French colony was left intact. The new French governor, Jean Ducasse, proceeded to reorganize the region by creating companies of militia to confront further Spanish attacks. He also asked his government for reinforcements, including two ships.

For the next four years, both governors made constant preparations to take control of the whole island. Official correspondence indicates the efforts of the Spanish authorities to obtain support from the viceroy of Mexico and the British governor of Jamaica to expel the French. The French not only sought to occupy lands in Santo Domingo but also antagonized the British in the Caribbean as part of their general war strategy. The War of the League of Augsburg, which started in 1689, was fought in the Caribbean as well as in Europe. In this war, France was pitted against Britain, Spain, and Holland, and during those years French corsairs again resurged in the Caribbean.

Corsair incursions increased until the middle of 1694, when Ducasse launched a major attack against Jamaica. More than 100 English colonists were killed and wounded, black slaves were captured and more than 50 sugar mills, and 200 English homes were burned. This called for reprisal on a large scale. In early 1695, the governor of Santo Domingo, Ignacio Pérez Caro was invited by authorities in Jamaica to support an attack they were planning against the whole French colony. This campaign would begin against the French settlements of the north and would end in the south after the destruction of the French settlements from which the pirates operated.

Pérez Caro accepted, and in May 1695, 1,500 armed Spaniards waited for the British squadron in the northwestern border point of Manzanillo. The British armada did not stop for the Spaniards and arrived at Cap Français before the Spanish troops. The ships bombarded the area while the English troops sacked the town. The English troops then went to Port de Paix where, after a long battle, they managed to dislodge the French. In both towns, English sailors and soldiers pillaged everything leaving little booty for the tired Spaniards who came on foot in forced marches from their colony.

The disappointed Spanish soldiers refused to follow the British to the south. To the dismay of the English authorities, the Spaniards abandoned the campaign and returned to their colony leaving the French in possession of their southern settlements. The governor of Jamaica complained that although the establishments of the North had sustained great damage, those in the south that were the nearest to Jamaica were left untouched.

The damage to the northern territories did not discourage Ducasse. He ordered all the inhabitants of the north, who had fled to the mountains, to return to Cap Français to reestablish French domination. Ducasse had received word that Spanish authorities had requested that the Crown send reinforcements and allow the immigration of 6,000 Andalusian families to help evict the French from the island and repopulate the west.

Ducasse was forced to change his plans for retaliation against Santo Domingo when the French government ordered him to put all the colony's resources at the service of a French corsair attack against Cartagena. This order completely disheartened Ducasse since the main objective of his strategy had always been Santo Domingo yet, Ducasse organized the expedition to Cartagena. The attack was succesful. Ducasse and his men took Cartagena in mid-1697 and sacked it completely, leaving it only after collecting a handsome booty.

Ducasse returned to Saint-Domingue, as the French side was called, just when the war between France and Spain was ending with the signing of the Peace of Ryswick in September 1697. The signing of the Peace of Ryswick made an immediate impact in the island for it allowed the renewal of commercial relations between the French and the Spanish colonists. With the capital represented by the booty taken in Cartagena, Ducasse and his men dedicated themselves to sugar production as many other settlers were doing in the Lesser Antilles and Jamaica. The turning of the French filibusters into sugar planters contributed to the economic development of the French colony and stimulated trade with the Spanish colony, despite the old monopoly laws. As the 17th century closed, the two colonies entered a new era of conflict and cooperation.

4.
The frontier
(1697-1789)

THE FRENCH AND THE CATTLE TRADE

Commercial relations between the French and Spanish colonies of Española resumed soon after the Peace of Ryswick was known on both parts of the island. With slaves captured from the English in Jamaica in 1695, Governor Jean Ducasse had began the construction of sugar *ingenios* on the northwestern plains of Española. Three of these *ingenios* were already in operation in 1698. Their construction produced important changes in the French colony. Due to the increase of sugar-cane fields in northern Saint-Domingue, the French moved the ranches which had been established in Guarico since 1685 to supply cattle to the colony.

The new *ingenios* needed land. To obtain it, Ducasse annulled many concessions to establish cattle ranches and granted the best lands to the new sugar-mill owners. In exchange, Ducasse assigned marginal lands to the colonists interested in continuing raising livestock. New ranches were established in the region of La Limonade, and in the basins of the Caracol and Yaquesí rivers, with cattle bought from the Spaniards. Investment in livestock was profitable, and little by little the number of ranches increased. The cattle propagated and the haciendas extended up to the banks of the Masacre River. In 1712, there were more than 10,000 cattle in La Limonade region. By 1714 the number of cattle had reached 14,000.

Such an increase in the number of French livestock would have been sufficient to satisfy the demand for meat if the *ingenios* had not multiplied the population of indentured workers and slaves. In September 1701, there were in the French colony 35 sugar mills functioning at full capacity, besides other 20 ready to begin production at the end of the year, plus 90 other *ingenios* undergoing construction. Thus, despite the increase in their own livestock production, the French remained in constant need of Spanish cattle.

Another reason the demand for livestock could not be satisfied with local production was that the French did not want to dedicate their best lands to raising livestock. They preferred plantation agriculture with higher productivity than cattle ranching. After comparing their profits with those of the sugar factories and indigo plantations, there was little enthusiasm for cattle raising among most French colonists. As time passed, the ranches originally established to substitute imports from the Spaniards gave way almost completely to plantation agriculture. This transition was officially promoted in 1711, when the French authorities decreed that all the lands between La Limonade and the Rebouc River should be dedicated to agriculture. As a result of this policy, by 1716 the French had built more than 100 *ingenios*.

The new *ingenios* demanded meat for their workers, as well as horses and mules to move their machines and carry the cane and sugar loads. As the number of mills, plantations, and slaves increased, so did the demand for livestock. The *ingenios* were not the only centers of demand for livestock in the French colony. The rest of the population also needed meat. Since the

French ranches were incapable of supplying all the necessary meat, dependence on Spanish cattle grew. Beef production became one of the most important businesses in both colonies. On the French side, the leasing of slaughterhouses, the numbers of which increased continually, brought benefits both to their operators and to the colonial government.

The colonial authorities of Santo Domingo opposed trade with the French. Often the opposition was based on the formal compliance with old monopoly laws. In other cases, especially in the towns near the French colony, the opposition was merely a ruse to obtain payoffs. The venality of the Spanish authorities of Santo Domingo was common knowledge among both the Spaniards and the French during this period. The governors arbitrarily enforced the laws prohibiting all commerce with foreigners. They continually used the armed forces along the frontier to extort ilegal fees from the cattle exporters who also imported large amounts of merchandise from the French colony.

In December 1720 and January 1721, for example, the cattle traders of Santiago, La Vega, Cotuí, and Azua complained that the governor wanted to tax each head of cattle sold to the French, with some of the proceeds eventually going into his own pockets. To enforce this measure, the governor stationed troops in Dajabón to prevent the passage of animals without his permission. This action prompted the people of Santiago to rise up in rebellion against the governor.

The people of Santiago declared themselves in open disobedience and elected Captain Santiago Morel de Santa Cruz as their governor and Captain Pedro de Carvajal as lieutenant governor, aided by Captains Juan Morel de Santa Cruz and Bartolomé Tiburcio. These four captains went to the border outpost of Dajabón and removed the guards placed there by the governor. For several weeks the city of Santiago was in state of turmoil until troops sent from Santo Domingo were able to reestablish order.

The "revolt of the captains" was only put down by means of terror and by instituting military rule in Santiago. The official documents prepared by those near the governor of Santo Domingo hid the true causes of the rebellion, putting the emphasis on the "treason" of the captains who were even accused of calling on the French to aid them with weapons while trying to deliver that part of the colony to the enemy. Nevertheless, it was clear in the testimony of the local witnesses that the rebels had removed the guards from Dajabón "because they charged four reales for each cargo that passed, and one peso for each pair of cows."

The needs of both colonies undermined official attempts to impose fiscal duties on the cattle trade. Although disputes and hostilities continued along the frontier areas, little by little the island's colonial economies became complementary. Spain could not supply its colony with manufactured goods, but France could. Spain could not maintain regular trade and navigation with its colony, but France could. France could not secure the meat and other provisions needed by its colony, but the Spanish colonists could.

This intercolonial trade was the result of natural demands arising from two different economies which evolved into two totally different land-use systems, antagonistic within the same area, but complementary in terms of the necessities of both colonies. While the French developed a plantation export economy that required the intensive use of land and labor, the Spaniards continued with their traditional system of production that consisted in the extensive utilization of the land for raising livestock.

Yet, the French put pressure upon the Spanish possessions every day because of their tremendous economic expansion and the quadrupling of their population. The demographic difference between the two colonies was enormous. In 1718, the Spanish colony contained 18,410 inhabitants of whom only some

3,705 were capable of bearing arms. Meanwhile, the French population was growing rapidly. By 1716, the French colony had 30,000 free persons and 100,000 blacks and mulattos. Among the first group there were 10,000 men capable of bearing arms, but if need be, some 20,000 blacks could be summoned to bear arms without seriously depleting the *ingenios* and plantations of their labor force.

Thus, despite the increasing communication and trade between both colonies, the struggle for the border lands was a permanent ingredient of the island's life in the 18th century. This was a struggle between the opposing interests of two different societies and two different economies, between the plantation and the cattle ranch. The shaping of the border was a slow, conflictive process in which the French wanted to extend their holdings to the maximum, trying at times to occupy the whole island while striving to preserve what they had already conquered. That is why the border between the French and Spanish colonies was never a simple line drawn up in official cabinets, but a living element in the social fabric of Española.

REPOPULATION OF THE BORDER AREAS

The residents and the governor of Santo Domingo became seriously concerned with the French expansionist tendencies and kept requesting the Crown to renew the Canarian immigration. From the moment in which the French presence became permanent on the west of La Española, the Spaniards knew they had to reinforce the defenses in the border areas if they wanted to keep a check on French expansion. Thus, from the very beginning, the importation of *canarios* was connected to the colonial frontier. This policy served not only to halt the French advance in Española, but also served as a solution to the problem of poverty in the Canary Islands.

As has been noted, the importation of *canarios* began in 1684. Between 1684 and 1691, some 323 families totaling over 1,615 individuals were brought to Española from the Canary Islands. During the 1680s these immigrants founded the towns of San Carlos on the outskirts of Santo Domingo and Bánica right on the border. However, after founding Hincha in 1704, west of Bánica, immigration from the Canary Islands was stopped primarily because between 1702 and 1713 the War of Spanish Succession made Atlantic navigation extremely dangerous. *(See map No. 5)*

In 1715, the *cabildo* of Santo Domingo complained that for 16 years the ships from the Canary Islands had not called at Santo Domingo. In 1718, the Consejo de Indias agreed that the shipments of families be renewed. The king then decreed that the shipowners of the Canary Islands should send one shipload of poor families periodically to Santo Domingo, Puerto Rico, and Caracas. On arrival at their destination, these families were to be given lands, livestock, and seeds. In 1720 the first 50 families arrived, and between 1721 and 1725 other 28 families arrived in Santo Domingo and were settled in various places on the island.

The Canarian immigration was interrupted in 1725. The governor of Santo Domingo was still writing to the Consejo de Indias in 1728 requesting families and soldiers from the Canary Islands to populate and fortify the ports of Montecristi and Samaná that the French were trying to settle. Furthermore, he expressed his desire that among these families some of Galician origin were sent, because he thought they were more adaptable to the humid tropical climate. The families requested by the Governor were not sent, and the question was not considered again until 1735, when the colonial authorities wrote two more letters to the Consejo de Indias requesting more families.

In 1735, the Consejo again ordered the *Juez de las Indias* in the Canaries to renew the shipment of families. Forty families arrived in 1737. The governor of Santo Domingo used them to repopulate the abandoned city of Puerto Plata. This second founding of Puerto Plata was disastrous because the authorities had sent the families without the necessary preparation and without enough supplies and provisions. Very soon, most of these people died of malaria. Perhaps because of this experience, the governor once again proposed that in addition to the Canarians, some Galicians and Catalonians should also be imported.

The efforts to repopulate the frontier continued for decades. In 1733, the village of San Juan was founded in the valley of La Maguana on lands that were coveted by the French. In 1735, the village of Neiba was established in a zone containing some wild cattle to prevent the French from continuing to hunt in this region. In 1740, the parish of Dajabón was created on the border "for the spiritual aid of the many *vecinos* which are in the border with many rural haciendas that have been formed there." Eleven years later, in 1751, the town of San Fernando de Montecristi was founded with a new contingent of 100 Canarian families. In that year, 100 other families were again sent to settle Puerto Plata.

In 1756, other Canarian families were sent to the new town of Samaná, located in a strategic point in the northeast. In 1760 these families were joined by another 60 families with a total of 240 persons. Some of these families crossed the Bay of Samaná and founded the town of Sabana de la Mar. In the following year, the Spaniards founded another town named San Rafael on the frontier. They also settled 26 other Canarian families in the coastal town of Azua "that needs residents for its development and defense in case of some insult on the part of enemies in times of war." For this same reason, the Spanish governor also wished to establish a town at the mouth of the strategic Haina River, several miles west of Santo Domingo. This was not possible for the moment, despite the fact that in 1762 there were 292 immigrants from the Canary Islands in Santo Domingo waiting to be settled there. These families were taken instead to the Sabana de Baní, where the town of Baní was founded in 1763.

The movement of families from the Canary Islands to Santo Domingo, and from this city to the interior of the island, cost money. To meet these expenses the Crown ordered the necessary funds to be allocated from the Cajas Reales in Mexico in 1741. The Viceroy of New Spain should annually send to Santo Domingo 16,000 pesos for each 50 Canary families settled on the island. The project was to cover all the zones of the island that had been depopulated during the *devastaciones*. This money was regularly sent to Santo Domingo for the following 20 years. During this time, according to the *Contaduría* of Santo Domingo, 225 immigrant families went to the island.

The Mexican colonial government suspended the money transfers in 1763. Under these circumstances, the Spanish governor asked that no more Canarians be sent because he did not have sufficient funds to complete the plan. Thus concluded the settlement program of the uninhabited zones of the Spanish colony of Santo Domingo that had been abandoned more than a century before. Only one further Spanish settlement was made during the colonial era: San Miguel de la Atalaya, founded in 1768 in the westernmost area of the Spanish colony, adjacent to the French settlements.

THE POLITICS OF THE CATTLE TRADE

Meanwhile, the trade of livestock and manufactured goods between both colonies continued along the border. A border agreement in 1731 stabilized relations between the French and Spanish residents of the island. Although on many occasions these relations were marred by land disputes along the border, there were permanent communications between the two colonial governments after 1731. Little by little, the French had succeeded in getting the Spaniards to accept the reality of the French occupation of the western part of the island despite the official Spanish argument that regarded the French presence as technically illegal.

The border agreement of 1731 tacitly legalized the French possessions once and for all, and both colonial governments promised to maintain the best relations possible. They did this not only because they were ordered to do so by their metropolitan governments now united in a common front against the British, but because it was convenient for the residents of both colonies. That was clearly seen during the war that Spain fought against England from 1739 until 1748. Navigation in the Caribbean immediately became difficult and dangerous. In 1740, the Spanish authorities had to ask the French governor to send a French ship to pick up the *situado* that had been deposited in Santiago de Cuba.

Despite this collaboration, the livestock trade was disrupted during the war by various measures adopted by the new governor, Pedro Zorrilla de San Martín. This officer arrived on the island in 1741, aboard a French ship that had first made a port call at Cap Français. During his stay in this French town, Zorrilla de San Martín discovered that the French had established a duty on the meat sold to their slaughterhouses, a measure which seemed illegal to him since it meant that a foreign government was enriching itself by taxing goods produced in Spanish territory.

Immediately after arriving in Santo Domingo Zorrilla de San Martín categorically prohibited the export of livestock to the French colony, thus aggravating the scarcity of meat existing there because of a drought which had been affecting the island for more than two years. This measure forced the French governor to beg Zorrilla de San Martín to permit an export quota of at least 200 head of cattle per month until the ranches of the French territory had recovered from the drought. The Spanish governor complied, but added that "in order to have this toleration accepted by the Court of Spain he believed he should establish a duty on the export of animals and fixed that tax at five pesos for each pair."

This measure caused an increase in meat prices in the French colony and the hostility of the Spanish ranchers who, harmed by this quota, chose to drive livestock as contraband into the French colony. This traffic, although difficult, was carried out along the hidden trails opened by the French in previous years to elude the payment of the duties established by former Spanish governors. When Zorrilla de San Martín learned of this contraband in 1744, he threatened the French authorities with totally cutting off all official trade. To calm his suspicions and contain his threats, the French governor named a commission to investigate the charges of misconduct of those in charge with buying livestock in the Spanish area.

These conflicts continued through 1760. Throughout all this period, the official export quota varied according to the convenience of the various Spanish governors, while many animals crossed the border in contraband through hidden roads. All this changed in 1761, when France and Spain renewed the Family Compact to protect themselves from the British. To confront this alliance, Britain declared war on Spain in 1762, and in the following year after a rapid series of victories, attacked and took the city of Havana which remained in English hands for eleven months.

During the Seven Years' War, the French sent additional troops to Española to protect both colonies against a possible British attack. At the beginning of June 1762, the two governors received orders from their respective government and were forced to sign a treaty that established that the Spaniards should supply the French 800 head of cattle per month without interruption. The price of these animals, some 9,600 head per year, was fixed at 35 pesos each pair. This represented a trade value of 168,000 pesos annually.

The duty of five pesos per pair established by Zorrilla de San Martín 20 years before remained in effect. Since this was an onerous burden on the French colonial economy, a French delegate arrived in Santo Domingo in 1763, with the permission of the Spanish Court, to negotiate with the Spanish governor a new arrangement regarding the cattle supply. His intention was to get the tax abolished and the monthly export quota raised to at least 1,000 animals per month, but the Spanish governor categorically refused.

The discussion continued and the French even sought permission to import livestock from the eastern part of Cuba where there was a great quantity of livestock that the Cuban colonists did not consume. Before this could be arranged, an order of the Spanish king arrived in Santo Domingo giving the French permission to buy from the colony all the livestock they needed. Hence, in May 22, 1764, the Spanish and the French authorities signed a treaty that permitted the free trade of cattle "without any extraordinary toll and without any other precaution than that to assure reproduction."

Despite the treaty's stipulations, the Spanish governor Manuel Azlor ruled that Spanish ranchers had to pay an export duty of 10 French pounds for each ox or cow; 3 for each hog, dead or alive; and 20 for each horse, mule, or donkey. Violation of these orders carried a penalty of death and confiscation of the transgressors's property. Although the French governor protested this measure, Azlor calmly answered that he would leave the matter as such until he received new instructions from his government.

Something similar occurred in 1766 and in 1769 when the authorities of both colonies renegotiated new treaties for the export of livestock. In the latter year, Governor Azlor established a new regulation stating that the trade could not be conducted without a permit to the exporter issued directly by him and not by the border officials. He also ordered his officials to prepare an annual statement that would inform the ranch owners of the quantity of cattle necessary for local consumption, and the amount that should be kept for breeding purposes. This report was designed to allow only surplus cattle to be exported, and it was used to closely monitor cattle production and inventories in each ranch of the Spanish part.

Because these regulations produced many difficulties for the French as well as for the Spanish cattle ranchers, the French authorities again sent another emissary to Santo Domingo to negotiate a treaty less harmful to their interests. These events took place at a time when diplomatic relations between the two colonies were extremely tense because of frontier disputes and conflicts. Therefore, the new agreement for the supply of livestock to the French was signed as a clause of a new general border treaty signed June 4, 1770. For the Spanish authorities the commerce of livestock could not be considered separately from the frontier problem.

The issue was further complicated in 1772 when Governor Azlor was replaced by José Solano Bote. This new governor intended to establish in Santo Domingo a branch of the Compañía de Cataluña, which had been founded in Barcelona in 1755 for the purpose of monopolizing Spanish trade with Española. This company was organized on the model of the Compañía Guipuzcoana de Caracas that had been operating in Venezuela since its founding in 1728, and the Real Compañía de Comercio de La Habana, which had been in operation since 1740. Although the Compañía de Cataluña never managed to undertake great business transactions in Santo Domingo, it named its representatives in the city and tried to intervene in the cattle trade.

Solano Bote, previously the governor of Caracas, was accustomed to serve the interests of the Compañía Guipuzcoana and believed that the interests of trading companies reflected the interests of the Crown since members of the royal family were stockholders in these ventures. Solano Bote obtained a promise from the Compañía de Cataluña to send six ships each year to the colony and, in return, promised to guarantee its monopoly. But to do that he had to prevent the Spaniards from buying from the French. To accomplish this, in January 1773 he decreed a prohibition of the livestock trade with the French under penalty of imprisonment.

The effects of this arbitrary measure were soon felt, and the French colonists again suffered a serious scarcity of meat as had happened on previous occasions when trade had been interrupted by the order of the governor. In the Spanish colony, the ranch owners reacted in the customary way, by smuggling their animals to the French. The French authorities had their metropolitan government complain against these regulations before the court in Madrid. The Consejo de Indias gave orders for the exportation of animals to be carried out in accordance with the Convention of 1766 that permitted the slaughterhouses and meat sellers in the French colony to freely enter Spanish territory to buy the animals that they needed, paying the corresponding duties.

The situation remained unchanged until a definitive border treaty was signed in 1777. This treaty, signed in Aranjuez by high-level representatives of France and Spain, established that the Spanish governor should issue the necessary passports to the French slaughterhouses to buy livestock in the Spanish colony without any obstacles whatsoever, while the French would pay the corresponding duties. From then on, the French came and went freely to provision themselves with livestock in the Spanish colony while the Spanish residents amply bought all sorts of European and North American merchandise imported through Cap Français and other ports on the western part of the island.

The Treaty of Aranjuez also definitively solved the long standing question of the border limits that had kept the French and Spanish colonists intermittently at war for more than a century. The first treaty of limits signed in 1731 by the colonial governors had just defined the border in its northernmost and southernmost sections, taking advantage of the existence of two rivers that had traditionally served as de facto limits between the two colonies. But the interior border areas, crossed by other rivers and mountains, and dotted with many fertile valleys, were a constant source of disputes that provoked hundreds of violent incidents and military clashes.

Intercolonial trade was one matter, but the occupation of lands by the French was quite another. Both the military watch and the resettlement of the frontier with Canarian immigrants had served to detain the French along a so-called "line of toler-ance," but this line of demarcation was increasingly called into question as the French coffee plantations advanced over the mountains that served to define it. The violent confrontations between French colonists and Spanish military patrols finally prompted the colonial authorities to recommend that Spain and France appoint representatives to negotiate a permanent border.

The negotiations that started in 1764 were linked to the cattle trade by the Spanish governors. Similarly, the French authorities linked the negotiations to the very old problem of the runaway slaves who were welcomed and freed by the Span-ish authorities. The frontier was finally drawn and fixed with stone landmarks in August 1776 by a Franco-Spanish commis-sion of surveyors who worked in the field for almost five years. Its charts and maps were approved in 1776 by the colonial gover-nors. This agreement to "put an end to all difficulties for ever" was officially sanctioned by especially appointed French and Spanish ambassadors in Aranjuez, Spain on June 3, 1777.

The Treaty of Aranjuez was a decisive turning point in the history of both colonies for it opened a new era of cooperation and increased trade. Not only did the commercial exchange in-crease in the following years, but the Spaniards also agreed to return all runaway slaves who crossed the newly defined bor-der. The Spaniards also committed themselves to protect the stability of the slave regime in the French part. The treaty also bound the authorities on both sides of the island to detain and return deserting soldiers and other people who would illegally cross from one colony to the other.

The American Revolution and the French support of the rebelling English colonists brought France and Britain to war in 1778. In the following year Spain allied with France to try to recover what had been lost in the Seven Years' War. During this period the French colony received large contingents of troops that were to defend the island from a possible British attack. These troops protected both Santo Domingo and Cap Français, and, because of this, the export of livestock was increased. Although the war ended in 1783 and the presence of the soldiers was no longer necessary, the volume of animals sold to the French did not diminish.

The French government eliminated all monopolies on meat in 1787, and the free buying of livestock permitted a noticeable increase in consumption that forced French buyers to penetrate further into the Spanish colony to obtain animals. Because the total population of the French colony had increased to 520,000 in 1789, the demand for Spanish cattle kept increasing. According to contemporary calculations, between 1783 and 1789 the flow of cattle from the Spanish colony was 15,000 heads per year with a price of 30 pesos each. This produced an annual gross income for the Spanish ranch owners of 450,000 pesos, not including the 10 percent received by the colonial government from duties.

IMPACT OF THE INTERCOLONIAL TRADE

The positive effects of the French demand for livestock on the economy of the Spanish colony became evident during the third decade of the 18th century. In 1728, the *cabildo* of Santo Domingo wrote the Crown informing that for the first time in about a century it was not necessary to seek money from the rich residents to defray the expenses of the colonial government. According to the *cabildo*, the military expenditures were duly satisfied, the militias were well disciplined, and the troops of the northern and southern coasts were well paid. The satisfaction of the *regidores* made them exclaim that never had the royal exchequer increased so much in a place so poor.

When Zorrilla de San Martín arrived as governor in Santo Domingo in 1741, the livestock trade was the main factor behind the economic reactivation of the colony. According to a contemporary witness, Governor Zorilla de San Martín allowed the Dutch and Danish traders to freely provision the colonists during the war between 1739 and 1748. This measure was beneficial because the Dutch and the Danes competed and thus their prices were lowered. Slaves were again made available, and some investors ventured into agriculture, especially sugar cane.

During this period the Spanish colonial population grew significantly. From 1718 to 1768, the population of the Spanish colony quadrupled. This demographic increase was stimulated by the importation of families from the Canary Islands, and by immigration from other parts of the Caribbean, including the French colony of Saint-Domingue. In 1718, there were only 18,410 inhabitants. Almost 20 years later, in 1739, the population had increased to 30,158. In 1769, the parochial records estimated the population in 73,319 persons. In 1783, the population surpassed 80,000 individuals, with the city of Santo Domingo containing about 25,000 inhabitants.

The economic revival was particularly evident in Santo Domingo. According to Antonio Sánchez Valverde, a contemporary writer, in 1737 more than half the buildings of the capital were entirely ruined, and of those still standing the majority were uninhabitable. By 1785, many buildings had been rebuilt with new stone fixings, and many others with strong mud walls, while the principal residents had beautified their houses inside and out. The city had been repopulated to such an extent that some people who moved in had to spend many days looking for a house. A similar change took place in the towns of the interior, especially in those which profited from the cattle trade, like Santiago.

The Martinican traveler Moreau de Saint-Méry also witnessed the improved condition of Santo Domingo in 1783. The population dedicated itself not only to trade and livestock raising, but also to sugar production in the old plantation zones surrounding the city and in the southern river basins. Between the Nizao and Ozama rivers 11 mills operated, powered by oxen and mules, while another 20 functioned around the capital. Yet these were still very small compounds. One of the most important, which had belonged to the Jesuits, employed 50 black slaves.

In the areas surrounding Santo Domingo some *vecinos* developed cacao plantations. More to the west of the Nizao River where the sugar fields ended, there were new plantations of indigo and cotton. A similar phenomenon could be observed in the towns of the interior. In Santiago and La Vega, for several decades cattle raising was supplemented by tobacco cultivation. So, by 1789, both colonies had already solved their most pressing economic problems complementing each other very well, exchanging cattle for manufactured goods, and expanding their plantations and ranches to satisfy the demand of both the international and Española markets.

5.
The French Revolution in Santo Domingo (1789-1809)

THE HAITIAN REVOLUTION

The outbreak of the French Revolution in 1789 had a disruptive effect on both colonies of Española in spite of the efforts of the French revolutionary leaders to maintain the status quo in the West Indies. The French bourgeoisie had invested large sums of capital in the colonies during the 18th century, making them an important source of profit. The fact that France had lost Canada to England during the Seven Years' War gave additional importance to the maintenance of French colonies in the Antilles. This was particularly true of Saint-Domingue, its the most prosperous one.

Many French merchants and industrialists had been actively participating in the slave trade since the 17th century. The French mercantile groups sold goods to the rulers of the African coasts where they purchased black slaves to be sold to the colonists in Saint-Domingue, Martinique, and Guadeloupe. France also exported large quantities of manufactured goods and food products to Saint-Domingue where consumption of imported goods had a tremendous impact on the expansion of French commerce in the 18th century. The French economy was strengthened by the considerable profits received from the triangular trade of European manufactured goods, African slaves, and West Indian tropical products.

The profitability of Saint-Domingue made the French investors resistant to any changes in the colonial status, but there were areas of discontent within the colony. The white planters and merchants resented the colonial system which kept most of the profits in France. Despite the enormous volume of exports, the economy of Saint-Domingue was burdened with debt. Many planters resented the fact that the monopoly established by the French investors denied them the liberty to trade with allied nations like the United States.

For several years, the planters demanded that the monopoly be abolished. In 1784, the French government complied and opened eight ports in the colony to foreign commerce. This measure put Saint-Domingue in direct contact with the United States, creating a new market for the colonial products. Attracted by new business possibilities, various metropolitan capitalists made additional investments in Saint-Domingue leading to increased production.

Despite the prosperity of the colony, some planters organized the Club Massiac in Paris, where they lobbied to obtain political autonomy and form their own government, thus breaking the French monopoly, as the United States had recently done with England. By 1789, there was a spirit of clear disaffection toward the French colonial system on the part of many of the white planters whose goal was to attain complete independence.

The free mulatto population, which had reached 28,000 by 1789, was also dissatisfied with the French colonial system. The mulatto class owned one-third of the colony's property, but was subjected to the political domination of the whites, who treated the free mulattos as second-class citizens. The rich mulatto planters, too, resented the metropolitan monopoly, and professed a deep aversion of the whites, who in turn resented the

fact that descendants of slaves had reached a preeminent position in the colonial economy. The mulattos felt they had more
right than the white colonial rulers to control the colony since
they were true natives of the island.

The mixture of races in Saint-Domingue was caused primarily by the permanent scarcity of white women. In the beginning, unions between masters and slaves were little more
than passing encounters, but as the colonial society developed,
the female slaves discovered that concubinage with their white
masters was the easiest way to acquire liberty for themselves
and their descendants. The offspring of these unions became
free people who could acquire full citizenship rights in accordance with Article 59 of the Black Code dictated in 1685. Among
the rights the mulatto sons acquired was the right of succession, as long as they were recognized by their fathers. In this
way, many of the properties passed into the hands of the mulattos, some of whom could be counted among the richest landowners of the colony.

The whites, who resented the social and economic mobility
of the mulattos, promulgated a series of discriminatory laws. To
defend their rights, the wealthy mulattos living in France organized the Societé des Amis des Noirs. This society attained notable prestige among liberal bourgeois groups in France who were
also fighting for recognition of their rights denied by the French
nobility. At the outbreak of the French Revolution, a close relationship already existed between important revolutionary leaders and representatives of the rich mulattos living in Paris.

The mulattos' goal in 1789 was to obtain from the French
Assembly a decree that would force the colonial authorities to
recognize their full rights of citizenship which had been cur-
tailed by discriminatory colonial laws. The French bourgeoisie
vacillated in their deliberations. The Assembly permitted the
whites to initiate a repressive movement against the mulattos
in Saint-Domingue, while claiming that the whites should be

granted the right to govern themselves through a colonial assembly. On March 8, 1790, the right to organize a colonial assembly was conceded, but this assembly, dominated by whites, would allow for no change in the status of the mulattos.

The Societé des Amis des Noirs sent two of its members to Great Britain in search of aid from the abolitionist societies. From there they went to Saint-Domingue to obtain by force what had been denied them by law. Vincent Ogé, the Societé's envoy, arrived in the colony in October 1790 and tried to organize an armed rebellion with another mulatto activist named Jean Baptiste Chavannes. Due to the small number of mulattos, Ogé and Chavannes failed in their attempt and fled to the Spanish colony, where they requested asylum. The French pressed the Spanish authorities to comply with the provisions of the Treaty of Aranjuez of 1777 regarding the restitution of runaway slaves and deserters, and Ogé and his companions were returned to Saint-Domingue and delivered to the French authorities, who promptly executed them along with other conspirators.

The execution of Ogé inflamed the mulattos who had begun to organize against the French authorities and the white colonists. The disputes between the whites and the mulattos became violent in the colonial assemblies. While the whites sought independence, the mulattos sought political equality and independence. Neither group was concerned with rights for the black slaves who comprised the majority of the population. As the blacks were exposed to revolutionary propaganda, they eventually became aware of their potential for freedom. Little attention was paid to the unrest among the slaves until August 14, 1791, when a revolt broke out on the Bredá plantation in northern Saint-Domingue.

The whites and mulattos were forced to forget their differences and unite against the slaves. In 1792, the whites and mulattos, backed by the French government, allied against the blacks. The slaves fought against all landowners since destruction of the entire system was their only chance for freedom. With their common interests threatened, the most important white planters also sought the assistance of Britain.

In its desire to secure the colony away from France, the British Parliament forgot about the abolitionist campaign and the drive to end slavery. The blacks also discovered their own foreign ally in the island: Spain. During 1792, black leaders entered into close contact with Spanish frontier leaders. The Spaniards saw their great opportunity to recover the whole island and promised freedom to the slaves. In March 1792, the French government recognized the equality of mulattos with whites, and that action immediately divided the population in three clear and opposing camps: white planters seeking British support; mulattos with French support; and, rebellious blacks with Spanish support.

In September 1792, when a Civil Commission appointed in Paris arrived in Cap Français to impose the decree of equality, the whites declared themselves openly against the French government and sought the assistance of the British in Jamaica. In the midst of this chaotic situation, important political changes were occuring in Europe. By 1793, England, Holland and Spain had become enemies of the French Revolution. Taking advantage of this opportunity, the British sent troops to Saint-Domingue where they occupied the southern and western coasts. The Spaniards in Santo Domingo, managed to conquer territories in the north in a rapid military campaign. The complete defeat of the French seemed imminent in August 1793, when Léger-Felicité Sonthonax, one of the French commissioners, in a desperate effort to save the colony for France, dictated a decree abolishing slavery in the colony once and for all.

This decision had immediate effects. The blacks became divided among themselves, since many of their principal leaders preferred to continue fighting as auxiliary soldiers of the

Spanish, while others turned back and joined the French who now appeared to favor their cause. Toussaint L'Ouverture, one of the most powerful leaders, crossed over to the French side with 4,000 men. Some mulattos supported the French government, others supported the white planters alliance with the British. In a matter of months, the Spanish lost most of their newly won possessions in the French colony to Toussaint. Having checked the Spanish, Toussaint and the French directed all their forces toward expelling the British. And so began an international war that would last nearly five years.

This struggle was a reflection of the larger war taking place in Europe. Spain was dragged into the war for reasons of European dynastic policy. Spain entered the war to defend itself against the eventual spread of French republicanism onto the Iberian Peninsula. Spain was too weak to win the war. By the middle of 1795, Spain was forced to sign a peace treaty with France. Under the treaty, Spain recovered its lost peninsular possessions in exchange for surrendering the eastern part of the island of Española to France.

The cession to France worried the British government, which then sent troops to the eastern part of the island. The British troops managed to penetrate the Spanish territories but they soon lost ground to Toussaint. Toussaint had been named General after rendering his services to the French government. One of his most outstanding services had been preventing mulatto slave owners from deposing the French governor, General Etiènne Laveaux. A third civil commission arrived in May 1796, and together with Toussaint and Laveaux began to work for the reconstruction of the country by forcing the blacks to return to work on the plantations.

Slowly but surely, the northern territories controlled by Toussaint managed to recuperate from the devastations of war, but production never returned to prerevolutionary levels. In the south, the mulatto leader, General Rigaud, maintained power and managed to force the blacks back to the plantations under a regimen of salaried labor, the severity of which resembled slavery. Meanwhile, the war against the British continued, but after a bloody and disastrous campaign in which the British lost more than 25,000 troops, Britain finally ordered its army out of the island in April 1798. By then, Toussaint had become the master of the entire colony and his military power went uncontested by anyone, including the French commanders.

After the departure of the British, Toussaint reorganized the colony. Just as he was leading the colony toward recovery, the mulatto partisans of Rigaud rebelled. As free men and land owners, the mulattos could not accept being governed by a former slave. In February 1799, civil war broke out between the blacks and mulattos who fought for more than two years for the control of the colony. The numerical superiority of the blacks, under the brillant military leadership of Toussaint, led to the defeat of the mulattos in August 1800. Rigaud left the island and Toussaint struggled to return the colony to its former economic splendor.

More than the hostility of the whites and mulattos, the real threat facing Toussaint came from the government of France, specifically from Napoleon Bonaparte. France needed the resources of its colonies. However, French control over Saint-Domingue would be impossible unless the blacks were subdued. Therefore, the French felt it was necessary to restore slavery and depose Toussaint. When Toussaint heard of Napoleon's plans in late 1800, he decided to protect his eastern flank by occupying the Spanish colony, which had not yet been deliverd to France. On January 26, 1801, Toussaint arrived with his troops in Santo Domingo, where he immediately began to unify the former Spanish colony under his government. However, Napoleon had no intention of changing his plans to put down the slave rebellion, and proceeded to send a fleet of more than 80 ships with 58,000 men to wrest the colony from the blacks.

The fleet arrived off the eastern coast of the island on January 29, 1802. Toussaint, who witnessed their arrival in Samaná, rushed back to the west to organize the resistance. Throughout 1802, the blacks took a heavy beating from the French forces, and on June 7, Toussaint was captured and imprisoned. This created great consternation among his followers, but his lieutenants decided to continue fighting. The blacks elected Jean Jacques Dessalines and Henry Christophe to replace Toussaint. For 21 months, the French tried to subdue the blacks. Yet, the blacks found an ally the French had not forseen: yellow fever and malaria. According to French sources, when the campaign ended, over 52,000 French soldiers had lost their lives. In November 1803 there were only 1,200 French troops surviving on the entire island.

Dessalines and the black generals decided to abandon Toussaint's policies of accommodation with France and proclaimed the independence of Haiti on January 1, 1804. Once again, the blacks had to begin the reconstruction of their devastated country, this time without Toussaint, but also without the whites, for Dessalines and Christophe decided to annihilate them all lest they could do further harm to their revolution.

CESSION TO FRANCE

When the Spanish authorities learned of the agitation in Saint-Domingue caused by the French Revolution in 1789, the governor of Santo Domingo, Don Joaquín García y Moreno, put his troops on alert. By 1790 the Spanish troops had been reorganized with headquarters in the north and in the south. Military operations were to be directed from these two points if necessary.

When war broke out between France and Spain in March 1793, the Spanish authorities once again began accepting the

rebelling black slaves. The slave rebels Jean François, Jean Bias-
sou, and Toussaint L'Ouverture, were aided by Spanish frontier
commanders who joined in the fight against the French. The confusion in the French colony led the Spaniards to believe that if
the French could be expelled from the island, Spain could recover the lands lost to the French over a hundred years before.

The Spanish alliance with the slave rebels worked for less
than a year. After the French authorities abolished slavery in
September 1793, Toussaint L'Ouverture abandoned the Spaniards. In May 1794, he moved with his men to support the
French. After the defection of Toussaint, the Spaniards lost the
major part of their early territorial conquests along the border.
In 1794 the French forces, primarily composed of Toussaint's
black troops, forced the Spaniards to abandon the important frontier posts of San Rafael, San Miguel and Hincha, and to regroup
in the towns of Las Caobas and Bánica in the South, and in Dajabón, Bayajá, and Montecristi, in the North. *(See map No. 6)*

Alarm spread among the residents of Santo Domingo and
the interior when they learned that Toussaint's troops had evicted
the Spaniards from their best grazing lands, and had forced
them to take refuge in San Juan de la Maguana and Azua, where
the Spanish commanders had concentrated their troops. At this
critical juncture, news arrived from Spain that the war with
France had ended in Europe and that a peace treaty had been
signed on July 22, 1795, in Basel, Switzerland.

The news was received in Santo Domingo on October 18,
1795. The Treaty of Basel stated that the King of Spain would
cede and abandon to the French Republic all property in the
Spanish part of the island of Santo Domingo. It further stipulated that Spanish troops would promptly evacuate the towns,
ports, and establishments and would surrender them to French
troops when they arrived. It was conceded that the inhabitants
of Santo Domingo would have one year, from the date of the
treaty, to relocate.

This news was a devastating blow for a population who had spent more than a century in constant battle against the French. Their efforts during the previous two years had been specifically aimed at expelling the French from the island. Now the French had become the masters of the whole island by means of a treaty in which the Spanish colonists had had no participation. The repercussions of the Treaty of Basel were felt immediately, as many people quickly made plans to emigrate. In 1795, the first group of emigrans was sent to Cuba where the authorities said they would be given lands equivalent to those abandoned in Santo Domingo.

The first families arriving in Cuba encountered many difficulties. They found there was no high quality land available nor did Havana have facilities to accommodate them. The city, already heavily populated, barely had living quarters for its own inhabitants. The cost of living was so high that only the rich emigrants could live comfortably. Since the best available lands in Cuba, those of Havana and Pinar del Río, were already occupied, the emigrants were offered inferior lands. When this became known in Santo Domingo, the colonists, reluctant to relocate, wrote to the king requesting he concede them more than one year to relocate. They also requested that he permit them to go to other areas, including Puerto Rico and Venezuela.

To facilitate the transfer of the colony, the French government commissioned Phillipe Roume to go to Santo Domingo and work with the Spanish authorities. Roume had to work quickly since the British were about to break the military cordon along the frontier and threatened to take control of Santo Domingo. In June 1796, approximatly 1,800 people left the island. The majority were military personnel with no economic stake in the colony. Many landowners chose to stay, especially after learning the fate of those who had emigrated to Cuba. Others requested the period for emigration be extended to three or four years so they would not be forced to sell their holdings at low prices.

Most landowners were also concerned about the French policy toward slavery. The Spaniards knew that in December 1795 Governor Laveaux had declared the slaves found in the Spanish colonies would be freed. Many Spanish slave owners took their slaves with them when they left the colony. To complicate the situation, in October 1796 two hundred slaves of the ingenio of Boca de Nigua, the biggest in the colony, rose up in arms, burned the cane fields and buildings, and killed the livestock. This revolt was promptly suppressed, but the fear of rebellions would continue.

Confusion prevailed among the Spanish population: British corsairs posed a threat to those leaving the colony and, to make mathers worse, there was little certainty of finding a new home in other Spanish territories. Moreover, slave holders faced threats from the French policy and the slaves themselves.

Only Governor García and Commissioner Roume knew what they wanted: to accelerate the delivery of the Spanish colony. During the first year after cession, García worked hard to protect the Spanish frontiers from British attacks. García surrendered Bayajá to the French and was eager to concentrate the Spanish troops in Santo Domingo where they could be embarked once the French troops arrived. The Spaniards were forced to surrender Las Caobas to Toussaint. This town soon became a new war zone as the British attacked and occupied it. From there, the British prepared to invade the Spanish colony focusing on the nearby towns of Neiba and San Juan, which they occupied by March, 1797. In April, 1797, Toussaint counterattacked and evicted the British.

García continued with his plans to surrender Santiago and Puerto Plata to the French. He concentrated his troops in the city of Santo Domingo where the situation was critical due to lack of food, supplies, and money to pay salaries. There was little hope of receiving shipments since the British squadrons dominated the Caribbean waters. Puerto Rico was blockaded for several months, and the *situado* was detained there for over a year. In September 1797, García informed Madrid that for five months the soldiers had been paid only half their salaries. The economic situation in Santo Domingo convinced more people to emigrate.

The formal surrender of the colony to the French seemed extremely remote. The French had no white troops to take possession and did not dare occupy the colony with Toussaint's troops because of the terror which the former slaves instilled in the Spanish residents. In the two and a half years since the announcement of the cession to France, the Spanish colonial government had come to a complete stop. Without the *situado*, the garrison of Santo Domingo, now reduced to 1,320 men, had become violent and tumultuous.

García's problem was totally dependent on events in Saint-Domingue and in France. When the defeated British began to evacuate their positions in the French territory in April 1798, new hopes arose that the official delivery of the Spanish colony would take place soon. A long awaited French commission finally arrived in Santo Domingo at the end of March 1798. To the dismay of García, the leader of this commission, General Gabriel-Theodore-Joseph Hedouville, did not wish to speak of surrender. His main concern was to wrest political and military power away from Toussaint, who had become too powerful for French designs. Hedouville failed and was forced by Toussaint to abandon the island or lose his life. To aggravate the problem further, the white French troops who had arrived in Santo Domingo with General Hedouville were left totally idle since Commissioner Phillip Roume had to travel to Saint-Domingue to occupy the post vacated by Hedouville.

Hostility between the blacks and mulattos intensified critically after the departure of the British. The ensuing civil war between blacks and mulattos forced Roume to return to the western part. Given these circumstances, the surrender of the Spanish colony to France was indefinitely delayed. The only person with sufficient force to occupy the Spanish area was Toussaint, but he was too involved in the struggle against the mulattos to take possession of the eastern colony.

Meanwhile in Santo Domingo, Governor García continued his efforts to abandon the island. In November 1799, several ships from the royal Spanish armada arrived with the delayed *situados*. The members of the Real Audiencia and their families embarked on these ships and left the governor behind with the last 1,165 men. By December 1799, word had spread in Santo Domingo that Toussaint was making plans to occupy the Spanish zone despite the official opposition of the French government.

Another problem facing the Spanish authorities was the question of the departure of the archbishop and the clergy. According to the instructions from Madrid, everyone was supposed to leave except the archbishop, who was to wait until the top colonial authorities and the Real Audiencia left. The archbishop, Don Fernando de Portillo y Torres, who had a deep hatred for the French, tried every means available to hasten his own departure and that of the clergy. His most difficult task was to convince the nuns and friars of the various convents in the city to leave the island. Although the Clarisse nuns accepted the orders to leave immediately, they later reconsidered upon realizing they would lose all their properties and revenues.

The same occurred with the other religious orders, including the Dominicans. In 1795, the Dominican order had four convents in the colony that provided them with significant revenues through mortgages on lands, alms, chaplaincies, and ecclesiastical annuities. The Dominican prior alleged that none of the members of his community wished to go to Ocoa, an isolated harbor, to await transfer and shipping since it was known that a malaria epidemic had broken out aboard the ships destined to transport the emigrants to Cuba. Other religious communities also argued they could not leave without receiving orders from their superiors and therefore excused themselves from obeying the archbishop.

Governor García urged the archbishop to force the religious clergy to leave. The secular clergy were to time their departure with that of the archbishop, while many of the clergy simply wished to stay on the island despite the changes taking place. Some did not wish to leave for financial reasons, others had been won over by the ideas of the French Revolution, some were reluctant to abandon their families, and some felt they should stay to attend to the spiritual needs of the remaining residents.

Knowing that without church support it was going to be more difficult to govern the colony, the French encouraged the clergy to remain. The French authorities published several documents guaranteeing that the religious practices and customs of the Spaniards would be respected. In mid 1796, the archbishop, trapped by both the French propaganda in favor of religious toleration and the clergy who refused to leave, gave consent for the regular clergy to remain until they sold their properties. The archbishop finally gained the governor's permission to embark and left the island in April 1798. He left behind a population in crisis and a clergy more interested in saving their revenues than in obeying the king of Spain.

The unity of the whole island was an important objective of Toussaint, but he had been forced to wait until the pacification of the French colony. After receiving the news of Napoleon Bonaparte's plans to reinstitute slavery Toussaint requested authorization from Roume to take possession of Santo Domingo. Roume argued that he could not authorize the takeover of the Spanish colony without specific instructions from France. Toussaint replied to Roume that he should sign the decree or all the whites remaining in the colony would be beheaded.

Roume gave in to his demand, and signed the decree for the occupation of the Spanish part on April 27, 1800.

Toussaint immediately sent this decree to Governor García in Santo Domingo. After learning that the surrender was going to be consummated, the Spanish residents and many French colonial exiles requested that the unification of the island be postponed. The residents asked the government not to surrender the city until the order arrived directly from Bonaparte in France. They urged García to send delegates to Madrid to ask for the intercession of the king of Spain. García could do nothing but accept the petition of the city's residents who had weathered the last five years and had begun doubting that the formal surrender would ever take place.

Sending the delegates to Madrid in search of a postponement of the surrender had calmed the residents of Santo Domingo, although some began searching for arms to repel an eventual invasion by Toussaint's forces. In June 1800, García reported to the court in Madrid that the residents of the interior towns were arming for defense and were forcing him to prepare for battle. However, since the civil war continued in Saint-Domingue, Toussaint could not yet distract his soldiers into the unification.

Hearing about the Spanish residents' resistance to his forthcoming rule, Toussaint wrote to the governor of Santo Domingo and told him that it was fitting to await the decision of France. On June 26, Roume dictated a new decree annulling the previous one regarding the surrender. Yet, in December 1800, news began to arrive in Santo Domingo that in the vicinities of San Juan and Neiba Toussaint had been mobilizing troops, provisions, and weapons. During all of December, restlessness and uncertainty pervaded Santo Domingo. Finally, on January 6, 1801, the Spanish governor received a letter from Toussaint, dated two days earlier, announcing that he was proceeding to San Juan de la Maguana with the necessary forces to take possession of the Spanish territories. In another message Toussaint stated that the properties and religious practices of the Spaniards who wished to stay on the island would be respected.

García argued that the decisions of Napoleon and the Spanish Court were still pending, but Toussaint was already on his way. Many residents began preparations for battle. As news of the advance of Toussaint was received, many defenders were overcome with fear and fled leaving their commanders with poorly armed, inadequate forces. In the area surrounding the Nizao River, Toussaint's troops destroyed the weak resistance. After obtaining the capitulation of the capital with Governor García, Toussaint marched, without opposition, into Santo Domingo with his troops on January 26, 1801.

While the capitulation was being negotiated, all the French colonial exiles residing in Santo Domingo left for Venezuela or other parts of the Antilles. Since early January, the Venezuelan colonial authorities had been aware of the military mobilization of Toussaint and had been pressed into sending ships to aid the inhabitants of Santo Domingo. Thus, when Toussaint entered the city, there were sufficient ships in the harbor to transport most of the people who wished to depart. Between January and February 1801, nearly 2,000 residents fled to Venezuela or other neighboring islands.

Once Toussaint had entered the city, the French tricolor flag replaced the Spanish one, and Toussaint officially replaced García as the colony's governor. This ceremony ended the Spanish domination over the eastern part of Española. A new era had just begun.

FRENCH RULE IN SANTO DOMINGO

After taking control of Santo Domingo, Toussaint abolished slavery, and took several measures to integrate the Spanish colony into the political and economic structure of Saint-

Domingue. The most radical reform Toussaint attempted was in agriculture, and he passed a series of decrees limiting the granting of lands to new proprietors. He declared that agricultural workers should receive one forth of the profits of farms, ranches, and plantations, as he imposed in the west. Toussaint also ordered the inhabitants to work on the lands already settled since it would be imprudent to permit new settlements while the old ones decayed. Anxious to increase production, Toussaint announced that he would severely punish those who were defficient in their work.

Toussaint's agricultural policy was an attempt to end the traditional Dominican system of labor that was known for the excess of leisure time that workers enjoyed, the lack of interest in hard work, and indolence. More perceptive than the majority of his contemporaries, Toussaint realized that the Dominicans' indolence was primarily a result of the livestock economy which had been the sustenance of the Spanish colony for almost three centuries. He believed that by transforming the economic structure, the Dominican working habits would also be transformed.

In order to encourage this change, Toussaint ordered all the landowners to cultivate sugar cane, coffee, cotton, and cacao for export. Toussaint sought to transform the former Spanish colony based on livestock raising and subsistence agriculture, into a commercial agricultural colony where the land was to be intensively planted with crops oriented toward external markets, as the French had done in Saint-Domingue. To facilitate this transition, Toussaint decreed the unification of the monetary system in both parts of the island.

Throughout 1801, Toussaint worked to turn his ideas into reality. Main roads and trails were repaired to improve transportation. Incorporation of the Spaniards into the political life of Saint-Domingue was encouraged by requesting the Spanish and Dominican creole residents to elect deputies for the draft-

ing of a political constitution that would ratify the recent political and economic changes. Toussaint was adamant about maintaining the freedom of the blacks. Slavery had been abolished
automatically on his arrival in Santo Domingo, and abolition
was ratified by the new colonial Political Constitution promulgated in Santo Domingo on August 27, 1801.

Opposition from Napoleon and powerful interest groups in
France to Toussaint's leadership frustrated these proposed
changes and led to a new French invasion to restore the colony
to its prerevolution status. In February 1802, while Toussaint
was in the city of Santo Domingo reviewing the military situation and preparing to receive the expected French expedition,
news arrived that the first ships were casting anchor in Samaná
Bay. With the arrival of the massive French expedition, the domination by the former slaves on the Spanish part of the island
came to an end since the Spaniards and Dominican creoles soon
allied themselves with the French and helped the invaders to
expel Toussaint's troops from the eastern part. Slavery was again
instituted by the French generals who occupied Santo Domingo on February 25, 1802.

Once the French troops had firm control over the military
situation in Santo Domingo, they sought to put down the blacks'
resistance. Many Spaniards and Dominican creoles supported
the military action. Long accustomed to identifying themselves
as white, the racially mixed population of Santo Domingo had
not been able to accept the governance of the blacks. It was
well known that the primary cause for Spanish opposition to
French occupation was their fear of liberation of the slaves.
Spanish colonists accepted the French only after discovering
they had changed their policy regarding slavery.

Throughout the next two years of war, the former Spanish
colony was relatively tranquil. However, not everyone was satisfied with the military government of General François-Marie
Kerversau in Santo Domingo. The commander tactlessly ordered

the closing of churches in the city until the parishioners accepted a French bishop who had arrived to replace the old archbishop, Portillo Torres. Pressed by the lack of troops, he ordered
the conscription of many residents. The French had barely tak-
en possession of the colony when Kerversau imposed a variety
of new taxes on the already impoverished population. Yet, they
considered French rule a lesser evil than Toussaint's.

The war in the west was extremely bloody and destructive,
and ended with the spectacular defeat of the French army. More
than 50,000 French soldiers and more than 100,000 blacks died
in 20 months of fighting. Again, malaria, yellow fever, and bac-
terial infections wrought havoc among the French troops. The
survivors took refuge in Cuba and Jamaica or fell into the hands
of the British who had aided the blacks. It was the British naval
commanders who received the official capitulation of the French
on November 28, 1803.

General Kerversau saw no alternative other than to obey
the order of capitulation when the British presented themselves
in Santo Domingo. However, General Jean Louis Ferrand, who
commanded the French troops in Montecristi, refused to surrender and decided to march to Santo Domingo. After 18 days
of forced marching, Ferrand brought his men to the capital. On
January 1, 1804, the same day as the proclamation declaring
the independence of Haiti, Ferrand executed a coup d'état, deposed Kerversau, and declared his command over the remaining French troops on the island.

Ferrand sent proclamations to the other islands in the West
Indies to the soldiers of the defeated French army and invited
them to return to defend the colony against an eventual Haitian attack. About 300 soldiers returned to Santo Domingo to
join Ferrand's troops and about 500 Spanish guards. Together,
all these soldiers formed a force of 1,800 men and prepared to
defend the city. The entire year of 1804 was a period of intense
military and administrative activity in Santo Domingo.

Ferrand found there was almost nothing in the city with which to maintain his troops. Therefore, on January 22, 1804, he dictated a decree confiscating the property of the inhabitants of the former Spanish colony who had emigrated without passports. Those living in Puerto Rico had to return within the next 40 days, while those in Venezuela had to do it within the next three months. With this measure the French colonial government managed to induce some of the former residents to return. At the same time, Ferrand confiscated the properties of many of those who did not return and tried to sell them and convert them into cash.

To further stimulate the return of the emigrés, Ferrand cancelled all their debts to the state. Without increasing taxes, Ferrand sought other resources by every available means while awaiting news from France. In the south, he promoted the cutting of mahogany and *guayacán* (lignum vitae) since these woods were highly sought after by Europeans and North Americans. Wood cutting became an important source of revenue for Ferrand's precarious colonial administration. Ferrand also promoted the cultivation of coffee in the interior of the colony and granted lands to some French colonists to that effect.

The situation in the interior was not as calm. Once the cities of Santiago, La Vega, and Cotuí, in the Cibao region, were evacuated by the French army in 1804, the Haitian ruler Jean Jacques Dessalines sought to incorporate these towns into Haiti. Dessalines also imposed a tax on the inhabitants to aid the Haitian government in repaying the expenses suffered during the war. Some wealthy families in the area emigrated to Cuba. Those who stayed sent two commissions to Haiti to request a delay of three months in the collection the money demanded. Both commissions failed and on May 8, 1804, Dessalines published a proclamation to force the inhabitants of the interior to declare their loyalty to Haiti.

At this critical juncture, troops organized by Ferrand to expel the Haitians from the Cibao area made a surprise attack on Santiago on May 15. After a battle which lasted only that afternoon and night, the Haitians were forced to evacuate the city. Despite this triumph, the inhabitants and troops decided to abandon the city for fear that Dessalines would immediately send an army in reprisal. By May 18, Santiago appeared deserted and remained so for almost two months during which time the majority of families with sufficient means emigrated from the region.

Finally, in July 1804, some dared to return and began building up a military organization to confront an eventual Haitian attack. The rest of 1804 passed quietly and, with the assistance of the French military officers sent by Ferrand, Santiago became an armed fortress. Thus, the inhabitants of the interior remained under French domination.

In Haiti, Dessalines was too busy with the reorganization of the army and the reconstruction of the devastated country to pay much attention to the eastern section of the island. But in February 1805, a commission sent by Haitian general Henri Christophe, arrived in Santiago demanding the passage of his army to Santo Domingo. This army was to join forces with another army commanded by Dessalines that was then moving with little opposition through the south.

The Haitian invasion was a direct response to Ferrand's proclamation on January 6, 1805 that authorized armed incursions into Haiti for the purpose of hunting black children less than 14 years old to be sold as slaves in the colony and abroad. With this measure, Ferrand believed he could compensate the soldiers for their services and enhance the financial position of the French colonial government. Until this moment, relations between the Haitians and the French governments had been tense, but they had not formally confronted each other. However, the publication of the decree precipitated Dessalines's reprisal.

Some 200 people in Santiago decided to fight against the 2,000 men commanded by Christophe. As the Haitians outnumbered the Spanish and Dominican creoles by ten to one, the city fell into the hands of the Haitian troops who completely sacked the area and beheaded most of the prisoners. Those who fled to the neighboring town of Moca managed to save their lives when Christophe accepted their plea for clemency on the condition that they did not oppose the march of the invading army.

When Dessalines and Christophe arrived in Santo Domingo with their armies, Ferrand had already prepared the city's defenses by burning the town of San Carlos on the outskirts, raising the wall, storing food, and arming all able men. But Ferrand's troops barely reached 2,000. On March 8, 1805, the siege began with the city blockaded by an army of 21,000 Haitians who tried to erase any vestige of French power remaining on the island. The blockade lasted three weeks. After the first two weeks of the blockade, the food supply was exhausted. The population of 6,000 residents and military men was forced to consume all available animals including horses, donkeys, dogs, and rats.

The French did not surrender, however, since Ferrand had news that a French naval squadron was in the Caribbean area and could arrive in Santo Domingo at any moment. On March 26, the sails of the French squadron appeared on the horizon. Observing that the frigates continued moving west, the Haitians decided to end the siege and return to Haiti to defend their own soil. In reality, the frigates did not go beyond Azua, some 75 miles west of Santo Domingo, but their presence was sufficient to prevent the city from falling into Haitian hands.

The towns of the interior were not spared the wrath of Christophe and Dessalines. After having attacked and burned Monte Plata, Cotuí, and La Vega, the Haitians arrived in Moca where, on the morning of April 3, they killed the entire population and burned the town. The same was done in Santiago where more

than 400 persons were massacred. Aside from Santo D
only the towns of Bayaguana, El Seibo, and Higüey, in the east-
ernmost part, remained standing. All the rest were deserted and
would remain so for many years.

Ferrand tried to reconstruct the colony by means of a paternal system of government which carried out the stipulations
of an 1803 decree by Napoleon whereby the French were ordered to respect Spanish laws, practices, and customs. Dominicans accepted this form of domination out of apathy more than
loyalty. Nevertheless, there was collaboration between the population and the authorities, but eventually the relative tranquility was interupted by two events. The first was Ferrand's order
to suspend all commercial dealings with the Haitians, especially the sale of livestock across the border. The second was Napoleon's invasion of Spain at the beginning of 1808.

In that year, Napoleon took advantage of the political crisis
afflicting the Spanish monarchy. The Spanish king, Fernando
VII was lured to France by promises of French support. Once
there, he was taken prisoner and forced to abdicate in favor of
Napoleon's brother, Joseph Bonaparte, who was then placed on
the Spanish throne. Napoleon's act of treason was known almost immediately in the Spanish colonies where it provoked a
great deal of indignation. This was especially true in Santo Domingo where the French governed a population that still considered itself Spanish.

Many important landowners considered themselves doubly humiliated since the mother country had fallen under French
domination and their businesses were being harmed by the
French prohibition of livestock sales to the Haitians. These proprietors decided to take action. Don Juan Sánchez Ramírez,
who was involved in the mahogany trade as well as in livestock
production, sought the collaboration of the governor of Puerto
Rico and of the Dominican emigrant population on that island
to remove the French from Santo Domingo. Sánchez Ramírez

began traveling throughout the island to arouse the pro-Hispanic sentiments of the population and to incite them to rebel
against the French.

During this period, Sánchez Ramírez maintained an intense
correspondence with Don Toribio Montes, governor of Puerto
Rico, who promised aid. Sánchez Ramírez pledged to send sufficient shipments of mahogany to Puerto Rico to cover the cost
of the operation. In August, Ferrand received a message from
Toribio Montes declaring war on the French. In vain, Ferrand
pleaded with the Dominicans to remain calm. For several weeks
secret envoys of Governor Toribio Montes arrived with revolutionary proclamations that were widely circulated among the
population. Montes even sent 300 troops to reinforce Sánchez
Ramírez.

In October, Ferrand sent troops to the eastern region where
he knew an uprising was being planned. By early November,
Sánchez Ramírez had gathered an army of about 2,000 men
and grouped them in the town of El Seibo, a cattle producing
center. His purpose was to march with this army against Santo
Domingo. Governor Ferrand arrived at El Seibo personally commanding 600 troops with the purpose of deterring the march.
Ferrand was confronted by Sánchez Ramírez, and a decisive
battle took place on the savanna of Palo Hincado on November
7, 1808. The French troops were almost entirely annihilated,
and Ferrand, ashamed by the unexpected defeat, committed
suicide. Thus began what the Spanish-Dominican population
called the War of Reconquest.

A military messenger took the news of the French defeat to
Santo Domingo on the day after the battle. The French forces in
the city immediately began preparations to resist the oncoming
attack. On November 12, the city was declared under a state of
siege by Ferrand's replacement, General Dubarquier. On November 27, Sánchez Ramírez arrived in the area and installed his
camp on the opposite side of the Ozama River. To further weak-

en the French position, three days after the battle of Palo Hincado, the British appeared with three frigates and two brigantines
in Samaná and forced the French commanders to capitulate and
surrender to the insurgents. From then on, British collaboration
became a decisive factor in the fight against the French.

The siege had hardly begun when the British initiated a naval blockade that was to last until July 1809, when the War of
Reconquest ended. The British ships left the port free for several weeks at a time to return to their bases. Thus the French
could send their schooners and brigantines to the French islands or to the United States in search of provisions, but the
intermittent Bristish blockade prevented the French from supplying themselves with more than a minimum of goods. Once
again, hunger became the worst enemy. For eight months, the
French troops resisted the siege, and in the last months the scarcity of food was so serious that the remaining soldiers resorted
to eating horses, donkeys, rats, pigeons, parrots, and even boiled
cowhide.

Sánchez Ramírez proved capable of maintaining order among
his troops despite discontent and the shortage of food. More than
30,000 cattle were consumed in the South, while the cane fields
were destroyed to provide feed for the horses. By early July 1809,
the French could resist no longer. Once again the British benefited since the French chose to surrender to them rather than accept defeat by the Spanish regiments. On July 11, 1809, the British naval commanders took possession of the city after agreeing
to the terms of surrender with the French commanders.

Sánchez Ramírez entered into negotiations with the new
occupants of Santo Domingo for the surrender of the city. But
the British refused to relinquish control until the Spanish promised to compensate them for the expenses incurred in the blockade. It was not until August that Sánchez Ramírez and his men
took complete control of the colony after granting the British
the right of free entry for their ships into the ports of the colony

and after granting imported British products the same tariff treatment given to Spanish products.

The War of Reconquest took place at a time when Spain was without a king, without resources, and without the possibility of effectively governing its Hispanic American colonies. Just when these colonies began revolting against Spanish rule, the Spanish-Dominican population of Santo Domingo was waging a war against the French to reimpose Spanish rule in the island. Twenty years had passed since the beginning of the French Revolution, and during those two decades, Santo Domingo underwent the ordeal of a slave revolt, two Haitian invasions, massive emigration, a British occupation, and the total destruction of its cattle and sugar mills, all of which left it in economic ruin.

The population of the Spanish part of the island, which had reached about 180,000 inhabitants by 1789, was reduced to less than half by 1809. In those 20 years, Santo Domingo not only lost its sense of national direction after being ceded to France in 1795, but also lost most of its educated elite and the colonial entrepreneurs who had been responsible for its economic revival during the second half of the 18th century. The blow struck by the French Revolution on the eastern part of Española was such that it would take its economy more than 40 years to recuperate.

Socially, the loss would be irreparable. The most enterprising towns of the interior had been burned to ashes and had lost most of their population. All the clergy had left the island, with the exception of about a dozen priests. The university was closed for several years, and all convents remained closed for more than a century and lost their lands and properties forever. The few schools that existed lost all their teachers. Exports were reduced to negligible quantities. Poverty again became universal, and a deep pessimism fell on the populace composed mainly of colored people who perceived themselves as white, Hispanic, and Catholic, and who did not want to be abandoned by Spain.

6.
The Haitian domination (1809-1843)

At the end of the War of the Reconquest the eastern part of Santo Domingo was completely devastated. In 1809, the situation of the entire Spanish colony was one of desolation and misery. News was received that the Junta Central of Seville had accepted the reincorporation of its former colony to Spain and recognized Sánchez Ramírez as governor. Sánchez Ramírez lowered the few existing taxes and invited the colonists who had emigrated to return, but very few went back.

The economic recuperation would take decades. Since most of the livestock dissappeared during the revolutionary period, tobacco and mahogany now replaced hides as the main export products. Tobacco exports became the economic base of the Cibao region, and helped it to recover from the devastation left by Dessalines in 1805. Mahogany exports in the south also provided foreign exchange to help pay for imports.

Export taxes did not produce enough revenues to defray government expenses. Compensations and aid expected by the victors of the Reconquest were limited to one *situado* that arrived in 1811 and did little more than dress and feed a few of the troops. When Sánchez Ramírez died in 1811, poverty and the government's lack of money had become very pressing problems. Sánchez Ramírez had placed many people on the state's payroll, and this group now constituted a serious financial burden. Confronted with this situation, his temporary successor, Licenciado José Núñez de Cáceres, was forced to issue paper money in 1812, but within a short period this currency devalued by 75 percent.

The desperate situation became worse in the midst of an atmosphere filled with conspiracies. In 1811, four French seargents attempted a coup to restore the colony to the French government: they failed and were shot. In August 1812, a group of free blacks and slaves in the vicinity of Santo Domingo tried to provoke a general uprising among the colored population, with the intent of killing the white population. The revolt was crushed and the ringleaders were killed.

When Carlos Urrutia, a peninsular governor named by the Junta de Gobierno in Spain, arrived in May 1813, he decided to replace the paper money with copper coins in order to please the military who demanded their salaries in metal. This was not easy to implement since landowners and merchants had accumulated most of the currency in circulation. Urrutia also tried to implement a new economic policy based on agriculture, and promoted the creation of food farms around Santo Domingo to help feed the city's residents. Local agriculture was not intended for export, but to satisfy the city's demand for food. The only area where land was cultivated for export was Cibao, where tobacco was the basis of the economy. Thus, after three and a half centuries of colonial domination, Spain had not been capable of developing commercial agriculture in Santo Domingo.

Due to lack of money the colonial administration could not function regularly. During Urrutia's five years as governor, Spain was unable to send any subsidies to Santo Domingo. When the new governor, Sebastián Kindelán, arrived from Cuba in 1818, he found that the impoverished public treasury only collected duties at the customs houses of Puerto Plata and Santo Domingo from the trade of mahogany and tobacco. But its revenues were barely enough to cover half of the government's expenditures. There was little Kindelán could do to solve this problem. He directed his efforts at obtaining aid from Havana and Madrid, and tried to cope with the monetary crisis by printing paper money, unwittingly provoking worse consequences than the earlier issue. By July, 1821, Kindelán faced increasing pressure from the colonial officials and the military.

The unstable international situation during those years further complicated matters. South American corsairs, at the service of Simón Bolívar, were sailing in Dominican, Cuban, and Puerto Rican waters, disrupting Spanish navigation in the Caribbean. The crown ordered the military mobilization of Santo Domingo. The military maneuvers drained additional funds at a time when there was not enough money to pay the regular salaries of the soldiers. Kindelán found it nearly impossible to maintain an operational military force in the middle of this monetary crisis.

The Haitian government, too, became anxious when it received news about a forthcoming French invasion. These reports were alarming since the French had already made two attempts to regain Haiti in 1814 and 1816. Anxiety increased in 1820 when Haitian President Jean Pierre Boyer was informed that French ships had arrived in Martinique for the sole purpose of invading the Spanish colony and using it as a base for the reconquest of Haiti. The garrison in Santo Domingo did not have sufficient forces to resist an attack from the outside and, furthermore, the neutrality of the Spanish colony was suspect. Therefore, the Haitians were suspicious that the Spanish government would give official support to French attempts to recover its lost colony.

Boyer's reaction to the news of a newly planned French invasion of Santo Domingo and Haiti was twofold. In Haiti, he made military preparations to repel the attack, while at the same time he tried to convince the inhabitants of the east to rise up against Spain and incorporate their colony into the Haitian Republic. In December 1820, rumors were heard in Santo Domingo that one of Boyer's agents was visiting the frontier towns of Las Matas de Farfán, San Juan de la Maguana, and Azua, proposing that the Haitians living in these areas mobilize and declare the incorporation of those regions into the Haitian Republic. The Haitian government let it be known that if the Dominicans did not join Haiti willingly, it might use force to unify the island.

The Haitian rulers never lost sight of their objective to unify the entire island under one government. For them, this would facilitate defense against an eventual French attack. Boyer's interest in acquiring the eastern part of the island was also directly related to internal problems. The fall of Emperor Henri Christophe, in October 1820, had left Haiti with a great number of unemployed and disgruntled military officers who were a constant threat to the government. By taking control of the eastern territory, Boyer would both secure the national borders and consolidate his regime by dispersing the excess officers into new areas.

Governor Kindelán discovered that some of his own military in Azua and Santo Domingo had already become part of the plan for unification with Haiti. Kindelán also discovered that Boyer's propaganda had already spread fear among the free colored population of being enslaved by the French. A letter written to Boyer was intercepted in January 1821, confirming Kindelán's suspicions that the Haitian president was using the pretext of a French invasion to intimidate the Dominican colored population, although some Dominican mulattos who lived along the border favored the unification with

Haiti for simple economic reasons. Haiti was the natural market for their products.

Besides the pro-Haitian party in the east there were other groups interested in deposing the Spanish colonial government. In 1819, a subversive letter written and printed in Caracas, but addressed to the Dominicans, was circulated in the colony. This letter called on the Dominicans to revolt against Spain and join the revolutionary movements in South America. The Venezuelan contacts, as well as the news arriving from Mexico and South America, made several high-ranking military officers, bureaucrats, and merchants consider the Hispanic American emancipation movements as the example to follow. At least twice during the spring of 1821 the bureaucratic creole party in Santo Domingo attempted a coup d'état but failed because of Kindelán's preventive measures.

Governor Kindelán was replaced in May 1821 by Pascual Real. Despite the information he received from Kindelán and the government's confidants, the new governor Pascual Real lost track of the conspiracy. Knowing that he could not count on the loyalty of his troops, Real decided not to confront the suspects directly but to watch them closely. Yet, the colonial government had lost most of its popular support and the conspirators had increased in number under the secret leadership of Licenciado José Núñez de Cáceres, the lieutenant governor of Santo Domingo. Núñez de Cáceres represented the dissatisfied military officers and bureaucrats who had already decided to proclaim the independence of Santo Domingo and seek confederation with the Gran Colombia under Simón Bolívar's leadership.

At the same time, agents of Haitian President Jean Pierre Boyer were making preparations to support those Dominicans who wished to be independent from Spain and wanted to join the Republic of Haiti. On November 15, 1821, the pro-Haitian party proclaimed their independence from Spain in the border towns of Dajabón and Montecristi. The leaders of the movement wrote to the commander of Cap Haitien announcing their decision to place themselves under the protection of Haitian laws and asking for munitions and weapons to defend themselves.

The news of this momentous event traveled quickly to Santo Domingo where Núñez de Cáceres and his group were caught by surprise. Realizing that they were losing control of the situation and had to act quickly, they provoked the impending coup. On November 30, 1821, troops loyal to Núñez de Cáceres took the fortress of Santo Domingo and imprisoned Governor Real. From there they occupied the storehouses and other military posts. On the morning of December 1, the cannon shots fired from the fortress announced the political change to the city's residents. Núñez de Cáceres and his followers then proclaimed the creation of the "Estado Independiente del Haití Español," which would eventually become part of the Gran Colombia.

Just as the installation of the new government was being carried out, three high-ranking Haitian officials sent by Boyer arrived in Santo Domingo with instructions to inform the Spanish authorities about the political change at the border. Finding the Spanish colonial government already overthrown, the chief of the Haitian mission contacted Núñez de Cáceres and led him to believe that Boyer would support the new government. But Boyer was planning otherwise, for now the eastern part was weaker than before and could be more easily taken by the expected French invasion.

By January 11, Boyer had made all the necessary preparations and on that day he wrote a long letter to Núñez de Cáceres explaining the impossibility of maintaining two separate independent governments on the island. According to Boyer, the difficult circumstances that Haiti had undergone during the last 18 years had prevented the Haitians from paying closer attention to the question of unification. Now that all those problems had been overcome, said Boyer, the Haitian Republic was ready to undertake the union to preserve the independence of the whole island.

Núñez de Cáceres was appalled when he received this message, but he realized that he could not win. Like Boyer, he knew the majority of the population was mulatto, and many were favorably disposed to the unification with Haiti. To them, the Haitian government promised land, the abolition of taxes, and the liberation of the few remaining slaves. Likewise, Núñez de Cáceres knew he could expect no support from people of his own class who blamed him for overthrowing the Spanish government. He was defeated and he knew it. Núñez de Cáceres had no alternative but to accept the entrance of Boyer's troops when the time came. On January 19, 1822 he wrote to Boyer accepting the protection of the Republic of Haiti. In his message, he recommended to both his followers and enemies that they receive the Haitian president as peacefully as possible.

Despite assurances of friendship, Boyer marched into Santo Domingo with an army of 12,000 men who had been preparing for the invasion since January 1. Boyer knew that the Dominicans were divided into at least three factions: One pro-Haitian, one pro-Colombian, and one pro-Hispanic. The first party was his guarantee of success, but he had to beware of the other two groups since his revolution was going to affect their interests. This revolution would consist of the abolition of slavery and the institution of a new land-tenure system based on French and Haitian practices, as well as the social and juridical equality of whites, mulattos, and blacks.

Because Boyer was aware that he was going to uproot a centuries old tradition, he knew he would have to use military force against the colonial elite. Following the example of Toussaint and Dessalines, he divided his army into two columns, and on January 28 set out for Santo Domingo. On February 8, he reached the city's outskirts, where the two columns united.

On February 9, the ruling Dominican creole elite awaited President Boyer at the gates of Santo Domingo to accompany him to city hall and the cathedral where they rendered him honors as President. *(See map No. 7)*

THE LAND QUESTION

Boyer's first public decision after taking possession of the eastern part of the island was to order the abolition of slavery and promise land to all the freed men. He immediately marched to the eastern bay of Samaná, where the French invasion was due to arrive. Boyer was able to deter the invasion by attacking the first arrivals and taking them prisoners. The French expedition, which had been badly organized with mercenary soldiers and nonmilitary men, was easily defeated. Boyer allowed the ships to depart with several hundred French planters who had been producing coffee in Samaná since Ferrand's times.

Boyer instructed his military commanders in the East to encourage the former slaves to grow coffee and foodstuffs. At the same time, the inhabitants of the eastern part of the island were to be made aware of the property law effective in Haiti. Boyer understood that Spanish property law and the system of land tenure in Santo Domingo was radically different from the French-Haitian legislation that provided for absolute private ownership guaranteed by titles issued by the state.

In the Spanish part of the island, from the middle of the 16th century, the predominant system had been that of communal lands commonly called *terrenos comuneros*. Under this system, land was simultaneously owned and used by multiple owners. The *terrenos communeros* originated as the island became depopulated in the 16th century. Then it was useless to divide the land for the purposes of inheritance since the total Spanish population only numbered 7,000 people. The original land grants from the Spanish Crown were legitimized by a deed, whereby the Crown guaranteed the ownership rights to the original owner and his successors. When that person died, his land was divided among his wife and children in equal parts, but it was neither surveyed nor partitioned for there was no real demographic pressure on the land. Low population density, and low exploitation associated with cattle raising and woodcutting made land surveying unnecessary and expensive.

For these reasons Santo Domingo had not had a single land surveyor for centuries. Most people defined boundaries of their lands according to the course of the rivers, mountains, trees, or other relevant landmarks. If the family did not migrate, its members usually kept their holdings. When title holders died, new heirs claimed their rights to the land, but only by writing their names on the original deed, not by actually partioning the land. To complicate matters further, when the new owners wanted to sell their rights, they could freely do so, but they had to be paid in cash the value of their shares in the original deed. This was normally estimated without any reference to the market, for there was nothing like a market for land. The buyer guaranteed his claim by writing it down on the deed or by a notary act legalizing the buyer's signature on the deed.

For Haitians, accustomed to the clear and systematic French legal system, the Spanish system of *terrenos comuneros* seemed confusing and backward. They saw it as an obstacle that should be removed at once in order to give land to those who needed it, particularly the recently emancipated slaves. The question to be resolved was which land to distribute.

How to determine land ownership in Santo Domingo presented a problem. Proprietorship could not be established immediately without alienating the landowning class. The freed people had to wait some time before receiving the land as promised. On June 15, 1822, Boyer reaffirmed his promise, proclaiming that he would make good their right to acquire state land on which to grow coffee, cacao, sugar cane, cotton, tobacco, and foodstuffs. Meanwhile, a new battalion –Battalion 32– was created to absorb those former slaves who wanted to be immediately free of their masters. This battalion became the principal military security force responsible in the Spanish part of the island.

Boyer's policy was designed to bring about the unification of the island as quickly as possible. His proclamation of June 1822 was followed on August 26 by the naming of a commission to investigate which properties in the former Spanish area should fall to the state. Among the properties claimed by the state were those whose owners had abandoned the island before political unification; the properties whose owners had left with the government's authorization but who had no intention of returning; and those that had been abandoned because mortgages or other debts had not been paid.

On October 12, the commission submitted its report declaring that the state was entitled to the properties belonging to the former Spanish colonial government, the convents of Santo Domingo, San Francisco, La Merced, Regina, and Santa Clara, as well as the various houses, ranches, animals, lands and lots which belonged to them; the buildings and accessories of the ancient colonial hospitals of San Andrés, San Lázaro, and San Nicolás, located in Santo Domingo, and the properties attached to them; the properties of Frenchmen seized by the Spanish government and that had not been restored to their prior owners; the properties of people who cooperated with the last French invaders at Samaná and who left with the French squadron; all the mortgages which through lapse or default had fallen into the hands of the archbishop, and had been donated to be used as an income for priests who had died or were absent; the mortgages raised for the cathedral; and all funds collected from construction.

Boyer submitted the report to the Chamber of Deputies and the Senate. On November 7, both houses gave it their full approval. The new Haitian commander and governor of Santo Domingo assumed the report had the force of law, and immediately began to confiscate properties that had belonged to the church in colonial times, but which had been in private hands for more than 20 years. The Haitian military governor gave some of the confiscated lands to some former slaves. He also sold other properties at low prices to friends, and freely granted others to Haitian soldiers, officials, and other functionaries. Those who were dispossessed of their properties by these actions vainly raised their protest before the Haitian government, and became bitter opponents to the island's unification.

There was confusion relating to the rights of the complainants who were in actual possession of the land, as well as to the rights of those who had left the island. In order to clarify the issues and make a positive decision, Boyer appointed a new commission on January 22, 1823 to study the problem and settle the land problem. Based on the commission's findings, Boyer issued a decree on February 8, 1823, setting a time limit of four months within which the proprietors of the former Spanish colony who had migrated before February 9, 1822, could return to the country to repossess their properties. The decree also empowered the military governors of Santo Domingo to confiscate the properties of Dominicans who had not returned to the country by June 8, 1823. The majority of the emigrants did not return, and those in actual possession of the lands in question were understandably uneasy. Many occupants were relatives or friends of the absentees. They were not regarded as proprietors in terms of Haitian law since they had no property titles, but, according to the system of *terrenos comuneros*, they had already acquired property rights.

The Haitian land policy deeply hurt the interests of the white proprietors of Santo Domingo. The archbishop of Santo Domingo saw in the Haitian legislation an imminent danger to the conservation of the church's properties. The archbishop could not conceal his anger at the policy of nationalization of ecclesiastical lands and properties, and he was equally enraged by Boyer's order of January 5, 1823 suspending payment of the salaries that the government paid to him and other members of the clergy. The Haitian government's opinion was that priests should maintain themselves on their ecclesiastical incomes. If these were not sufficient, they should take charge of the parishes on the southern coast, which were in great need of religious personnel.

On July 8, 1824, Boyer ordered the promulgation of a law that was to crown all his previous attempts to find a legal and practical solution to the land question. This law incorporated into the patrimony of the state all properties in the eastern part of the island that before February 9, 1822 did not belong to private owners; all movable and real properties, territorial incomes, and their respective capital that belonged to the Spanish colonial government; all religious convents, monasteries, hospitals, or churches; and all the movable and real property belonging to individuals who being absent from the territory when the union was achieved, had not returned by June 10, 1823. In addition, the state claimed the property of those who left after the unification.

According to this law, all the inhabitants of the republic would have the right to own their own lands, protected by a title given by the state. But the execution of the law required the definition of the boundaries of existing properties, for which Boyer authorized a committee to undertake a general survey. This survey would also indicate which properties would become permanently attached to the state.

The determination of the proprietors was extremely difficult, for in the Dominican system of land tenure the title holders were not invariably the owners of all the land, and most of the land titles from the colonial era were affected to a greater or lesser degree by multiple degrees of possession, division, usufruct, sale, and participation within the communal land system. Boyer tried to solve this problem by authorizing his agents to examine the property titles in existence so that they could determine the property rights of each person and could issue new titles to replace the old ones. The new titles should correspond with individually owned parcels of land.

According to the law, the state would distribute land to all who needed it, but no new proprietor could have fewer than 5 *carreaux* of land (approximately 15.5 acres). In the event that a smaller quantity was received, the new proprietors could ask the state for the necessary quantity of land to reach the established minimum. On their new plots, the owners were to produce mainly for the export market. If a farmer failed to keep the whole unit in production, he was required to surrender it to other proprietors, since the interest of the Haitian government was to have the land cultivated with export crops. Hence, livestock could not be reared on units of less than 75 acres, which was the minimum quantity necessary to raise cattle economically.

In short, the law of July 8, 1824 sought to eliminate the system of *terrenos comuneros* and the control of the church on the land. At the same time, it sought to make each rural inhabitant a *campesino* who owned his own land, and was obliged to cultivate it. This law directly challenged the Spanish system of land tenure in Santo Domingo. Execution of this law meant that Dominicans with titles to large properties would find their properties fragmented and shared with others. Many large landowners were in debt because of the decline of the livestock market. Boyer wished to win them over by reducing their debts to one-third of the total. To facilitate payment of the debt, Boyer granted them three years in which they were to cancel their mortgages and reimburse the state in six semiannual installments.

The church, which was to be the institution most affected by the loss of property rights, would be compensated by the state, which would pay an annual salary to each of the priests connected to the Cathedral of Santo Domingo. The state would also give an annual salary to the monastic orders. The archbishop, whose interests had been particularly affected, would also receive a salary. In spite of this, the archbishop never forgave Boyer for ruining the Dominican church and he refused the assigned salary, raising his opposition to the Haitian government.

To the surprise of Boyer and his military commanders, it was not only the archbishop who refused to collaborate but also the *campesinos* of Spanish origin. The Dominican *campesinos* were not sympathetic to orders to cultivate cacao, sugar cane, and cotton. Rather to engage in plantation agriculture, they preferred to pursue other economic activities that for several decades had proven more profitable because of the assurance of a foreign market: cutting mahogany in the south, planting tobacco in the north, and raising cattle in the east.

THE RURAL CODE

In the west, the Haitian peasants also resisted the government's pressures to practice commercial agriculture. This was an unforeseen consequence of the Haitian policy of distributing lands after the revolution. The policy led to the gradual fragmentation of the Haitian plantations and to the emergence of an independent Haitian peasantry. The peasants, who had no obligation to work other people's land, preferred to dedicate themselves to living peacefully on the foodstuffs they produced on their small parcels. At first, the policy of land distribution had been universally popular even among the Haitian mulatto proprietary class. But with time it became clear that for lack of rural labor the state's poverty increased as plantation agriculture declined.

The Haitian mulatto elite grew increasingly disenchanted with the general situation and exercised its influence on Boyer to adopt corrective measures. Their argument was strengthened by the fact that the policy of export promotion had failed even in Santo Domingo, where the population was subject to military government. For the mulatto elite the obvious solution was to revert to the policy of compelling *campesinos* to do plantation work. On May 1, 1826, Boyer presented to the Haitian Senate a set of laws designed to reorganize the agricultural economy of Haiti on the principle that the *campesinos'* work on plantations was obligatory under threat of punishment.

The Rural Code, as this body of laws was called, was designed to enable the Haitian economy to recover the levels of productivity achieved under Toussaint, Dessalines, and Christophe. The code's provisions were to help overcome the problems of seasonal shortage of labor and the tendency of farmers to evade work and leave the plantations to till their own land. The code established that no one was exempt from working the land, except government servants and citizens in recognized professions. No proprietor could abandon the plot on which he lived without previous authorization from the local justice of the peace or military chief. Children of agricultural workers were not to attend school at the expense of abandoning their parents' plot without the permission of the authorities, and no worker could leave the countryside to engage in commerce under any circumstances. Nor, according to the code, could any worker construct his own dwelling and leave the plantation with his family.

Once an agriculturist was employed by a plantation owner, he was obliged to serve him for a minimum of three years. Vagrancy was absolutely forbidden. In order to apply these measures, the army would assign soldiers to each of the plantations

to supervise the workers. The soldiers would be fed and maintained by the plantation owners. Further, women were obliged
to work up to the fourth month of pregnancy and to return to
work four months after childbirth. All these measures were to
apply equally to the mulatto-owned plantations of the west and
to the great proprietors of the east, whose support Boyer wanted to ensure.

The code, which was considered a masterpiece of Haitian
legislation at the time, failed for a variety of reasons. The main
reason was that rural Haitian workers simply ignored its provisions and invariably refused to obey any suggestions that would
restore servitude on the plantations. Over the years, an independent Haitian peasantry had emerged, but Boyer and his elite
seemed to have lost sight of this phenomenon. The main interest of this new peasant class was a comfortable subsistence.
There was a contradiction between the interests of this peasantry and those of the big landowners, since the development
of the latter depended on a labor force bound to the plantations. Boyer and the government could do nothing to make the
peasants work. The majority of the Haitian people owned small
parcels of land and had little inclination to be employed as peons on other people's lands.

Boyer and his collaborators soon discovered that there was
no way of forcing the peasants to work for the big planters. The
army was not in a position to enforce the code for two reasons:
the majority of the soldiers and their families were small proprietors of rural origin, and they would not take action against
their own families in order to favor an elite of large proprietors; and, in 1825, the Haitian government had reached an
accord with France whereby the latter recognized the independence of Haiti.

This agreement removed the enemy that had served as a
pretext to maintain army discipline. The soldiers relaxed their
military habits and occupied themselves with their personal

affairs and properties rather than with policing the country-side. Consequently, when the Rural Code was promulgated, military discipline was undergoing a process of decline. The irony was that the code had been conceived as the instrument that would increase export production in Haiti in order to pay France the 150 million francs indemnity established as a condi-tion for France's recognition of Haitian independence.

Boyer's interest was centered on agriculture since both he and the Haitian elite were convinced that in Haiti, without in-dustries or commerce, only agriculture could provide a lasting foundation for wealth. The Rural Code faithfully reflected this philosophy. The protection Boyer gave to agriculture did not in any way imply that farmers were exempt from fiscal controls. The laws of May 3, 1826 and December 23, 1830 established that the farmers should pay the state 5 percent of their produc-tion not bound for export. The owners of pottery shops, the woodcutters, matchmakers, and owners of saltworks had to pay a similar tax.

ECONOMIC CRISIS AND POLITICAL UNREST

Boyer's agricultural policies produced unrest in the eastern part of the island. A law passed in July 1828 authorizing farm-ers to kill the animals of other people that damaged their crops gave rise to continual quarrels between cultivators and cattle owners. Also unpopular was the limitation on the amount of time to be dedicated to traditional religious celebrations im-posed by the government in 1826. The government resented the considerable time lost in the numerous religious *fiestas*, but that decree clearly ignored the Dominican popular character. In a rural society with a long tradition of cattle ranching, people preferred to employ their free time attending cockfights with their neighbors, rather than engaging themselves on plantation work. Boyer's decree in February 1830 closing the cockpits once and for all, except on Sundays and holidays, proved equally unpopular.

The anti-Haitian prejudice that Boyer had noted when he arrived in Santo Domingo continued in 1830. The control exercised by the Haitians over the Dominicans was sustained more by military power than by voluntary submission. The majority of the population never communicated fully with the Haitians, whose language and customs were different. Despite the good intentions of the president, the Haitian political economy, the legal organizaiton of property ownership, and the agricultural labor policies had alienated the majority of the Dominican population.

In the south, restrictions and control over the cutting and sale of mahogany disgruntled the biggest landowners who resorted to contraband. When the Haitian government realized that mahogany cutting was eluding its control, Boyer issued a series of orders in 1830 to facilitate the creation of a legal wood market so that the state could profit through tax collection.

As mahogany forests on the main river banks became exhausted, wood cutters moved to the lands that now belonged to the state, but which they considered communal lands. Boyer attempted to restrict this activity, but despite restrictive regulations passed to prevent the illegal cutting of mahogany, the proprietors in the south and east never abandoned their business. Eventually, Boyer realized that mahogany exports were aiding the Haitian ailing economy and ended the prohibition, allowing the cutting of mahogany in state lands.

By 1830, discontent was prevalent on both sides of the island. To the natural rivalries that marked the relationship between the ruling mulatto elite and the black population, a new problem was added: the currency devaluation caused by the creation of paper money that had been printed to help pay for the compensations owed to France since 1825. Devaluation led

to a fictitious increase in coffee prices, but the financial uncertainty clearly affected the interests of the Haitian elite.

Finally, the crisis found political expression in the Senate
and the Chamber of Deputies, where some congressmen tried
unsuccesfully to question Boyer's economic policies. As the situation deteriorated, the struggle among the congressmen and
the government increased in strength and violence. In August
1833, Boyer expelled the two main leaders of the opposition
from Congress.

To make matters worse, in 1834 Boyer made a final effort
to force the proprietors of Santo Domingo to submit their titles to authorities for the delimination of land boundaries. The
landowners continually resisted, filtering their protest through
prominent Dominicans attached to the Haitian government.
Boyer was only able to incorporate into state property what
had belonged to the church and what had been confiscated
from Dominican exiles who had not returned. More complaints
about land confiscation were raised by the families of the exiles who could not meet the demands of the government, since
they did not possess titles but considered themselves, in accordance with Dominican tradition, the legitimate owners of
those lands.

By 1834, the Haitian government had not been able to per-
suade the great landowners to submit their titles, in spite of
the insistent demands of President Boyer. Therefore, on April
7, 1834, Boyer set a new date for the Dominican landowners
to meet with Haitian officials to verify their titles. The new
deadline imposed by Boyer was December 31, 1834, after which
all rights would be lost by those who failed to verify their land
titles with the official commission appointed for that purpose.
This was seen by the Dominicans as the ultimate threat to their
property rights, with the final purpose of abolishing the traditional system of the *terrenos comuneros*. The large landowners of Santo Domingo became increasingly alarmed and im-

mediately appealed to the authorities entrusted with its execution.

Since Boyer wanted to avoid friction, he accepted the landowners' arguments and published another proclamation recognizing the impediments to compliance with the law. There were
simply not enough surveyors in the country to undertake the
enormous task of measuring all the private lands in order to
assign to each proprietor a legal deed. Boyer continued to insist
on the transformation of the land-tenure system, declaring the
need for a national land survey and forbidding the sales of rural properties in both parts of the island.

In April 1835, the Haitian deputies returned to the battle.
Boyer's opponents referred to the unfavorable economic situation and argued that the improvement in coffee cultivation had
not been accompanied by similar improvements in other crops.
Furthermore, they said, commerce was declining daily due to
the devaluation of money and an unfavorable trade balance
which limited Haiti's capacity to import. The pro-Boyer congressmen responded this criticism arguing that the merchants
were responsible for the depreciation of money, and accused
them of systematically introducing counterfeit and debased
currency that threatened to ruin the economy.

In 1836, the opposition sensed increased support from the
merchants in their struggle against the government. This support was given additional stimulus around mid-year when Boyer passed a law that closed five western ports to foreign commerce. This law affected important trading houses whose business depended on foreign trade. At the end of 1836, a group of
military officers in northern Haiti sought to mobilize the peasant masses in a rebellion against Boyer. Colonel Izidor, the leader
of the conspiracy, had been a large landowner since the era of
Christophe and was particularly hostile to Boyer's agrarian policies. By January 1837, it was clear that there was a military
movement in the north. Izidor issued an anti-government proc-

lamation. He criticized the lack of discipline among the soldiers of the republic, who preferred to remain on their plots rather than perform military service of any kind.

With that proclamation, Izidor made a grave error; the soldiers and peasants understood that the aim of the rebel chief was to restore the system of compulsory labor. They abandoned their rifles, and in a short time the rebel leaders found themselves alone and without popular support. Boyer and the loyal troops liquidated the movement without difficulty. Boyer wrongly interpreted the lack of popular support for the Izidor movement as proof of the dedication of the people to the constitutional government. In reality, the failure was caused by lack of political tact among the leaders of the conspiracy.

Opposition to the government increased daily. The reelection to Congress of the deputies who had been expelled the previous year was a clear example of the intensification of opposition. Leaders of the opposition made their presence felt at the opening sessions in April 1837 when they demanded the government improve the economic situation. A commission that had been set up to review the national accounts exposed the continued stagnation in agricultural production. More importantly, coffee production, the base of the economy, had dropped alarmingly over the previous three years. The president of the commission blamed the government's policies for the decline in production.

The Chamber of Deputies sent a message to the president of the republic to explain that the country's commercial situation was a result of the 1835 law requiring payment of import duties in foreign exchange. In July 1837, shortly after receiving the message from the deputies, Boyer issued a proclamation in which he accepted the opposition's diagnostics. But Boyer's proclamation implied that the problem afflicting Haitian commerce was a consequence of the financial crisis that was being suffered in Europe and the United States. He said that the complete unavailablity of overseas credit had led to import restrictions; the scarcity of foodstuff imported from the United States had caused prices to rise, and subsistence had become more difficult for the people.

Boyer did not accept the demand of the Chamber of Deputies to abolish the law regarding the payment of customs duties in foreign currency. He believed the Chamber was dominated by the opposition, and he persuaded the Senate to reject the proposals on the law. Among the most important reasons for Boyer's refusal to revoke the law was the necessity of assuring foreign exchange to fill the Republic's depleted treasury to pay the national debt. By resisting the demands of the deputies, Boyer increased the opposition that had been growing on both sides of the island among the mercantile establishment. These frustrations were powerfully expressed in May 1838, when a group of soldiers opposed to the government tried unsuccessfully to assassinate the president and his secretary-general.

THE OVERTHROW OF BOYER

In the eastern half of the island, on the other hand, there were also constant pretexts for new conspiracies. The conspiracies and congressional debates in the west, fed by the commercial crisis of the previous two years, activated a group of young men in Santo Domingo to form a secret society called "La Trinitaria" in July 1838. La Trinitaria's goals were to organize Dominican resistance and to separate the eastern part of the island from Haiti. Very quickly, the *Trinitarios* succeeded in attracting the majority of the youth of the city of Santo Domingo. The leader of this secret group was Juan Pablo Duarte, the son of an impoverished Spanish merchant who had seen his father's business ruined under Haitian domination.

The roots of Dominican dissatisfaction with the Haitian regime went deeper than the single issue of land tenure in Santo Domingo. For about two centuries, two different societies had been evolving independently in both parts of the island under very different, economic, and social conditions. By the fourth decade of the 19th century it was evident that two different nations coexisted, one beside the other, with their differences based not only on dissimilar economic systems but also on racial, cultural, and legal dissimilarities.

Boyer failed to integrate both parts of the island, not only because Dominicans were opposed to his agrarian policies but also because his own countrymen were opposed to them. The Haitians had developed into a black peasantry much more interested in cultivating their own plots than in serving as salaried workers for the plantation owners. The ruin of the Haitian economy was evident in 1826, when Charles Mackenzie was appointed consul of Great Britain to Haiti and described statistically the decline of Haitian agricultural exports as related to the development of the peasantry. That ruin brought political instability to Haiti as the mulatto planters and the merchant class were hurt by the devaluation of the currency, triggered by the printing of debased paper money, and by falling export prices during the economic crisis that hit the United States in 1837 and 1838.

As his land policy failed, Boyer's fiscal objectives in the east required increasing the state's share of the mahogany trade on which the Dominicans had been concentrating in recent years. In March 1838, Boyer returned to his former position and decided to press for the enforcement of the law of July 8, 1824, issuing a new proclamation intended to force the proprietors to verify their titles and allow the authorities to split the *terrenos comuneros* among the actual coowners. The deadline was fixed as July 1, 1838. Once again, the Dominican landowners resisted, and the government could not force them to verify their land titles with the authorities. After this last attempt, Boyer finally desisted and recognized the right of the Dominican landowners to keep their inherited lands.

Instability grew as Boyer's regime proved incapable of tolerating political dissension within the Chamber of Deputies, thus alienating those mulattos who exerted leadership in the south of Haiti. In 1839, Boyer again expelled the most outspoken deputies from Congress and triggered a new political crisis among the mulatto elite. When the 1840 congressional elections were held, the same deputies were reelected, and despite Boyer's opposition to them, they were again reelected for the 1842 legislature as representatives of the Department of Les Cayes, the center of the mulatto opposition. By expelling them from the Congress for a fourth time, in April 1842, Boyer left them with the only road open to gain access to power: a military plot.

Boyer's political situation worsened after May 7, 1842, when a strong earthquake shook the whole island and nearly destroyed Cap Haitien and Santiago. The opposition accused the government of not doing enough to assist the country, and restlessness followed for the rest of the year. Finally, in September 1842, the most important mulatto leaders in Les Cayes formed a "Society of the Rights of Man and the Citizen" which was to articulate political opposition to Boyer. The society issued a manifesto bitterly attacking Boyer and the subservient congress and denouncing Haitian economic and political malaise caused by 22 years of one-person rule.

The manifesto contained most grievances expressed by the opposition leaders in the Chamber of Deputies in the previous eight years, and called for a military commander of patriotic intentions to lead the country toward change. The military officer secretly chosen to lead the movement was General Charles Hérard, alias Rivière, commander of the batallion of the regiment of artillery in Les Cayes. His title, while he carried out his revolutionary mission, would be "Chief Executor of the People's Will." During the following months, military preparations were secretly made and the Haitian "reformists" endeavored to coordinate their movement with the secret organization of La Trinitaria in the eastern part of the island.

Curiously enough, the military governor of the department of Les Cayes, General Maximilien Borgella, former governor of the Dominican part of the island, did not take any measures against the conspirators despite the evidence he had regarding their revolutionary activities. Borgella's leniency allowed the movement to grow, and he even hosted in his own house the Dominican envoy to Les Cayes, the Trinitario leader Ramón Mella, who arived there on January 26, 1843, the day before the revolt started.

On January 27, Hérard gathered his army at his farm in Praslin, near Les Cayes, and began a military march throughout the southern towns of Haiti gaining increasing support to eventually attack both Les Cayes and Port-au-Prince. Several weeks later, it became evident that the mulatto leadership had entirely abandoned Boyer despite the president's efforts to impress them with military parades in Port-au-Prince. On March 4, Borgella surrendered Les Cayes without fighting, and his desertion forced Boyer to accept his defeat on March 13. Boyer resigned the presidency and secretly boarded an English ship that took him and his family to exile in Jamaica. The news spread quickly throughout the country, and the revolutionaries pressed their march to Port-au-Prince, where they would assume control of the country, which was now at their disposal.

7.
Separation
from Haiti
and Independence
(1843-1844)

News of the overthrow of Boyer reached Santo Domingo on the afternoon of March 24, 1843. The atmosphere there was of agitation, conspiracy, and expectation. The news served as a signal for Boyer's opponents to take to the streets shouting "Long live independence and reform!" Before long, a crowd formed under the leadership of Dominican merchant and Trinitario leader Juan Pablo Duarte, Haitian opposition leader Alcius Ponthieux, and the anti-Boyer general, Etienne Desgrotte. These men directed the rioters toward the fortress which they intended to take by force. On arriving at the plaza of the Cathedral, the group was detained by government troops, and after a brief verbal exchange, shooting broke out leaving two dead and five wounded.

Confronted with this resistance and recognizing their military inferiority, the rebels fled the city and sought refuge in the neighboring town of San Cristóbal, where they forced the local commander to side with the *reforma* movement. From San Cristóbal they sent emissaries to the neighboring towns of Baní and Azua where they obtained a favorable response. Two days later, after having assembled a motley army of some 2,000 men, the revolutionaries returned to the city of Santo Domingo. Upon seeing the popularity of the rebels, the Haitian commander capitulated and surrendered the city to the Junta Popular which had been formed on March 30 by the leaders of the revolt.

Throughout the following two months news and instructions were sent from Santo Domingo and Port-au-Prince to various towns in the east where the liberal leaders formed committees and juntas to defend the *reforma* movement. The provisional government in Port-au-Prince called for these juntas to elect deputies to a constitutional assembly that was to meet in the Haitian capital on September 15 to prepare a new constitution. The provisional government ordered municipal elections to be held on June 15, 1843. This convocation was well received by the Dominicans. As the elections drew near, relations between the liberal Dominicans and the liberal Haitians deteriorated. The Haitians soon discovered that the Dominican collaboration to overthrow Boyer had been merely a tactical measure in their strategy toward separation and independence.

The situation worsened on June 8, 1843, when a group of Dominicans at the Junta Popular denounced that despite Dominican collaboration in the *reforma* movement, Haitians were quartering troops and their patrols fostered unrest, especially during the days prior to elections. The signers also stated that since the eastern part of the island was not conquered territory, they should be permitted to write their official documents in Spanish. They also requested that the Junta Popular instruct the soon-to-be-elected deputies to the constitutional assembly to demand the observance of their Catholic religion and the conservation of their Spanish language and native customs, "since this neither opposes, nor contradicts, nor weakens the simple and indivisible union of the democratic Republic." Consideration of this document in the Junta Popular caused serious debates and heated discussions between Dominicans and

Haitians and split them into two irreconcilable parties, which brought separate candidates to the elections.

The week before the elections was extremely tense and, as expected, the Dominicans won almost everywhere in the east. In the Cibao area, the separatist spirit was so great that the residents of San Francisco de Macorís and Cotuí took advantage of their victory to depose the Haitian military commanders and exercise power independently. In Santiago, the local leaders were in contact with the separatist leaders of Macorís and Cotuí where Trinitario leader Ramón Mella had gone to coordinate the movement.

In El Seibo and Higüey, two brothers, *hacendados* Ramón and Pedro Santana, organized an extensive conspiracy to overthrow the Haitians, while in Baní a similar movement was organized under the leadership of two youngsters, Jacinto de Castro and Hipólito Billini. Political excitement was high and led to a proliferation of pamphlets and leaflets containing satires, proclamations, and other writings calling for a revolt and the separation from Haiti.

To avoid rebellion, Haitian authorities in Santo Domingo asked General Charles Hérard to march with his army to the east as soon as possible. Hérard was in Cap Haitien with his army and set out for the border after receiving the news. Arriving at Dajabón, Herard learned for the first time that the population did not speak French and that its customs differed from those of the Haitians. Hérard then went to Puerto Plata, where he learned that Haitian officers had been stealing Dominican lands and property titles for a long time. Therefore, he dismissed those officials and appointed new authorities, while taking measures to reinforce Haitian rule.

On his arrival in Santiago the pro-Haitian party denounced the separatist conspiracy. Hérard detained the implicated Trinitario leaders and sent them as prisoners to Port-au-Prince. He also learned that several families from Santiago had lost their lands and property titles to Haitians through violence. In an attempt to win the Dominicans's support, Hérard replaced the Haitian authorities and ordered the restitution of the stolen properties to the previous owners.

Hérard then went to La Vega where he also dismissed the local commander and reinforced the security of the Haitians who were there. Then he went on to San Francisco de Macorís, another center of conspiracy where the Haitian commander had been removed by the newly elected municipal government. After interviewing the municipal leaders implicated in the conspiracy, Hérard became convinced that the Dominicans did not love the Haitians. He was informed that the local priest was planning to assassinate him and his companions. According to Hérard, the priest kept in his house a revolutionary manifesto and a Haitian flag with the words "Down with the tyrant" written in it in big letters. The manifesto said that the new Haitian government would be more tyrannical than Boyer's, and that the time for rebellion had arrived.

After imprisoning the local priest and reinstating the Haitian authorities, Hérard then went to Cotuí where the local records had been burned to cover up the conspiracy. The local priest was also arrested for being the friend and accomplice of the priest in San Francisco de Macorís. Hérard also detained the Trinitario leader Ramón Mella, who had been sent from Santo Domingo to Cotuí to coordinate the plans to destroy the Haitian army. Both were sent as prisoners to Port-au-Prince along with the other conspirators.

After taking control of Cotuí, Hérard left for Santo Domingo where he arrived at 11:00 a.m. on July 12 and found that "all the doors of the citizens of Spanish origin were closed; only those of the citizens of French origin were open." With the city occupied by Haitian troops, the Trinitarios moved out of the city to escape the search that Hérard was about to begin. The separatist movement was soon disbanded. Hérard took advantage of the situation to send some troops to other towns with orders to seize all separatists implicated in the conspiracy. Among those arrested were the brothers Ramón and Pedro Santana, two important landowners and cattle ranchers in El Seibo.

Hérard and his troops spent several more days in Santo Domingo where he reorganized the municipality, the tribunals, and the national guard according to Haitian interests. During his stay, the Haitian troops terrorized the city and violently searched all the houses looking for the principal Trinitario leader Juan Pablo Duarte. On August 2, Duarte escaped secretly on board a schooner headed toward Saint Thomas, leaving behind a completely disorganized and demoralized party. After expelling two other priests involved in another separatist plot in favor of Spain, Hérard had a Te Deum sung and then departed the city, taking with him several dozen prisoners.

Despite this defeat, the Trinitarios were gradually able to recover under the leadership of a young mulatto named Francisco del Rosario Sánchez, who had managed to avoid capture by feigning illness and sudden death. During the months following Duarte's exile, the Trinitarios acted in extreme secrecy and divided into two groups, one headed by Ramón Mella and the other by Sánchez and Duarte's brother Vicente. Mella returned to Santo Domingo at the end of September 1843, after having been admonished and then liberated by the Haitian government, along with the other political prisoners taken by Hérard in July. The following months were a time of little danger for the conspirators, since in the West the Haitians were now deeply divided.

Two issues divided the Haitian leaders in Port-au-Prince. One was a disagreement regarding the organization of the Constitutional Assembly. The other was a proclamation issued by Hérard assuring Dominicans that their religion, language, and customs would be respected and guaranteed in the new Constitution. According to the Haitian politicians, Hérard had no right to impose the lines of conduct that the Constitutional Assembly should follow. They saw this proclamation as a part of a plan to have himself elected president.

Control of the assembly gradually fell to Hérard in December 1843. After three months of discussions, Herard employed his troops to force the deputies to finish the Constitution within a limited number of hours, and was elected president of the Republic by an overwhelming majority of votes. Just as Hérard had promised in his proclamation to the inhabitants of the east, the assembly produced an extremely liberal constitution. It was so liberal that the very members who wrote it publicly stated that it would be inapplicable. During his trip to the east, Hérard had come to realize how unpopular and unsuccessful Boyer's measures had been among the Dominican population.

In an effort to please the Dominicans and avoid a confrontation that could imperil his liberal revolution, in the last days of December 1843 Hérard abolished all the laws, circulars, and decrees that had piled up as a consequence of the law of July 8, 1824. He also abolished other dispositions that had offended Dominicans for years, like the one forbidding them to write public and legal documents in Spanish.

But it was too late. The Dominicans had decided to separate themselves from Haiti. The political truce offered to them by the unrest provoked by the Constitutional Assembly in Port-au-Prince allowed the separatist groups in Santo Domingo a breathing space, since there was little fear of new mass arrests. However, there was little chance of action. The Trinitarios, the most noted of the separatists groups, had still not completely recovered from the imprisonment of their leaders and the exile of Juan Pablo Duarte. Furthermore, there were four independent groups struggling to separate from Haiti.

First, there was a pro-Spanish group whose leaders wrote to the Spanish authorities in Puerto Rico and Cuba on several occasions to denounce the Haitian domination. Its leaders asked the Spanish government to send troops to evict the Haitians and offered their services to help in the venture. The Spanish government never showed any real interest in these offers, although during the first half of 1843 the French consul in Port-au-Prince was convinced that Spain actually was interested. The second separatist group was seeking British protection, but their efforts failed because of Great Britain's lack of interest.

A third group was made up of individuals who had held administrative posts within the Haitian government. Familiar with French legislation and acquainted with the French consul in Port-au-Prince, these men believed that it was possible to shed Haitian domination with the aid of France in return for some political, commercial, and territorial privileges. The visible leaders of this group were Buenaventura Báez, a rich property owner and mahogany exporter in Azua, and Manuel Joaquín Delmonte, an important lawyer and merchant.

The fourth separatist group, the Trinitarios headed by Juan Pablo Duarte, sought pure and simple independence without any foreign aid or intervention. Given the exile of its leader, all that this group could do was continue to organize and wait for an opportunity to shake loose from Haitian rule.

Meanwhile he Trinitarios developed a new strategy. Duarte would obtain arms and other provisions in Venezuela and Curaçao and charter a ship that would land on or before December 9 on the beach of Guayacanes, east of Santo Domingo. According to Francisco del Rosario Sánchez and Vicente Duarte, who created the plan, this was of the utmost importance since it would precipitate action by other separatist groups. This plan fell through as Juan Pablo Duarte was unable to obtain arms and military supplies. This forced Sánchez and his group to follow the tactics laid out by Ramón Mella to gain new supporters among the conservative population of Santo Domingo who could help them to organize a *golpe*. The conservatives, had previously treated the Trinitarios with skepticism, but now began to perceive that separation from Haiti was possible.

Mella's tactics bore fruit. At the end of 1843, the Trinitarios were able to win over Tomás de Bobadilla, an influential bureaucrat since the colonial days who had continuously collaborated with the Boyer government in important positions, but who had been removed from public administration by the new Haitian rulers. Bobadilla now considered himself an opponent of the Haitian liberal government. His collaboration proved to be very valuable as the Trinitarios needed someone with practical political experience.

In the meantime, the pro-French faction was working silently in Port-au-Prince. Buenaventura Báez and Manuel Valencia, the main leaders of this faction, had been elected as deputies to the constitutional assembly and took advantage of the occasion to contact the French consul, André Levasseur, whom they urged to support the separatist movement. In return for French protection, they promised to cede Samaná Bay and Samaná Pensinsula to France. Levasseur, who had at first encouraged separatist ideas among the Dominicans, hesitated. After Boyer's overthrow, the Haitian provisional government had declared bankruptcy and refused to make the annual payments to France. Under these circumstances, the consul had to act more conservatively since he knew the debt with Haiti was partially defrayed through the export of mahogany and tobacco from the East.

The situation changed again in the middle of December with the arrival of a special envoy from France to Port-au-Prince. This plenipotenciary, Mr. Barrot, was charged with negotiating the debt with Haiti, and demanded as a guarantee some territorial concessions which included Samaná Bay. On hearing these instructions from his government, Levasseur accelerated his plans to enhance French influence on the island and acquire the Samaná Peninsula for France via the Dominicans. On December 16, he informed his government that he had received a petition from the seven deputies representing the east requesting the placement of their territory under the protection of France in exchange for Samaná. Although Levasseur did not explicitly commit his government, Báez and the other members of the pro-French group anticipated the French support and set April 25, 1844 as the date for a coup against the Haitians.

News of these secret negotiations soon leaked. One of the deputies, Manuel María Valencia, wrote to one of his friends in Baní about the plan, and this person spread the news among his friends. José María Serra, one of the Trinitarios who was in Baní at that time, soon learned of the plan. Serra immediately set off for Santo Domingo where he informed Francisco del Rosario Sánchez and the other Trinitarios of the plan. After some discussion, the Trinitarios all agreed upon the need to preempt the pro-French coup, and declare the East a free and independent state before the pro-French or *afrancesados* could do so. The coup was set for February 20, 1844, two months before the date set by the *afrancesados*.

On January 1, 1844, the pro-French group issued a manifesto stating the reasons for separating from Haiti and seeking the protection of France. On January 16, the Trinitarios issued their own document calling for a rebellion and listing a series of grievances suffered by the Dominican people during the previous 22 years. These two manifestos were a clear expression of the views of the eastern population who considered themselves completely different from the Haitians, especially regarding language, race, religion, and domestic customs that, despite official regulations and pressures, had remained unchanged under Haitian domination. Both documents circulated widely throughout the country and stirred up more animosity against the Haitians who were accused of the most horrible crimes. By mid-February, 1844, the Dominican population, especially that of

Santo Domingo, was keyed up by the separatist propaganda and ready for action.

The Trinitarios were unable to act on the prescribed date as they had not received word from the ranchers of El Seibo under the leadership of Ramón and Pedro Santana. Thus, they waited until February 26, when word finally arrived that the night before the Santana brothers had resolved to march to Santo Domingo with a small army made up of the region's landowners and their peons. This news set the conspirators in motion in Santo Domingo, although with the greatest secrecy. Arrangements were made to meet at one of the city's gates at 11:00 p.m. on the 27th, and then move on to the rampart and main gate of El Conde where a Dominican lieutenant in charge would be waiting with his men and others to reinforce the conspirators. The *coup* was executed rapidly, and on the following day, February 28, the people of the capital crowded before the gate of El Conde to await the results of the negotiations between the Haitian authorities and the "insurrectional committee" headed by Francisco del Rosario Sánchez.

Negotiations ended at nightfall on the 28th with the mediation of French Consul Eustache Juchereau de Saint-Denys, who had recently been transferred from Cap Haitien to Santo Domingo by Levasseur with instructions to favor plans to place the east under France's political protection. As the Haitian authorities became convinced that they could not oppose the popular insurrection, they capitulated. The capitulation guaranteed the peaceful surrender of power to the Dominicans and the departure of all deposed Haitians under honorable conditions. The following day, the Haitians surrendered the archives, government properties, and military equipment to the new Dominican authorities.

The insurrectional committee solemnly proclaimed the Dominican Republic and constituted a provisional "Junta Central Gubernativa" to run the affairs of the state. Various dele-

gates were appointed to visit the other towns of the East to convey news of the separation and to ask for additional proclamations of independence. During the next 15 days, all the towns of
the east announced their decision to separate from Haiti, and
thus the Dominican Republic was born.

INDEPENDENCE

The coup of February 27 produced an immediate reaction
in Haiti. President Hérard could not permit the separation of
the East in the midst of his liberal revolution. This would deprive Haiti of the necessary resources to pay France the remainder of its debt. Hérard decided to subdue the Dominicans by
force as he had done in the summer of the previous year. On
March 10, after issuing a proclamation asking the Dominicans
to return to the Haitian Republic, Hérard summoned his army
and prepared for another march into the East.

The Dominicans ignored Hérard's call and prepared for war.
An army composed of any one having an available weapon was
rapidly organized. Pedro Santana was named military chief.
Santana was able to gather 3,000 men, and with these troops
he moved quickly to Azua, some 80 miles to the west of Santo
Domingo. There he prepared to resist the approaching Haitian
attack. Another army was in readiness in Santiago, where fear
dominated the population.

In Santo Domingo the population was also terrified. Many
sought refuge with their families in the French consulate, while
others embarked on any available ships. The Junta Central
Gubernativa made desperate efforts to achieve more decisive
support from the French consul who, since his arrival in Santo
Domingo two months earlier, had been encouraging the Dominicans to separate from Haiti. This officer had hinted that
France would offer military aid. But since he had no authority

to commit his nation's naval forces, France's warships were kept a short distance off the Dominican coast.

On March 18, the Haitian army led by President Hérard arrived before the town of Azua and took up positions along the banks of the Jura River. On the 19th, Hérard's vanguard troops attacked. The entrenched Dominicans confronted the Haitians with cannonshot while their infantry fired at close range killing several Haitian soldiers and officers. After a two-hour battle the Haitians picked up their dead and wounded and retreated to their camp.

This short battle helped the Dominicans to temporarily detain the Haitians. During the night, Santana gathered his troops and the local population, and abandoned Azua to retire to Baní, a location closer to Santo Domingo, but separated from Azua by the mountains of El Número. On the way, he left various guerrilla groups stationed at the narrow mountain passages. By putting the rugged hills of El Número between his poorly equipped army and the 10,000 troops of Hérard, Santana avoided certain defeat. Azua was a little town of thatched wooden houses situated in the middle of a plain and could easily be surrounded and torched by the enemy. Finding the town deserted, the Haitians occupied it and immediately attempted to cross the mountains, but found their path blocked by guerrilla fighters. Some Dominican schooners equipped with cannons off the coast also prevented the Haitians from attacking by sea.

Meanwhile, the population of Santiago awaited the attack of another Haitian army under General Jean Louis Pierrot. News of the Haitian advance was spread by an English merchant who lived in Santiago, but who had been in Cap Haitien when the troops were being mobilized for the invasion. This allowed the Dominicans sufficient time to prepare for the coming attack. On March 30 the Haitian army set out to take the city through an assault in open formation. Since Santiago was situated on a hard-to-reach promontory from which all the maneuvers of the Haitians could be seen, the battle was particularly easy for the Dominicans. From various improvised trenches and ramparts they freely used their artillery against the attackers. The battle lasted throughout the afternoon of March 30, with the Haitians suffering 715 casualties as opposed to only 1 for the Dominicans.

At the end of the day, General Pierrot asked for a truce to pick up his dead and wounded. A commission of Dominican officials came down to talk with the general and brought with them a printed sheet that had been published in Santo Domingo a few days earlier. According to this paper, President Hérard had been killed in combat in Azua on the 19th. When this sheet was shown to Pierrot, his first thoughts were about the upcoming struggle for the Haitian presidential succession. Pierrot decided to break camp that very night and the next day he retreated with his troops in such haste that many of the wounded were left abandoned.

Hérard did not died in Azua. The printed sheet had been merely propaganda designed to raise the morale of the Dominicans who had seen some high-ranking Haitian officers in ornate uniforms fall in combat. When Pierrot reached Cap Haitien, he learned that the President was still alive and fighting in Azua. Hérard learned of Pierrot's retreat and ordered him to bring his troops to reinforce him in the south. Pierrot refused, seeing that Hérard's political position had been greatly weakened by the agitation provoked by Boyer's old political friends in Port-au-Prince during Hérard's absence. Pierrot joined with Hérard's enemies on April 25, 1844, favoring General Phillipe Guerrier as a replacement for Hérard. On May 2, a coup in Port-au-Prince overthrew Hérard and the army declared Guerrier president.

Realizing that his position in Azua was hopeless, Hérard returned to Haiti to fight for the presidency. Before abandon-

ing Azua the Haitians set fire to the town, but found their retreat hampered by guerrilla raids that harassed them up to
the border. Before reaching Port-au-Prince, Hérard realized
that his cause was lost and that he was unable to remain in
power. On a beach near the Haitian capital he embarked for
exile. On May 3, General Guerrier was installed as president
of Haiti, but the complications that arose during his term in
office were so great that he never had the opportunity to invade the east, although he did manage to issue some ineffective manifestos calling for the Dominicans to reintegrate into
the Republic of Haiti.

    While the war was being waged, the Dominicans began their
initiation into the problems of politically organizing an independent country. One of the first acts of the junta was to send a
schooner to Curaçao to bring the Trinitario leader Juan Pablo
Duarte back to the country. Duarte arrived in Santo Domingo
on March 15 and was named brigadier general and incorporated into the junta. When news arrived that Santana had retreated to Baní after the battle of March 19, Duarte asked for authorization to go to the south to aid the army. The junta complied
by charging him with the mission of assisting Santana, and also
authorized him to take over command if necessary. Duarte arrived in Baní on March 23 and tried to get Santana to change
his defensive strategy to an offensive one. Santana completely
rejected this suggestion and instead asked the junta to accelerate its efforts before the French consul to obtain military and
political support from France.

    Duarte and Santana disagreement over strategy and tactics
deepened. Duarte insisted that the Dominican army should attack the enemy. Confronted with Santana's refusal, Duarte then
asked the junta for authorization to direct offensive operations
himself. The junta foresaw the risks of such tactics and decided
to recall Duarte to Santo Domingo with only his staff to accompany him. Having more trust in the military judgment of San-

tana, the junta sided with the army and left Duarte and the Trinitarios without military support.

Thus, from the very beginning political differences between liberal Trinitarios and conservatives caused serious confrontations. When the Junta Central Gubernativa was organized on March 1, the conservatives outmaneuvered the young Trinitarios. Tomás de Bobadilla was elected as the junta's president instead of Francisco del Rosario Sánchez, the leader of the separatist coup. Although Sánchez remained as the military commander of the city, his party had to accept the fact that the separatist movement was now under the direction of the very person who, for over 20 years, had worked to keep the country under Haitian domination.

The crisis created by the clash between Santana and Duarte in Baní decisively changed the alliance between the Trinitarios and the conservatives. Bobadilla, the head of the former Boyerists and now president of the junta, openly supported Santana's policy of requesting military and political protection from France. As early as March 8, 1844, the junta had sent a message to the French consul ratifying the terms of the plan for a French protectorate in exchange for the bay and peninsula of Samaná. As the weeks passed, the conservatives intensified their efforts, but this policy caused a major rift between the conservatives and the Trinitarios.

Duarte protested on several occasions. He was opposed to any understanding which involved the cession of the peninsula and bay of Samaná to France or to any other power. Duarte believed it would violate the sovereignty of the new Republic. Since his opinion in the junta was not decisive, relations between the Trinitarios and the conservative members of the junta became more and more strained. Finally, on May 26, 1844, a political crisis exploded at one of the junta's meetings when the archbishop of Santo Domingo and the junta's president expressed their preference for a French protectorate. The ensuing debate was so violent that the meeting was adjourned without reaching any agreement. This event made it quite clear to the Trinitarios that they had eroded their influence by letting the conservatives take over the junta's presidency as well as the command of the army.

Duarte and his followers then tried to recuperate their lost power. After meeting with the city's garrison on May 31, they managed to have 56 active officers sign a document addressed to the junta asking that Duarte be named general-in-chief of the army, and that four prominent Trinitarios be named division generals or brigadier generals. With this plan, the Trinitarios wanted to position themselves with ranks higher than Santana's in order to take control of the armed forces. The junta was not impressed by this demonstration of the city's military and responded to the petition by stating that since the hostilities had already ceased there was no place for promotions within the military ranks. Furthermore, the junta declared that it would not appoint more generals in order to comply with the principles of the manifesto of January 16.

On the following day, June 1, the junta again requested the political and military protection of France to defend the Dominicans from the Haitians. This time, the junta managed somewhat to conciliate the positions for Sánchez and Duarte also signed the new communiqué. This unity went no further than appearances, and during the week of June 9 the more radical Trinitarios met again with the garrison and decided to carry out a military coup to depose the conservatives who had compromised the nation's sovereignty by maintaining negotiations with France. After the *coup*, Francisco Sánchez was named president to replace Bobadilla. The other conservatives were replaced by the most radical Trinitarios. Besides retaining his seat on the junta, General Duarte was named military commander of the Department of Santo Domingo, thereby gaining control of the country's main garrison.

Once in power, the Trinitarios acted to remove Santana from the command of the Southern Army, which was then the main military force of the Republic. Santana had been suffering from depression and ill health and had previously asked the junta to be temporarily relieved of his charge. When his brother died suddenly on June 15, Santana repeated his request and added that now he had to take care of his brother's affairs. Sánchez and the Trinitarios took advantage of this opportunity. On June 23, the junta ordered Colonel Esteban Roca to temporarily replace Pedro Santana as head of the Southern Army.

After these bold moves, the junta soon found the situation out of hand. On June 20, Duarte had set out for the Cibao region to put an end to the internal discord over the issue of a French protectorate. On his arrival there, Duarte found that his Trinitario friend Ramón Mella had been working to proclaim him as President of the Republic. Duarte accepted the proclamation in Santiago on July 4, and in Puerto Plata a few days later. A chain of such proclamations then followed, and the junta found itself in the embarrassing situation of having to recognize that a new government had arisen in the Cibao under Duarte. These events divided the Trinitarios for Sánchez was still the junta's president.

The situation became even more complicated on July 3 when Colonel Roca arrived in Azua and prepared to replace Santana. To Colonel Roca's surprise, both the officers and soldiers refused to obey the order and insisted they would not be separated from General Santana. They had come with him and would only follow him. Under these circumstances, Colonel Roca joined Santana's forces and informed the junta of the difficulties that had arisen. The refusal of the troops to accept Roca's command lay in the very nature of Santana's army. This army was in effect a personal one comprised of the peons who worked on the haciendas of Santana's friends, *compadres*, and relatives. Thus, in spite of his stated intention to retire, Santana was not willing to be deprived of his command surrendering it to Duarte and the Trinitarios, nor were his men willing to remain at the battlefront without their leader to whom they were bound by personal ties.

After learning about Duarte's proclamation as presidente in the Cibao region, Santana marched with his troops to Santo Domingo to reestablish the political order that had disappeared with the June 9 coup. Sánchez tried to detain Santana by force and ordered the local military commander, José Joaquín Puello, to prepare the city's defenses. Puello, however, refused. He was pressured by the French consul who threatened to withdraw from the city along with his warships if the government used force to repel Santana. Sánchez then had no alternative but to go to San Cristóbal, 20 miles west of Santo Domingo, and seek a political solution by bargaining with Santana. In this meeting, Santana violently accused the Trinitarios of denying the army the support needed in the campaign at Azua, and told Sanchez how displeased he was with it. Sánchez could do nothing but assure Santana that he would be allowed to enter Santo Domingo with the Southern Army.

On the morning of July 12, 1844, Santana entered the city heading some 2,000 men completely loyal to him. He gathered his army in the *plaza de armas* where one of his officers harangued the troops, while the soldiers shouted "down with the junta, long live General Santana, supreme head of the people!" A new military coup was taking place. At first Santana wished to proclaim himself dictator, but the French consul convinced him that it would be better to preserve the junta without the illegal Trinitario members, and reinstitute the conservatives ousted on June 9, for the junta was the legitimate government since the foundation of the Republic.

During the ensuing days, the movement against the Trinitarios gained force. Santana issued a proclamation making it clear that he was prepared to end all influence of Duarte's party. It was not so easy to replace the Trinitarios, however. On July 15, Santana almost lost his life at the hands of one of the Trinitarios, Juan Isidro Pérez, who, in a state of exaltation attempted to assassinate him saying that as Rome had its Brutus so, too, would the Dominican Republic. This incident culminated in the imprisonment of all the Trinitarios who had played an active role in the events since June. At 3:00 p.m. on July 16, with the city under his control, Santana reinstituted the Junta Central Gubernativa, with the original members ousted the previous month, while keeping the presidency for himself.

Meanwhile, in the Cibao Duarte and his friends were unaware of the events in Santo Domingo. On July 19, an enthusiastic Ramón Mella sent a communiqué to the junta to officially inform it of the proclamation of Duarte as President of the Republic. On the 20th, Duarte appeared in Puerto Plata to express his gratitude for the public demonstrations in his favor. On the 24th, the commission sent by Mella arrived in Santo Domingo and informed the junta of the nomination of Duarte as President. The junta, under the leadership of Santana, responded with a manifesto stating that it did not recognize the nomination of General Duarte or of any other person as President unless it be made by the Constitutional Congress. It then added that General Ramón Mella had been dismissed as commander-in-chief of the department of Santiago and the frontiers of the northwest. It also stated that General Duarte's appointment had been canceled and he should discontinue his functions as delegate of the government.

This manifesto also declared Duarte and Mella traitors to the country. On receiving it, Mella set out for Santo Domingo, but when he arrived there he was detained and jailed along with the other Trinitarios. On the same day, the archbishop issued a pastoral letter stating that it was an offense to God not to obey the mandates and orders of the General of Division and Supreme Chief Santana as well as the Junta Central Gubernativa. According to the archbishop, those who disobeyed the provisions of "our wise government" would be excommunicated.

Moreover, on August 1 the Southern Army, now called the Liberation Army, issued another manifesto signed by 628 officers and soldiers demanding that Santana exercise "justice against the assassins of the Fatherland," and requesting him to apply the strongest punishments against them. Two days later, another manifesto was circulated in the city by 68 family heads who also asked that the Trinitarios be punished and sent to exile. Santana agreed. On August 22, the Junta declared Duarte, Mella, Sánchez, and other five high-ranking Trinitarios traitors to the country and decreed their exile for life.

These events forced Duarte to hide in the countryside near Puerto Plata for almost the entire month of August until he was finally captured and imprisoned on the 27th. A few days later he was transferred to Santo Domingo, from where he was expelled from the country on September 10. The Trinitario movement was now completely dismantled. The junta took the precaution of sending the main leaders to Germany, England, the United States, and Venezuela to prevent any communication among them. The conservatives enjoyed total political power now.

The triumph of Santana, Bobadilla, and the pro-French group gave them time to work on the organization of the government and the writing of a political constitution. On July 24, on the same day the junta published the manifesto against Duarte and Mella, it also dictated a decree convoking the electorate to choose deputies for the assembly that would write the constitution. Elected between August 20 and 30, the deputies met in San Cristóbal on September 21, and continued working until November 6, when they presented the junta with a draft constitution based on the Haitian Constitution of 1843 and on the United States Constitution, both of which established the separation of powers and the preeminence of the legislature over the executive.

When Santana and his advisers studied the project, they disagreed immediately because the document left little room for the President to act swiftly in times of war. Santana refused to accept the presidency if the Constitution were not altered. He argued that in the Dominican Republic political power should belong to the military rather than to the civilians since the state of war with Haiti demanded speedy decisions. At first, the Congress was reluctant to accept Santana's demands and the tensions between the Constitutional Assembly and the Junta Central Gubernativa ran high. This crisis was finally resolved at the suggestion of Tomás de Bobadilla who proposed the inclusion of the following article into the Constitution:

"Art. 210: ...during the current war and while peace has not been signed, the President of the Republic can freely organize the army and navy, mobilize the national troops; and consequently be able to give all orders, decision, and decrees which are fitting, without being subject to any responsibility."

This article instituted a political and military dictatorship which completely invalidated the democratic provisions of the new Constitution. One of the few who protested against the inclusion of this article was Buenaventura Báez, who had been one of the principal framers of the original document and had participated in the debates that led to the drafting of the Haitian Constitution during the previous year. This protest found little support among the other deputies. Santana, who wanted the article approved at any cost, sent a battalion of soldiers to San Cristóbal where the assembly was still in session. While the deputies were deliberating inside, the soldiers surrounded the building in a threatening manner and advised them of the convenience of complying with Santana's desires.

Placated by the inclusion of the article, Santana then accepted being elected president of the Republic for two consecutive terms of four years, which would keep him ruling the country until February 15, 1852. He was sworn in and he appointed his first cabinet on November 13, 1844. He also chose loyal military men of proven experience as governors for the various provinces of the country. Simultaneously, the junta was dissolved since it had accomplished its task of producing the first constitutional government of the Dominican Republic.

8.
The first caudillos:
Santana and Báez
(1844-1856)

PEDRO SANTANA

The first government of General Pedro Santana was plagued with difficulties. One of the first problems he had to confront was a conspiracy planned by friends and relatives of the Trinitarios who wished to overthrow his government and bring back Duarte and his followers. This conspiracy was discovered at the beginning of 1845. Its leaders were sentenced to death and executed on February 27, 1845, the first anniversary of national independence.

Another difficulty facing Santana was the growing opposition of the upper clergy who insisted that the state return all the properties which the Haitians had confiscated from the church in 1824. On May 17, prominent priest José María Bobadilla published a pamphlet defending the rights of the church and demanding the restitution of the church properties. He was immediately rebutted by the administrator and inspector general of finance, Manuel María Valencia, who pointed out the problems that would arise if the state returned those properties that had already been bought and sold many times to third parties.

Valencia's arguments justified the government's policy expressed in the Ley de Bienes Nacionales of June 7, 1845, which ratified the Haitian confiscations. This was a true law of *desamortización* that forever eliminated all ecclesiastical annuities, chaplaincies, capitals, and rents on any lands and buildings in the former Spanish colony, and left these properties exempt from all liens and mortgages held by the Church. This law thus removed all hope for the Church to recover not only its former properties but also the interest that might have accumulated since 1824.

The government's refusal to return the Church's assets soon turned the clergy against the President. Santana responded by threatening some church members, and Father José María Bobadilla fled into exile. This kept the church hostile to Santana and produced another grave political consequence. Tomás de Bobadilla, Santana's most capable minister, became highly displeased by his brother's exile and left the government nine months later. Bobadilla then joined the ranks of the opposition that had been gaining strength in the Congress where various deputies and senators resented Santana's dictatorship.

In July 1845, Santana also had to confront a popular revolt in Santa María, a rural community 20 miles west of Santo Domingo composed almost entirely of black families of Haitian descent. Believing the Haitian propaganda that the Dominican government was going to reinstitute slavery among the black population, the inhabitants of Santa María revolted when the government called the young male population to join the Southern Army and go to the border to defend Dominican independence. The revolt was repressed by Santana who could not allow any sedition to gain ground at a time when the Haitians were again invading the country.

This new Haitian invasion came as a result of the ascension of General Jean Louis Pierrot to the presidency of Haiti following the death of Phillipe Guerrier on April 15, 1845. Pierrot, who had been defeated by the Dominicans in Santiago the year before, had decided to avenge this defeat. On May 10, 1845 he issued a proclamation calling the Dominicans to reunite with Haiti and stated that he would never renounce the indivisibility of the Haitian territory. In this second military campaign, the Dominicans were much better prepared than in the previous year. Resistance to this new invasion was overwhelmingly successful.

The Haitian advance was detained along the northern and southern borders where numerous battles were fought during the rest of the year. Finally, the Haitians were soundly defeated on September 17 in a site called La Estrelleta, and thus had to retreat, leaving the south in peace. On October 27, Dominicans also defeated Haitians on the northern front at the Sabana de Beler. As the invasion by land had failed, the Haitians attempted to invade by sea in December, 1845. But their squadron was poorly commanded and on nearing the coast off Puerto Plata ran aground and sank. The crew was taken prisoner on December 21.

With these victories, the Dominican Republic saved itself for a second time from submission to Haiti. Despite his failures, General Pierrot wished to counterattack. On January 1, 1846 he announced a new campaign, but his officers and soldiers, who had grown tired after eight months of unproductive fighting, received this new call to arms very coldly. When Pierrot ordered the troops to march on the Dominican Republic the following February 1847, the army mutinied and proclaimed his dismissal as President. The new Haitian president, General Jean Baptiste Riché, realized that the war against the Dominicans had become extremely unpopular. Facing at the same time a violent peasant rebellion in the south, Riché dropped all plans for any new invasion.

Despite the fact that the Haitians had been thoroughly defeated in the campaign of 1845, the Dominican conservative leaders clung to the idea that it was not possible to save the

Republic from a new Haitian invasion without the aid and protection of a foreign power. In May 1846, the Dominican government sent a diplomatic mission to Spain, France, and England to negotiate the recognition of the Dominican Republic as an independent country, but at the same time with the intention of placing the country under the protection of the power with the most to offer. These negotiations produced limited results. The Spanish government still believed it could exert its sovereignty over its former colony and refused to recognize Dominican independence. The British government postponed taking any decision until it was better informed as to what was transpiring in the Dominican Republic. But France found it fitting to keep a consul in the city of Santo Domingo.

Meanwhile, the economic situation was going from bad to worse. A long drought occurring in 1846 severely damaged the tobacco crop, thereby depriving the government of important fiscal revenues. This difficult economic situation was further aggravated by growing military expenditures and by the poor management of the minister of finance, a fact widely publicized by congressional opposition now led by Tomás de Bobadilla who had been elected to Congress upon leaving his post as minister.

The opposition became stronger in March 1847, when the accounts of the various ministers were read before Congress. Great controversy arose over the annual report of the minister of finance, who was accused of misappropriation of public funds by several members of Congress. This accusation completely enraged Santana who threatened to resign on the grounds that he was tired of encountering so many difficulties in the exercise of power, especially those problems created by the Congress led by former Minister Bobadilla.

Santana's threat to resign alarmed his supporters. General Merced Marcano, Santana's private secretary, presented Congress with a petition signed by 92 army officers and 4 public officials requesting that Bobadilla be dismissed as congressman and exiled from the country within 48 hours. Santana openly supported his army in its confrontation with Congress, while his cabinet warned the legislative body that if the military's demands were not accepted they would all resign thus aggravating the political crisis. Bobadilla chose to resign and went into exile. As soon as Santana received news of Bobadilla's departure, he and his ministers appeared before Congress while his troops were quartered nearby ready for combat. He said that his desires were to follow the Constitution and that he hoped that the congressmen would do everything possible to sanction the laws which the country needed.

As the economic situation worsened throughout 1847, Santana's cabinet was incapable of solving the growing number of problems. Opposition to the government became even more evident. The political tensions increased even more after the government accused prestigious General José Joaquín Puello and his brother Gabino of conspiring to overthrow Santana. The two brothers, with extensive connections with the Trinitarios, were taken prisoners and sentenced to death. They were executed on December 23 along with their accomplices.

Despite this repression, little by little a climate of civil disobedience grew. Santana handled it with a complete lack of diplomacy. In some cases he ordered the execution of poor peasants accused of stealing a simple bunch of plantains, as happened with a man named Bonifacio Paredes who was executed on October 22. At other times, the government went as far as censoring the opinions of some congressmen with regard to the country's financial situation. Moreover, on February 17, 1848, the government attempted to control movement within the country by decreeing a law requiring Dominicans to use an internal passport to go from one place to another.

The economic crisis and the political malaise, coupled with the growing congressional opposition which the exile of Bobadilla made worse, affected Santana, who became ill and depressed. At the end of February 1848, he retired to his hacienda in El Seibo leaving the executive power in the hands of the cabinet. During Santana's seclusion in El Seibo, the opposition became even more active in Santo Domingo, and congressional sessions were characterized by political demonstrations where the government's economic policy was mercilessly attacked.

By the middle of the year it was clear that Santana's government lacked popular support. The disfavor became more obvious during a military crisis in July 1848. On this occasion, Santana wanted to remove a colonel with some links to the Trinitarios on the grounds of indecorum, but could not find any witnesses among the military to substantiate the accusation. Therefore, the war council in charge of judging the colonel declared him innocent. With this incident Santana realized that he had lost support even within the army in Santo Domingo.

On August 4, 1848 Santana resigned before his cabinet. This body exercised the executive power until September 8, when General Manuel Jimenes, the minister of war, was sworn in as president. Jimenes was unanimously chosen to replace Santana because of his apparent control over the army and because of his former affiliation with the Trinitarios. The congressmen who voted for him thought he would give the country a liberal government different from that of his predecessor. Nevertheless, Jimenes was not an apt ruler and he quickly undermined his position by decreeing the army infantry disbanded on the grounds that the men were needed in the countryside to stimulate agriculture.

Jimenes concurred with the opposition's demand for a general amnesty for all political exiles. On September 26, 1848, he decreed that all those exiled for political reasons, especially Duarte, Sánchez, Mella, and the other Trinitarios, be allowed to return. But he angered many of his sympathizers when they discovered that he still bore grudges with some Trinitarios and was not allowing some exiles to return.

Jimenes's political position also began to wane as a result of the efforts of Buenaventura Báez and other Dominican diplomats in Europe who were working to have France sign a treaty of recognition of Dominican independence. Haitian President Riché had died suddenly on February 27, 1847, and had been replaced by Faustine Soulouque, an obscure, illiterate officer born in Africa who had been chosen by Haitian politicians who wanted to govern the country using him as a figurehead.

During his first year as president, Soulouque had to confront so many conspiracies and other difficulties just to stay in power that the Dominicans could breathe more easily and spent their time in organizing the country. However, in 1848, when France finally recognized the Dominican Republic as a free and independent state through a provisional treaty of peace, friendship, trade and navigation, the Haitians immediately reacted and protested that the treaty threatened their own security since they suspected that France had been authorized to occupy Samaná Bay. Moreover, the Haitians objected that if France recognized Dominican independence, they would have no more chances to reoccupy the eastern two-thirds of the island and could not collect from Dominicans the money and resources needed to pay the debt that they had contracted with France in 1825.

Soulouque decided to invade the Dominican territory before the treaty was officially ratified by the French government. On March 9, 1849, an army of 15,000 men crossed the border and divided in several columns led by the most important Haitian military leaders. In a sweeping march the Haitians occupied all the frontier towns. Within a few days Soulouque arrived in San Juan de la Maguana where he established his general headquarters. The Dominicans could do little to stop this advance despite their frequent guerrilla raids. On April 7, when Soulouque moved on to Azua, the Dominican commanders evacuated the city and took cover in the mountains of El Número where they reorganized and sent out guerrillas to ambush the Haitians.

The weakness and lack of energy with which President Jimenes directed the military operations created a profound crisis of confidence in Congress. Having lost faith in the military ability of Jimenes and forgetting their former grievances, the congressmen then recalled General Santana to head the army. Jimenes tried to prevent the return of Santana, but Congress was adamant and granted Santana full power over the Southern Army. Santana again repeated his strategy of waiting for the Haitians behind the mountains of El Número, while keeping some guerrillas to harass the invaders.

On April 17, the Haitians were resisted on El Número, but this time they managed to cross the mountains passes. Soulouque then prepared his troops for the decisive battle against the mass of the Dominican army under the command of General Santana who waited with his troops at a crossing of the Ocoa River called Las Carreras. On April 21 the two armies were poised on opposite sides of the river. A violent and bloody encounter followed. The Haitian army suffered a crushing defeat and was forced to retreat by Santana's forces. While fleeing to Haiti, Soulouque's forces sacked and burned the towns of Azua and San Juan de la Maguana as well as all the other small Dominican settlements in their path.

With his victory in the Battle of Las Carreras, Santana again recovered his political prestige. Once the war was over, Santana had the army issue a manifesto authorizing him to not lay down arms until a new government was established to impose law and order and remove political discord. Santana accused Jimenes of endangering the integrity of the Republic by disorganizing the army and demoralizing the national spir-

it. Jimenes responded to this accusation with a decree dis-
charging Santana. Congress now recognized its mistake in
electing Jimenes as president and nullified the presidential
decree while supporting Santana and his march to the capital
to overthrow the government.

On May 17, 1849, Santo Domingo was sieged by Santana's
forces. A short but violent civil war broke out in which the neighboring town of San Carlos was burned. Jimenes quickly lost all
support and capitulated, going into exile on the 29th. On the
following day, Santana entered the city with his expeditionary
army and took over the executive power "by mandate of the
people and the army." Then followed a witch hunt of his political opponents who were again sent into exile as soon as they
were captured.

This time Santana convoked presidential elections to be held
on July 5, 1849. A private citizen, Santiago Espaillat, was personally selected for this position by Santana and was subsequently elected. Espaillat, however, as a matter of conscience
declined to accept the presidency since he would only be a puppet for the chief of the army. Consequently Congress was forced
to call for new elections on August 5 while Santana recommended that the electors vote for Congressman Buenaventura Báez
who had been responsible for his own political rehabilitation
and had aided in the overthrow of Jimenes.

Báez had an impressive political background. He had been
a congressman during the Haitian occupation, one of the secret negotiators of the French protectorate, and had headed the
Dominican diplomatic mission that went to Europe in 1845 to
garner the political support of England, France, and Spain. On
August 18, Báez was officially elected president while Santana
preserved his army command and, again, retired to his hacienda in El Seibo.

BUENAVENTURA BAEZ VS. PEDRO SANTANA

When Buenaventura Báez assumed the presidency on September 24, 1849, one of his first acts was to organize the army and navy to undertake an offensive campaign against Haiti. At the same time he began a lengthy process of negotiations with Great Britain, France, and the United States to mediate before the Haitian government to prevent more invasions. These efforts were rewarded by the ratification of a treaty of recognition, peace, friendship, trade, and navigation between Britain and the Dominican Republic on September 10, 1850. The British government wished to increase trade with the country and found it in its best interests to promote peace and strengthen the sovereignty of the Republic so as to decrease the influence of Spain, France, and the United States.

The rivalry of the various powers to influence Dominican politics was quite acute at this time. Both France and the United States wanted to eventually take control of the peninsula and bay of Samaná, thus preventing the other from accomplishing it first. Great Britain had no desire for more possessions in the area and, instead, wanted the Dominican Republic free from all foreign interference since Great Britain had the most trade with the country and knew it would lose its commercial privileges if France or the United States occupied Samaná.

After Soulouque's first invasion, the British tried to get Haiti and the Dominican Republic to sign a truce so that the Haitian threat would not force the Dominicans to seek foreign support. The British consul worked with his colleagues in Santo Domingo to force Soulouque to sign a ten-year truce with the Dominicans. Although Soulouque only accepted a truce for two months, diplomatic pressure prevented him from invading the Dominican Republic for several years and limited his military operations to simple mobilizations on the other side of the border. Thus due to this mediation the period of Báez's first government from 1849 to 1853 was a time of relative peace with Haiti.

Freed from the Haitian threat, Báez was able to act independently from Santana in both his international and domestic policies, and could consolidate his own political leadership. During the four years of his presidency, Báez granted amnesty to several groups of political exiles and protected many of those formerly persecuted by Santana. He also took advantage of his office to reorganize the military command and to favor various officers who had not received Santana's support.

Báez also favored the negotiation of a concordat with the Holy See to regulate relations between the church and the government and to placate the clergy who had been hostile to Santana since the exile of Father Bobadilla. This move greatly angered Santana who, little, by little, was discovering that the man he had chosen as president was using the executive power to form his own party and free himself from Santana's political tutelage. Trying to recuperate his vanishing power, Santana maneuvered to replace Báez as president of the Republic once Báez stepped out of power at the end of his term.

Because General Santana was the only military and political leader recognized on a national level, it was natural for him to replace Báez as president once the latter's term ended in February, 1853. Once in power, the Santanista party encouraged Santana to send Báez out of the country to avoid political competition. Already jealous of the political independence of Báez, Santana fully agreed with his party and acted accordingly.

In March 1853, Santana's newly inaugurated government provoked a crisis with the Church aimed at breaking the clerical support behind Báez. Archbishop Tomás Portes e Infante was accused of inciting the people to rebel against the government, and was forced to appear before a public session of the

National Congress to pledge loyalty to the Constitution of the Republic. At first the Archbishop refused to bow to Santana's pressures. However, when the President showed him a passport and threatened to expel him immediately from the country, the archbishop, with his mental health impaired by old age and several weeks of tension, finally submitted. Santana also took advantage of this confrontation to expel three priests who were accused of instigating a plan "to invest the clergy with rights and powers which were the exclusive resource of the powers of the State."

Believing he had destroyed a conspiracy within the Church and had deprived Báez of political support, Santana decided the time was ripe to issue a manifesto against his political rival. In July 3, 1853, Santana publicly accused Báez of the worst crimes against the security of the Republic and made special reference to the supposed agreement between the former President and the ecclesiastical authorities "to mutually aid each other in oppressing the people in offense to the Constitution and to justice." Báez was also accused of wishing to use the clergy and army to remain in power as president for life. By virtue of these accusations, Santana dictated a decree expelling Báez forever from national territory. Báez did not wait to be captured and quickly fled for Curaçao.

With his rival out of the way, Santana was ready to exercise power with his customary absolutism. After reconciling with Trinitario General Ramón Mella, Santana sent him on a diplomatic mission to Spain to obtain Spanish recognition of Dominican independence and to seek political and military protection to guard it from Haiti. Mella left in December 1853, and stayed in Spain until May 1854. Eight years had passed since the first failed mission to Spain, but the Spanish government had not changed its position. The Spanish minister of state informed Mella that his government was not interested in intervening in Dominican affairs.

The Spanish government radically changed its policy the following year when news arrived in Madrid that the U.S. President Franklin Pierce had sent Texan General William Cazneau to the Dominican Republic with instructions to negotiate about leasing some land on the Samaná Peninsula for the purpose of establishing a U.S. naval station. Spain wished to prevent the presence of the North Americans in Santo Domingo at any cost since it would jeopardize her hegemony in the Antilles. Thus, on February 18, 1855, Spain entirely reversed its policy and agreed to sign a treaty of recognition, peace, friendship, trade, navigation, and extradition with the Dominican Republic. This treaty was approved by the Dominican Senate on April 30, 1855.

Santana's success abroad was not matched on the domestic level. From the beginning of his second term as president, he experienced great opposition to his authoritarian methods, especially among congressional representatives who firmly demanded a more liberal constitution to remove the excessive presidential powers granted by Article 210. In July 1853, Santana was finally forced to call a constitutional assembly to write a new constitution. This assembly, convoked during the middle of January, 1854, was dominated by several liberal thinkers who introduced significant changes in the constitutional text of 1844.

According to the new constitution, the Senate was invested with more powers, among them the ability to grant military promotions and to mobilize the armed forces during times of war and peace. Also, the office of vice-president was created, and the municipal system was modified to allow the *ayuntamientos* greater political and economic control over the city governments. Although Article 210 was omitted, thereby preventing the president from exercising power in an absolutist or irresponsible manner, a special transitory law was introduced that allowed General Santana to hold two consecutive terms as president that would end on February 28, 1861.

Another transitory disposition permitted the president to grant all the military promotions he considered necessary until a definite peace was signed with Haiti. Such a provision clearly invalidated those articles that conferred this right on the Senate, and, once again, placed the absolute command of the armed forces in the hands of the President. Yet, this constitution was promulgated on February 25, 1854, despite the reservations of Santana, who continued to find the elimination of Article 210 disagreeable.

During the following months Santana consolidated his power base and began asserting his influence in Congress. At the beginning of August, the legislature dictated a decree authorizing him to adopt all measures he judged necessary to guarantee order and security of the state, thus reviving the spirit of Article 210. With these powers in his hands, and after this show of congressional weakness, Santana called an extraordinary session of the Senate and Chamber of Deputies to meet on November 1, 1854, to discuss writing another constitution since he considered the February document too weak to assure the stability of the country because of the formal restrictions imposed on the executive power. When Congress met on the assigned date, Santana read a brief speech in which he admonished the representatives about the dire consequences that would ensue if the constitution were not drafted according to his wishes.

Frightened, the congressmen met and worked under the influence of Santana's agents in Congress. Human rights and the exercise of fundamental civil liberties were omitted from the new constitutional text. These would be regulated by special laws that could be modified according to the government's will. Elections would be conducted through indirect votes and electoral colleges. Congress, which had previously been bicameral with more than 30 representatives, was now reduced to one so-called "Senado Consultor" of only 7 members with legislative, judicial, and consultative powers. This Senate could be reelected indefinitely and would meet in legislative sessions lasting only three months each year. Outside of these sessions its function was limited to being a mere advisory body for the executive power.

Under the new constitution, the provincial governments remained under governors directly dependent on the president who had jurisdiction over the *ayuntamientos*. Although the new constitution did not contain Article 210, the Dominican political system was now organized in such a manner that the country was led by a political oligarchy represented in one legislative of only seven members at the disposal of the president. This constitution was promulgated on December 23, 1854, and later became the preferred text of all 19th-century Dominican dictators. As soon as the constitution was passed, Santana retired for a few weeks to rest on his hacienda in El Seibo and left the power in the hands of newly elected Vice-President General Manuel de la Regla Mota.

The following year, 1855, was one of intense revolutionary activity on the part of Báez and other Santana's opponents who were exiled on the island of Saint Thomas. Forgetting their former disagreements, these exiles accepted Báez's leadership and planned their return to the homeland to overthrow Santana. One of the chief targets of the exiles was a projected treaty of friendship, trade, and navigation that Santana was negotiating with the United States involving the cession or leasing of the bay and peninsula of Samaná to the U.S. government. The supporters of Báez and other enemies of Santana disliked the new treaty with the United States since, once implemented, it would greatly decrease the possibilities of removing Santana, who could then count on U.S. military, economic, and political support to strengthen his position.

The exiles sought the support of the British and the Spanish governments who, like the Haitians, feared the extension of

U.S. military influence to the island. Britain did not wish to see the United States receiving trade privileges in Dominican Republic for it would mean the loss of the commercial hegemony it had recently acquired through the favorable trade treaty in 1850.

Haiti's fear was based on the fact that the United States was a slave power and its presence in Dominican territory could threaten Haitian independence. In November 1855, Soulouque once again organized the Haitian army, which was divided into three columns, to invade the Dominican Republic through Dajabón, in the north, Las Matas de Farfán, in the center, and Neiba, in the south. By December the units of the south and center were already on the march, making a sweeping advance and occupying several border towns. General Santana, on his part, occupied Azua where he established his headquarters and sent out two columns to dislodge the Haitians.

On December 22, two important battles took place. These were two of the bloodiest battles ever in the Haitian-Dominican war. The battle of Santomé was particularly decisive. After four hours of intense combat in which the Dominicans made extensive use of their machetes and lances, the Haitians were defeated, leaving at least 695 dead and many wounded on the battlefield and in the surrounding woods. Terrified by the fury of the Dominican attack, the Haitian troops, under the personal command of Emperor Soulouque, fled toward the border. They were persistently harassed by Dominican troops who, during the following months, raided the enemy forces as far away as the small Haitian fort of Cachimán near Las Caobas.

These triumphs in the south were followed by an equally decisive and important Dominican victory at Sabana Larga in the north on January 24, 1856. After a disastrous defeat on the battlefield, the fleeing Haitian troops were so viciously attacked on their rear guard by the Dominican troops that there was a trail of Haitian dead and wounded up the border. Soulouque attributed the Haitian defeat to the incompetence and treason of

his officers and brought his most important military commanders to a martial court, finding them guilty and executing them.

The Haitian defeat strengthened Santana's ability to continue his negotiations with the United States while the new
Spanish consul, Antonio María Segovia, arrived in Santo Domingo in the middle of the war on December 27, 1855. To Santana's surprise, Segovia worked publicly to prevent the consum-
mation of the treaty with the United States. Segovia openly offered political support to all the enemies of Santana who opposed the treaty with the United States. He opened special reg-
istry books in the consulate to allow all Dominicans who wished
to declare themselves as Spanish citizens to freely do so, even
though this action clearly violated Article VII of the treaty signed
by Spain and the Dominican Republic the year before.

The move proved effective since many of the President's opponents, now declared themselves Spanish citizens and felt politically protected from the authorities. Segovia's activities coincided with a new monetary crisis created by the excessive printing of paper money on the part of the government to finance the
war expeditures. Since Santana had returned to his former dictatorial ways, his popularity had been deteriorating rapidly.

Particularly damaging was the nationalist propaganda of
the opposition that continually denounced the government's
plans to surrender part of the national territory to the United
States, a slave power with different customs, language, and religious beliefs. Although the government harassed and jailed
many of its opponents, a significant part of the population of
the capital, where the opposition was greatest, registered as
Spanish subjects in the books of the Spanish consulate. Thus
the government suddenly found itself governing a city where
many of its most influential inhabitants had declared themselves
citizens of another nation.

Santana finally protested to the Spanish government about
the interference of its consul in internal Dominican politics.

While these protests were being delivered diplomatically by his envoy in Madrid, civil resistance to the government became so evident that Santana, seeing himself abandoned by many of his former supporters, became severely depressed and, arguing ill health, retired again to his hacienda in El Seibo to prepare his resignation. Before departing, he declared the country in a state of emergency and put the armed forces on a state of alert to prevent any uprising.

The retreat of Santana further discredited his government, and on May 26, 1856, he resigned in favor of Vice-President Manuel de Regla Mota. With the country in ruin because of the recent war that had been financed by the government's printing of worthless paper money, the new president was forced to discharge the very soldiers who were needed to back his regime because he was unable to raise sufficient funds to pay their salaries.

The dismissal of the army left Regla Mota practically powerless. Spanish consul Segovia took advantage of the situation and went to Saint Thomas where he met with Báez, whose safe return was guaranteed so that he could again become president. Báez returned, and Regla Mota, under pressure from Segovia and the opposition, named Báez vice-president so that he himself could resign, leaving Báez to become president by constitutional means. After receiving a general amnesty for himself and all the other political exiles who wished to return, Báez took over the presidency on October 6, 1856.

It was now Báez's turn to seek revenge for the injuries done to him by Santana by 1853. In the following months he and his partisans prepared various political intrigues to make Santana appear as a conspirator and the instigator of a supposed military plot. Santana was accused of the vilest crimes against the citizenry and institutions of the Republic including tyrannical government, economic ruin through the squandering of the treasury, and execution without trial of his political adversaries. In early January 1857, when the case against Santana had been sufficiently publicized, Báez gave orders for his arrest and a few days later sent him into exile.

With Santana out of the country and the government on a state of alert because of the recent political crisis, Báez changed his former liberal policies. Using the supposed conspiracy as a pretext, he unleashed an implacable political campaign against Santana's partisans who were forced to resign from the Senate and other public posts which they occupied so that the vacancies could be filled with Báez's own followers.

The Constitution of 1854, which supported the absolute power of the president, fit Báez's designs perfectly as he now came to power imbued with the spirit of reprisal against those he believed responsible for his previous political disgrace. The tobacco merchants of the Cibao would be his next victims, and the continuing monetary crisis that the country had been experiencing since 1844 would be his pretext.

9.
The Revolution
of 1857
(1857-1858)

Under Haitian domination the Dominican population recuperated and grew to 126,000 people in 1844, while the Haitian territory contained about 800,000 people. Despite complaints of both the Haitian and the Dominican elites, during
this period wood exports increased, particularly in the Dominican south, while tobacco continued to be planted in increasing
quantities in the Cibao.

This created an important difference. Since there were no
roads to link the south with the Cibao, the two regions existed
much as two different countries. Boyer's agrarian policy stimulated the *campesinos* to plant more tobacco in the Cibao and
encouraged the large landowners of the South to cut more
wood for export. During the Haitian domination, the sale of
mahogany, brasilwood, and lignumvitae increased at such a
rate that woodcutting became the economic base of the entire
southern region.

Trade in Santo Domingo was dominated by a minority of
Jewish and Spanish merchants who controlled the import and
export business. Such foreign merchants were wholesalers and

financiers of the small retail merchants since Haitian law forbade noncitizens from becoming involved in the retail business. These merchants were the channels of foreign trade and were the only ones with sufficient capital to meet all contingencies, including the constant demands for credit from the government.

In the northern harbor town of Puerto Plata, trade was likewise controlled by foreigners, mostly Germans, who represented tobacco manufacturers in Germany. There were also several Jews representing firms from Saint Thomas and Curaçao that bought large quantities of tobacco for resale in Europe. Trade in the interior was mostly handled by native Dominicans who depended on the large import houses of Santo Domingo, Puerto Plata, and Santiago.

Santo Domingo was merely an administrative center surrounded by large cattle ranches. The city imported most of its food from San Cristóbal and the surrounding countryside. There the peasants cultivated yucca, plantains, sweet potatoes, and yams, and produced a limited amount of raw sugar and molasses for further processing into rum. Farther to the west, in Baní, the people exploited the natural salt ponds, raised goats and cattle, and cut mahogany wood for export. Farther westward, in Azua, the population made raw sugar and rum, cut mahogany and hard woods for exportation, and raised some livestock. The inhabitants of San Juan de la Maguana, on the central road to the west, were still involved in livestock trade with Haiti. A similar situation characterized the towns of El Seibo and Higüey, where the population eked out a living from the extensive cattle herds that roamed freely on the vast southeastern savannas.

In contrast, the economy of Santiago, in the heart of the Cibao valley, was much more diversified. The Cibao had the best land in the island, and there Boyer agricultural policies really made a difference by stimulating tobacco and food production. Santiago contained a large group of artisans, mechanics, and tailors, plus a very active group of retail merchants.

There were also some tanneries and many cigar factories. Besides the cultivation and preparation of tobacco, which constituted the main commercial crop, most peasant families cultivated yucca, plantains, yams, and sweet potatoes, and also raised hogs and cattle. Around Santiago, the land was well cultivated by a relatively independent peasantry that constituted an assured market for the city's imports.

The sierra towns of San José de las Matas and Jarabacoa contained only a handful of families. These cultivated tobacco, raised cattle, and practiced subsistence agriculture. Down in the heart of the Cibao valley, in the humid, fertile triangle between La Vega, Moca, and Salcedo, the land was still used for livestock rising. Its inhabitants had only recently started to raise tobacco as a commercial crop and, of course, cultivated the usual food crops on subsistence farms.

Farther to the east, in San Francisco de Macorís the population produced corn, rice, and beans that they sold in the neighboring towns, although most people still concentrated on cattle raising. In Cotuí there was a small population that lived in extreme isolation and raised hogs and cattle for its own consumption. Still further to the east, the people of Samaná, practically segregated from the rest of the island, practiced extensive fishing and cultivated coconuts, as well as yams and other roots. They even managed to export small quantities of hides, coconuts, and tobacco. Samaná was one of the few exporting towns in addition to Santo Domingo, Azua, and Puerto Plata.

Some isolated natural harbors like Montecristi, Cabarete, and La Romana were used only to export wood. In the northwestern villages of Montecristi and Guayubín, almost all the inhabitants lived from raising cattle and goats that they traded in the northern sections of Haiti. In Puerto Plata, mahogany cutting alternated with livestock raising, and with an incipient subsistence agriculture, although cultivation had started to take off under Haitian supervision. The town's population also profited from the harbor's activity since Puerto Plata became the main outlet for the exportation of tobacco and was also the main port of entry of European and U.S. imports. Its population enjoyed a higher standard of living than the inhabitants of the other towns, with the exception of Santiago.

THE MONETARY QUESTION

The first year of independence, 1844, was an extremely hard year for the Dominican Republic. Because of the invasions and the threat of a new Haitian domination, the merchants stopped importing while exports were paralyzed due to the fact that the war occupied all the labor force normally dedicated to agriculture, cattle raising, and wood cutting. Moreover, when the Haitians were finally expelled in March 1844, the treasury in Santo Domingo and Puerto Plata only held 6,068.64 dollars and 5,093.77 Haitian *gourdes*, barely enough to cover the primary expenditures of the troops needed to confront the invasions. Within a few days, the Dominican government was without any ready cash and had to seek loans from the large landowners and the local merchants, especially those of foreign affiliation.

During the first year of independence the Government borrowed 12,000 dollars and 95,591.77 Dominican pesos from these sources. During the following years borrowing became a common practice and was combined with the printing of paper money without backing to keep the bureaucracy functioning. These practices kept commerce in a continual state of crisis, caused the ruin of the treasury and helped explain much of the political unrest of that time.

When Santana came to power on July 12, 1844, the country was suffering from a "dreadful financial crisis." The little remaining Haitian money in circulation was in the hands of the merchants. The public held almost nothing. In 1846, new printings put more than 2 million pesos into circulation and the Dominican peso lost 90 percent of its value. The administration of the treasury was poor because of economic ignorance. For example, in March 1847, Congress became alarmed by the crisis and asked the minister of finance to submit accounts. He could present no documents to clarify the situation. The congressmen then strongly attacked the minister and the government, and accused them of incompetent administration.

The real cause for this financial crisis was more ignorance than corruption, and the same members of Congress later judged that the depreciation of national currency "comes from the same causes which have produced the same results in all countries whose state of war has caused more expenditures than revenues, where the difference has been filled by printing of paper money which, found in excess of what the needs of the mercantile movement demand, begins to depreciate later. Such is the state of the actual circulation of paper money which we desire to remedy; that is, there circulates ten times the quantity of pesos which the commercial movement of the country can use; therefore each peso has fallen in real value, and represents in the monetary circulation, ten cents."

This economic and financial malaise alienated Santana from the little support he still held in Congress and was one of the main causes for his resignation in August 1848. President Manuel Jimenes, his successor, proved even more incapable of handling the Dominican monetary problem. Jimenes followed none of Congress's suggestions and ignored a plan for loans and consolidation of the public debt so that the currency in circulation was funneled into the hands of the richer merchants. When Soulouque invaded in 1849, the government again had to mobilize the army. But there were no funds to confront the emergency. By mid-1849, there was not one cent in the public coffers to cover the new war expenditures so that the government had to issue one million pesos.

When Buenaventura Báez became president in September 1849, there had already been at least ten printings of paper money. The first of these had been "exclusively reserved to provide arms, war equipment, leather straps, uniforms and other such materials in the shortest amount of time possible." Later printings were made with the same pretext, although the government adopted a new financial policy of issuing national money to exchange it for dollars that were deposited in a bank in Saint Thomas where that money earned between 3 and 6 percent interest annually. From Báez's administrative point of view this seemed like a sound measure since it created a contingency fund to cover emergency expenses.

The measure was not popular, though. The producers and exporters who generated wealth said it forced them to receive depreciated paper money instead of sound foreign currency. For this reason Benigno Filomeno Rojas, the representative of the tobacco industry in Santiago and the Cibao region protested ardently in March 1853, saying that "this policy of issuing five or more millions pesos in paper money to reduce it to a hundred thousand dollars, and deposit the money in a bank in Saint Thomas, is an inconceivable measure, an erroneous act, and one only has to read the first pages of a treatise on political economy to know that it should be qualified as such."

When Báez was replaced by Santana in February 1853, the country had a little more than 100,000 dollars deposited abroad as backing for the national currency. Although this was not a huge sum, it was the largest reserve ever accumulated by the government since the founding of the Republic. As the country now enjoyed a truce with Haiti, the pretext of a Haitian invasion to print more bills was replaced by the need to collect the older bills that had deteriorated because of the poor quality of paper. Thus, Santana began by issuing eight million new pesos in two printings. In the following years, he made three additional printings, one of which he justified by saying that the Haitians were preparing to invade and that it was necessary to have funds to cover the expenses of the approaching war. The Haitians invaded in 1855, the money was spent, and again the government had to resort to issuing new bills to replace the old bills that had deteriorated.

By the time Báez returned to power in 1856, as a result of the schemes of Segovia and the economic crisis that Santana's financial policy had created, there had been 23 monetary printings so that the value of the Dominican peso was well below that of the Spanish *peso fuerte* or of the U.S. dollar, although not as weak as ten years earlier during the founding of the Republic. The exchange rate of 68.75 pesos to one dollar when Báez took office improved to 50:1 on the eve of the tobacco crop in the spring of 1857 when gold and silver coins from abroad circulated in abundant quantities in the Cibao.

It was at this juncture that Báez precipitated another major monetary crisis. After having the seven-member Senate extend the presidential powers to issue paper money, he authorized the printing of 18 million more pesos on the pretext that the old money was badly deteriorated and that there was a dangerous lack of currency to cover the needs of the tobacco dealers in the Cibao. The new bills were then divided among his favorites and protégés who then travelled to the Cibao to buy as much tobacco and gold as they could. When this scheme was discovered, it was already too late for the Cibao merchants to recuperate their money. The Cibao farmers and merchants who had accepted the old paper money at an exchange rate of 50:1 soon found themselves ruined by the flood of new bills that greatly decreased the value of the national peso. Báez had not been popular in the Cibao since 1849 when he had attempted to set up a tobacco monopoly with some French associates, and now the tobacco growers and dealers decided to revolt.

THE REVOLUTION

On the night of July 7, 1857 the main military leaders of Santiago met in the local fortress along with the most important merchants, landowners, and intellectuals of the region. In view of the recent monetary measures, they issued a manifesto declaring their purpose "to shake off the yoke of the government of Señor Báez which they do not recognize from this point on and they declare themselves governed by a Provisional Government with its seat in the city of Santiago de los Caballeros (until a Congress elected by direct vote, constitutes a new power)."

The new government was installed with General José Desiderio Valverde as President and the lawyer, Benigno Filomeno de Rojas, as Vice-President. After receiving the prompt backing of almost all the inhabitants of the Cibao provinces, these two men organized an armed movement to march on Santo Domingo and overthrow Báez. The Santiago government placed its revolutionary troops under the command of General Juan Luis Franco Bidó, and in a few days the capital was surrounded and the civil war had begun. With all the resources at his disposal Báez could not be easily expelled from the capital.

Protected behind the walls of the city and fortified by the hundreds of thousands of dollars in gold and tobacco that his agents had swindled from the people of the Cibao in the previous weeks, Báez prepared to resist the revolt. Encouraged by the resistance of the forces loyal to the government in Samaná and Higüey, Báez tried to break the siege and used his money to import arms and provisions from Curaçao and Saint Thomas.

Confronted with the power that Báez demonstrated from the very beginning of the war, the Cibao government decreed a political amnesty to favor the return of General Padro Santana and his partisans from exile. As soon as he received news of the amnesty, Santana reentered the country on August 25, 1857. Because of his military experience and his ability to gather troops in the east, the Cibao government asked him to aid General Franco Bidó who had not been able to take Santo Domingo due to Báez's powerful resistance.

This invitation to Santana proved to be the biggest mistake committed by the Cibao government. Seeing their old enemy at the front of the revolutionary troops, Báez's forces were even more determined to resist and not be conquered because they knew that Santana and his party had returned for vengeance. Thus a revolution that might have triumphed after a brief siege of the city was denied an immediate victory by the tenacious resistance of its enemies who in no way wanted to fall into the hands of Santana.

Further, by assigning Santana as an aide to General Bidó, the Cibao government undermined its own military leader. Within a few weeks of his arrival, Santana was able to gather together his own forces through rapid recruitment of those troops who had been loyal to him since 1844 and who were working on ranches and in forest areas of the east and south awaiting his return. Santana's own military force, comprised of a docile and servile peonage familiar with war, weakened Bidó's command. In contrast, the Cibao troops, far from their homes, felt strongly the need to return to their land to reinitiate the planting of tobacco for the next year. Thus, in a short time Santana supplanted Franco Bidó and by September 18 he was the master of the situation.

The war raged for almost one year as both sides fought with great tenacity. During this period both governments in Santiago and Santo Domingo continued issuing large amounts of paper money to finance their expenditures, and these new printings totally bankrupted the state and ruined the country. Báez printed 59.7 million pesos in one year alone, while the Cibao government had issued approximately 20 million pesos. In consequence, the value of the national peso depreciated and fluctuated between 3,125 and 4,750 per dollar.

Despite this tremendous economic crisis, the Cibao government worked to give the country a democratic constitution that would replace the autocratic one of December 1854. On September 25, the country was summoned to elect deputies, with the election date set for December 7. The constitutional assembly was soon filled with the most illustrious intellectuals of the country whose thoughts were fully in line with the liberal ideas that had inspired the revolution. As soon as they began their work, it became clear that these men were bent on establishing the first Dominican democratic and representative government since independence.

The new Constitution, written in Moca, was proclaimed on February 19, 1858. According to it, the death penalty for political crimes was abolished. Dominicans were guaranteed their civil liberties without restrictions, especially the rights of free speech, free travel, and public meetings. The government was to be civilian, republican, popular, representative, elective, and responsible. Every citizen with the right to vote would do so secretly and directly instead of indirectly as established in the previous constitutions.

According to the new constitution, the president could not hold office for two successive terms, and the provincial governors could no longer be military commanders. Municipal power was fully restored. The armed forces were declared essentially obedient to the civil power, without authority to deliberate and with the duty to defend the sovereignty of the nation and public order, and to observe and comply with the laws and the Constitution. The Constitution also declared that the capital of the Republic should be established in Santiago de los Caballeros, while a transitory law ordered that the new government should be elected by the representatives to the Constitutional Assembly.

Thus, on March 1, 1858, General José Desiderio Valverde and Benigno Filomeno de Rojas were again chosen to govern the country. But things did not go as expected. The new Constitution totally displeased General Santana and his partisans who were perfectly content with the Constitution of 1854. They did not believe that it was proper to reorganize the state in the midst of a bloody civil war. Moreover, according to their beliefs, the state had already been properly constituted in 1844.

Santana considered the Constitution of Moca completely divorced from the true situation of the country, its society, customs, religion, and economy. Santana's displeasure was of vital importance. His troops were just waiting outside the capital for the moment when Báez would abandon the city so that they could again seize power. Meanwhile, the Santanistas were speaking of reestablishing their former government in Santo Domingo.

The Baecistas, protected behind the walls of the city, still had to be subdued. Their resistance gradually weakened by desertions and the demoralization of the remaining troops who barely numbered 400 when the foreign consuls began to mediate an armistice that would assure the departure of Báez and his followers from the country, guaranteeing their lives and properties. These negotiations began the first day of June, and by June 12 conditions had already been set for a surrender that was accepted reluctantly nine days later by the government in Santiago. Under the terms of the agreement Báez was allowed to take all the money, gold, and tobacco he had stolen from the people of the Cibao, plus the state's brigantines and schooners used to transport him and his followers to exile.

As soon as Santana and his troops entered Santo Domingo after Báez's departure, his party mobilized to abort all the efforts of the Cibao liberals to control the government. For the Santanistas, this was the proper moment to return to power. Thus, on July 27, 1858, the most prominent of Santana's representatives and some Baecistas who had reconciled with Santana at the last minute published a manifesto in Santo Domingo. Acting as "organs of the will of the people," they visited Santana and demanded on behalf of the southern provinces the restoration of the old political order based on the Constitution of December, 1854.

In the following days a series of similar manifestos appeared in each of the towns of the Republic requesting Santana not to recognize the Cibao government nor the Moca Constitution. In those manifestos Santana was asked to take charge of restoring the rule of the Constitution and laws and to comply with "the sovereign will of the people." Before these manifestos were even published, Santana issued a proclamation accepting the new mandate which "the city of Santo Domingo has presented to me through a large and respectable commission."

The people of the Cibao did not immediately accept the treason of the man whom they had politically rehabilitated. They prepared to resist the march that Santana was organizing with his army to restore the old order in the Cibao provinces. Although President José Desiderio Valverde himself marched with his troops toward the capital, the Cibaeños soon realized that the only truly effective army with full combat capacity was that which General Santana had organized in the revolutionary camps with his former troops who had been blindly following and obeying him since 1844. Santana's march to the Cibao with these troops was reason enough for many of the generals who had previously supported the revolution to now abandon President Valverde and the civilian leaders of the Cibao Revolution.

During August and the first three weeks of September 1858, the experiment in democratic government completely collapsed in the Cibao, while Santana and his troops visited the various towns where they installed military commanders to help in the consolidation of the new dictatorship. On September 23, Santana was again in Santo Domingo with his followers, and on the 27th he dictated two decrees reestablishing the Constitution of 1854 and all the laws and provisions promulgated during his previous government.

10.
Annexation to Spain and republican restoration (1859-1865)

FINANCIAL AND POLITICAL CRISIS

The Revolution of July left the country in ruins. A severe economic crisis occurred in the following two years. The profits of one full year of agricultural activity in the Cibao, the richest region of the country, had been stolen by Báez and his protégés, and another year of labor had been lost because of the civil war. The paper money in circulation was completely worthless, and the government had to abstain from printing new bills in order not to worsen the situation.

In May 1859, the government fixed the exchange rate at 2,000 pesos to the dollar, but the foreign merchants and others who held the paper money refused to accept it. The foreign merchants asked their consuls to obtain a more beneficial exchange rate, but the government refused and argued that the rate set was the market value and that the market should rule the rate. As negotiations proved fruitless, the consuls left the country and in November returned accompanied by the warships of France, England, and Spain that threatened to bombard the city if the government did not accept their demands for an exchange rate of 500 pesos to one dollar. This threat forced the government to decree a new exchange rate favoring all those who held paper money, the most important of which were the foreign merchants.

While these monetary problems were bearing down on Santana's government, another problem also threatened the security of the country. As soon as the war ended, Maxime Raybaud, the former French consul in Port-au-Prince, arrived in Santo Domingo as a special envoy of Emperor Soulouque to propose an understanding between Santana and the Haitian government. Raybaud made it clear that if the Dominicans did not accept a new confederation with Haiti, either the United States would attempt to annex the Dominican Republic or Haiti would take over the country by force. The terms of this proposal were so offensive to Santana and his ministers that they forced Raybaud to leave the country without receiving a response.

Once Raybaud departed, the worry remained that Soulouque was planning a new invasion, and the country did not have the resources to undertake a new military campaign. This worry was not unfounded since Soulouque was indeed trying to mobilize his army for a new invasion. However, the Haitian officers, aware that many of their counterparts had been executed after the failed campaigns against the Dominicans in the past, promptly organized a conspiracy at the end of December 1859, under the leadership of General Geffrard. After a brief military campaign, Soulouque was overthrown and forced into exile at the beginning of January 1860.

One of Geffrard's first acts after taking power was to inform the Dominican government that he was not planning any new invasion of the Dominican territory. Skeptical of Haitian promises, Santana continued his preparations for a new war. He ordered new printings of paper money to cover the expenses for mobilizing the army using the pretext of withdrawing old bills. The first of these new printings of 10 million pesos was ordered in January 1860, and produced an immediate disaster since the new bills were refused by the public. Although the government was forced to withdraw these bills immediately, they were successfully put back in circulation a few weeks later.

In March, the Senate secretly authorized the issue of another 10 million pesos which was followed by another printing of yet another 10 million in August, and 8 million more in December. Thus, within a few months the third government of Santana printed almost 40 million pesos in new bills inundating the money market. Although many of these bills were used to replace old ones that had deteriorated, they primarily served to aggravate the already catastrophic monetary problems.

In the 17 years since the founding of the Republic, its governments had made no less than 33 monetary printings amounting to some 148 million pesos. Although part of this sum had been collected and burned, there were still 83 million pesos in circulation at the end of December, 1860. On March 16, 1861, Santana and his ministers decided in favor of an exchange rate of 250 pesos for one dollar, but this measure failed to resolve the basic financial problem of the country.

The difficulties after the Revolution of 1857 were so overwhelming that Santana and his advisers decided to revive the old idea of seeking the aid of a foreign power. Raybaud's mission had greatly influenced this decision since Santana feared a new Haitian invasion would surprise the government, now without resources. Santana was also worried that the United States would take advantage of the government's weakness to overthrow his government as William Walker had just done in Nicaragua. At the same time, the problem of paper money was growing more serious every day, and Santana and his ministers were convinced that the only way to solve this crisis was with the aid of Spain.

ANNEXATION

Santana took advantage of the fact that General Felipe Alfau was vacationing in Europe, and appointed him as extraordinary envoy and plenipotenciary minister. Alfau was instructed to inform the Queen of Spain of the critical situation of the
Dominican Republic and to solicit the aid necessary to fortify
the various points and ports along the coast coveted by the
United States. Santana wanted to negotiate an agreement whereby Spain would establish a political and military protectorate
over Santo Domingo as a means of preserving Dominican independence against the Haitians.

Alfau was received by the Queen in the middle of April, 1859.
He spent the rest of the year contacting various Spanish officials with whom he negotiated and discussed the possibilities
and conditions for signing either a treaty, convention, protectorate, or alliance in which Spain would provide men, equipment, and loans to the Dominican Republic in exchange for a
mortgage on customs receipts and the reduction of import duties on Spanish ships entering the country.

These negotiations proceeded more rapidly than expected
since the Spanish government recognized the advantages of
establishing a protectorate over Dominican territory that would
strengthen Spain's strategic position in the Antilles. As Alfau
kept the Dominican government well informed of his activities,
Santana became more and more enthusiastic. At the beginning
of 1860 he began to believe that a protectorate was not sufficient to assure the country's stability and security, and asked
the Queen to consider incorporating Santo Domingo as a province like the islands of Cuba and Puerto Rico. On April 27, 1860
Santana wrote to the Queen that his government was interested in being annexed to Spain, from which the Dominicans
should never have separated.

This was a time of extreme difficulty for the Santana government. It is true that the Haitians had abandoned their former policy of invasions, but they were now cajoling the Dominicans living along the border to re-establish trade relations. Because the Haitian market was very attractive to many frontier inhabitants, it was easy for the Haitians to receive a favorable response. After several years of truce and with the expressed promise that there should be no new invasions, many Dominicans lost their former fear and within a few months the frontier trade grew to an unusual intensity. According to the Dominicans, Geffrard wished to use this trade to "Haitianize" the frontier economy in order to increase Haitian penetration and domination in these areas in a peaceful and gradual manner. In May, 1860, the minister of finance and commerce reported that this frontier trade had acquired colossal proportions and that the people of Azua were alarmed at the rate at which the frontier inhabitants were becoming Haitianized.

Santana was also preoccupied by the conspiratory activity of the Baecistas who, since the previous year, had been trying to organize rebellions in the south. Although these plots had been discovered and severely repressed by the government, Báez continued to incite other conspiracies from Curaçao and Saint Thomas. Some of his followers also maintained contact with the Haitians, whom they urged to invade the Republic in order to oust Santana. One of the main participants in the frontier trade with Haiti was Báez's cousin, General Valentín Ramírez Báez, who was very influential in the border areas. This alliance between the Baecistas and the Haitians greatly worried the government.

What most disturbed the government, however, was an incident that occurred between April and October 1860, on the small rocky islet of Alta Vela, off the southwestern coast. A group of North American adventurers landed on the island, planted the U.S. flag, and declared the island a territory of the United States in order to exploit its guano deposits. As peaceful diplo-

were not enough, the Dominican government
warships to take the Americans and their labor-
and bring them back to Santo Domingo. The
lent caused by these adventurers was very serious. Although the Dominican government received U.S. recognition of its sovereignty over the islet, it also discovered that
Samaná was not the only national territory coveted by the U.S.
adventurers.

These threats, plus the overwhelming financial crisis, led
Santana to change the course of the negotiations with Spain
and to insist on a treaty or agreement that would reincorporate
or annex the country to Spain. This course was much more
agreeable to the Spanish officials negotiating with Alfau since,
in their judgment, the annexation offered more advantages than
a protectorate.

Throughout the rest of 1860, the bases for annexation were
established, and by the beginning of November Alfau and the
Spanish diplomats had agreed that if annexation were chosen
Spain would promise to: 1) never reestablish slavery in Dominican territory, 2) consider Dominican territory as a Spanish province, thus permitting it to enjoy the same rights as other provinces, 3) employ the services of the greatest possible number of
Dominican civil and military officials in the new government,
4) amortize all paper money then in circulation in the Dominican Republic, and 5) recognize as good and valid all the acts
passed by the Dominican government since 1844.

At times it appeared that the negotiations would fail. In December 1860, the Prime Minister of Spain, Leopoldo O'Donnell, declared that his government wished to postpone the reincorporation, which had already been agreed on, until the outbreak of the U.S. Civil War. But this last-minute hesitation was
soon overtaken by the enthusiasm of the colonial government
of Cuba and many Spanish officials in Madrid who saw the
annexation as a new step leading to the recovery of Spain's pres-

tige and power in Latin America. Negotiations thus continued at the instance of the captain general of Cuba, General Francisco Serrano, who received orders from the Spanish government to conclude them and begin the annexation process making it appear as a spontaneous act of the entire Dominican population.

Spain did not wish to create suspicions among the other powers that the act was inspired by motives of conquest. Accustomed to rule by giving orders rather than by seeking a consensus, Santana acted surreptitiously. On receiving the favorable sign from Serrano, Santana secretly informed each local military commander who shared his confidence, so that if the annexation was signed they would be prepared to back it and force the inhabitants of their respective areas to also support it. Thus, between December 1860 and March 1861, most of the government's activities were directed toward ensuring the success of the political change that was being prepared without the knowledge of the majority of the Dominican population.

Some suspected what the government was plotting. Former Trinitario leader, General Ramón Mella, declared his opposition to the annexation policy, but was arrested in January 1861, and later expelled from the country. As rumors increased over time, the Baecistas in Curaçao began to denounce the annexation proposals. Another former Trinitario leader, General Francisco del Rosario Sánchez, in close association with the Baecistas, began to organize an invasion through Haitian territory despite the fact that he was then gravely ill. Nothing, however, could stop the government, which since January had been receiving military assistance from Cuba and Puerto Rico and had been inviting immigrants from Canary Islands in Venezuela to settle in Dominican territory.

When everything was ready on March 4, 1861, Santana sent a circular ordering all the military commanders in his confidence to inform the authorities and notable persons of the country about the negotiations and the conditions under which the annexation was to take place. This done, the government immediately sent one of its ministers to the towns of the interior to collect manifestos prepared by the government with signatures supporting the annexation obtained by the local military commanders.

On March 16, Santana dictated a decree setting a new exchange rate for paper money at 250 national pesos to one dollar. This rate was much more favorable than the old rate of 500 to one. This decision threw new light on Santana's policy of the past few months of printing enormous quantities of paper money. Many of his partisans would reap great benefits once Spain began to amortize it. Santana also distributed as payoffs among his principal followers the properties that the Haitians had abandoned and that now belonged to the state. At the same time, he lavished military promotions on those officers who supported annexation, assuring them that the Spanish government would respect their new rank.

As soon as the annexation was solemnly proclaimed in the Cathedral Plaza on March 18, 1861, the manifestos forged at the insistence of the government began to be published, thus giving the impression that the whole country supported the reincorporation to Spain and that all Dominicans wished to renounce their sovereignty. But soon the voices of opposition surfaced. On May 2, General José Contreras and a group of his followers, the majority mulattos of Baecista political affiliation, rose up in arms protesting against the political change and charged that the Spaniards had returned to the country in order to restore slavery. This rebellion was soon quelled and its leaders were shot.

In June, Francisco del Rosario Sánchez finally invaded the country from Haiti, but he was trapped by an ambush set up by government forces. Wounded, he was taken prisoner and later shot along with many of his companions. The other leader of this invasion, General José María Cabral, managed to save his life by fleeing to Haiti. Meanwhile, Father Fernando Arturo de Meriño, the catholic vicar, also attempted to organize a rebellion against annexation. This attempt also failed, and when his plot was discovered, the priest was imprisoned and later expelled from the country.

Santana was appointed captain general of the province of Santo Domingo in May 1861. Assisted by a large group of civil and military Spanish officials, he then reorganized the government using the money, arms, and provisions sent by Spain. This abundance of resources limited Santana's power because his authority now depended on that of the captain general of Cuba, Francisco Serrano, and was supervised by Serrano's representative, Brigadier Antonio Peláez de Campomanes, the second in command in the province. As he had to consult Peláez de Campomanes before making any decision, it soon became clear to Santana that he could no longer exercise absolute power and that he was now part of a colonial administrative system in which his government was but one part of a network of Spanish interests in the Antilles. Thus, as the Spanish officials and military personnel began arriving to fill their posts in the new province, Santana discovered that power was slipping through his hands.

Many of Santana's partisans, both civil and military, were gradually removed from their former positions and replaced by Spanish officials coming from Cuba and Puerto Rico. Their removal caused serious conflicts between Santana and the high-ranking Spanish officials in 1861, particularly when they tried to replace the military personnel who had been loyal to the former president since independence. The Junta Clasificadora, a commission established on August 6, 1861 for the purpose of studying military service records, simply found many of Santana's old companions-in-arms unacceptable for membership in the Spanish army.

By the end of the year, Santana knew that his power had disintegrated and that he was nothing more than another official subject to the same rules and regulations as the other Spanish officials. Because his authoritarian personality could not adjust to this situation, on January 6, 1862 Santana presented his resignation as captain general of the province, citing reasons of poor health.

The Spanish government accepted Santana's resignation without hesitation. For several months, officials of the Spanish government in Santo Domingo had suggested that Santana be relieved of his post because he had become an obstacle in the path of the Spanish administration. Santana remained in office until July 19, 1862, when his replacement, General Felipe Ribero, arrived. Although the Spanish government distinguished him with the title of Marqués de las Carreras and gave him a generous retirement pension, Santana was very depressed in the following months as he realized that his plans to remain in power with the help of the Spanish government had failed.

While Santana and his cohorts did not find the annexation as rewarding as expected, the Spaniards were also finding a few surprises. As soon as they began arriving in Santo Domingo, they discovered that the people they had come to govern were not as Hispanic as they had been led to believe. The majority of the population were mulattos, and their customs varied enormously from Spanish tradition because of the centuries of isolation during the colonial period, and particularly after 22 years of Haitian domination and 17 years of national independence. Soon the differences between the Spaniards and the Dominican population became clear.

Some of these differences proved serious from the very beginning of the annexation, especially those pertaining to the race and color of the Dominicans. This was a constant topic of conversation among everyone because the Spaniards continually offended the Dominicans who were reminded that in Cuba or Puerto Rico they would be slaves. This attitude of superiority had its effects on the Dominicans themselves. The lighter-skinned people began to avoid contact with their darker skinned friends for fear of being associated with them or of being considered inferior by the new, Spanish rulers. Incidents of this type were frequent and produced grave social conflicts, especially in Santiago where most of the inhabitants were light-skinned but of mixed racial background.

Another matter which rankled the Dominicans from the beginning was the policy of the Junta Clasificadora. After studying the merits of the former officers of the Dominican army, many were left completely outside the Spanish militias and others were placed in the reserves and often waited to receive their salaries for months at a time. This caused great anger and created serious political problems for the government in Moca and Santiago at the end of 1862. Moreover, the prohibition against using Spanish uniforms for officers and chiefs of the reserves deeply wounded the pride of these men and aroused hatred toward the peninsular soldiers.

The Spanish government also adversely affected the economic interests of the Dominican population, particularly the merchant class, when, in April 1862 it refused to unconditionally redeem the paper money as Santana had anticipated. The officials in charge of collecting the paper money refused to accept any bills deteriorated by use. Because the paper used to print the money had been of very poor quality, almost everyone held dilapidated bills. Thus, the majority of the population who had already been greatly harmed by the numerous monetary printings now discovered that the paper money that they believed was going to be redeemed at a better exchange rate was not accepted at face value by the Spanish authorities. The residents of Santiago sent a commission to the government in Santo Domingo to request a better deal for those who held paper money. This commission finally managed to have the paper money accepted on better terms, but the resulting compromise did not remove the distrust created by the incident.

Moreover, the so-called system of *bagajes* put in practice by the Spanish army also alienated the rural population, especially in the Cibao. This system consisted in requisitioning without any guarantee of return, all the beasts of burden needed by the Spanish troops to undertake their military mission. In an area such as the Cibao where the tobacco economy depended on the availability of animals to transport the tobacco from the countryside to the cities and from the cities to the Puerto Plata harbor, the loss of these animals could mean ruin for many farmers. As a regular occurrence, the *bagaje* began to pose an economic threat to the whole peasant population. According to a Madrid newspaper, the system of *bagajes* was so offensive that "the cargoes which the *campesinos* bring on their horses are thrown into the middle of the streets signifying that the urgency of the Royal Service is so great that there is no time for anything else...."

The arrival of a new archbishop, Bienvenido de Monzón, to head the Dominican church also had negative psychological effects on the population. As soon as he arrived, he resolved to modify the customs of the Dominicans, which he believed to be in a deplorable state owing to the infrequency of ecclesiastical marriages in the country. The reason for the limited number of religious marriages had its roots in the colonial life of the 17th and 18th centuries when poverty and the lack of roads prevented inhabitants from using the services of the extremely small number of clergy who remained in the country.

The majority of the population, including the priests, thus came to accept concubinage as natural. Monzón, however, considered this an immoral situation that needed to be corrected and wanted the Dominicans to marry within the Church and within a prescribed period of time. This irritated the majority of Dominicans whose marriages, while not canonically legal, were socially valid and accepted. Moreover, in a country where the majority of people were born outside of legal matrimony, Monzón's ruling seemed totally unfair.

Beside this attempt to force couples to formalize their unions, the archbishop also tried to reform the morals of the Dominican clergy, which he likewise found in a deplorable state. Many priests had children or were masons. Also, while many received generous fees for ecclesiastical services in their parishes, their contributions to the Church were minimal. Monzón attempted to force the clergy to retain only 50 pesos per month as a fixed salary and to surrender the rest of their income to the archbishopric. The clergy refused, and they too came to dislike the new colonial government imposed by the annexation.

Just as the clergy was displeased with these impositions, the elite of the various towns and cities was angered when the archbishop attacked the masonry in his pastoral letters and ordered the masonic lodges closed. Dominicans found such demands both unacceptable and senseless since freemasonry in the Dominican Republic had none of the anti-monarchical or anticlerical characteristics that it had in Spain, Italy, and some other Latin American countries. Instead, Dominican freemasonry limited its activities to works of social assistance and to the education of its members. Moreover, many Dominican priests were masons and were not willing to obey the archbishop in the persecution of their lodges.

These and subsequent measures created a general state of ill will toward the annexation among merchants, landowners, military, and *campesinos*. The malaise was further increased when the government tried to impose limitations on foreign trade to benefit Spanish interests. Duties on non-Spanish merchandise and ships were fixed at much higher rates than those paid by Spanish merchants and ships. In addition, the government attempted to establish a monopoly on tobacco in favor of

Spanish interests, thus harming the interests of the tobacco export merchants. By November and December 1862, political resentment was becoming overt, and some Spanish officials began to fear the outbreak of a rebellion in a short time.

THE RESTORATION WAR

The first rebellion broke out in early February 1863, in the southwestern town of Neiba. There a group of some 50 men attempted to assault the house of the local military commander. Although this isolated revolt was quelled almost immediately by government forces, a much larger conspiracy that had been in the planning for several months was being directed from the northwestern town of Sabaneta by General Santiago Rodríguez. This new rebellion, which would include the entire population of the Cibao region, was set to explode on February 27, the anniversary of the founding of the Dominican Republic.

Despite Rodríguez's secrecy and caution, the plan was discovered on February 21, and led to the mobilization of the Spanish forces under the military commander of Santiago. While this officer was marching toward the northwest, the conspirators in Santiago rebelled against the Spanish government on February 24, 1863 forcing the officer to return. He quelled this rebellion with little effort and then once again marched to the northwest to combat the other rebels who fled toward Haiti. In the following months, Rodríguez's followers spread out through the countryside and organized guerrilla units to keep the spirit of rebellion alive, while Rodríguez sought arms, munitions, provisions, and money in Haiti.

The Spanish government declared a state of siege and kept its troops on alert, sending reinforcements under the command of General Pedro Santana to Santiago to strengthen the local garrison. After subduing the local rebellion, the government issued a general pardon on March 16 to appease the population. Nevertheless, the ringleaders of the movement in Santiago were kept in prison and then executed on April 17. Although many *campesinos* accepted the pardon and returned to their homes, the leaders of Rodríguez's group continued operating in the countryside near Dajabón, under the protection of the Haitian government.

Haitian President Fabré Geffrard was more than willing to help the Dominican rebels. The annexation had placed Haiti in a highly uncomfortable position by having as a neighbor a slave power such as Spain whose colonies in the Antilles created a hostile environment for Haitian independence. Moreover, the annexation endangered the Haitian territories snatched from Spain by Toussaint L'Ouverture in 1794, for now, by virtue of a royal order of January 14, 1862, the Spaniards intended to regain those territories.

In pursuit of the Dominican rebels, the Spanish troops decided to carry out this royal order and evicted all the Haitians living in the the border areas of Dajabón and Capotillo. Since this royal order also covered the towns and outlying areas of Hincha, Las Caobas, San Rafael, and San Miguel de la Atalaya, Geffrard also expected a Spanish invasion of this territory that had been controlled by the Haitians for almost 70 years. This threat against Haitian security led Geffrard to help the Dominican rebels as much as possible.

With this aid, on August 16, 1863 a group of 14 Dominicans led by Santiago Rodríguez crossed the border back into Dominican territory and raised the Dominican flag, signaling the beginning of a new war for independence and the restoration of the Republic. In the following days, the inhabitants of the Northwest joined the movement, while Spanish troops sent from Santiago were greeted in the first battles of the war. The revolutionary push soon forced the Spaniards to retreat. One town after another in the Cibao proclaimed their adhesion to the revolutionary movement. La Vega, Moca, Puerto Plata, San Francisco de Macorís, and Cotuí gave their support to the revolutionaries and prepared their men for a coordinated attack on Santiago, the capital of the Cibao, which had been partially occupied by the rebels on September 1.

On September 6, 1863, the attack began on Fort San Luis where the Spaniards had taken refuge. The Dominicans now had some 6,000 men from the whole Cibao area, while the Spaniards had 800 well-armed soldiers sheltered behind the walls of the fort. The following battle was extremely violent, and, as a consequence, the city of Santiago was almost completely destroyed by a gigantic fire. Although reinforcements arrived from Puerto Plata, the besieged troops could not break the encirclement. After several days of combat and negotiation, an armistice was drawn up whereby the Spaniards were allowed to leave the city on September 13.

The next day the revolutionaries met in a house near Fort San Luis, which had been spared from the fire, and decided to constitute a provisional government to restore the Republic. General José Antonio Salcedo, who had distinguished himself as chief of operations in the recent fights, was elected president, with Benigno Filomeno de Rojas chosen as vice-president. The ministers for the new government included many of the foremost leaders of the Revolution of July, 1857. As soon as the government was formed, its members wrote an Act of Independence that explained their motives for taking up arms and denounced Santana's treason in annexing the Republic to Spain. This act circulated throughout the Cibao where it was signed by some 10,000 people, more than double the number who had signed the manifestos in favor of annexation fabricated by Santana.

The establishment of the provisional government was followed by almost two years of war, which cost Spain more than 10,000 casualties and some 33 million Spanish pesos, while the Dominicans suffered the loss of hundreds of men and the complete ruin of their economy. With the exception of such well-fortified coastal cities as Santo Domingo, Puerto Plata and Samaná, which remained under Spanish control, the whole country rose up in rebellion against annexation. Other towns like Azua, El Seibo, Hato Mayor and Higüey, were precariously retained by the Spaniards as they were regularly attacked by the revolutionaries who dominated the countryside.

What began as a peasant revolt soon became a racial war, since the black and mulatto Dominicans who constituted the majority of the population feared being enslaved again by the Spaniards. The Restoration War became a truly popular war as it directed all the energies of the nation toward achieving independence and restoring sovereignty.

With few material resources available, and taking into account the geography of the country, the Dominicans could only fight the Spaniards in one possible manner: guerrilla warfare. From the beginning, each rural community and each region of the country organized its own forces and named its own leaders to coordinate operations with the revolutionary government. In many cases, these leaders acted on their own, attacking when possible and retreating when necessary.

At times they were united under the command of the main leaders, who were charged by the revolutionary government to undertake special missions with large contingents that stayed together until the mission was completed. Afterward, they returned to their own areas and continued their operations in small groups that raided and pursued the Spanish troops and temporarily disbanded when the Spaniards pursued them with superior forces. The war was a nightmare for the Spanish troops who could never find a compact and visible enemy to confront except at certain strategic points such as the pass into the Cibao called El Sillón de la Viuda, where, from the beginning, the provisional government dispatched permanent forces to block the path of enemy troops.

The Spaniards were never successful in their plans to penetrate the Cibao since the Dominican guerrillas held all the mountain passes, and the Spanish troops could not cross without suffering numerous casualties and dangerously stretching their supply lines. Furthermore, as soon as the war started, the Spanish soldiers became ill and died in huge numbers. Dysentery, vomiting, and malaria produced by contaminated water and mosquitoes cost the Spaniards around 1,500 soldiers monthly. These soldiers, once ill, were sent to hospitals in Puerto Rico and Cuba so as not to die in Santo Domingo. Although there were some 107 battles during the war, the majority of Spanish casualties were caused by illness. Toward the end of the conflict, the captain generals of Cuba and Puerto Rico were almost without replacements for their men lost in Santo Domingo.

Confronted with these calamities, the Spanish governors could do nothing. The first to realize the impossibility of winning the war was Santana's replacement, General Felipe Ribero, who, from the beginning, tried to make the Spanish government see the futility of the struggle. His replacement, General Carlos de Vargas, who took over on October 23, 1863, planned to bring in massive reinforcements to concentrate in the north, take Montecristi, and from there continue on to Santiago. The plan could not be completed because when the Spaniards took Montecristi on May 15, 1864, they discovered that the advance to Santiago would be impossible. Enormous resources were needed to lead an army of 6,000 soldiers through a semidesert region full of cacti where the scarce water supplies would not sustain the several thousand mules necessary to carry the provisions, artillery, munitions, food, clothing, medical supplies, and other equipment for the large army.

A study of the costs of the operation and of the foreseeable Spanish casualties, that were calculated at ten percent per month, caused the minister of war in Madrid to give orders suspending the operation and to concentrate all troops in the cities and coastal points until the Queen's government decided whether it should continue the war. Opposition to the occupation of Santo Domingo was then strong in Spain and had already produced several political crises leading to the downfall of Prime Minister Leopoldo O'Donnell. His replacement, General Manuel Narváez, wished to submit the matter for the consideration and decision of the Cortes.

The impossibility of a Spanish military victory was demonstrated by the fact that General Pedro Santana had still not been able to enter the Cibao through El Sillón de la Viuda, where the revolutionary forces put up steady resistance because they knew that if Santana reentered the Cibao the consequences would be fatal for everybody involved. Santana had been reintegrated into active military service shortly after the war erupted and sought to break through the passage to the Cibao region. Despite all his efforts, Santana could do nothing because in his camp at Guanuma near Monte Plata the Spanish troops under his command were sick and dying en masse. Each day his forces were weakening. Nevertheless, he attempted to fight and break the resistance.

At the beginning of March 1864 Santana received orders from General Vargas to concentrate his forces near Santo Domingo in compliance with instructions from Madrid. He refused to obey orders and was severely admonished by his Spanish superiors. This rebuke depressed Santana, already suffering the effects of age, poor health, and the unpopularity of the annexation. In these circumstances, General José de la Gándara replaced General Vargas as governor of Santo Domingo and relieved Santana of his command two months later.

Santana's troops were then placed under Spanish military commanders instead of the Dominicans officers whom Santana believed would succeed him. This led Santana to confront La Gándara in open disobedience, and forced the governor to order him to leave for Cuba to give an account of his actions before a military court. However, Santana did not have to face this disgrace. On June 14, 1864 he died suddenly in his home in Santo Domingo amid rumors that he had committed suicide. He was quickly buried the following day in the courtyard of the Ozama Fortress because his family and friends feared that his body would be desecrated.

Meanwhile, General La Gándara, who had to accept the orders from Madrid to retreat to the coast, planned to win the war by diplomatic means. In September 1864, he let the revolutionary government know of his intention to negotiate peace, or at least an exchange of prisoners. President Salcedo responded that he was willing to talk and sent a commission to Montecristi to discuss peace terms. These first negotiations amounted to nothing and were suspended as neither side could reach an agreement due to the fact that their respective representatives only wished to negotiate on the basis of the other side's surrender. When Salcedo was planning to send a new commission to interview La Gándara, he was overthrown by General Gaspar Polanco and various other disaffected military leaders on October 10, 1864, accused of betraying the revolutionary cause by means of these talks.

The real reason for Salcedo's overthrow was the fear among the revolutionary leaders that he would resign and recall Buenaventura Báez, a traditional enemy of Cibao interests, because in a speech a few days earlier, Salcedo, tired of the disobedience of his subordinates, had threatened to resign and spoke in favor of Báez for president. To mention Báez's name among the very men who had led the Revolution of July, 1857, was almost an anathema of which Salcedo had not foreseen the consequences. The gravity of his declaration was even greater in view of the fact that Báez had supported the annexation from exile and had obtained his own nomination as Field Marshall of the Spanish Army. The hatred that the Cibao elite had for Báez was only comparable to the hatred that Santana had awakened as the war gained intensity.

Polanco only remained in power for three months. He was an illiterate man of arms who ruled tyrannically from the beginning. He had former President Salcedo assassinated, and those whom he believed to be his enemies were cruelly harassed. Despite all advice to the contrary, in December, 1864, he made a suicidal attack on the Spaniards in Montecristi. This venture ended in total failure. What most irritated the residents of the Cibao was Polanco's attempt to establish a monopoly on tobacco in favor of several of his friends. At the beginning of January 1865, the other revolutionary generals overthrew Polanco who was accused not only of tyranny but also of Salcedo's murder. Along with the civil leaders of the Restoration movement these generals then organized a provisional junta with Benigno Filomeno de Rojas as president and General Gregorio Luperón as vice-president.

This provisional junta immediately issued several decrees lowering the war taxes that the government had been collecting from the tobacco producers. They also declared that the 1858 Constitution of Moca would be in force until a national convention could meet on February 27, to write a new constitution adjusted to the existing circumstances and to elect a constitutional president of the Republic. The work of this convention was relatively easy because the writers were men convinced of the validity of the liberal ideals contained in the Constitution of Moca. Thus the new constitution was simply a new version of the older document. As soon as the work of the convention was completed the new constitution was proclaimed and General Pedro Antonio Pimentel was elected president. Pimentel immediately named a council of war to investigate the death of Salcedo.

While the convention was meeting, the Cortes in Spain were also in session. After long and heated debate, the Cortes finally decided to abandon Santo Domingo since the war had become a project supported by the entire Dominican population and continuing it would give the appearance of a war of conquest over a territory Spain did not really want. On March 3, 1865 the Queen signed a decree annulling the annexation. Although La Gándara tried to obtain some advantages from the negotiations relative to the departure of his troops, the Dominican government was firm in defending its rights and refused to agree to anything except the departure of the Spanish troops, the return of prisoners, and security for the sick and wounded. On July 10, 1865, the Spanish soldiers started embarking for Cuba, Puerto Rico, and Spain, and within 15 days not a single Spanish soldier on military duty remained on the island. The War of the Restoration had ended.

11.
Caudillo politics and political instability (1865-1879)

POST-RESTORATION POLITICS

The Restoration War left the country devastated. The cities of Santiago, Montecristi, and Puerto Plata were almost destroyed. The majority of the *campesinos* were up in arms. The economy was totally ruined as the men seldom attended their fields, and the few crops that were cultivated went to feed the guerrilla fighters. Only tobacco continued to be exported, but the export revenues received by the government were rapidly spent for military equipment and other war-time necessities.

To keep the economy functioning, the government of Santiago had to resort to new printings of paper money, thus diminishing the value of the Dominican peso continually. In order to have sound money to pay for the importation of arms and other merchandise, the government had to follow the tradition set by previous governments and borrow money from the merchants of Santiago and Puerto Plata.

The most serious problem was the tremendous political fragmentation produced by the war. As the struggle against the Spaniards had been carried out by guerrilla warfare, once the conflict ended the country remained dominated by several dozen military leaders with little or no education who soon began to squabble for power among themselves. Because the country still had no roads or highways linking the south with the Cibao, the two regions existed much as two different countries.

In each of the major cities and towns, rivalries existed among the local elite for personal, family, or social reasons. The internal disputes had been laid aside temporarily to fight the Spaniards, although they reappeared at such critical junctures as during the coups against Salcedo and Polanco, and later when President Pimentel ordered the persecution of all those he believed to be his enemies.

The Restoration War had been successful because the local and regional leaders had been able to form a temporary alliance against the Spaniards. As soon as the Spaniards left, the precarious nature of this alliance became clear. The guerrilla leaders of the south who had been operating largely on their own did not wish to recognize the government of Santiago and were opposed to the presidency of Pimentel. Dominican politics had always been based on personalism and *caudillismo* because the population was primarily rural and illiterate, and their loyalty was only possible through a system of personal connections. Under such a system there was little understanding of the liberal philosophical principles behind the Restoration War or the 1858 Constitution of Moca.

The liberal constitutions elaborated by the Cibao intellectuals were an expression of the existing socio-political structure of this region where the power of the many medium-sized landowners was always the result of alliances or arrangements with other proprietors of the area. In 1865, as in 1858, the leaders of the south did not want to accept either the political leadership of the Cibao or the direction taken by the Santiago government. The southern leaders had always opted for a constitution that would permit the free exercise of power by a small oligarchy of large landowners or their representatives.

When President Pimentel decided to move his government to Santo Domingo in August 1865, he learned in Cotuí that the southern Baecista generals José María Cabral and Eusebio Manzueta had denounced his government and had declared Cabral as supreme chief with the title of "Protector" of the Republic so that he could install a new government that would give the country a new constitution.

As Valverde before him in 1858, Pimentel was thus forced to return to Santiago where he learned that many of the military leaders of the Cibao were also against him because of his ruthlessness in persecuting his enemies. Finding himself without support, he resigned. Meanwhile, the opposition of the local military leaders to Pimentel had brought many of them to support Cabral, who was then setting up his government in Santo Domingo under the terms of the Constitution of February 1854. Thus as in 1858, the southerners, united under a single leader, managed to impose their will over the Cibaeños by taking advantage of political divisions among the latter.

Cabral's government was nevertheless shortlived. Santana's death had left the southern oligarchy deprived of one of its two main leaders, and many of its members had now begun to look toward Báez as the natural candidate to fill the political vacuum left by Santana. Therefore, a few weeks after the installation of Cabral's government, a rebellion broke out in the east under General Pedro Guillermo, who sought to bring Báez back to the country and make him president again.

Cabral, who was himself a Baecista and lacked the willpower to put up much opposition, finally bowed to the pressures of his party. On November 15, 1865 he resigned and left executive power in the hands of General Guillermo until Báez could return from Curaçao. The constitution was modified to permit this political change. When Báez arrived, he immediately took over the presidency on December 8, 1865. As the latest constitutional modifications were not agreeable to him, Báez promptly had the National Congress reinstitute the Constitution of December 1854.

While Báez was taking up the presidency for the third time, the people of the Cibao, especially the tobacco merchants, were taking up arms to prevent the return of the man who had once swindled them and who had even supported Spain during the annexation. As the Baecista party was restructuring the government, the Cibaeños could see that the same men who had governed before with Báez were resuming their former positions.

Supported now by some old Santanistas, the Cibaeños grouped behind the Restoration leaders and formed a political alliance called the Partido Nacional Liberal, or Partido Azul, to distinguish it from the Baecista Party, or Partido Rojo. These names appeared during the Revolution of 1857, when the soldiers of both sides recognized each other by the use of blue or red bands in their hats. This practice continued in the revolutions which took place in the years after the Restoration.

The ensuing struggle between the Baecistas and the Azules was to last 14 years, until 1879. It was fought with amazing fury, since the two sides represented opposing interests and two totally different conceptions of the state. While Báez and his followers wanted to control the government in order to use the treasury to enrich themselves, the Azules sought to use the state to favor the development of industry, trade, and education through the implementation of the Constitution of Moca and the reforms of 1865. The Azules represented the interests of the tobacco cultivators and merchants of the Cibao region, while the Baecistas represented the great latifundia of the cattle ranchers and the woodcutting interests.

In the following years, the conflict between Baecistas and liberals, between the north and the south, between Rojos and Azules, engulfed the Dominican Republic in more than 50 uprisings and revolts resulting in some 21 changes in government. Each time the Azules came into power they reinstated the Constitution of Moca with some minor variations. Each time the Rojos took power they reestablished the Constitution of December 1854, which facilitated political control through a one-man dictatorship.

Báez originally enjoyed some advantages over the Azules. When the War of Restoration ended, he was the only nationally recognized political leader because of his previous two terms as president. The Azules did not have a single national leader, but many important regional leaders who shared the same liberal ideas but who could not coordinate their political activities rapidly due to their geographical dispersion and poor communication links within the country.

Báez's leadership rested on a network of personal loyalties which he, as the only caudillo of his party, had been able to develop over the years. The Azules depended upon the capacity of their leaders to reach agreements through informal democratic negotiations, a practice that was highly inconvenient when immediate decisions were needed and that gave Báez a clear operational advantage.

The social structure of the Cibao made the consolidation of leadership on one man extremely difficult. Nevertheless, political talent, ambition, and military courage gradually brought the leadership of General Gregorio Luperón to the forefront. As soon as Báez took power in October 1865, Luperón met with the other Restoration leaders and declared himself opposed to the government. Despite several failures, this revolt did not end until Báez was forced to resign on May 28, 1866.

The directors of this revolt constituted a military triumvirate, which on May 30 created a Junta Auxiliar over which they presided to handle government affairs. After overcoming the resistance of some Baecistas in the northwest, the triumvirate installed itself in Santo Domingo on August 10, 1866, dissolved the junta auxiliar, and decreed the convocation of a national convention to draw up a new constitution and duly elect a new president.

Meanwhile, the capital was a political boiling pot since each of the Restoration generals there was accompanied by a large staff, and their old rivalries were constantly disrupting public order. Of all these generals, the one with the most troops at his disposal was none other than General José María Cabral, a decided enemy of Pimentel. Cabral could not forgive Pimentel for his part in his removal from power the year before. He now counted on the support of the Capital's merchants whom his troops had protected after the departure of the Spaniards from the restoration forces, particularly from Pimentel's men. In the following weeks, Pimentel tried on various occasions to overthrow the government and take over the presidency to take vengeance on Cabral and the merchants, but he was stopped by the maneuvers of Luperón and Cabral.

Given this climate of enmity among the generals, the political situation and public order deteriorated each day and the Triumvirate steadily lost power due to the lack of troops to defend the government. Searching for a compromise, Luperón proposed that Cabral return to the presidency but with the stipulation that he would keep Báez out of the country. This suggestion was accepted, and in the following month artificial elections were held whereby Cabral again became president. After taking office on September 29, 1866, Cabral integrated several Azul leaders in his cabinet to guarantee political stability.

This compromise did not work. On the day following Cabral's inauguration the Baecistas rose up in arms on the grounds that Cabral had betrayed them by allying with the Azules. The Baecistas in Curaçao quickly organized an expedition that landed on October 24. Although this expedition was liquidated, the revolt continued both within the country and on the other side of the border. The Azules had been clearly able to separate Cabral from Báez. Now Cabral found it necessary to seek the backing of the Cibaeños to run the government.

In November 1866, Cabral made a trip to the Cibao in search of political support, but at the same time he began carrying on secret negotiations with the United States to sell or lease Samaná in exchange for military and financial aid that would allow him to resist political opposition and solve the urgent monetary problems inherited from the War of Restoration. These negotiations failed when various members of the government learned about them and stated their opposition.

The new Haitian president, Silvain Salnave, who had overthrown Fabré Geffrard at the beginning of 1867, accepted Cabral's overtures of friendship and in July, 1867 agreed to sign a peace treaty on the condition that Cabral promise not to cede or mortgage any part of Dominican territory to any foreign power. Nevertheless, the damage had already been done. The accusation that Cabral was planning to sell Samaná Bay to the United States barely two years after the war against annexation to Spain caused the president to lose what little popularity he had left.

By the end of 1867, when Cabral's envoy in Washington attempted to continue the negotiations, a Baecista rebellion was already at the point of victory with troops dangerously approaching the capital. During the first days of the new year, the Baecistas movement further weakened the government. Finally, on January 31, 1868 Cabral had to capitulate, allowing the rebel troops to enter the capital.

Cabral left the country while a new Baecista triumvirate was installed on February 15. This triumvirate unleashed a reign of terror and persecution against all the Azules politicians and generals who had supported Cabral. Meanwhile, the new government appointed a commission to go to Curaçao to seek out Buenaventura Báez, who was to be given the presidency. Báez returned on March 29 and formally took office on May 2, 1868, after holding fake elections designed to legalize the political change.

ANNEXATION TO THE UNITED STATES

The junta of generals that brought Báez once again to power in 1868, also convoked a national convention to write a new constitution that, as expected, ended up as being merely a copy of the Constitution of December 1854. The convention also recognized as a public debt the money that Báez had borrowed from the firm of Jesurum & Zoon in Curaçao to cover the expenses of the movement that had brought him to power.

Before closing, the convention conferred on Báez the title of "Great Citizen" in continuation of the tradition which had proclaimed Santana "Liberator" and Cabral "Protector" of the Republic. Leaving no doubt as to the course the new government would take, on June 18, 1868, Báez decreed that the authorities were to execute all armed opponents of the government. This decree was directed at the remaining generals of the Azul party who were preparing to fight against Báez.

The most noted generals to carry on the struggle against the government in the South were the Timoteo brothers, Andrés and Benito Ogando, while the Restoration governor, José Cabrera, organized the opposition in the Northwest. With these allies, Generals Luperón and Cabral could keep their revolutionary movement alive for quite some time in these zones, although it soon became apparent that Báez had superior political resources and that internal divisions within the Azul party would prevent any unified action that could bring the party to power.

Báez also counted on aid from Haitian president Salnave who, in alliance with the Dominican government, agreed to surrender Dominican rebels who crossed the border. This alliance was convenient for Salnave as he, too, was fighting a rebellion organized by Haitian General Nisage Saget. To protect themselves against this official alliance, Luperón and Cabral allied with Saget for mutual aid along the border. Opposition to Báez's government became stronger as Dominicans realized that Báez had overthrown Cabral so that he personally could direct negotiations over the sale or lease of Samaná in order to gain the greatest benefits for himself.

A few days after having been sworn in as president, Báez informed the U.S. government that he was willing to sell the bay and peninsula of Samaná for $1,000,000 in gold and $100,000 in arms and munitions. Báez also requested that the United States send him three battleships to keep him in power while the negotiations progressed because he had received news that Luperón and Cabral had allied with the Haitian rebels to overthrow Salnave in exchange for future aid against the Dominican government. By August the battle cry of Báez's enemies was opposition to the sale or lease of Samaná.

Báez's proposals to the U.S. government were being considered with great secrecy by Secretary of State William Seward who did not dare make any move at the time as his project to buy the Danish Antilles was then being seriously challenged in the U.S. Senate. Seward did not let Báez know that his government was interested in Samaná, but in December, 1868, the president of the United States himself declared his support for the acquisition of this part of Dominican territory.

Báez's urgency to win U.S. support was caused by a serious lack of funds which prevented his government from taking any decisive action against the rebels. As an immediate understanding with the United States was impossible, Báez decided to look elsewhere. First, he resorted to another printing of paper money which was devalued rapidly. Then, he sent his Curaçaoan associate Abraham Jesurum to the United States to seek a loan that would provide quick funds to pay his political and military expenses.

Jesurum was not able to obtain a loan in the United States and had to go to Europe. There an English financial adventurer named Edward Hartmont expressed his interest in lending

£420,000, or about $2,000,000, in exchange for a commission and an interest rate so high that only the very desperate would have accepted it.

Báez was desperate. The Hartmont loan was negotiated at the beginning of 1869 and furnished the funds so urgently needed, although it left the country completely mortgaged to a British financial firm. In his eagerness to obtain money at any cost, Báez agreed to recognize the debt of £420,000 at an annual interest rate of 6 percent for 25 years and a commission of £100,000 paid immediately to Hartmont. The customs receipts, coal mines, state lands and forests, and the guano deposits on Alta Vela island were all mortgaged.

In addition to the liens on the Dominican economy on which Báez agreed, the Government would end up paying £1,472,500, or some $7,000,000, when the loan matured. To make matters worse Báez did not even receive the entire £420,000 since Hartmont could only procure £38,000 as an advance. As the contract had already been signed by the Dominican government, Hartmont had to obtain the rest of the money so he then authorized a London bank to issue bonds based on the Dominican loan for the sum of £757,700, which was £337,700 more than the amount stipulated in the contract.

Báez was unconcerned by Hartmont's fraudulent action since the £38,000 were sufficient in the short run to buy arms and pay off his generals and political followers needed to resist the rebellion led by Cabral and Luperón. With this loan Báez was able to remain in power and take advantage of the fact that the new U.S. president, Ulysses S. Grant, was very interested in acquiring Samaná. With circumstances working in his favor, Báez began to change his ideas about selling Samaná into a plan to annex the whole country to the United States.

To prevent these new negotiations from succeeding, the Azules gave all the economic support they could to Luperón and lent him enough in hard currency so that he could buy a small warship of 500 tons to transport rebel troops along the coast. With the steamer Telégrafo Luperón spent almost one year harassing the northern ports and towns, particularly Puerto Plata, which was attacked on June 1, 1869, although it remained under government control. Both the Telégrafo and Luperón were declared pirates by the government and were closely pursued by the Dominican Navy and some U.S. warships giving aid to Báez. Unable to continue maritime operations, Luperón was forced to sell the Telégrafo, at the end of 1869.

Meanwhile negotiations for annexation to the United States continued with greater intensity. In the middle of July 1869, President Grant sent a confidential agent to Santo Domingo at Báez's request. After several weeks of conversations with the Dominican minister of foreign affairs, this agent returned to Washington with a rough draft of the project to annex the country in exchange for the immediate shipment of $100,000 in cash and $50,000 in arms to keep Báez in power. As Grant wished to complete the project as soon as possible, he sent another agent to sign the treaty as outlined in the rough draft.

This treaty was signed on November 29, 1869, but did not take effect immediately since it needed the approval of the U.S. Senate and the consent of the Dominican people. Báez prepared a plebiscite and through intimidation wrested some 16,000 votes from the Dominicans, the majority of whom were poor and illiterate. The Senate vote was not so easy because Grant had neither the power nor personal support to obtain rapid approval. When the treaty was presented for consideration, the senators voted to send an investigatory commission to the Dominican Republic to verify that the Dominicans wished to be annexed and to ascertain what advantages and disadvantages could be derived from this annexation.

Grant and Báez spent the entire year of 1870 discussing and plotting with various members of their respective governments until finally, at the beginning of 1871, the Senate investigatory commission left for Santo Domingo. After traveling throughout the country for several weeks and investigating those matters that interested them, the senators returned to Washington where they gave a favorable report because several of them had been bought off previously by Grant and his associates.

Despite the committee's approval, the U.S. Senate was divided over the project because of an internal campaign conducted by Dominican exiles and the opposition of several senators. One of the leading Senate opponents of the plan was Charles Sumner, chairman of the Foreign Relations Committe, who considered the Dominican annexation an immoral attempt by presidents Grant and Báez on behalf of some U.S. adventurers who for years had been after the land of the Samaná peninsula. After a long series of debates the Senate turned down the treaty in July 1871. This failure was a serious blow to Báez as his Haitian ally, President Salnave, had been overthrown in January 1870, and the new Haitian president, Nisage Saget, was giving the aid he promised to the Dominican rebels led by Cabral and Luperón operating along the border.

As the prospects for getting more money directly from the U.S. government disintegrated, Báez began negotiating with the very adventurers who had contrived the whole annexation plan in the first place. The chief adventurer, Joseph Fabens, was seeking to lease Samaná to a private U.S. company that had been formed for this purpose under the name of the Samaná Bay Company. The original idea of Fabens and his partner had been to lease the peninsula to promote colonization and to offer the bay to the U.S. government for the installation of a naval base.

Now the plan was to cede to this company all the privileges that the annexation treaty of 1869 would have granted to the U.S. government. Accordingly, the company was to have the power to name all the executive, legislative and judicial authorities in the territory of Samaná and was to be given for each mile of railway or canal constructed, a square mile of state lands bordering these routes "without any cost whatsoever." Such an agreement would leave Samaná in a completely anomalous juridicial state and the sovereignty of the Republic would be seriously affected.

With the jails full of political prisoners, hundreds of opponents dead and as many others exiled, and with the mass of the population frightened and passive, Báez had little opposition and quickly got the Senate to ratify the contract that Minister of Foreign Affairs Manuel María Gautier had signed with the Samaná Bay Company on December 28, 1872, to lease the peninsula and bay of Samaná for 99 years. In the plebiscite that Báez prepared on February 19, 1873 to approve the lease, there were only 19 votes against the measure.

Nevertheless, Báez's control started slipping throughout the course of 1873 since, as the government's economic position continued deteriorating, the leaders of his own party began to realize that the growing rebel movement would end with the overthrow of the president. Thus many of Báez's followers began withdrawing their support, especially as the new presidential elections, to be held at the end of the year, approached. Several of the more important Rojo leaders wished to succeed Báez, and several individuals, particularly Vice-President Manuel Altagracia Cáceres, began to be mentioned as candidates. But these same leaders soon became convinced that Báez would never be replaced through elections because a recent modification of the Constitution permitted the indefinite reelection of the president.

A new conspiracy then arose within the very heart of the Baecista party. Its leader was the governor of Puerto Plata, Ignacio María González, who, foreseeing the triumph of the Azul rebellion and not wishing to be forced into exile, suddenly declared himself against the government and began forming what came to be called Movimiento Unionista on November 25, 1873. This movement immediately gained the backing of all the Baecistas of Puerto Plata and soon spread throughout the country.

The Azul leaders who had played an important part in under-
mining the government now saw power slip through their fingers
since the majority of the population, including many prominent
civilian leaders of the Azul party, approved of González's movement as a means of ending Báez's regime once and for all. The
signers of the Revolutionary Manifesto of November 25, 1873
named González as "supreme chief" of a new provisional government and commander of the revolutionary army that was ordered
to march to Santo Domingo to remove Báez from office.

Faced with the overwhelming support that the whole country gave to González, Báez decided to negotiate his capitulation
through the mediation of the English, German, and Danish consuls on December 31, and on January 2, 1874, formally resigned
before the Senate. Since the victors had previously been his own
partisans, he was allowed to go abroad quietly to enjoy the fortune that he had amassed during his years in power.

Thus ended a corrupt government characterized by tyranny, assassinations, embezzlement of public funds, censorship,
political persecutions, and the lease of Samaná Bay to the United States. This period lasted six years during which Dominican
political life was degraded by the actions of their president who
became an opportunist, his only goal being to acquire his share
of money from the sale of the Dominican Republic to U.S. political adventurers who operated in close association with President Ulysses S. Grant in Washington.

ROJOS, VERDES, AND AZULES

After overthrowing Báez, González and his followers set up
headquarters in the capital. To prevent Luperón, Pimentel, and
Cabral from putting any impediments in the way of his power,
he dictated a decree prohibiting them from entering the country until the next government was formed. Because these three

generals had all served as presidents in the past, González feared their competition in the forthcoming election. Therefore, it was not until after the elections had been held and he had been sworn in as president in February 1874, that González permitted these generals to return to the country.

The elections were held after the Constitution of 1854 had been replaced by a new liberal constitution that guaranteed universal suffrage through direct vote. González made a sweeping triumph in these elections over the other Baecista candidate, former Vice-President Manuel Altagracia Cáceres, thanks to the manipulation of votes and to the fact that the majority of Azules voted for him out of gratitude for having rid the country of Báez's dictatorship. It was clear to everyone that a vote for Cáceres was simply a vote for Báez, for it was said that Cáceres was an illegitimate son of Báez.

At the beginning, the new government enjoyed immense popularity since both Rojos and Azules proclaimed the victory of national unity over party interests. This popularity increased tremendously when the government decided to rescind the contract with the Samaná Bay Company. The company was behind in its annual payments and, as the contract stipulated that in case of arrears the Dominican Republic could cancel the agreement, González took advantage of this clause to annul the entire contract. This action was highly satisfactory to the majority of Dominicans, especially members of the Azul party.

González also wished to negotiate a treaty of peace, friendship, trade, and navigation with the Haitian government, and to definitively resolve the border problem. This problem had been vexing Dominican political life for the last 30 years, first with the Haitian invasions, and recently with the revolutionary activities carried on along both sides of the border. The treaty took almost a year to negotiate and was not signed until November 9, 1874. According to its stipulations, the borders were to be determined to the satisfaction of both countries, while free trade was to be established between the two nations.

The treaty opened the door to new Haitian encroachments onto Dominican territory in the name of free trade. To González what mattered most was to secure a source of additional revenues to keep his government in operation. Haiti was to pay an annual indemnity of 150,000 pesos for eight years to the Dominican government in exchange for the tacit recognition of sovereignty over the extensive grasslands of the Plaine Centrale in the western part of the island that were occupied by Tousaint L'Ouverture in 1794.

The most notable acts of the González's government were related to the economic policy of granting concessions to favor foreign investment in agricultural and industrial ventures. During his two years in power, González expedited tax concessions for the production of textiles, soaps, candles, bricks, sugar cane, starch, chocolate, gun powder, wood, coffee, and salt, while he exempted from the payment of customs duties the importation of galvanized metal to roof the houses which until then had been covered primarily with palm bark, thatch, or boards. Of all the concessions, that which produced the greatest economic impact was the opening up of new lands to create sugar cane plantations and built sugar mills.

González was unable to govern according to the manifesto of the Movimiento Unionista because after losing the elections the Baecistas decided to impose Manuel Altagracia Cáceres by force. On learning of this conspiracy, González set off in the middle of July for the Cibao provinces where the majority of Cáceres followers were located. After González had imprisoned some of Cáceres's partisans, Cáceres gathered some thirty of his supporters and made a surprise attack on Fort San Luis in Santiago on August 5. He then declared himself in rebellion against the government.

The government troops were able to quickly defeat Cáceres

with the support of the Azul party which had no desire to return to Baecista rule. Despite this victory, the whole experience led González to change the nature of his regime. Believing that the uprising was caused by the liberal character of his government, the president began to listen to the advice of some of his own supporters who recommended that the government should use a stronger hand.

On September 10, 1874, González proclaimed himself "Supreme Representative of the Nation by the Will of the People," and decreed that the Constitution should be modified as it did not fit the existing conditions in the country. A new Constitutional Assembly was convoked to effect this change. The old liberal constitution of the Azules was now to be supplanted by a new authoritarian document written at the insistence of González, a former Rojo leader who now decided to gather his personal followers into a new party that he baptized as the Verdes or green.

Well before the new constitution was promulgated at the beginning of March 1875, González's despotic manner had alienated the Azules. Their distance from the government was further increased when González refused to recognize as a national debt the loans incurred by Luperón in his long struggle against Báez's dictatorship. Rather than satisfying Luperón's demands, González's Baecista supporters undertook a press campaign to discredit the Azul leader. The Azules came to Luperón's defense and denounced that the antiliberal stance of the government was endangering domestic tranquility.

These accusations and counteraccusations were aired publicly in the newspapers despite González's desire to control the press. When the governor of Puerto Plata stated that he wished to imprison Luperón and even have him assassinated, the Azul party, acting under a patriotic association called La Liga de la Paz, prepared to confront the government. At this time, the financial situation of the government had already deteriorated because the president had spent practically all the revenues of the treasury in gifts and rewards to the military personnel and politicians whom he wished to incorporate into his own party to the detriment of the Azules and Rojos.

In view of this situation that the Azules considered unfair, particularly for the public employees who had not been paid for several months, the Liga de la Paz and the literary Sociedad Amantes de la Luz issued various manifestos against the president, who was accused of having violated the Constitution by becoming a dictator and by misappropriating public funds with his recent financial mismanagement. The manifestos provoked a new round of political activity. The main Azul generals prepared for another rebellion at the beginning of February 1876, while they waited for Congress to recognize the accusations against González.

Within a few days, the Azules mobilized public opinion and even obtained the backing of many Rojos in case it became necessary to resort to arms. However, since no one wanted another civil war, the political leaders of the various parties met on the outskirts of the capital on a farm called El Carmelo. There, they signed a pact whereby Congress would acquit González of the accusations made against him if he promised to renounce the presidency and leave the executive power in the hands of his cabinet. The cabinet, in turn, would surrender power to the leaders of the revolt so that they could organize elections to choose a new president. And so it was done, despite an attempt by one of González's military protégés, General Villanueva, to conduct a coup in Báez's favor on February 27. This movement was quickly suppressed by the Azul generals whose troops had already arrived in the capital.

The Azul party was now united. Little by little the Azules had come to realize that they formed the only nucleus of coherent political ideas capable of organizing the Dominican government according to liberal principles. Under Luperón's initiative, the Azules agreed to name Ulises Francisco Espaillat as president. Espaillat was a politician who had distinguished himself for his democratic ideas in the Revolution of 1857, during the Restoration War, and in his opposition to Báez's tyranny. Espaillat was formally elected president on March 24 1876, in the elections organized by his party.

From the very beginning Espaillat tried to put into practice his old liberal economic ideas. In line with his liberal creed, Espaillat also wanted to keep the press free from censorship and to favor the free play of ideas. His government began with the great expectation that the Azules would at least exercise power and that the rebellions would end. But circumstances were totally contrary to the experiment that Espaillat hoped to put into practice. The country was almost bankrupt, the treasury was empty, and there was no money to pay public employees.

In order to save money to pay public employees, Espaillat had to suppress payment on all political expenses such as allowances and gifts that were, in more than one sense, the guarantee of stability for the various governments of the period. Espaillat, unlike most Dominican presidents before him, had no organized personal army at his service. Moving from their own military nuclei, the other presidents possessed the capacity to structure more or less permanent alliances with the other caudillos by bargaining on a political market of personal services and economic gratifications. Thus a president who had sufficient funds to keep these generals well paid and busy could ensure their loyalty, at least until someone else could offer more.

On coming to power, Espaillat acted against the market character of the political clientele of his party by declaring that he would only use government funds to pay public employees. He thus automatically lost the support of those who had brought him to the presidency. González was able to stay in power for two years because he knew how to use state funds to form a political clientele loyal to himself only. González was overthrown when these funds ran out and it was no longer possible to re-place them with the issue of bonds to which he had resorted to several times during his presidency. Before González, Báez had stayed in office six years through the money obtained from the Hartmont loan and through the support offered by the U.S. government. Now Espaillat came to power declaring that he did not intend to follow the pattern set by the previous presi-dents. This intention was soon to be put to the test.

After naming Gregorio Luperón as minister of war, Espai-llat wished to organize a professional army. However, Luperón was more of a merchant than a bureaucrat, and neglected the affairs of his ministry. During his ministry, Luperón went to live in Puerto Plata to attend his personal businesses. At that time he was heavily in debt from the obligations he had con-tracted with various Dominican and foreign businessmen to finance the revolt against Báez. As soon as he came to power, Espaillat declared Luperón's loans, which amounted to $170,000, as part of the national debt. Espaillat attempted in vain to create a bank to alleviate the critical lack of govern-ment funds. He vainly tried to resolve the disquieting problem of the public debt that had been growing at an increasing rate during the past few years.

The Rojos completely opposed Espaillat's policies, and var-ious manifestos appeared accusing Luperón and Espaillat of corruption. These manifestos were followed by military upris-ings by the Rojos and verdes who sought to return to power. Once again the country was in the midst of civil war. Without the support of the military to whom Espaillat refused to give their customary gratifications, the Azul cause was lost. Two re-bellions broke out, one int the north, under the leadership of Ignacio María González and another in the south under Mar-cos A. Cabral on behalf of Buenaventura Báez. In July, Espai-llat declared the country in a state of emergency and named Luperón chief of government operations.

Everything was useless. Ignacio María González appeared with his army before the gates of the capital on October 5. Believing that surrendering power to the Verdes was the lesser of two evils, Espaillat proceeded to replace his ministers with González partisans to preserve constitutional appearances. With González in control of the situation, Espaillat handed in his resignation on December 20 and sought asylum in the French consulate after only seven months in power.

Espaillat's resignation did not satisfy the Rojos, and the Baecista forces immediately encircled the capital. Since the Azules refused to support González, he, too, was forced to resign. The Baecista generals quickly advised their leader to return to Santo Domingo. Báez arrived within one week of the resignation of Espaillat and took office as president on December 27, 1876. A furious persecution of the Azules and Verdes was promptly initiated.

Although this new government of Báez was only to last 14 months, the old dictator tried again to revive his plans to annex the country to the United States. However, the U.S. government was no longer interested, and Báez gained little from his efforts. Meanwhile, the Azules began another revolt along the border with the aid of the Haitian government, which did not want to see its neighbor annexed to the United States. At the beginning of 1878, the Azules, under the leadership of Father Fernando Arturo de Meriño, organized their guerrillas and prepared a strong offensive.

By February, Báez realized that he was rapidly losing support, and prepared to leave the country. But before departing, he forced the merchants of Santo Domingo to pay him their customs duties in advance and thus gathered 70,000 pesos. With this sum and another 300,000 pesos that he had accumulated the previous year by withholding the salaries of the troops and public employees, he left the country on March 2, 1878.

At Báez's departure, two different governments were formed. In Santo Domingo, the so-called Junta de Gobierno was established by the Baecista general, Cesáreo Guillermo, whose troops first occupied the capital, while in Santiago a so-called Gobierno Provisional was set up by the followers of González. Wanting to avoid the continuation of the civil war, the Azules began negotiating a new understanding with González who was asked to appoint various Azul leaders as ministers and generals in his new government in exchange for their recognition of him as president.

After a conference with Luperón, González announced a reconciliation with the Azules and accepted their offers. With this agreement and with the withdrawal of Guillermo's troops to an area outside the capital, González was again sworn in as president on July 25, 1878. A few weeks later, he reneged on his promises to the Azules and ordered Luperón and several of his partisans imprisoned.

This betrayal led to a new rebellion by the Azules. Unable to resist, González capitulated on September 2, while the troops of Cesáreo Guillermo approached the capital. The president of the Supreme Court, Jacinto de Castro, then became the provisional president and set up an interim government until new elections could be held. Guillermo served as minister of war for this government, and arranged to have himself elected President. He took office on February 27, 1879. Luperón, who now wished to stay out of politics, set sail for Europe as soon as Guillermo had announced his desire for the presidency.

Guillermo's government, meanwhile, proved no better than that of his predecessor. Both a military leader from El Seibo and a Baecista politician, Guillermo had been attracted to the Azul party little by little by Father Fernando Arturo de Meriño, although his Baecista past prevented him from being accepted by many of the Azul generals. Once he gained power, he forgot his agreements with the Azules and took advantage of his office to embezzle the treasury and divide its funds among his partisans and friends to the detriment of the Azul generals and public employees who no longer received their salaries.

When the Azules protested, Guillermo followed the example set by Báez and unleashed a brutal reign of persecution against all those who were not his followers. Finally, to assure his complete power, Guillermo decided to dismiss all the Azul generals who held posts in the government, particularly Luperón's representative, General Ulises Heureaux. When Luperón returned from Europe, the Azules agreed to overthrow Guillermo and make Luperón president of a provisional government.

After issuing a manifesto, the Azules set up a new government in Puerto Plata on October 6, 1879. The ensuing rebellion had widespread support, especially among the Azul generals, and Guillermo was defeated in battle. Guillermo took refuge in the capital, which was promptly surrounded by enemy troops. The revolt was too strong for him to resist, and on December 6, 1879, Guillermo had to take refuge aboard a Spanish warship then in the harbor and went into exile.

With Guillermo's fall ended the most unstable period of Dominican political history, and one in which caudillo politics became the norm of Dominican life. The Restoration had bequeathed to the Republic hundreds of armed men who, once the war was over, remained organized under their guerrilla leaders and made the sale of their military services into a political profession.

The Dominican armed forces were not a coherent, organized institution. Rather, they were a diverse ensemble of guerrilla groups obedient to several dozen generals who had enough prestige and resources to rise up in arms and keep a sizable group of men for or against some political cause. Normally the causes amounted to little more than a struggle of personalities or a dispute over local or regional interests, or the control of the national treasury.

Thus during the 19th century the exercise of military power and political activity in the Dominican Republic clearly acquired a market character. The two largest political groups that fought for power, the Azules and Rojos, needed the public treasury to keep themselves in office. Only the most educated civilian leaders of the Azul party were inspired and motivated by an ideology other than the desire for economic advantages. However, since the Azules functioned as an alliance of very dissimilar ideas and groups, the implantation of their progressive ideology was limited by the personalities and individual interests of their military leaders.

The struggle between Rojos and Azules was a struggle between two different modes of thought: one liberal, the Azul, and the other, the Rojo, reactionary and dictatorial. From 1879 on the Azules would rule the Dominican Republic for 7 years, but the market character of caudillo politics did not disappear. To understand this, it is necessary to look at the first stable Azul goverment under the presidency of General Gregorio Luperón. Once his provisional government was set up, Luperón began to organize the country along the liberal principles that had been espoused by Azul leaders since 1857. A new era was now beginning in the political life of the country since the governments of the ensuing years were all dominated by members of the Azul party.

The Rojo party was in decline and disbanded. Its former leader, Buenaventura Báez, was already old, rich, and ill in Curaçao, and had no interest in returning from exile to live in a country where his very name was discredited and only served to arouse hostility. The governments of González and Guillermo had weakened Báez's control over the Rojos since they, along with Cáceres, had taken over the Baecista leadership to enhance their own personal fortunes and had subsequently destroyed the party's unity through their personal rivalries.

The battles of the past years also ruined the image and influence of the Rojo and Verde leaders because, like Báez, they had shown they were only interested in personal gain and not in the progress of the country. The only exception had been the brief period when González had governed in alliance with the Azules and had made concessions to favor industrial and agricultural investments. The Azules, on the other hand, had interests and ideals to fight for beyond their own personal ambitions. As the most important merchants and landowners of the Cibao and the north, they saw the state as an instrument of progress to promote free enterprise and maintain public order so as to guarantee the development of economic activities.

The Rojo party had also lost strength by becoming the party of a generation that had entered politics before 1844, so that its main leaders were not only discredited but also old and tired. The Azules embodied the ideals of a new generation that had entered politics during the Revolution of 1857, and had matured during the War of the Restoration under the inspiration of the great liberal thinkers of the Cibao.

Of all the disciples of these men, the most outstanding was the young general Gregorio Luperón, who possessed a special mixture of military valor and political skill. These characteristics along with a lively business mentality, allowed him to become the leader of the Partido Nacional Liberal that dominated Dominican politics after the period of instability that followed the Restoration, but which was unable to attain power with stability until 1879. Now, under Luperon's leadership, a new political era began in the Dominican Republic.

12.
The liberals
in power
(1879-1886)

THE AZUL GOVERNMENTS

General Gregorio Luperón took control of the provisional government of Puerto Plata on October 6, 1879. Because he preferred to govern from that city, he appointed his long-time assistant, General Ulises Heureaux, as government delegate in Santo Domingo and as minister of war to handle political and military matters in the capital and the south. On the day after he took office, Luperón decreed the suspension of payments on the public debt that overwhelmed the government.

Luperón then created various lending companies called Juntas de Crédito to make loans to the government. These groups lent money at a lower interest rate than the old credit institution that operated in the capital and charged the government interest rates of up 28 percent. By reducing the rate to 10 percent per month, Luperón was able to reorganize public finances. Yet Luperón was a stockholder in the Juntas de Crédito and profited amply from their operations.

To provide greater revenues for the government, import and export taxes were increased on many articles. However, to benefit the Cibao region, the export tax on tobacco was reduced from 75 to 25 cents per hundredweight on the grounds that the decrease would stimulate the growers to increase their production. Luperón also wished to pass a stamp act to provide revenues through internal taxation, but the new Congress rejected it because the public only accepted as legitimate those taxes derived from customs receipts.

In accordance with his liberal philosophy, Luperón also instituted a subsidy of 40 pesos per month for all newspapers founded or published in the country thereby assuring a free press to educate public opinion in the exercise of democracy. But to prevent his enemies from conspiring against him, on December 8, 1879, Luperón decreed the death penalty for all those who took up arms to overthrow the government. Since there were no armed conspiracies during this period, this penalty was never applied.

Seeing the need for a new liberal constitution, Luperón summoned a new national convention on January 7, 1880. The new constitution was to be based on any of the former documents "excepting absolutely that of December 1854" that had served as an instrument of tyranny for the Rojo party. The convention met during the following months and produced another modified version of the Constitution of Moca, similar to the one passed the previous year. The new constitution was officially promulgated on May 28, 1880. Among its articles was the stipulation that the term of presidency was to be limited to two years so as to give opportunity to a greater number of aspirants.

During the following months, Luperón also worked to improve the postal system, create new schools, and promote the creation of professorships for higher education in the capital. One of his most notable achievements was the foundation of the Escuela Normal, a senior high school, under the direction of Puerto Rican intellectual Eugenio María de Hostos, then living in exile in the Republic.

All of the military posts and their fortifications were also repaired, and buildings were constructed to house the civil governments and military commands of the various cities and towns. Arms and other new equipment were bought to restock the arsenals that were empty after so many years of wars and revolutions. Schools were furnished with books and other materials, while new European-style uniforms were bought for the soldiers. With the funds made available by his fiscal policy, Luperón was also able to pay the salaries of the public employees and soldiers, which amounted to over 200,000 pesos and which had been in arrears since the governments of Báez, González, and Guillermo.

Another of Luperón's important moves was to force the Haitian Government to honor the Treaty of 1874 that the Haitian President Lysius Salomon was attempting to invalidate before his Congress. According to this treaty, Dominican goods were to enter Haiti duty-free, but Salomon gave orders requiring that all Dominican products arriving by ship or on mule back to pay the same duties as other nations. Since this maneuver was part of Salomon's plan to aid the Baecistas to overthrow the Azul government, Luperón ordered the suspension of all trade with Haiti.

A serious commercial crisis then arose in Haiti, which was dependent on Dominican cattle for food and on Dominican resin, wood, wax, and honey that Haitian merchants bought from the Dominicans to be later exported to other countries. Haitian merchants were particularly injured by the cessation of the rum trade, which was quite voluminous. Haitians then rose up in protest, and their Congress tried to force the president to maintain a friendlier attitude towards the Dominican Republic. Salomon finally agreed to respect the treaty and to pay the installments on the debt that were in arrears.

The basis for the continuation of Azul governments had been established since the Constitution now limited the presidency to a two-year term. Luperón began to look for a new candidate within the ranks of the party. After several prominent civil leaders declined the responsibility, Luperón finally recommended Catholic Father Fernando Arturo de Meriño. Following the Azul tradition of private consultations and agreements between the various party leaders who always complied with the recommendations of Luperón, who controlled both the party's financial machinery and military power, Meriño's candidacy was accepted by the other party members. Meriño was officially elected president by popular vote on July 23, 1880.

Meriño took office on September 1, 1880 and continued his predecessor's policies. The Azul party now worked as a team, and the most prominent members strove to achieve the goal of conserving peace and reconstructing the nation within a liberal framework. The armed forces remained under the control of Luperón's trusted representative, General Ulises Heureaux, who was now named minister of the interior. Heureaux also exercised great influence over Meriño's new minister of war, Francisco Gregorio Billini, after the seat of government had been moved from Puerto Plata to Santo Domingo. Other Azul leaders occupied posts in the local governments, the military, the cabinet, and civil service.

Meriño inherited the treasury with enough money to continue the public works initiated by Luperón. Increased attention to the customs administration also allowed the government to receive more revenues than in previous years. At the same time, the Haitian government began making regular payments on the debt owed to the Republic. Luperón, while on vacation in Europe in 1878, was named extraordinary envoy and plenipotentiary minister of the government in order to negotiate a loan of 12 million francs to be used in the introduction of immigrants for the nascent sugar industry. Although this loan was contracted, it was later canceled because of the opposition of the Juntas de Crédito whose members financed most of the government's operations and feared the loss of their business in the capital.

Meriño maintained Luperón's liberal style of government until he discovered that the Baecistas were conspiring in the south under the leadership of General Braulio Alvarez. He also learned that Cesáreo Guillermo was preparing an invasion with the aid of Puerto Rican authorities who feared the Dominican support given to Cuban and Puerto Rican exiles who were conspiring for the independence of those islands. As a means of preventing the Baecistas from disrupting his government, Meriño decreed on May 30, 1881 that any person found armed against the government would be punished by death, despite the prohibition against such actions found in the new constitution. This provision, known as the Decree of San Fernando, failed to deter the Baecista conspirators.

In July, Generals Alvarez and Guillermo rose up in rebellion. Meriño detached General Heureaux to one of the fronts, while he personally took charge of the other forces. The struggle against the rebels lasted two months. All enemies falling into the hands of President Meriño or General Heureaux were shot. Fearing that the executions would cause new uprisings and that the Constitution was too liberal to ensure stability, Meriño forged various manifestos requesting him to become dictator and abolish the Constitution. This was done without much hesitation, and an authoritarian government was soon set up under the control of Meriño and Heureaux.

This dictatorship did not last long, however, and ended as the Baecista threat subsided and Meriño's term of office expired. On Luperón's recommendation, General Heureaux was then elected president with General Casimiro Nemesio de Moya as vice-president. The office of vice-president had not been included in the Constitution of 1880, but was now established in the new constitution to allow more political participation among party members.

Heureaux took office on September 1, 1882. According to Luperón, the ascension of Heureaux was the result of his many meritorious acts for the party and the Republic since his days as a soldier in the Restoration War. In the previous 20 years Heureaux had been Luperón's trusted confidant in both military and political affairs. Between 1879 and 1880, Heureaux had been Luperón's delegate in the southern provinces and later had served as Luperón's minister of war and the interior. Heureaux's victory in the campaigns against Guillermo and Alvarez had also given him a decisive superiority in the military over the other Azul generals, and placed him in a position unequaled by any other leader in the party since he alone was chief of the armed forces and head of the party while Luperón was again traveling in Europe.

Although his first government in most respects followed the lines laid down by Luperón and Meriño, Heureaux diverged from his predecessors by using his position to attract the Rojo leaders who had been looking for a new chief since the death of Báez in Puerto Rico on March 4, 1884. Under the protection of the president, these Rojos convinced Heureaux that he should become leader of the Azul party with the support of the Baecistas who were politically dominant in the south. Therefore, when the elections of 1884 drew near, Heureaux decided that he himself should name the next president of the Republic.

During the course of the elections Heureaux made full use of his power and position. Although Luperón wanted the civilian Azul ideologist Pedro Francisco Bonó to accept the presidency, Bonó refused on the grounds that he would only be a puppet for Heureaux who was in complete command of the army. Following Bonó's refusal, Luperón then sought other civilian candidates, but they also refused. Luperón saw no other recourse than to state that he would not declare himself in favor of any particular candidate. Meanwhile, Meriño and Heureaux were working to promote the candidacy of Francisco

Gregorio Billini and Alejandro Woss y Gil as president and vice-president. Both were Azul politicians from the capital and the south.

Heureaux's candidates soon found competition from General Segundo Imbert and the Vice-President, Casimiro Nemesio de Moya, from the Cibao and the North. As Imbert was the oldest of the Azul generals, as well as a favorite of the Cibao, Luperón declared himself in his favor. Because Heureaux and Meriño insisted on backing Billini and Woss y Gil, the Azul party was unable to present a unified candidacy. The elections were finally held and, according to Luperón, were actually won by Imbert and Moya, although Heureaux, "who grossly violated the law by adding 15,000 votes in the ballot boxes," had Congress declare Billini's victory and swear him in as president on September 1, 1884.

Imbert and Moya's supporters sought the support of Luperón in an effort to invalidate the fraudulent elections. He refused on the grounds that it would lead to civil war and hopelessly divide the party. Before leaving for Europe, Luperón therefore advised the losers to join the cabinet and unite the Azules within the government so as to preserve peace and continue the party's work. Although this advice was followed, it soon became evident that the maneuvering of Heureaux and Meriño had already definitely split the party. It also became clear that Heureaux was controlling the party's political machinery. Under his protection, the former Baecistas were conspiring to destroy Luperón's leadership within the Azul party.

The more liberal Azules now wished to stop Heureaux's growing military and political power that had made the fraudulent elections possible in the first place. From the very beginning of Billini's term, the press of Puerto Plata and Santiago made a fierce attack on the government. This campaign was also directed against Luperón who was held responsible for the electoral fraud because of his patronage of Heureaux. The press in Puerto Plata was under the direction of the governor, a personal enemy of Luperón. Thus, when Luperón returned from Europe some months later, he met with open hostility and even feared for his own personal safety.

Billini sought to protect himself from these attacks by declaring a general political amnesty and by calling in the aid of another of Luperón's enemies, Cesáreo Guillermo, then living in exile in Saint Thomas. Billini's call for Guillermo was too much for Luperón. Guillermo was widely considered a traitor to the country because of his collaboration with the Spaniards. Luperón reacted harshly and threatened to overthrow Billini in a coup. This threat, along with the continual demands of Heureaux who was intent upon controlling the government from his ministry of war, led Billini to resign and hand over his office to Vice-President Woss y Gil on May 15, 1885.

With the fall of Billini, Heureaux now controlled the government since the new president was completely obedient to this man to whom he owed his position. Luperón was then named government delegate in the Cibao so that the military wing of the Azul party now completely dominated the country. Nevertheless, alarmed by the absolutist tendencies of Heureaux, the liberals realigned their forces backing Casimiro Nemesio de Moya and former President Billini as candidates for the next presidential elections.

These activities caused discipline to deteriorate within the Azul party. It was now clear that the Rojos had succeeded in dividing their opposition by converting Heureaux into an opponent of liberalism. According to Luperón, some of the most notorious Rojos, joined Heureaux who then placed them in important positions while working to cause a division between Heureaux and Luperón. The Rojos steadily infiltrated into the Azul party without the Azules realizing their ability to split the party. All this became evident when the time came to present candidates for the elections of July, 1886.

Again, the senior Azul leaders Pedro Francisco Bonó, Don Casimiro de Moya, and José María Glass declined to be candidates as Luperón urged. They all foresaw that the elections would again be manipulated by Heureaux. Only General Casimiro Nemesio de Moya, spurred by his liberal friends within the Azul party who wanted to retaliate for the fraud of the previous elections, dared to openly oppose Heureaux. Moya had been vice-president under Heureaux from 1882 to 1884 and had shared power with him in all the Azul governments since the Meriño government.

Luperon recounts that according to the tradition established within the Azul party, Moya should have received the party candidacy, but the attacks leveled against Luperón by Moya's supporters in the previous months had caused Luperón to resent the liberal faction and moved him to support Heureaux's candidacy for a second presidential term. When election day arrived the party was clearly divided into two irreconcilable factions, with Luperon supporting the antiliberal cause. Although Luperón proposed to reunite the party by running Heureaux and Moya on the same ticket, Moya's supporters refused despite the fact that Moya favored it.

The tensions reached their height in the weeks before the elections. Moya's supporters were persecuted and jailed in many parts of the country. On election day they were not able to vote in the capital and the surrounding towns because of the persecutions undertaken by government troops directly under the command of the official candidate, Ulises Heureaux, who was also minister of war. Besides the clear use of political terrorism, a colossal fraud took place when it was time to count the votes. According to Luperón, Moya held the majority of the country and the immense majority of the Cibao. Both men and women favored him. But Heureaux's supporters managed to change the results and stole the elections.

Finding themselves tricked and their votes changed, Moya's

followers, who had expected an overwhelming victory, now clamored for open rebellion. According to Moya, he did not wish to make any armed protest that would once again involve the country in a civil war, but his military followers who held an old grudge against Luperón organized a rebel movement in Moya's name. Moya then felt compelled to support them. The rebellion broke out on July 21, 1886, and during the following weeks the fighting was extremely violent, with over 600 men killed in combat. Luperón offered his services to the government and helped Heureaux fight the rebels. At first Heureaux lost ground, but soon he realized that he could defeat the rebellion by buying off several of the opposition generals who had no real attachment to liberalism.

With the money borrowed from a Puerto Plata merchant, Heureaux bribed various key men in the rebellion so that after a few weeks the Moyistas were reduced to a few regions and had to capitulate. Moya and the main liberal leaders had to flee the country, along with their families, because the government troops commanded by Hereaux pillaged their houses, farms, haciendas, and other properties in La Vega and the Cibao region. It was popularly said that the rebellion that Heureaux had not been able to win with lead had been won with silver.

President Woss y Gil gave all his support to Heureaux to combat the rebellion that ended on October 31, 1886. The elections of July were then legalized. Heureaux used his troops to impose order throughout the country, and finally took over the presidency on January 6, 1887, a few months later because the civil war had kept him busy in the interior of the country. The Azul party was now permanently split, while all political power had fallen into the hands of Heureaux who would remain in power until his assassination in July, 1899.

THE AZUL PARTY AND THE ECONOMY

The rise of the Azul party to power in 1879 did not occur by chance. For 20 years, the people of the Cibao had been fighting against the oligarchic and bureaucratic groups of the south in order to establish a political order based on liberal theories and doctrines. It was an arduous struggle because the Cibao had to confront the steady opposition of the southern provinces that refused to accept the democratic organization postulated by the Constitution of Moca.

The Azules also had to fight for two years against Santana and the Spaniards to restore the Republic and the Constitution of 1858. Later, they had to struggle against Báez and his followers in the Rojo party to prevent the country from being sold to the United States. Theirs was a permanent fight against various tyrannies instituted under the postulates of the 1854 Constitution that Santana composed to fit the interests of the southern oligarchy. There were also struggles within the Azul party as some of the Azul generals, imbued with a pernicious military *caudillismo*, had also tried to take the authority away from the liberal leaders who led the party after the War of Restoration.

Throughout this period, the Azules were the party of the Cibao tobacco interests. It best represented the nature of a rural mercantile society based on an agricultural economy. Structured on the intensive exploitation of small parcels of land, the Cibao's products were traded through a complicated network that involved the entire population of the north. On the other hand, the Rojo party was the party of the large landowners in the south and east where cattle and timber were the principal products. These large landowners derived their fortune and personal authority from the possession of extensive territories that were exploited by peons. Debt peonage kept the rural population of the southern and eastern region completely dependent on the big landowners, without the possibility of becoming an independent peasantry.

During the First Republic and the period following the Restoration, the Cibao and the south functioned as two different and independent countries, politically and socially segregated. The lack of roads made communication between the two areas extremely difficult, and the inhabitants thus became closely linked to the individual merchants who bought their products. As the two regions produced different merchandise for different markets, the south and Santo Domingo were oriented toward England, Curaçao and Saint Thomas, while the Cibao and Puerto Plata directed their trade toward Hamburg, Bremen, and also Saint Thomas. Just as tobacco was the basis of the Cibao economy, mahogany and hardwoods became the economic base of the south.

Mahogany constituted the backbone of the economy in the capital. The most conspicuous representatives of the south made their fortunes through the exploitation and export of wood. Before becoming president, Buenaventura Báez lived for many years off the extensive mahogany forests that he had inherited from his father. In the south, many trees were felled but there were few owners. Tobacco, on the other hand, became the lifeblood of the Cibao economy and the entire population of the region. Tobacco was produced by thousands of family units who exploited small parcels of land, but these small quantities of tobacco added up to a great annual production. In the Cibao, virtually every family worked by and for itself, and ultimately many were dependent on the tobacco financiers who were the large import-export merchants of Puerto Plata acting on behalf of the tobacco buyers of Saint Thomas, Hamburg, and Bremen.

These two products, tobacco and mahogany, developed out of diverse ecological and economic conditions and ended up forming two dissimilar societies with correspondingly different attitudes. According to reports of travelers and foreign consuls, agriculture in the south was virtually undeveloped, where-as in the northern provinces agriculture was the principal eco-nomic activity. The southern economy, based on cattle ranch-ing and lumbering, did not stimulate the creation of productive jobs among the region's population, and did little to arouse in-terest in commercial agriculture.

In the Cibao, tobacco agriculture had been established since the 18th century and kept the entire population occupied al-most all year, bringing into play all the energies of the region. Tobacco production was an industry that multiplied work and income, thereby having a democratizing social effect. The *campesinos* who planted the crop were not the only ones who worked in the production process. There were also women who harvested and prepared the tobacco, men who cured and packed it, and the owners of the animals that transported it to the towns and later to the ports. In the towns, shops employed many indi-viduals to work on the fermentation and packaging of the to-bacco until it was loaded on the ships for export.

The entire process required the labor of a large number of farmers and their families, muleteers, peons, rope and bag manufacturers, packers, balers, cigar and cigarette manufac-turers, merchants, financiers, and trade brokers. It also gave rise to a dynamic cycle by putting into circulation a large amount of cash. This, in turn, stimulated the importation and sale of merchandise to satisfy the demands of a large population who regularly earned money and consumed all types of products.

The Cibao was an active, enterprising, and industrious re-gion. It was the Cibao's capacity to finance itself that allowed the consolidation of the Azul party between 1865 and 1879 de-spite many difficulties. And it was the Cibao's tobacco-based wealth that supplied Gregorio Luperón with a steady stream of credit from the merchants of the Cibao and Saint Thomas. These merchants financed the continuous rebellions that he and his party launched against Báez. Luperón eventually became the financier for his party and the successive Azul governments as he was made a partner of the merchants who invested their money in the rebellions. The final triumph of the Azules was the triumph of tobacco over mahogany and consequently the triumph of the Cibao over the south.

It is the economic diversity of the Cibao that explains the receptiveness of the *Cibaeños* to the ideas of equality and freedom propagated by the European and U.S. liberals of the 19th century. In a society such as the Cibao where wealth was more equitably divided than in the south, it was more natural for the population to be more inclined towards democracy than in the south, where wealth and political power were concentrated in an extremely small number of landowners. These landowners, who had inherited land, prestige, and social and political power from the old colonial landed elite, were able to recover from the impoverishment of the colonial era by the trade of mahogany and even managed to retain their influence during the period of Haitian domination. However, the southerners were not willing to share this influence as demonstrated by the events of 1844, 1848, 1858, and 1865. Thus the struggle between the Rojos and the Azules from 1865 to 1879 was a war for supremacy among two different societies with two dissimilar economies, two modes of thought, and two antagonistic political conceptions.

There was an economic crisis faced by mahogany exporters shortly after the end of the Restoration War due to the disappearance of accessible forest areas along the rivers. As a result, the resources needed to finance the Rojo political machinery disappeared. The leaders of the Rojo party, particularly Buenaventura Báez, were then forced to seek foreign loans that eventually submerged the Republic in a sea of international complications. Báez and the Rojos systematically embezzled treasury funds to keep their political machinery running. In the long run, the mahogany crisis favored the Azules because they

relied on a permanently productive economy based on intensive cultivation of land and not on exploitation of forests that
were eventually depleted. Consequently, after the Restoration
War new timber fellings were developed in the north along the
coast near Puerto Plata, and in the northwest, in the Yaque River valley where the timber could be easily shipped through
Montecristi.

The Azules attained power in 1879 at the same time that a
new industry was beginning to develop in the south as an indirect result of the War of Restoration. This war had incited the
Cubans nationalists to launch a similar effort against Spanish
colonialism in 1868. Hence, during the next ten years the first
war of independence was fought on Cuban soil. From the beginning of this war, many Cubans emigrated to the Dominican
Republic so that within a few years there were some 5,000 exiles living in the country. Many of these Cubans were openly
persecuted by Báez and later by Ignacio María González in their
attempt to remain on good terms with the Spanish colonial government. But once Báez was overthrown and the Azules were
able to act freely, Luperón and his political allies offered both
aid and acceptance to all Cuban and Puerto Rican exiles who
arrived through Puerto Plata in search of either refuge or support for their independence movements.

These immigrants had important effects on the Dominican
Republic. Both Santiago and Puerto Plata benefited greatly from
the presence and activities of professionals, businessmen, and
intellectuals who created an atmosphere of cosmopolitanism
and cultural refinement previously unknown in the country.
Many educated Cubans married Dominicans and formed families. However, the most important effect of this immigration
was the investment made by some Cubans who bought land to
establish sugar cane plantations and modern sugar mills that
used steam power and railroads. The construction of these sugar mills began in the south and in the east, where land was less

expensive and where the tradition of sugar production was still alive in certain zones near the capital. *(See map No.8)*

The first concessions to construct these sugar mills were granted by the first González government, but the real stimulus came from the Azul liberal policy of promoting and protecting foreign investment as a means to encourage the social and economic development of the country. Progress, they believed, was only possible if the Dominicans could attract a sufficient number of immigrants and capital to develop agriculture and industry. These economic theories were accepted by the majority in the Azul party so throughout this period, foreigners could obtain all the concessions they wanted to establish themselves in the country.

The first to establish a modern sugar *ingenio* was a Cuban investor, Joaquín Manuel Delgado, who in 1875 bought 5,000 *tareas* (1 hectare=16 *tareas*) near San Carlos and imported new machinery and railroad equipment to process and transport the sugar. From this point on, the number of investments multiplied so that within seven years 30 sugar plantations and *ingenios* were established representing an impressive investment of 21 million pesos or 6 million dollars, an amount which was several times greater than the national budget. The owners of these mills were all foreigners because the Cubans were followed by American, German, and Italian investors who eventually controlled the entire sugar industry.

The impact of these investments was immediately felt in the south. Landowners sold their properties at unprecedented prices, high by national standards but cheap in comparison to land prices in Cuba, Puerto Rico, and Louisiana. Many of the owners who sold their land were *campesinos* who were attracted by the salaries offered by the sugar mills that were much higher than their earnings from their farms. Many chose to sell their lands to the *ingenios* and then work there as peons. Within a short period of time, the population near Santo Domingo was dispossessed of its land.

The new sugar industry was already well developed by 1880 and caused the bankruptcy of many small *ingenios* or *trapiches*, particularly those in the areas near San Cristóbal, Baní, and Azua. These small establishments could not compete with the tremendous quantities of sugar produced at lower prices and of a much better quality that the modern *ingenios* produced.

The development of the sugar industry also came at a time when Dominican tobacco was beginning to be rejected in its traditional European market because of its poor quality. The rudimentary methods used to treat and cure the tobacco led the buyers to prefer better quality tobacco from other areas of the Caribbean. Ironically, when the Azules attained power as a result of the tobacco trade, Dominican tobacco was losing its European market and was being replaced by sugar as the principal export product.

In addition to sugar, Dominicans also began to produce coffee and cacao for export that were then selling at good prices in Europe and the United States. Even Luperón, after traveling through Europe as the government's envoy decided to close his business in Puerto Plata and begin several plantations of sugar cane, coffee, cacao, and other fruits with the intention of exporting these products to the New York market. The Azul party's most important intellectual, Pedro Francisco Bonó, warned that the neglect of the tobacco industry and the consequent support given to the sugar industry would jeopardize the social well-being of the country. According to Bonó, sugar was the business of large landowners with great amounts of capital and was therefore injurious to the small independent farmers on whose progress the traditional wealth of the country depended.

Bonó believed that the sugar industry was stripping the peasants of their lands in the south and the east and was converting them into a mass of rural proletarians with no future, subjected to the ups and downs of the international sugar market. Once removed from their farms where their subsistence agriculture provided enough for daily sustenance, these peasants would be completely dependent on the sugar *ingenios* where they were only assured work during the harvest period. The rest of the time they would be left in misery and indebtedness. A noticeable effect of the growing sugar industry was a general scarcity of fruits and vegetables in Santo Domingo as the small farms in the surrounding areas disappeared.

As a result of the growth of the sugar industry, the country's economic center which had revolved around tobacco in the Cibao for several decades began to shift toward the sugar region which had Santo Domingo as its main center. Thus in a few years Santo Domingo became an important financial center, even more important than Puerto Plata. The decline of the tobacco industry forced government leaders to turn to the sugar industry to increase the financial support needed to maintain power.

The political implications of these changes were eventually unfavorable to the Azul party. When Luperón set up his provisional government in Puerto Plata in 1879, he appointed General Ulises Heureaux as government delegate in Santo Domingo, the south, and the east. Heureaux was also appointed as minister of war, a position that he kept in the Meriño government and one that gave him full control of the armed forces. During his own presidency from 1882 to 1884, Heureaux did everything in his power to attract prominent Rojo partisans who were left without a leader after Báez's death. Two of these leaders, Generoso de Marchena and Manuel María Gautier, became important political assistants to Heureaux who allowed them to recover part of their lost influence in exchange for their personal loyalty and that of the other Baecistas who desperately sought to return to power.

While Luperón and the other Azules were content with influencing the selection of the succeeding presidents, Heureaux was busy incorporating Rojo politicians into his service. With a power base consisting of Báez's southern partisans, Heureaux saw the advantage to be gained in separating himself from Luperón who until then had been the recognized leader of the Azul party. With the support of these southern Rojos, Heureaux snatched the Azul political machinery away from Luperón and instituted a personalistic regime that differed little from the previous governments of Báez. By 1886, when he clashed with the liberal wing of the Azul party, he had already built his own political machinery, and was ready to use it to perpetuate himself in power.

13.
Ulises
Heureaux
(1886-1899)

INSTALLING THE DICTATORSHIP

Ulises Heureaux was popularly known as General Lilís, a name that resulted from the mispronunciation of Ulises. As a youth his friends had called him Lilises, but as time passed Dominicans suppressed the two final letters and simply called him Lilís. Heureaux gracefully accepted this nickname in both his private and public life.

As soon as he was again in power, Lilís urged his supporters to publicly demonstrate in favor of Congress convening a national convention to modify the Constitution so that the presidential term would be extended from two to four years and presidential elections would be held indirectly through electoral boards as was done under Báez and Santana, instead of by universal suffrage i.e. through direct and secret votes practiced by the Azules. With the opposition crushed and Luperón away in Europe, it took Lilís little effort to make Congress modify the Constitution.

The Rojos were the most enthusiastic promoters of these constitutional changes. They immediately carried out a campaign to have Congress confer on Heureaux the permanent title of "Pacifier of the Homeland," in recognition of his role during the recent civil war. From the very beginning, Lilís let it be known that he would govern with men from all parties, thus ending the political exclusiveness of the Azules who had only used party members in high government posts. This new government of national unity was one of the pretexts used by Heureaux to complete the destruction of the Azul party and to create a political machinery loyal only to himself.

Heureaux's reward to the Rojos for their political support was to name the former minister of foreign relations under Báez, Manuel María Gautier, as secretary of foreign relations and to appoint the Baecista general Wenceslao Figuereo as secretary of the interior and the police. General Miguel Andrés Pichardo was named secretary of war as payment for his treason against the Moyistas during the civil war of the preceding year.

The war had cost the government dearly. Since Lilís had always worked through an extensive network of spies and informers who required money to operate, there were few funds available to carry on the routine tasks of government. To resolve this problem Heureaux sent another Rojo politician, General Generoso de Marchena to Europe to negotiate another loan that would cover the enormous expenses involved in maintaining an extensive political clientele of Rojos and Azules loyal to the new party.

De Marchena was connected to the Sephardic Jewish community of Curaçao. He traveled to London and Amsterdam where he met with various financial groups. In June 1888, he managed to put together a loan for £770,000 at 6 percent interest per annum, payable in 30 years. From this sum the Dominican government allocated £142,860 to repay the £38,095 received by the Hartmont loan contracted in 1869 by Báez. Another portion was used to redeem part of the internal debt left by former governments. The rest was used to keep Lilís's new political machinery operating, to buy new arms and uniforms for the army, and to order construction of warships that could transport troops rapidly around the island.

The loan was contracted with Westendorp & Company of Amsterdam, Holland. As a guarantee for the money received, Heureaux mortgaged 30 percent of the revenues of the customs houses to the company. To collect the quotas on the amortization of capital and interest, the company sent several financial agents to work in the country. These agents were charged with collecting all customs revenues and, after deducting the portion stipulated for the repayment of the loan, they were to deliver the remainder to the Dominican government. The contract was officially ratified by Congress on October 26, 1888 and was the beginning of a series of financial deals put together by Lilís that ended up ruining the economy.

While the loan was being negotiated in the summer of 1888, the Azules began to react to Heureaux's absolutist tendencies. With the jails full of political prisoners, the press persecuted and terrified, and a weak Congress, the liberal Azul leaders who still remained in the country asked Luperón to return from Europe and lead the party in order to prevent Lilís's reelection during the coming elections to be held on October, 1888. Luperón returned to Puerto Plata and met with his partisans who were thoroughly convinced that only he, because of his longstanding relationship with his former lieutenant, could convince Heureaux not to seek reelection.

Because the majority of the Azul party was in favor of Luperón, Lilís himself wrote to his former leader and offered support for his candidacy. Believing in the sincerity of Lilís, Luperón published his political program and began an active campaign until he realized that Heureaux was only playing for time until he was sure the loan would go through so that he could launch his own campaign.

As soon as Heureaux informed Luperón of his intention to also run in the elections, he unleashed a wave of persecution and terrorism against Luperón's supporters that was even more violent than that launched against Moya in 1886. This time Heureaux's vice-presidential nominee was Báez's former minister of foreign relations Manuel María Gautier, who had been elected over another Baecista, Wenceslao Figuereo, who also sought the office.

It was evident that these elections would not be free either. In July 1888, Luperón, was forced to issue a manifesto in which he withdrew his candidacy because of the violence against his followers and electoral committees in several parts of the country. When election day finally arrived, only those who had been bought off by Heureaux, some 11,000 out of a total of over 100,000 voters, cast their ballots while there was an almost complete abstention by the urban voters.

Almost all the Azules wanted to rise up in arms against the government and asked Luperón to head a new movement. Luperón refused on the pretext of not wanting to appear dominated by vulgar ambition. After having spent much of his money on the campaign, he simply could not compete in an armed struggle with Lilís, who had the funds to buy all the military support he needed. Financially ruined and betrayed by the very man whom he had raised to the presidency, Luperón requested his passport and went into exile.

Meanwhile, the electoral campaign had allowed Lilís to pinpoint his opposition. As soon as Luperón was out of the country, a new wave of persecutions, imprisonments, and assassinations began. The number of political exiles grew, and under the leadership of Casimiro Nemesio de Moya the exiles met in Haiti for the purpose of invading the country and overthrowing Heureaux. This invasion received the support of the Haitian government as Heureaux had been aiding the Haitian revolutionaries against President Louis Hippolyte. The exiles also collaborated with several groups of Azul youths who planned an uprising in Santiago to support the movement.

As soon as Lilís heard of the preparations for the invasion, he sent his minister Ignacio María González to Port-au-Prince to negotiate. The Haitian government subsequently agreed to deport Moya in return for the Dominican government's cooperation against the Haitian rebels. This pact ended the invasion scheme and caused the failure of the uprising in Santiago where several Azul youths sought to take over Fort San Luis in the middle of February 1889. This uprising also gave Lilís an additional opportunity to make more arrests and carry out executions, thus destroying the few remaining centers of opposition within the country.

In order to guarantee his security from any foreign threat, Lilís followed Báez's example of seeking the support of a foreign power. Lilís began by insisting to the U.S. government that the U.S. minister in Port-au-Prince be designated chargé d'affairs in Santo Domingo since there was no such office there. This objective was achieved during 1889, and in the following years Lilís offered the bay and península of Samaná for lease to the United States in return for economic aid and military protection against any foreign threat, especially from Haiti.

The negotiations with the United States were filled with incidents. Before entering into Lilis's schemes around Samaná, the U.S. government preferred to first bring the Dominican Republic under the terms of a treaty of commercial reciprocity. Looking for U.S. support, Heureaux accepted the draft of the treaty. According to it, 26 U.S. manufactured articles were to be allowed to enter the country duty-free in exchange for similar treatment to a series of Dominican products and raw materials. This reciprocity treaty was signed and later ratified on June 14, 1891, but was not put into effect because of the open opposition of those European countries that had commercial ties with the Dominican Republic.

In response to the privileged treatment given to U.S., interests, the Germans, who had been the traditional buyers of Dominican tobacco, now refused to buy the leaf if the treaty with the United States went into effect. This measure was enough to lead the Cibao tobacco growers and merchants to the brink of war against the government. They would not tolerate losing their only market for the 1892 crop, which was calculated between 175,000 and 200,000 hundredweight.

In the Cibao, the government's unpopularity increased when rumors spread that Lilís was planning to lease Samaná to the United States. These rumors arose from news in the U.S. press about the negotiations being undertaken by the government's envoy, Manuel de Jesús Galván. Heureaux had to publish official declarations denying that any such negotiations were being conducted, but he was not believed in the Cibao region. The representatives of the Cibao tobacco interests, the liberal wing of the Azul party now prepared for war. Worse yet, the Germans presented Lilís with an ultimatum made in agreement with France, Italy, and Holland demanding the abrogation of the reciprocity treaty. Facing this political resistance, Heureaux was forced to yield, and asked the United States not to put the reciprocity treaty into effect.

Meanwhile the country was going even further into debt because of Heureaux's policy of seeking loans locally and abroad to pay for his network of spies, and to keep up with his policy of payoffs and gifts to his followers who required money in return for their support to the government. As in the past, politics and the state were the easiest sources of income. Politicians and military men sought to be sustained and maintained by the president in return for their loyalty. Lilís believed that political stability was bought through gifts and fear, and he was ready to pay the price. That stability cost him dearly and fully indebted the country, but he reasoned that in the long run he would not live long enough to pay the final bill.

In September 1890, he secured a new loan of £900,000 from Westendorp & Company with the intention of building a railroad linking Santiago and Puerto Plata. Despite the fact that each day his loans constituted a heavier burden upon the government's finances, he did not hesitate in going to the Juntas de Crédito throughout the country in search of more money. This he was granted in return for giving merchants a free hand in bringing into the country whatever contraband they wished. He also began the fraudulent marking of silver money under a 1891 law that brought further economic ruin for many and totally discredited the national currency. Then in 1892, he obtained a new loan from Westendorp. *(See map No. 8)*

By this time Westendorp was on the verge of bankruptcy due to the drop in import revenues resulting from contraband and could not pay its shareholders and bond holders any dividends. To avoid total bankruptcy, Westendorp took advantage of Lilís's Samaná schemes with the United States and sold its interests in the Dominican Republic to a group of U.S. capitalists, among whom were the secretary of state and other U.S. government officials. This group founded the San Domingo Improvement Company to buy up Westendorp's credits in the belief that the United States would soon establish a protectorate through the leasing of Samaná. Investors in the newly created company expected a handsome profit once the leasing of Samaná was formally concluded.

In March 1893, Lilís allowed the new company to take over Westendorp's interests. Since the last loan from Westendorp had been spent rapidly, he set as a condition for the new company that it would make new loans to the Dominican government, one for US$1,250,000 and another for £2,035,000 to cover payment on the Dominican internal debt. The company issued bonds of various denominations and at different rates of interest so that the Dominican Republic was buried under a mountain of national and international debts that reached 17 million pesos in 1893, a sum several times the national budget.

FINANCIAL EMBROILMENT

The entrance of the San Domingo Improvement Company into Dominican finances gave the United States unprecedented influence over the country. Not only did some New York broker firms control the sugar industry, but the Improvement Company had complete control over customs receipts. Moreover, Heureaux granted the Clyde Steam Lines Company an exclusive monopoly over the transportation of passengers and freight between New York and Santo Domingo. This growing influence of the United States over Dominican economy and finances greatly affected European interests that had traditionally dominated Dominican commerce and caused deep resentment on the part of European businessmen working in various cities of the country.

This resentment had become evident during the crisis caused by the Reciprocity Treaty. It was made even more obvious during the campaign preceding the elections to be held at the end of 1892. Although Lilís at first stated that he was tired and would not run for office again, what he really had in mind was to find out who were the ambitious ones within his own camp who wanted to be president. One was soon found in Generoso de Marchena, Lilis's own financial agent, and high officer of the National Bank of Santo Domingo.

This bank had been operating in the capital since the time of the Westendorp Company. It belonged to French capitalists associated with Marchena who viewed the growing U.S. influence with suspicion. The National Bank officers hoped to counteract this influence with a plan to consolidate the national debt with a new issue of bonds through a European syndicate comprised of investors from Germany, Britain, Belgium, the Netherlands, and Spain. This syndicate would also eventually lease Samaná and would fortify it within three years. Samaná was still thought as a strategic bay and peninsula where a naval base and coaling station could be securely established.

The plan was totally contrary to Heureaux's foreign policy of seeking an alliance with the United States. When it was made public during the electoral campaign of 1892, it gained such popularity that Marchena decided to run as a candidate in the next presidential election. As expected, Heureaux soundly defeated Marchena through coercion of the electors. Marchena then decided to conspire to overthrow Lilís to avenge the fraud. He ordered the National Bank of Santo Domingo to refuse all credit to Heureaux on the grounds that he was far behind in repaying his personal loans from the bank. Moreover, Marchena ordered frozen other funds held by Heureaux in the bank and placed an embargo on the guarantees offered by Heureaux to fulfill his obligations.

Lilís acted rapidly. Marchena was taken prisoner at the beginning of December 1892 and after a year in jail was executed in December 1893, along with a group of Baecistas who had sought to rebel in his favor in Azua. Meanwhile, the Improvement Company had taken control of the customs offices, and Lilís had begun a lawsuit that eventually forced the National Bank to leave the country, with the Improvement Company then taking its place.

Marchena's disgrace and the frustrated rebellion in Azua terrified Heureaux's Minister of Foreign Affairs Ignacio María González, who was also involved in the conspiracy. To save his own life, González fled to Puerto Rico where he issued a statement declaring that he had abandoned the country on discovering Heureaux's scheme to lease Samaná to the United States, although, as minister of foreign affairs, he obviously had known and supported those plans for some time.

González then went to Haiti to meet generals Luperón and Moya who were there preparing another invasion against Heureaux. The Haitian government supported this operation and President Hippolyte donated arms and ammunition to the exiles who were preparing to cross the border at the end of March

1894. Haitian support waned rapidly, however, once Lilís let his Haitian counterpart know that he would arm Haitian rebels if the invasion was not stopped. Once again the Haitian president betrayed the Dominican exiles, who were forced to leave the country within 72 hours. Moya and his followers then spread out to the Turk Islands, Saint Thomas, and other points in the Caribbean.

Although Heureaux had again triumphed over the rebels, he was still being pressed by financial difficulties. The mortgages placed on the customs receipts left the government with barely 90,000 silver pesos per month to carry on its operations. Nothing remained of the money from the previous loans. Lilís sought another loan outside the country. One such source was the Haitian government that was intimidated into paying part of the sum owed as stipulated in the Treaty of 1874. This money allowed the Dominican government in 1895 to pay France the compensations that it demanded for Lilís's illegal tampering with the National Bank of Santo Domingo at the end of 1892.

Lilís also dealt privately with the directors of the Improvement Company, who agreed to create two new subsidiary companies, the San Domingo Finance Company and the San Domingo Railways Company, to furnish money to the government in exchange for lucrative commissions for themselves and Lilís. In 1895 and 1896 various secret operations were transacted that left the Republic completely mortgaged to the Improvement Company without any hope of recuperating its customs revenues or without real ownership of the railroads that were being constructed with this money.

While the Improvement Company was handing out money to him, Heureaux continued accepting it to pay off the country's domestic creditors and to keep his political machinery operating. Eventually, the company stopped furnishing the government with fresh funds when the customs receipts stopped producing sufficient money. When this became known, the merchants who ran the Juntas de Crédito became more and more reluctant to lend their money to the government.

From then on, Lilís had to use his own fortune to cover the government's current expenses as well as the payments on the various debts contracted abroad. The president of the Republic thus became one of the most important money lenders to his own government, although he was careful not to charge higher interest rates than those of the Juntas de Crédito.

The growing financial chaos had no precedent. The interests of the Improvement Company became intimately connected yet in conflict with the personal interests of Heureaux and other government officials. In August 1897, it was necessary to draw a new plan whereby the foreign debt would be consolidated, and Lilís accorded the Improvement Company the right to issue new bonds to collect and pay all previous debts. This plan was put in operation with the sale of bonds for over £5 million, which only created a new debt since the old bonds were not recalled and the Dominican government made no effort to redeem them.

The government faced complete bankruptcy. Lilís continually wrote to his friends, to government officials, and to the directors of the Improvement Company about this "catastrophe" and the "disgrace" into which he had fallen through the many complicated fraudulent operations recently negotiated with the company. To obtain more money with which to pay the Juntas de Crédito, Lilís had to resort to printing some 5 million pesos in paper money. Since there were neither funds nor fiscal reserves to back these bills, they were not accepted by anyone and the attempt became famous as yet another of Lilís's schemes to reap benefits at government expense. To this day those bills are remembered as the *papeletas de Lilís*.

By 1898, the government was trapped in a terrible web of domestic and foreign creditors. Through its various agreements with the government, the Improvement Company owned credits over 15 million pesos. Many Juntas de Crédito that had continued doing business with the government were demanding their money. Several dozen merchants who had made private deals with Lilís since the beginning of his presidency were also seeking repayment on their loans. Government employees who were months behind in receiving their salaries were also demanding to be paid in hard currency rather than in worthless paper bills.

One of Heureaux's most pressing needs was to placate the ever-growing interests of the sugar industry in the south for the sugar producers had been another of the government's financial sources for the past decade. The sugar companies were intimately tied to the New York finciancial market, the source of the Improvement Company's dollars. The sugar elite had gradually replaced the Cibao merchants who were suffering from low tobacco prices and the loss of the tobacco market.

Over the years, Lilís had dried up the Cibao merchants of their liquid assets by constantly demanding new loans through the Juntas de Crédito. The sugar companies were forced to step in and started providing credits to the government. Since those credits acquired a new priority for Hereaux, he was willing to pay them back even in the middle of the crisis. Therefore, in 1898, when Heureaux managed to obtain a new loan in Europe for $600,000, he allocated the entire sum to pay back the merchants and industrialists of the sugar districts of Santo Domingo and San Pedro de Macorís, completely ignoring the Cibao.

This move roused the complete animosity of the Cibao, although fear of Lilís's ruthlessness prevented any immediate rebellion. Action was finally taken by an old Baecista named Juan Isidro Jimenes. Although at one time Jimenes had supported the Lilisista party, he had eventually been forced to leave the country because of Heureaux's financial depredations. After buying the ship Fanita in the United States and loading it with 3,000 guns and several million bullets, he invaded the country through Montecristi in June 1898 and tried to start a revolution in the northwest where he had been the most important businessman since Báez's time. This expedition failed, and Jimenes sought exile in France.

While in exile in Paris, Jimenes came in contact with several young Dominicans students whom he encouraged to organize a conspiracy. On his return to the country one of these youths, Jacobito de Lara, met with a group being organized in Moca by the merchant-farmer Horacio Vásquez and his cousin Ramón Cáceres, who were planning to overthrow Lilís.

Meanwhile, Heureaux was making desperate efforts to disentangle himself from the Improvement Company which now totally dominated the country's financial affairs. At the end of 1898, Heureaux finally reached a new understanding with some European financiers who agreed to make a new loan to buy the Improvement Company's interests and consolidate the debt. At the same time, Heureaux tried to negotiate a protectorate with the United States to insulate himself from another attack from abroad. But on this occasion he did not succeed, because the U.S. government did not trust his word after the failure in negotiating for the lease of Samaná and the collapse of the reciprocity treaty.

Ever careless of national sovereignty, Heureaux also took advantage of conversations held with the Haitian government regarding border problems to secretly sell to Haiti other territories that had been in dispute for nearly 100 years and that had been poorly defined by the Treaty of 1874. Thus, in October 1898, these territories were sold for a paltry sum of 400,000 pesos. Yet Lilís secretly signed a receipt for 1 million pesos that were never received by the Dominican treasury. The difference of 600,000 pesos was embezzled by those who negotiated the sale. Since the border was still illdefined, the Dominican and

Haitian negotiators agreed to submit the problem to papal arbitration.

These conversations had to be suspended, however. Before they could be resumed, Lilís was assassinated by Jacobito de Lara and Ramón Cáceres in Moca on July 26, 1899. That day the dictator was traveling through the Cibao in an effort to placate the local merchants and convince them to lend him even more money in exchange for new fiscal exemptions and financial privileges.

14.
Toward a U.S. protectorate (1899-1911)

Lilís left the treasury completely ruined, indebted, and with its revenues in the hands of a foreign company that had profited handsomely at the expense of the Dominican state. In the 14 years of his government, the Dominican Republic had undergone visible changes so that by 1899 it was a very different country from what existed in 1886. During this period, the economy had changed radically. Instead of exporting wood and raising cattle, the South now concentrated on the production of sugar for export to the United States.

The Cibao had expanded its production to include the cultivation of cacao and coffee, which developed rapidly because of increased consumption in the United States and Europe and because of improved transportation facilities offered by two railroads which connected Santiago with Puerto Plata, and La Vega with the port of Sánchez. During the Lilís era, Sánchez and San Pedro de Macorís became important export centers and changed from simple fishing villages to thriving commercial cities. Many capitalists, businessmen, and speculators introduced a new urban lifestyle previously unknown in these areas.

Many local merchants had been ruined under Lilís because of the continual financial crises, the printing of worthless paper money, and the subsequent devaluation of the peso. In their place appeared new merchants associated with Lilís in the business of making loans to the government. These merchants soon constituted a new economic elite whose fortune depended on their financial audacity and their loyalty to the regime. This elite shared power with a large group of politicians and the military who made their careers by directing Lilís's political machinery or by blindly executing the orders of the dictator.

At Lilís's death, the military men and politicians who had served him sought to perpetuate themselves in power under Vice-President General Wenceslao Figuereo, who automatically became president. Figuereo immediately decreed the persecution of Heureaux's killers, but the effort failed. At the time of Lilís's death the government was at the lowest point of its popularity and no one was willing to turn in the conspirators. At the call of the leader of the conspiracy, Horacio Vásquez, a rebellion broke out and expanded rapidly throughout the Cibao so that Figuereo's government was forced to resign on August 30, 1899. Power was then left in the hands of a Junta Popular that maintained order until Vásquez and his troops entered the capital on September 4, representing a provisional government that had been constituted in Santiago a few days earlier.

Vásquez permitted complete freedom of the press and called for the return of all political exiles. He also tried to put some order in the State's finances by withdrawing Lilís's paper bills from circulation. The exchange rate was fixed at 5 silver Dominican pesos for 1 dollar. The population reacted favorably to such economic measures and gave the government enough support so that it could easily organize new constitutional elections to choose a new president and vice-president.

Contrary to tradition, the provisional president refused to accept his selection as constitutional president. Still young,

Vásquez preferred to support the exiled merchant Juan Isidro Jimenes who enjoyed widespread popularity because of his expedition in the *Fanita* the year before. Filled with enthusiasm, the rebel leaders agreed to present a single ticket for the coming election: Juan Isidro Jimenes for president and Horacio Vásquez for vice-president. After an easy election, both men took office on November 15, 1899.

The new government set to work to untangle the financial chaos that Lilís had left behind. With the customs receipts mortgaged to the Improvement Company, the government was only receiving $60,000 per month, a sum insufficient to cover current expenses. The government's first measures were therefore aimed at clarifying the economic situation and recovering control over the customs office. The Improvement Company, however, claimed to hold its rights by virtue of contracts signed by the State and before ceding control to customs, demanded that these rights be recognized by the new government.

Public opinion considered these rights invalid because they had been acquired through secret and fraudulent dealings with Lilís. During Heureaux's government, the Improvement Company had floated bonds for each loan made to the government and for each debt consolidation scheme. Many of these bonds had been sold in Europe to hundreds of private investors at great discounts. These investors included a large number of Catholic peasants from France, Belgium, and Italy who had been led to believe that the bonds were for the Dominican religious order rather than for the Dominican Republic.

There were several groups of bondholders in addition to the Improvement Company: one in France, another in Belgium, another in Germany, another in Italy, and still another in Britain. In 1900, the Dominican government owed these investors the sum of $23,957,078, while the internal debt amounted to another $10,126,628. This meant that the country's total debt surpassed $34 million, while the customs revenues barely amounted to 2 million per year.

Once it was known in Europe that Lilís had died and that the Dominican government was in a state of economic ruin, the bondholders began to pressure their respective governments to force the Dominican Republic to pay the capital and interest that were now in arrears. The Dominican government could not do this. It had no money and the funds coming from customs went to the Improvement Company or to corrupt officials and politicians who supported the contraband trade. To escape this financial quagmire, Jimenes asked the Improvement Company to use the customs receipts to immediately pay the European bondholders who were working to have their governments recover the debts by force, but the company resisted.

With the Europeans threatening to send troops to take over the customs for themselves, Jimenes's government sought to reach an understanding with the Improvement Company and with the bondholders in such a manner that the state could pay them all an equal share. Plans for such a program were set up and soon turned out successfully. After a year of negotiations and agreements with the various parties involved, the Dominican government announced on January 10, 1901 that it was ready to remove the Improvement Company from the customs administration and deal directly with the bondholders by guaranteeing to use 40 percent of the customs revenues to pay off the debts.

The Improvement Company, which had been keeping most of the customs revenues for itself, immediately protested and took its case to the U.S. Department of State where it complained that the Dominican Republic had violated solemn contracts and agreements. Until then, the U.S. government had not offcially directly participated in the various deals and discussions. Now, with the interests of an American company being threatened, the State Department decided to intervene.

Because the Constitution of 1896 was still in force, Jimenes was to remain as president until November 1903. However, as soon as Jimenes took office the politicians began to argue over Jimenes' successor in 1903. At the same time, the Lilisistas were working to separate Vásquez from Jimenes by making the president think that Vásquez was trying to eliminate him in the next elections and that he should choose another candidate, perhaps a Lilisista, for vice-president. Meanwhile, a new party, the Partido Republicano, was created to enhance the political position of President Jimenes.

These intrigues ended up by distancing Vásquez and Jimenes. The two men were already physically separated since at the beginning of their term Vásquez had gone to Santiago to work as government delegate in the Cibao. As the leader of the anti-Lilís movement, Vásquez was surrounded there by Lilís's liberal enemies and by many who had been adversely affected by the financial policies of the dictatorship. Meanwhile in the capital, Jimenes was surrounded by many former Lilisistas who were trying to integrate themselves into the new government in order to return to public administration. As time passed, Vásquez began to believe that his life was in danger and on April 26, 1902 he called his supporters to war against the government. He then marched on the capital where, on May 2, he forced Jimenes to leave the country.

This rebellion, which made little sense beyond the personal rivalry of two caudillos, again divided the country under two political banners. From then on, and for the next 15 years, Horacio Vásquez and Juan Isidro Jimenes would head the two most important political factions of the country with each trying to attract as many followers from among the former Rojos and Azules who had been united under Heureaux. Jimenes, who was of Baecista origin, attracted the support of the Rojos, their descendents, and friends. Vásquez drew to his side what was left of the old Azul party, especially the liberal wing that had great admiration and affection for the man who had overthrown Lilís.

Nevertheless, after 14 years of dictatorship, one-party rule, and profound economic changes, the old party loyalties were almost meaningless. Many of the former leaders had died and a new generation was now entering the political arena. The new parties were named after the two new caudillos: one Horacista and the other Jimenista. At the time the national sport was cockfighting, and these parties were also popularly referred to as the two types of cock: the Jimenistas were called *bolos* (without tail feathers) and the Horacistas were called *coludos* (long tail feathers).

As soon as Vásquez took possession of the presidency after the overthrow of Jimenes, he began to persecute those Lilisistas who had worked with the *bolos*. As Jimenes was still popular because of his former prestige as a politician and merchant, resistance was widespread. Yet the Jimenistas were promptly repressed, and the jails were soon full of political prisoners, particularly the Lilisistas.

Vásquez was able to stay in power for several months. During that time, most of his energies were dedicated to solving the problem of the country's foreign debt that was increasing daily because of accumulating interest. The Improvement Company demanded that the Dominican government pay $11 million for the rights, properties, and full control of the Central railroad. Vásquez, like Jimenes before him, refused these demands on the grounds that these debts had been heavily inflated through Lilís's innumerable financial maneuvers and therefore should not be recognized.

The Improvement Company finally agreed to accept $4,500,000 for its alleged rights in the country and to sell some $4,525,000 in bonds it still held from the Dominican government at 50 percent of their face value. This agreement was formalized on January 31, 1903 with the signing of a protocol by means of which the Republic consented to allow a board of three arbitrators to set the form of payment. One of these arbitrators was to be chosen by the Dominican government, the second by the United States, and the third by common agreement by both governments. If the two governments could not agree on a suitable person, then the third arbitrator was to be a member of the U.S. Supreme Court. This agreement was harshly attacked by the Dominican press that voiced the public's hatred for a company that had so long supported Heureaux and who considered that the government was paying too much.

While this agreement was being negotiated, the Lilisistas were conspiring. The unpopularity of these negotiations along with the disturbances in the Northwest, where Jimenes was a true caudillo, kept the capital at a political boiling point, with the Ozama Fortress filled with political prisoners, especially Lilisistas. Finally, on March 23, 1903, when Vásquez and his chief ministers were away in the Cibao directing operations against the rebels, these prisoners took advantage of their absence and mutinied within the Fortress. With the aid of their followers in the city, they overthrew the government.

As President Vásquez set out with his troops to recover the capital, the Lilisista rebel forces chose as their leader former president Alejandro Woss y Gil who prepared to defend the city. A bloody civil war developed during the following weeks causing the death of many soldiers and the destruction of the suburb of San Carlos by fire. After several of the government's generals died in a fruitless attempt to take the city by force, Vásquez was forced to withdraw his troops, and he headed back to Santiago where he resigned from the presidency on April 23, 1903, less than a year after ousting Jimenes.

Woss y Gil then installed a provisional government and called for new elections to be held on the following June 20. He was the only candidate, seconded by Eugenio Deschamps, a former anti-Lilisista supporter of Jimenes, for vice-president. Jimenes and his followers supported this ticket as a means of participating in the new government. The new government was formally sworn in on August 1, and Jimenes was appointed as the government's financial agent in Europe.

Within three months a new rebellion broke out in Puerto Plata under the leadership of a Jimenista named Carlos F. Morales Languasco. This movement, called the Revolución Unionista, was directed at preventing Woss y Gil from establishing a new dictatorship similar to that of Heureaux. The pretext that Morales Languasco used to launch the rebellion was that Woss y Gil had not fulfilled his promises to Jimenes. With some support from the Horacistas, Morales's forces easily broke the government's resistance, and on November 24 Woss y Gil capitulated. By December 6 the rebel troops occupied the capital, and Woss y Gil and several of his Lilisista followers were forced to leave the country.

Morales now installed a new provisional government that included both Jimenista and Horacista ministers and called for new elections to be held at the beginning of 1904. However, once in command, Morales had no desire to relinquish the presidency. Contrary to his former promises to reinstate Jimenes to executive power, Morales now sought the support of the Horacistas who had no desire to see Jimenes return to power.

Thus, for the coming elections Morales set up a new ticket in which he was candidate for president and Ramón Cáceres, a first cousin of Horacio Vásquez, was the candidate for vice president. The Jimenistas immediately felt betrayed and rose up in arms to impose their candidate by force. Once again there was civil war. This time it was called the Revolucion Desunionista and lasted until March 1904. Throughout this new revolution numerous battles took place in the country.

U.S. FINANCIAL INTERVENTION

Morales held the upper hand in this struggle because of the support of the United States. In exchange for this aid, Morales accepted the demands of the U.S. government to respect the agreements made by his predecessors in regard to the Improvement Company and to allow the United States to build lighthouses along the Dominican coast to facilitate the navigation of ships passing through the Panama Canal that was then under construction. Protection of its interests in the Panama Canal was now a primary concern of the U.S. government, which began competing against the traditional interests of the European powers in the Caribbean.

The whole Caribbean area was of vital importance to the United States, which did not wish to see its navigation routes to the nearly completed canal threatened by unfriendly European powers. U.S. control of the Caribbean depended on stability in the area, but recent history had shown that countries such as Cuba, the Dominican Republic, Nicaragua, Honduras, Haiti, Venezuela, and El Salvador suffered from chronic internal political struggles and economic backwardness that often left them heavily indebted with European creditors. According to existing international practices, creditor nations had the right to use force against the debtor nations to make them pay. To protect its own strategic interests against any possible European interference, the United States invoked the Monroe Doctrine, which stated that it would not consent to any European power again occupying territory in Latin America.

The Dominican Republic was still of vital concern to the U.S. government, despite the fact that after the Spanish-American War of 1898, the United States had lost interest in Samaná as it now possessed Guantánamo in Cuba and several other bays in Puerto Rico. But after Heureaux's death the Dominican Republic was continually threatened with armed invasion by various European powers that insisted in collecting the debts it owed to the European bondholders.

On two occasions, in 1900 and 1903, the Italian, Belgian, and German governments had even sent warships to Santo Domingo to force rapid payment. To U.S. President Theodore Roosevelt these threats were unacceptable for the risks they posed to the Panama Canal's defense. He wanted to remove the Dominican Republic, as well as the other Caribbean countries, from the sphere of European influence and force the Caribbean and Central American governments to no longer contract loans in Europe.

In June 1904, the arbitration board set up by the Protocol of 1903 obliged the Improvement Company to accept the payment of $4,500,000 for its properties and interests in the Dominican Republic. At the same time, it imposed on the Dominican government the obligation to set aside revenues coming from the customs offices in Montecristi, Puerto Plata, Samaná, and Sánchez for payment of this debt. To collect these revenues the government of the United States was to name a financial agent who would act as counselor for the Dominican government and without whose consent no expense nor payment could take place.

This arbitration decision, called the Laudo Arbitral, was not acceptable to either the European bondholders or the Dominican creditors who saw their own possibilities of repayment decreased because the customs revenues of the nonsugar ports were now designated to serve the Improvement Company's debt. The Laudo Arbitral was also displeasing to the politicians in Montecristi and Puerto Plata since they would have little influence over the new financial agent. But what was most offensive to the Dominicans was the fact that the financial agent chosen by the arbitrators was John T. Abbot, a high official of the Improvement Company.

Despite this opposition, Morales's government eagerly accepted these initiatives of the United States. Having a precarious political base, Morales realized that the United States would have to use its warships in order to install the financial agent. From the very beginning, Morales worked to strengthen his government through an intimate alliance with the United States and in March 1904, he even proposed to the U.S. State Department a protectorate treaty for 50 years.

The elections, which had been postponed because of the civil war, were finally held on May 31, with Morales and Ramón Cáceres elected president and vice-president. Including both Jimenistas and Horacistas as ministers in an effort to present a front of national unity, the new government formally took office on June 19, 1904, while negotiations over the debt were still being conducted.

In view of Morales's inclination to reach an understanding along the lines set up by president Theodore Roosevelt, the United States decided to pursue the alliance even further. At the end of September, the U.S. secretary of state asked the Dominican government if it was willing to request that the United States take official charge of all customs offices in the country so as to distribute revenues equitably among both foreign and domestic creditors, including the Improvement Company. Although it took some effort to convince all of his officials to agree, Morales finally managed to have his ministers approve a new agreement that invalidated the Laudo Arbitral and left more income in the hands of the Dominican government.

This new agreement was negotiated rapidly and was formally signed by representatives of both governments on February 7, 1905. The U.S. government promised to take charge of all the obligations of the Dominican government, both foreign and domestic. In exchange for this service it was also to take charge of all customs receipts, distributing them in the following manner: 45 percent of the total was to be handed over to the Dominican government to attend to its administrative needs. The remaining 55 percent was to be used by the U.S. government to

pay customs employees and to amortize the foreign and domestic debt. The agreement also established that as long as the
entire debt was not completely paid, there could not be any
modification of the customs duties without the consent of the
president of the United States. The Dominican government could
abolish or reduce export taxes, but it could not increase them
nor increase the public debt without the consent of the U.S.
president. The government of the United States, at the request
of the Dominican Republic, would decide how to help the Dominican Republic reestablish its credit, preserve order, increase
the efficiency of the civil administration, and promote material
progress.

When Roosevelt presented this agreement for Senate approval, he justified the document by saying that in recent years
the conditions in the Dominican Republic had been deteriorating because of the many disturbances and revolutions, and because of the debts contracted beyond the capacity of the Republic to pay. He emphasized that certain foreign countries had
long felt aggrieved because of the nonpayment of debts due to
their citizens, and threatened to intervene to forcefully collect
their debts.

For Roosevelt, that was a legitimate procedure approved
by the International Court in Hague that had been recently applied in Venezuela. Therefore, the United States could not prevent its application without openly confronting the creditor
countries or without proposing some feasible alternative. Because the first course of action was not in the best interests of
the United States, he deemed necessary to exercise control of
the Dominican customs houses until the country was financially rehabilitated. He justified his action by reminding the U.S.
Congress that under the Monroe Doctrine the United States
could not see any European power seize and permanently occupy the territory of any of the American republics. In view of
this dilemma, Roosevelt added, the United States should not

adhere to its usual attitude of nonintervention, and should exercise its influence to help the Dominican Republic to get out of the financial embroilment.

The U.S. Senate refused to ratify this project on the grounds that it established a protectorate over the Dominican Republic and that was not the intention of the American people. The arrangement came to a standstill until the negotiators devised a legal formula to put it in operation as a *modus vivendi*, that is, as a temporary solution to the problem of collecting the customs duties and of paying the public debt of the Republic.

The concept of a protectorate that was implicit in the convention was suspended, but the other provisions were put into operation by a decree issued on March 31, 1905, in which President Morales authorized the president of the United States to appoint someone to receive the customs duties and distribute them according to the agreement.

The European greatly favored this arrangement because now the U.S. government guaranteed the repayment of their loans. The Improvement Company, however, protested since it lost control of the customs offices in the north and now would be treated as just another creditor without any special privileges. The administrator of the customs was now a U.S. official who had worked in customs receivership in the Philippines after these islands fell under American control during the Spanish-American War.

THE DOMINICAN-AMERICAN CONVENTION

Following the establishment of the General Customs Receivership, the Dominican government began to receive more funds than it had under the previous system. The 45 percent delivered in a regular manner guaranteed enough income for Morales's government to attend to the most urgent administrative needs for 1905, although it could not guarantee that Morales stay in power.

The negotiations over the Agreement and the *modus vivendi* had again stirred up interparty rivalries. The Revolución Desunionista had ended during the preceding year largely due to the temporary disembarking of U.S. troops that forced the rebels to lay down their arms. For example, in February 1904, a U.S. cruiser bombarded rebel forces besieging the capital from the eastern side of the Ozama River. In order to make peace in the Northwest, Morales had to please two Jimenista leaders, Demetrio Rodríguez and Desiderio Arias, who demanded that they and their partisans be appointed to the majority of public offices in their province.

Morales had great difficulty maintaining equilibrium within his government. The Jimenistas resented the power of the Horacistas over Congress and the cabinet and distrusted Morales for having betrayed them the previous year. The Horacistas strongly disliked the increasing efforts of the Jimenistas to attract Morales to their side and pressured the president to replace all Jimenistas in the government with Horacistas. Such pressures grew as time passed, especially after Horacio Vásquez's brother presented the thesis that the whole government should be made up of Horacista ministers and officials. Vice-President Cáceres supported his party on this point and on several occasions forced Morales to remove the Jimenista ministers.

By December 1905, Morales had lost all control over his government because his officials only obeyed Horacista Vice-President Cáceres. Morales tried to regain power through a demonstration of force utilizing several U.S. naval units that were anchored in the capital. Boats filled with U.S. marines armed with machine-guns were lowered to patrol the Ozama River. This maneuver only further irritated the Horacistas in the government who were willing to fight the marines in case they disembarked or fired on the city.

The first weeks of December were a period of intense political activity in Santo Domingo where it was evident that Morales was no longer in command. Under Horacista pressure, the president was forced to place the Army Headquarters of the city in the hands of a radical young Horacista general, Luis Tejera. The Horacistas also demanded that the general's father, Emiliano Tejera, be appointed as minister of foreign affairs. Other public positions and ministries were also placed in the hands of Cáceres's friends at his insistence.

Morales wanted to react by allying with the Jimenistas in a coup d'état against his own cabinet to expel the Horacistas. On December 24, 1905 he secretly left the capital for the neighboring town of Haina in the company of Enrique Jimenes, a nephew of Juan Isidro, expecting to find men, arms, and munitions awaiting him. Morales found nothing instead. On learning of the maneuver, the Horacistas detached troops to pursue the president.

On his flight to Azua, Morales fractured his leg and had to beg clemency from his enemies who, through the intervention of Emiliano Tejera and the U.S. minister, granted him his life in exchange for his resignation and departure from the country. The executive power was then held by the cabinet until Cáceres officially took over the presidency on December 29, and put the government under exclusive Horacista control.

Like other presidents before him, Cáceres had to handle the debt problem. The *modus vivendi* was functioning well and in the past eight months the Dominican government had enjoyed an unprecedented abundance of funds. However, the debt was still too high, and it was known that many of the claims were fraudulent. One study made by Jacob Hollander, a financial expert sent by Roosevelt to determine the real amount of the debt, established that in the middle of 1905 the Republic owed more than $40 million both in the country and abroad. According to Hollander, this sum could be reduced by more than half for lack of legitimacy.

At that time, customs revenues barely reached $2 million a year. Although some $100,000 was deposited each month in the National City Bank of New York to comply with the *modus vivendi*, it was clear to everyone that this sum was insufficient to satisfy all the claims. Cáceres and the U.S. government then decided to use Hollander's idea for an adjustment plan in order to lower the debt to less than 20 million.

Negotiations began in March, 1906, between the Dominican Finance Minister Federico Velázquez, and a U.S. financial expert. These two men examined each of the relevant documents, and with the support of the U.S. government forced the creditors to accept a reduction that, in many cases, was greater than 50 percent of their claims. Many creditors protested, but both governments remained inflexible and in September 1906, the majority of the claimants had accepted the adjustment plan that reduced the debt to only $17 million.

The next step was to consolidate the debt in such a manner that the Republic would have only one creditor. It was also in the interest of the United States to eliminate once and for all European interference in the Dominican Republic and to replace this influence with a U.S. financial protectorate as established in the 1905 agreement. On several occasions, Roosevelt had shown that this was the objective of his Caribbean policy, especially when construction of the Panama Canal reaffirmed the strategic value of the Antilles. The U.S. government therefore officially backed the Dominican government in its efforts to obtain a loan of $20 million from Kuhn, Loeb & Company, a New York bank. While $17 million of this sum were to be used to cancel pending debts, the rest was to be used in public works projects and other investments.

This loan was granted in September 1906 and at the beginning of December the Dominican government managed to have almost all its creditors sign the adjustment plan with the understanding that they would receive their money within a brief period of time. In return for the guarantee that the U.S. offered to Kuhn, Loeb & Company, the U.S. government imposed on the Dominican Republic similar conditions to those stipulated in the 1905 agreement. The Dominican government was to surrender the administration and control of its customs to the United States until the debt was paid, and also promised not to modify its tariffs nor increase its public debt without the previous consent of the president of the United States.

For payment of the debt, 50 percent of the customs revenues was to be deposited in a New York bank. Another 5 percent was allocated for the salaries of the customs employees, and the remaining 45 percent was to be delivered to the Dominican government to cover its administrative costs. These conditions were fixed in the Dominican-American Convention of 1907 that was approved by the Dominican Congress on May 3. The United States now had complete control over Dominican finances as well as the right to interfere in Dominican politics whenever it considered that the operations of the customs receivership or the compliance with the convention were threatened.

RAMON CACERES AND THE U.S. PROTECTORATE

Dominican negotiators Emiliano Tejera and Federico Velázquez argued that the Dominican-American Convention was the only practical response to the continual demands from both the European creditors and the U.S. government about the debt. As a financial tool, the convention was an effective means of untangling the debt. As a political agreement, the dependency on the United States that it imposed on the Dominican people was too high a price. But judging from the events that took place in other Caribbean countries at that time, there were not many ways to escape from the bankruptcy inherited from Heureaux.

The convention provided the same results as the *modus vivendi*. Contraband was liquidated, customs accounting systems were refined, leaks and embezzlement were checked, and the border customs houses were reorganized. These improvements meant a noticeable increase in revenues. In 1904, after the establishment of the receivership, customs duties provided an income of $1.8 million. In 1905, it rose to $2.8 million; in 1906, to $3.7 million; in 1907, to $3.9 million; in 1908, to $4 millon; in 1909, to $3.8 million; and in 1910, to $4.7 million. Thus, within five years customs revenues tripled, as did the revenues of the Dominican state.

There were other factors that also contributed to increase the country's wealth. Exploitation of new agricultural lands initiated by foreign and Dominican capitalists led to increased production and exportation of sugar, coffee, cacao, and tobacco. The rise in prices of these products on the international market also increased revenues and initiated a period of national affluence as yet unknown. Thus, the regime of Ramón Cáceres became the stable and rich government so long awaited by the Dominican people and it enjoyed ample popular support.

The Cáceres government did not begin smoothly, however. One of Caceres's first acts was to put down a revolt by the Jimenistas in the northwest that broke out as soon as they learned that Morales had been overthrown. For some time the northwest had been the main Jimenista bastion under the leadership of the caudillos Demetrio Rodríguez and Desiderio Arias. These two rebel leaders attacked the cities of Santiago and Puerto Plata at the beginning of January 1906. These attacks failed, and in one of the battles General Rodríguez was killed, forcing Arias and his followers to retreat to Montecristi and the northwest countryside. The rebellion spread in the following months as Arias and his men carried out guerrilla warfare against the government until Cáceres devised a plan of pacifying the northwestern region.

With Horacista troops recruited from the provinces, Cáceres arrived in Santiago. From there, he ordered the concentration of the northwestern population with their livestock into a certain number of towns within a given time period. After this period expired, the government troops combed the area and killed all remaining livestock to deprive the guerrillas of their main food source. At the end of the campaign, in which each of the commanders followed his orders as he saw fit, the northwest was strewn with the carcasses of animals and left with its economy ruined. The Jimenista leaders were then forced to flee to Haiti to avoid harsher penalties. Although the population had been militarily pacified, the campaign actually increased resentment against the Horacistas and against the U.S. government, which was accused of favoring Cáceres.

A few months later, a nephew of Juan Isidro Jimenes, Enrique, organized a maritime expedition that landed in the north and incited the Jimenistas to again rebel, but this revolt was also quickly repressed. By the middle of 1907, peace and order reigned throughout the country, and Cáceres continued to rule with a strong arm to prevent new rebellions. From the very beginning, he had invested large sums of money to purchase arms and other equipment to improve the combat capacity of the army that he wished to convert into a peacekeeping force at the service of the president and independent from the regional military caudillos.

Once peace was achieved, Cáceres proposed to reform the Constitution of 1896. This was done in 1907, but the president was displeased with the results and convoked a new constitutional assembly that worked in Santiago from November 1907 until April 1908. The new constitution reorganized the Dominican political system to create a strong executive power, but with juridical mechanisms to protect human rights. The vice-presidency was eliminated since it was considered a contributing factor to the continual political instability inasmuch as the friends and supporters of vice-presidents were always conspiring. The presidential term was set at six years, and a bicameral legislature with a Senate and Chamber of Deputies was established. Special executive powers formerly held by the cabinet were suppressed in order to make those powers the exclusive prerogative of the president.

One of the most important chapters of the new constitution pertained to the provincial governments. Until then, provincial governors had both political and military functions that gave them a free hand in the public administration of the provinces under their command. The new constitution created only civil governors who were to be in charge of administrative and political affairs, and military matters were left to army officials specifically appointed for this task. This article was thus part of Cáceres's plan to remove the army from local caudillo influences and turn it into a professional body under direct presidential control.

To effectively remove the old caudillos from politics and keep them out of his new presidentially-controlled army, Cáceres created a special account in the national budget entitled "For Generals at the Orders of the President of the Republic," from which the generals would receive a stipend or pension in return for their political neutrality. Those military men who could not be retired from active duty were transfered to regions where they had no local political ties and where they were used to strengthen the role of the army as a peace-keeping force. Cáceres also named young Cibaeño General Alfredo María Victoria as chief of the army of Santo Domingo in order to direct the reorganization of the Army. Thus, he snubbed the other young generals including Luis Tejera, governor of Santo Domingo Province and son of Emiliano Tejera, the minister of foreign relations.

The new constitution was put in force on April 1, 1908. Plans were then made for new general elections since Cáceres was concluding the presidential term begun by Morales Languasco in 1904. Because the major candidates were to be from the Horacista party, many wanted Horacio Vásquez to be the official candidate. However, Cáceres, at the urging of his friends, decided to run himself and he even received the indirect encouragement of Vásquez, who did not wish to present a separate candidacy. Elections were held on May 30 with the sole candidacy of Ramón Cáceres for president. The Jimenistas, knowing that they would lose, only ran candidates for Congress. On July 1, 1908, Cáceres was formally sworn in as president for the next six years.

Cáceres decided to invest the surpluses left each year from the customs revenues in the country's infrastructure. He began with the construction of a new branch of the Central Dominican Railway so that Moca was connected to the usual run between Santiago and Puerto Plata. He also installed new telegraph lines and reorganized the postal system so as to improve communications. The nation's most important ports and docks were also rebuilt, while new lighthouses were built along the coast. Work on two highways to connect the capital with the south and the Cibao was also begun. A Public Works Administration was created to direct these projects, while a U.S. engineer was appointed to oversee construction. Funds were also set aside for new schools, the number of which increased from some 200 in 1904 to 526 in 1910. Many of the new schools were located in rural areas.

As the government increased its reserves, it also began to recover various concessions that were deemed prejudicial to the national interest. The monopoly formerly granted to the Clyde Steamship Company to transport merchandise and passengers between Santo Domingo and New York was canceled, and the administration of the docks in San Pedro de Macorís was removed from private hands.

Once peace had been restored to the country, Cáceres concerned himself with legislation pertaining to many aspects of public life that had been ignored for years. In March 1907, he promulgated a road law whereby local residents were required to keep their roads in good condition. The following month he passed another law on the colonization and development of the unsettled border areas that had been left uninhabited for decades, allowing the Haitians to gradually take over the best lands. In 1909, a General Directorate of Agriculture was created to promote agricultural development. In 1910, two experimental farm schools were begun in Moca and Haina for the rational and scientific teaching of agriculture.

Cáceres's support of agriculture came as a result of the many changes that had taken place during the past 20 years with the development of the sugar industry and the new cacao and coffee plantations in the humid regions of the country. To further favor development of these export products, Cáceres passed a Ley de Franquicias Agrarias that placed under state protection all investments made in the planting, cultivating, manufacturing, and exporting of these products. Construction of factories, bridges, and docks, and the installation of aqueducts, telegraphs, telephones, and electrical plants were placed under the same protection and granted fiscal incentives.

For the first time since the end of the Haitian occupation in 1844 the government began to take agriculture seriously and to realize that the country's wealth was rooted in the cultivation of the soil. Although such traditional forms of livelihood as livestock raising were never completely abandoned, Cáceres's government marked the beginning of a period of active legislation in favor of agricultural development that would be the permanent concern of all successive governments. One law of particular impact was passed in April, 1911 for the partition of communal lands. This law was designed to regulate the buying and selling of cultivable *terrenos comuneros* which were now acquiring greater value as cacao, sugar cane, and coffee, as well as other crops such as bananas, were rapidly spreading all over the country.

As early as April 1906, Cáceres had decreed the complete exoneration from taxation of all sugar produced and exported from the country. By legislating in favor of the large foreign-controlled sugar companies, Cáceres believed that the country would benefit through increased production and new sources of employment. However, this law, along with the one passed to regulate the partition of communal lands, soon allowed these corporations to appropriate the best farmlands in the south and the east of the country. The sugar companies enjoyed the complicity of some native notaries and surveyors who discovered how to falsify the titles of these communal lands to allow the *ingenios* to buy them at extremely low prices or to appropriate them without paying compensation to their ancient owners.

Cáceres's economic policy created resentment among Dominican property owners and businessmen who saw that although the foreigners were exonerated from taxation, their own businesses were being forced to pay new taxes that were created to provide more funds for the state. The so-called Stamp Act of July 1910, greatly affected hundreds of producers of rum and other alcoholic beverages and created great unpopularity for both Cáceres and Treasury Minister Federico Velázquez. Another group highly displeased with Cáceres included merchants and moneylenders who had enjoyed privileges under the Lilís government. Although they had signed the Adjustment Plan, they now refused to receive any payments from the government and for several years insisted on a better treatment for their claims.

The former Lilisistas were not the only ones unhappy with the Government. The campaign in the northwest, the forced retirement of many old caudillo leaders, the slighting of certain Horacista generals, and the inability of the Jimenistas to share political power, all produced an atmosphere of opposition among politicians and military men. By 1910, both the Horacista and Jimenista parties were divided. Almost all the

Horacista military men who were displeased with Cáceres began to seek the support of Horacio Vásquez to rebel against the government.

Because Cáceres was Vásquez's cousin and the government was of Vásquez's party, Vásquez preferred to leave the country and live in New York to prevent the discord from continuing and the malcontents from using him to topple the government. Nevertheless, many unhappy Horacistas, former Lilisistas, and Jimenistas followed him to New York where they finally managed to convince him to sign a public letter denouncing various policies, especially the adjustment plan. This letter circulated widely in the country at the beginning of 1910 and definitely divided Cáceres and Vásquez, thus destroying the remaining unity of the Horacista party.

Though the Horacista party was divided, the civil and intellectual leaders of the Jimenista party supported the government's reconstruction efforts, and even Juan Isidro Jimenes spoke favorably of Cáceres from exile. However, the Jimenista military caudillos under the leadership of Desiderio Arias continued wanting to overthrow Cáceres and began supporting the dissident Horacistas. The *bolos* thus ended up divided into two groups now alluding to the feet of the rooster. The *bolos pata blanca* ("white-legged") were comprised of the civilian and intellectual wing, whereas the *bolos pata prieta* ("black-legged") represented the military *caudillos*.

Meanwhile, on learning that some of his own followers were planning to kidnap the president and force him and his army chief to resign, Horacio Vásquez left New York to retire in Saint Thomas. Foreseeing that some were planning to assassinate Cáceres, Vásquez let it be known that he would not participate in any subversive plots, much less do anything to put the life of his cousin in danger. But other conspiracies were already in progress. In 1909, the U.S. government discovered a plot to invade the country by former President Morales Languasco. In

Morales's documents captured by Puerto Rican authorities there was also clear proof that one of those implicated in the plot was none other than General Luis Tejera, who still resented being denied full control of the army.

Cáceres did nothing to detain Tejera, who was the son of his own minister of foreign affairs and had been governor of the Santo Domingo Province. Believing that no one in the capital wished to make an attempt on his life, Cáceres took no extra precautions, but his confidence soon proved fatal. On the afternoon of November 19, 1911, while taking one of his customary Sunday rides down the new highway to Haina, a group of conspirators led by Luis Tejera attempted to kidnap him. When the president's aide-de-camp opened fire, the conspirators returned the fire and fatally wounded the president.

The assassination ended Cáceres's five-year attempt to reorganize the country. The conspirators were pursued, captured, and executed on the orders of the chief of the army Alfredo Victoria, a personal rival of Luis Tejera. Although a wave of repression moved over the entire country, the Bolo leaders under Desiderio Arias took advantage of the power vacuum and organized a new rebellion in the hope of imposing one of their own men as president. Once again, political instability became the rule in the Dominican Republic.

15.
The collapse
of sovereignty
(1911-1916)

POLITICAL CHAOS AND U.S. INVOLVEMENT

The death of Cáceres created a political vacuum that Dominican caudillos and politicians immediately tried to fill. Their
long-repressed antagonisms erupted into violent confrontations
and dragged the country into an intense period of civil wars
which eventually allowed the resurgence of the Jimenista party.
Under the political and military preponderance of the guerrilla
caudillo, Desiderio Arias, the *pata prieta* faction of the Jimenista party took the revolutionary initiative. Both Juan Isidro
Jimenes and Horacio Vásquez refused to return from abroad
since neither wanted to be connected in any way to the conspiracy against Cáceres.

The most important task ahead was to elect a new president.
This was a serious problem because the chief of the army Alfredo
Victoria was opposed to the candidacies of both Jimenes and Vásquez as well as to that of the finance minister Federico Velázquez,
who for years had been the *eminence gris* behind the Cáceres administration. Meanwhile, the executive power remained in the
hands of the cabinet until Congress could elect a new president.
For two full months, December 1911 and January 1912, Congress

worked frantically without being able to choose Cáceres's successor, as the country again prepared for civil war.

Alfredo Victoria did not want to relinquish power but lacked
the constitutional age required for the presidency. Therefore,
he forced Congress to elect his uncle, Senator Eladio Victoria, a
former minister in the government of Morales. Victoria took
office on February 27, 1912, with the support of Juan Isidro
Jimenes and the bolos *pata blanca* who quickly joined the government. Because the decision of Congress was the result of
military threats, and the Horacistas had no desire to lose the
power that they had exercised for several years, Horacio Vásquez
returned from Puerto Rico and organized a rebellion that quickly
spread throughout the Cibao. The followers of Vásquez and Arias
then united for the following year in a common effort to overthrow the government.

Eladio Victoria was little more than a puppet for his nephew and did not question Alfredo's decision to confront the rebellion with the utmost violence. Repression became universal
in all areas controlled by the government. Jails were filled with
political prisoners, and government executions were carried out
by the dozens. This civil war, the bloodiest in Dominican history, became famous because of the violent battles in La Vega,
Santiago, and the northwest. The fiscal reserves of more than 4
million pesos left by Cáceres in the treasury were soon spent by
the government in its military operations. The payment of salaries for public employees soon had to be suspended. By the
middle of the year it was already evident that the government
needed more funds to end the war.

The United States believed that Victoria would soon squelch
the revolt and continued handing out the monthly allotments
of the customs receipts due to the government. Taking advantage of the war, Arias gained control of the customs houses along
the border, while the Haitians profited from the disruptions
caused by the war and made further encroachments into Do-

minican territory, causing the U.S. government to consider seriously the possibility of military intervention as established by the Convention of 1907.

At the end of September, U.S. President William Taft sent a pacification commission to Santo Domingo to negotiate with the end of the civil war and to fix a provisional border with Haiti that would guarantee customs operations and the removal of Haitian settlers from Dominican lands. Two years earlier the United States had agreed with both governments to act as a mediator in border disputes, and now, by giving a broad interpretation to the Convention of 1907, the U.S. president sought to resolve the two problems at once.

The commission arrived in Santo Domingo accompanied by 750 U.S. marines and it immediately began negotiations under the threat of direct military intervention if U.S. demands were not met. At first the commissioners tried to arrange an agreement whereby President Eladio Victoria would remain in power until 1914 while his nephew would be removed as chief of the army. But as both men were equally unpopular, the commission then reached an agreement with the rebels whereby a provisional government would be set up headed by Archbishop Adolfo Alejandro Nouel.

The archbishop, who had served as liaison in the negotiations and who was a respected clergyman, was soon accepted by both sides. Eladio Victoria resigned from the presidency on November 26, 1912 and Congress elected Nouel to replace him on November 30. Nouel was named provisional president and charged with the specific task of organizing free elections within one year.

No sooner had Archbishop Nouel taken office than Desiderio Arias declared himself in open disobedience to the government. This situation was made even more unstable because Arias then headed the Jimenista faction who controlled the northwest as well as the provinces of La Vega and Santiago. With this rebellion, Arias intended to force Nouel to find government positions for a huge number of his followers, but there were not enough positions in the entire government to fill Arias's demands. Although Nouel personally went to Montecristi to seek a truce in January 1913, the following month Arias brought several hundreds of his men to the capital to impose their demands on the president.

The Horacistas demanded that the government not surrender more control to their political enemies. Caught in the middle of this controversy, Nouel vacillated between the two groups, appointing and firing public employees and ending up not satisfying anyone. Realizing that he was incapable of governing, Nouel wanted to hand in his resignation that he had drawn up after only a month in office.

The United States, however, urged him to stay on and offered him both economic and military aid. The U.S. government offered him a loan of $1.5 million to help the Dominican government pay the salaries of public employees who had not been paid for six months. Depressed and on the verge of a nervous breakdown, Nouel had no desire to stay. At the end of March, he left for Barahona where he resigned for reasons of ill health. In the four months of his regime he had done little more than cede to the pressures of Arias and his supporters.

The Senate then met to elect a new provisional president to organize the coming elections. Once again, however, political divisions prevented Congress from reaching a majority for any of the three principal candidates, Vásquez, Jimenes, and Velázquez. Two weeks passed before Senator José Bordas Valdez finally suggested that they should choose a candidate independent of the three main contenders. Congress agreed and elected Bordas as a temporary solution to end the party rivalries. As soon as Bordas took office on April 14, 1913, the parties began their campaigns for the coming elections.

For a few months everything remained calm while the politicians prepared for the elections. The United States offered Bordas the same support that they had offered Nouel and began negotiations with various banks to procure the loan for $1.5 million. But, contrary to expectations, it soon became evident that Bordas wished to manipulate the coming elections to stay in power. The first to react were the Horacistas, as Bordas had belonged to this party and had promised to work harmoniously with Vásquez. Bordas now wished to become independent and to take advantage of the divisions within his party. To win support of the Jimenistas, Bordas named Desiderio Arias as government delegate in the Cibao. In order to gain popularity in the province of Azua which then stretched to the border, he appointed the region's main caudillo, General Luis Felipe Vidal, as government delegate in the South.

The Horacistas felt particularly betrayed when Bordas took away their control over the Dominican Central Railway and auctioned it off to one of Arias's supporters for $130,000, although everyone knew that Arias would never pay the government. This railway from Santiago to Puerto Plata had previously provided enough funds and jobs to keep the Horacista clientele in the Cibao satisfied after the U.S. government had taken over the administration of the customs receipts. Thus, while the Jimenistas had to resort to loans from local merchants and property owners to survive after the fall of Cáceres, the Horacistas had been able to preserve their control over the railroad even during the dictatorship of Eladio Victoria. To lose that control now, on the eve of new elections, was intolerable.

On September 1, 1913, Horacio Vásquez and his men again went to war in what was called the *Revolución del Ferrocarril* (the Railway Revolution) and proclaimed a new provisional government under Vásquez. This revolt was nevertheless short-lived since Bordas had the military resources of the Jimenistas led by Arias, and the military and diplomatic support of the

United States. The U.S government informed Vásquez that it would not recognize a de facto government and, in case he won, the Customs Receivership would suspend the delivery of funds to the Dominican government. At the same time the U.S. State Department ordered its minister in Santo Domingo to negotiate an agreement between the government and the Horacistas.

This mediation was successful. The Horacistas agreed to put down their arms with the understanding that the United States would guarantee free and honest elections, scheduled for the following December to select new *ayuntamientos* as well as the deputies for the constitutional assembly. The constitutional assembly, in turn, would make the necessary legal reforms for the presidential elections to be held in June of the next year. Bordas agreed to appease several Horacista leaders by appointing them to various political and military posts within the government.

The municipal and congressional elections were held as promised on December 6, 1915, but despite all guarantees, they were flagrantly fraudulent. In order to win them, Bordas sent troops to break up all political meetings held on the eve of the elections and jailed dozens of his political opponents. In addition, many of the votes already in the ballot boxes were changed and the results were totally altered. The reaction to this electoral fraud was so great that the constitutional assembly was unable to carry on its work normally as even the Jimenistas worked to prevent Bordas from being reelected.

At the beginning of January 1914, the Bordas government was suffering extreme financial difficulties. In addition to the $386,000 owed in back salaries, the government needed another $740,000 to pay pending claims. Even congressmen threatened that they would not continue working if the government did not pay them. To support Bordas, the U.S. State Department ordered the Customs Receivership to advance $40,000 from the customs revenues. And, in exchange for allowing the

Dominican government to use an additional $1,200,000 in unsold bonds from the loan of 1907, the United States made Bordas accept the appointment of a U.S. comptroller to supervise public expenditures. This "financial expert" arrived immediately in Santo Domingo and the Customs Receivership continued delivering funds to Bordas.

Meanwhile, the time period set for presidential elections expired on the anniversary of Bordas' ascension to the presidency without any elections being held. The Horacistas took advantage of this to proclaim that Bordas was no longer the legal president and again rebelled. Horacio Vásquez returned from Puerto Rico where he had taken refuge after his defeat the previous year and personally led his party in the rebellion. Bordas had enough money to buy off some of the Horacista military leaders and managed to keep the major cities under his control for several weeks. During that period, Bordas staged fake elections on June 15 by which he was elected president until 1920.

Because of these new farce, the revolt gained even more force and the revolutionaries even received aid from the Haitian government. The Horacistas were also joined by the Jimenistas and the followers of the Southern leader Luis Felipe Vidal, which were called Vidalistas in a common effort to overthrow Bordas. In July 1914 intense fighting took place throughout the country, especially in Puerto Plata. At the end of the month, the United States intervened again and forced the contenders to agree on a truce while a new mediation commission arrived from Washington with a truce proposal drawn up by President Woodrow Wilson himself, called the Wilson Plan. The United States threatened that U.S. marines would be sent from Guantánamo to protect U.S. interests in Santo Domingo if the Dominicans did not accept Wilson's plan.

According to the Wilson Plan, the rebels were to lay down their arms and agree on the selection of a provisional president. If not, the United States would choose a president and

keep him in power by force. The new president would then organize a government to hold elections that would be supervised
by the United States. The government resulting from these elections was to be respected by all parties and would receive the
support of the United States, which henceforth would not tolerate new rebellions.

Humiliating as these terms were, the Dominicans had to accept them. Bordas resigned, and the leaders of the Horacista,
Jimenista, Vidalista, and Velazquista parties (the latter were followers of Federico Velázquez) chose Dr. Ramón Báez, the son of
Buenaventura Báez, as provisional president with the task of organizing new elections within three months. Báez took office on
August 27, 1914 and set to work to constitute a new government.
He took advantage of his position to bring the remains of his
father back to the country. He also worked to find government
jobs for his friends and for members of the Jimenista party of
which he was a sympathizer although not an active member. This
policy later worked in Jimenes's favor as the electoral laws were
prepared by government officials of Jimenista affiliations.

JUAN ISIDRO JIMENES AND THE U.S. TUTELAGE

The elections were finally held on October 25, 1914. Despite some irregularities they were free and Horacio Vásquez,
the loser, accepted the results. Juan Isidro Jimenes won with
the support of the Velazquista party that had joined the Jimenistas in exchange for 25 percent of the public offices in the
new government.

The new president took office on December 5, and two days
later named a cabinet comprised of members from the victori-
ous parties. Because the elections were hard fought, Congress
was seriously divided. There was a prevailing element of Arias's
supporters who, although nominally Jimenistas, owed their di-

rect allegiance to Arias. Jimenes took into account Arias's majority position within the party and named him secretary of war, thus giving him complete control of the armed forces.

Whoever was elected president at this time owed his position directly to U.S. political intervention since each crisis that had occurred after the death of Cáceres had ended with some kind of U.S. mediation or imposition. The past elections had been such an imposition, as had been the governments of Nouel and Bordas and the appointment of an U.S. comptroller whom Bordas accepted in order to retain U.S. support.

In the past 15 years, the United States had been moving toward a policy of political tutelage over the Caribbean and Central America that left no alternatives other than military and diplomatic intervention. This policy was based on the conviction that only by managing the financial affairs of these countries could the continual political instability and revolutions in the area be suppressed. To enforce the policy, the United States resorted to open intervention both through diplomatic channels and through military force.

When Jimenes took office, the U.S. State Department expressly stated its desire that the Dominican government formally approve the appointment of the U.S. comptroller so as to regularize his official position within the country. Jimenes confidentially promised the United States to legalize the status of the comptroller once he was sworn in, but instead he only submitted the matter to Congress for consideration. The deputies and senators rejected the recognition of the U.S. official and openly defied the pressure of the United States. The U.S. government then reacted by imposing the comptroller by force and ordered him to stay in the country where he was to supervise the delivery of customs revenues to the Dominican government and to sign all checks paying public expenditures.

The United States was working on two levels. Though weakening the Dominican government through financial intervention, the U.S. government also pressured Jimenes' political enemies to accept the new regime. In January 1915, the U.S. State Department issued a stern warning to the Horacistas who were involved in new political disturbances in Puerto Plata. Moreover, the secretary of state threatened to send naval forces if the opposition tried to block the financial and political reforms that Jimenes was supposed to make at the insistence of the U.S. government.

Jimenes himself, however, was not willing to accept all the reforms laid down by the United States. One of the main sources of conflict was the U.S. proposal for the creation of a national guard directly under the control of U.S. military personnel. This guard was to replace the existing Dominican armed forces then under the command of Desiderio Arias. The U.S. government also insisted that the director of public works could not be removed without the consent of the U.S. State Department. Jimenes refused to accept either of these demands.

The U.S. pressure created a political crisis within the government. Since Jimenes could not remove the comptroller, Congress threatened in April 1915, to have him impeached by the Senate. Although Jimenes sent a high-level commission to Washington to seek a diplomatic solution, the State Department maintained its position. These pressures coincided with the appearance of discord within the Dominican government itself. The old rivalries between the *bolos pata blanca* and the *bolos pata prieta* again flared up as Desiderio Arias tried to eliminate from the cabinet his old political enemy, Federico Velázquez, who was once again finance minister.

Jimenes's position became even more precarious the following July when a group of Horacista generals rebelled in the north and east in protest against Jimenes's inability to grant them all the public offices they demanded in return for their allegiance. Although Horacio Vásquez himself was not involved in this revolt, and even encouraged his followers to lay down their arms, the United States took advantage of the occasion to again warn Vásquez of the dangers brought about by his revolutionary activities, and again threatened to send troops to maintain order if necessary. The revolt ended two months later after the government agreed to grant various road construction contracts to rebel leaders and appointed some of them at the public posts they demanded.

While this rebellion was still taking place, another event was occurring on the other side of the island that foreshadowed events in the Dominican Republic. On July 28, 1915, the United States militarily occupied Haiti to put an end to that country's financial chaos and political instability. Although this event alerted many Dominicans to the seriousness of U.S. threats, it also allowed the U.S. State Department to take a harder line on Dominican intransigence.

When he arrived in the Dominican Republic the following October 19, the new U.S. diplomatic envoy, William Russell, who was occupying this post for the second time, presented the Dominican government with a diplomatic note. The note insisted that the Dominican government should approve the appointment of the comptroller, dissolve the Republican Guard, and create a police force and a national guard under the command of U.S. military officers appointed by the U.S. government.

The elderly Jimenes could not answer the note immediately because he had been out of the capital for two months recuperating from the pressures of the presidency. On returning to the capital, he met with his cabinet, Horacio Vásquez, and other opposition leaders to decide how to respond to the note. Together, government and opposition leaders, resolved to refuse the U.S. demands with dignity. Thus, on December 8 Jimenes sent the U.S. government another note expressing the Dominican people's firm opposition to all foreign interference in its internal affairs.

By the end of 1915 and the beginning of 1916, Jimenes was in a highly precarious political situation. The United States refused to offer any extra economic assistance until Jimenes acceded to its demands. The lack of resources to undertake public works and to cover administrative costs greatly weakened the government's position. Almost at the same time, Arias became openly disobedient to the President after Jimenes took the Central Railway from Arias's partisans and placed it under the administration of the Directorate of Public Works.

In view of the President's poor health, Arias was a particularly powerful adversary as he could count on the firm support of all the Jimenista congressmen and that of the armed forces that he commanded as minister of war. The conflict with Arias reached its climax the following April while the president was resting on the archbishop's farm located 24 kilometers west of Santo Domingo. Tired of Arias's insubordination, as well as his continual fights within the government, Jimenes finally gave orders on April 14 to arrest the commander of the Ozama Fortress and the chief of the national guard, both loyal to Arias, so as to proceed later against Arias himself. Arias responded by taking over the fortress despite preventive efforts by Jimenes's partisans and some Horacistas.

Jimenes now found himself outside the capital with his own secretary of war in open rebellion against the government. This situation greatly alarmed the Horacistas and *bolos pata blanca* who immediately gathered troops to march on the capital to confront Arias. The United States, which had previously confronted Arias in the northwest and along the frontier, also found the new developments particularly menacing, especially because Arias now appeared as the probable successor to Jimenes.

At the end of April, Arias and his followers along with some Horacista legislators decided to remove Jimenes by impeaching him before Congress. The U.S. minister interpreted this move as a coup d'état and offered Jimenes troops from the U.S. warships anchored off the Dominican coast. Although Jimenes preferred to accept only arms and munitions, the U.S. government decided to land the marines "to protect the lives and interests of the foreigners then in the city." The marines then surrounded the U.S. Legation, the Customs Receivership, and the Haitian Legation where there were various persons seeking political asylum.

Faced with the pressure from the U.S. government that he use the marines to return to power, and not wishing to be impeached by a Congress that he felt was dominated by antagonistic forces, President Jimenes resigned on May 7, 1916. The executive power then passed to the cabinet, and the U.S. government tried to pressure Arias into surrendering. Arias continued to resist, however, until May 13. Then, the chief of the U.S. naval forces presented him an ultimatum to either lay down his arms or the capital would be bombarded. To avoid open confrontation with the U.S. troops, Arias gathered his weapons and his men and returned to the northwest to fight on familiar ground.

On May 16, 1916, the U.S. marines occupied the capital and began sending troops to other parts of the country. Despite resistance by Arias and his followers in Puerto Plata and Mao in the northwest, the U.S. troops continued to occupy the rest of the country throughout June and July. By the end of this period, the U.S. soldiers controlled all of the most important military headquarters in the country as the politicians in the capital debated over the election of a new president.

As soon as Arias had left the capital, Congress began seeking a successor to Jimenes. The senators and deputies met for several weeks trying to find a suitable candidate. Since Congress was strongly divided, it was impossible to attain the majority required for the election of a president. The U.S. government was determined that the presidency not go to a partisan of Arias or to someone who would not accept the military and financial reforms proposed by the State Department. The two candidates with the greatest possibilities, the president of the Supreme Court, Federico Henríquez y Carvajal, and Don Jacinto de Castro, both had to be discarded. The first met opposition from the U.S. government who considered him too close to Arias. The second was rejected because he was a follower of Horacio Vásquez.

While Congress was in the midst of this argument, the United States advised the senators and deputies that it would maintain its occupation forces in the country until its demands were satisfied. This meant that the election of a new president would have to take place through negotiations with the U.S. government. Congress then took the United States by surprise by agreeing on the election of Dr. Francisco Henríquez y Carvajal, a brother of the Supreme Court president. Although he had resided in Cuba for 14 years, Dr. Henríquez promptly accepted, returned to the country, and took office on July 31.

The U.S. State Department informed Henríquez that the United States would not recognize his election if he did not accept its demands concerning the appointment of the comptroller, and the establishment of a national guard commanded by U.S. military officers. The U.S. minister warned that all funds coming from the customs receipts would be retained by his government until the Dominicans complied with those demands. Because Henríquez refused, on August 18 the Receiver General of Customs informed him that in accordance with the instructions sent from Washington it would surrender no more funds to the Dominican government until there was an understanding regarding "certain articles" in the Dominican-American Convention of 1907.

The government of Henríquez y Carvajal got off to a bad start. There was not one penny in the treasury to cover administrative expenses, the country was occupied by foreign soldiers, and the United States was threatening to not recognize his presidency if he did not comply with its demands. Henríquez argued that these demands violated the Dominican constitution as well as the nation's sovereignty, but the United States remained adamant. Fortified by its success in Haiti the preceding year when the United States had managed to set up a puppet government that ratified reforms similar to those now demanded of the Dominicans, the State Department continued to pressure Henríquez in the belief that the Dominicans would finally yield.

Nevertheless, the Dominicans did not yield. Public employees, from the ministers on down, continued in their posts without salary and even bought office materials with their own money. Commerce gradually became paralyzed because of the lack of money in circulation, but still nobody gave in. In an effort to save the situation, Henríquez finally agreed to accept the financial expert, but insisted that the Dominican armed forces would remain under Dominican control. The State Department rejected this compromise and demanded the rapid dissolution of the existing armed forces and the creation of a national guard under U.S. military officers.

Finally, on October 31, 1916, high officials of the State Department and the Navy Department met in Washington to decide whether to withdraw from the country or legalize the occupation since the situation could not continue indefinitely as it was. The war in Europe was a key issue in these deliberations. Knowing that the United States would soon go to war against Germany and that Arias, as well as all the important Jimenistas were pro-German, the officials agreed that the military occupation of the Dominican Republic was an advisable course of action. To leave the country under the domination of Arias while they were fighting the Germans was considered a serious threat to the United States as the Dominican territory could be used as a base of operations for the Germans and thus endanger navigation through the Panama Canal.

On November 22, the secretary of state recommended to President Wilson that he make a definite decision on the Dominican case and that "the only solution to the difficulty" was to formalize the military intervention. On November 26, Wilson accepted these recommendations and gave immediate instructions for Captain Harry S. Knapp to officially proclaim the military occupation of the Dominican Republic.

Three days later, on November 29, 1916, Knapp published a proclamation in which he announced that from that date forward the Dominican Republic was "in a state of military occupation by the forces under my command and remains submitted to the Military government and to the exercise of the Military Law applicable to such occupation." Knapp also announced that "Dominican laws will remain in effect as long as they are not in conflict with the purpose of the occupation or with the necessary regulations established to this effect." Dominican sovereignty had just collapsed.

16.
The U.S.
military
occupation
(1916-1924)

IMPOSING MILITARY RULE

In the days that followed Captain Harry S. Knapp's proclamation, the military government took various measures to ensure the complete control of the country. The first prohibited the carrying or possession of firearms, munitions, and explosives by Dominicans. The second ordered a strict censorship of the press. All news about the occupation that the newspapers wished to publish had to be previously submitted for prior examination by a local censor. The publication of expressions that tended "to incite hostility or resistance to the military government" was prohibited. Publication of proclamations and circulars containing "unfavorable opinions to the United States of America or to the military government in Santo Domingo" was also banned.

On December 8, 1916 Knapp announced the dismissal of President Henríquez's cabinet and declared their posts vacant. A few days later, on December 12, he named various U.S. marine officers to take charge of the ministries. Thus, with all major Dominican officials dismissed and with the U.S. State Department deeply involved with events in Europe, the administration of the Dominican Republic was virtually in the hands of the U.S. Department of the Navy. Moreover, this military government believed itself seriously committed to a long-term mission to correct the economic, political, and social life of the country according to the U.S. Navy's conception of a more stable order.

Knapp immediately set to work to repair the chaotic financial situation plaguing the country, a task made much easier by the release of the funds that had been withheld by the Customs Receivership. One of Knapp's first measures was to resume public employees' salaries that had been retained for months because of disagreements between the Dominican government and the U.S. Department of State after Jimenes's fall. This measure was meant to neutralize part of the antipathy toward the North Americans and was used to point out the improvement of the American occupation over the previous Dominican regimes. From then on, public employees regularly received their salaries.

The resumption of salary payments to public employees and the release of the customs revenues for government use were coupled with drastic measures to disarm the Dominican population. Indeed, the disarmament methods, which included arbitrary arrests, imprisonment, and torture, were applied so thoroughly that very few people wished to run the risk of keeping revolvers, rifles, shotguns, and munitions in their houses. At the same time, however, Knapp attempted to diffuse some of the antagonism provoked by these measures by seeking the collaboration of the most respected Dominican leaders as consultants and advisors.

Once a certain degree of stability had been achieved, the military government was able to devote itself to a series of long-term goals. The public works projects that had been planned during the government of Ramón Cáceres, but suspended after his assassination in 1911, were quickly resumed. Other goals included the reorganization of the public administration, the creation of a system of internal taxation, the establishment of a more modern system of public accounting, and the creation of a national guard that would replace the armed forces comprising Cáceres's Republican Guard and the old navy. The U.S. military regime also made plans to continue and complete the network of highways initiated under Cáceres and to establish a system of primary education that would diminish or eliminate illiteracy.

In April 1917, the Dominican National Guard was instituted with the aim of creating a body of native troops that could control revolutionary movements once the marines had left. At the beginning of May, the guard's leaders and commanders were chosen from among the U.S. marine officers so that recruits would be trained according to the rules of the U.S. Marine Corps and thus be an extension of that body. Many former members of the Dominican Navy and Republican Guard joined this new National Guard, and many unemployed youths took advantage of the occasion to begin a military career. Among these new recruits was Rafael Trujillo, a former telegraph operator in San Cristóbal, and one-time camp guard for a sugar company in the east. Trujillo joined the guard on December 18, 1918. In June 1921 the name of this body was changed to Dominican National Police.

In order to increase collection of internal taxes, the military government dictated a series of executive orders regulating the application of taxes on the manufacture of alcohol and other Dominican products, and regulating the collection of these taxes by means of a system of seals and stamps that permitted control over the national manufacturing production. The new system of collection, which had antecedents in the Law for Alcoholic Beverages decreed by the Cáceres government in 1910, forced producers to concentrate their stills and distilleries in the provincial capitals in order to facilitate tax collection. Despite protests, which the censor did not permit to be published, the military government continued this fiscal policy and thereby greatly increased the state's revenues. To centralize the collection of these taxes, the government created the General Directorate of Internal Revenue in August 1918.

Two other important measures affecting the increase of internal revenues were the property tax of 1919 and the Land Registration Law of 1920. The latter measure was instituted not only to increase the state's revenues, but also to further the process of modernizing the system of landownership begun in the 1911 with the Law of the Partition of Communal Lands. Both this law and the 1910 Law of Agricultural Franchises had given increased incentives to the sugar companies that wanted to expand their acreage at the expense of the owners of *terrenos comuneros*. The 1920 law was designed as a culmination of a modern land policy that would break forever the colonial land tenure system.

With the official entry of the United States into World War I in April 1917, the military government issued a proclamation warning sympathizers of Germany not to demonstrate their sympathies. More important than this warning, which caused the incarceration of many Dominicans and foreigners, was the suspension of the Dominican Republic's trade with Germany and its allies. A commission was created to control imports, the distribution of merchandise and food stuffs, and exports so as to prevent any transaction whatsoever with Germany or its allies.

ECONOMIC CHANGE DURING WORLD WAR I

During the war, many commercial houses had either to close their doors or reorient their business towards the United States. Thus, by the end of the war almost all Dominican commerce was tied to North America. This reorientation of Dominican trade was officially sanctioned by the Customs Tariff Act of 1919, which favored the entrance of the U.S. manufactured goods. According to this tariff, more than 245 U.S. articles were declared duty-free, while some 700 more products had their duties drastically reduced.

The increase in state revenues through new taxes and tariffs was greatly aided by the general prosperity of the country, especially after the termination of World War I. Worldwide shortages of tropical raw materials caused prices of Dominican products such as sugar, tobacco, cacao, and coffee to soar. Since 1910, the Dominican economy had rested on the production of sugar and cacao. which constituted four-fifths of the country's foreign earnings, with tobacco and coffee making up the remainder. The war had damaged beet sugar production in France, Russia, and Germany causing an enormous increase in the demand for cane sugar.

The rise in sugar prices had a positive effect on the whole of the Dominican economy. Although most of the direct benefits remained in the hands of the foreign owners of the sugar companies, there was a considerable increase in the salaries of sugar cane workers and also considerable benefits for the *colonos*, or tenant farmers, who owned their own sugar cane lands. This same process occurred with the cultivators and exporters of tobacco, cocoa, and coffee who, upon receiving more money for their products, increased their capacity to consume. The great increase in the demand for manufactured goods led merchants to import enormous quantities of articles produced abroad. Thus, as the price of a hundredweight of sugar rose from $5.50 in 1914, to $12.50 in 1918, and $22.50 in 1920, the Dominican economy grew to levels never before imagined.

This sudden and gigantic expansion of the economy was called "Dance of the Millions." During this short period, towns such as Santiago, La Vega, San Pedro de Macorís, and Puerto Plata acquired new urban status. Sugar made San Pedro de Macorís into a city with large houses of reenforced concrete and streetcars to transport passengers. Favored by the railroads, Puerto Plata, Santiago, La Vega, and Sánchez were converted into lively commercial centers that managed most of the cacao, coffee, and tobacco exports.

Day after day new buildings and stores rose up, while the merchant class enriched itself almost overnight. Some cities even installed electric lighting, paved their streets, and constructed sewage systems for the first time. There was also a marked animation in the cultural life of the various communities as social clubs proliferated, literary societies were founded, and theaters and parks were built.

Meanwhile, the military government, favored by the rise in revenues, dedicated itself to finishing the three major highway projects initiated in Cáceres's time. With little worry about the means of repayment, a new loan for $1.5 million was authorized in 1918 by the Department of State. The ready availability of such funds facilitated the construction of the new highways so that by May 1922, the Duarte Highway was inaugurated between Santo Domingo and Santiago, linking the towns of Bonao, La Vega, and Moca. The construction of two other major highways was also advanced with the completion of the sections between Santo Domingo and San Pedro de Macorís in the east, and from the capital to Baní and later Azua in the south. *(See map No. 9)*

The general prosperity of the country enabled the military government to continue with its public works projects, especially the organization of a national primary public school system, and a national sanitation system. In order to develop primary education, the military promulgated a new education law in April 1918 and created the National Council of Education in charge of the general supervision of public instruction in the country. From 1917 to 1920, the military government constructed several hundred schools, both large and small, in the cities and in the countryside. The number of students enrolled rose from some 20,000 in 1916, to over 100,000 in 1920.

In sanitation matters, the military government also introduced important reforms by promulgating new laws and creating the Ministry of Sanitation and Welfare. This agency carried out various campaigns to combat malaria and venereal diseases as well as the intestinal parasites that affected the majority of the Dominican population. On many occasions abuses were committed in applying the sanitary regulations. One example of such an abuse was the treatment given to the prostitutes who were forced to live in certain zone of "tolerance" in the main towns. However, the sanitation policy of the military government did set the base for programs improving health conditions to be carried out by future governments.

NATIONALIST RESISTANCE

In November 1918, shortly before the end of World War I, Captain Harry S. Knapp was relieved of his charge and promoted to rear admiral. General B. H. Fuller occupied a brief interim government until the arrival of Rear Admiral Thomas Snowden, who then acted as military governor from February 1919 to June 1921. Knapp's replacement signified the substitution of the first officers who worked in the public administration by others more ignorant of Dominican life.

During the years of Snowden's government, Dominican hostility toward the occupation made itself progressively more evident. Snowden abandoned Knapp's policy of working in close contact with Dominican leaders, and, worse still, he publicly announced his conviction that the occupation should continue for 20 years or more until Dominicans learned to govern themselves and correctly administer their country.

Dominicans did not like being governed by U.S. soldiers, as they had not liked it when they were ruled by Spanish soldiers at the time of the annexation, by Haitian soldiers during Boyer's rule, or by French soldiers under the control of Ferrand. A long tradition of independence had made a foreign government intolerable. On many occasions, Dominican politicians and intellectuals let it be known that they preferred a free country with rebellions to an occupied country living under an imposed peace. Moreover, the censorship, the obligatory use of passports, the military courts of justice, the arrests of innocent persons, and the torture of prisoners accused of opposing the occupation created an atmosphere of patriotic resistance in the country.

The disarmament of the population kept most Dominicans engulfed in a spirit of defeat during 1917 and 1918, but there were two exceptions. One was the military resistance in San Francisco de Macorís. The other was a movement of nationalist peasant guerrillas, called *gavilleros*, in the east, especially in the province of El Seibo. The *gavilleros* confronted the U.S. occupation with guerrilla warfare for more than four years. This protracted struggle had its origins in the development of the sugar industry. For three decades foreign companies had been forcibly removing the *campesinos* or buying their lands at ridiculously low prices. The expansion of the sugar plantations had left many families with barely enough land on which to live or had forced them to move to the less fertile lands of the small mountain chains in the east.

Led by leaders such as Vicente Evangelista, Ramón Natera and Martín Peguero, the so-called *gavilleros* were pursued continually by U.S. soldiers between 1917 and 1921. However, despite the capture and execution of their leader Vicente Evangelista, they could not easily be subdued because they enjoyed the collaboration of the majority of the population of the region.

Even the sugar companies furnished the *gavilleros* with food and money in an effort to keep them from looting their mills and warehouses, or burning their cane fields. It was not until soldiers of the Dominican National Guard, who knew the territory and were familiar with native guerrilla methods, joined the campaign that the *gavilleros* could finally be suppressed. The *gavilleros* never extended beyond the eastern region of the country and therefore never posed a serious threat to the U.S. military occupation.

Equally subversive was the work of nationalist Dominican intellectuals Américo Lugo, Emiliano Tejera, Fabio Fiallo, and Enrique Henríquez who kept the people of Santo Domingo in a state of continual agitation against foreign domination. Former President Francisco Henríquez y Carvajal traveled throughout Latin America denouncing the occupation and the lack of liberties in the Dominican Republic. On receiving such information, several governments became concerned, fearing that the case could be repeated in other parts of Latin America. Throughout 1919, various Latin American governments protested before the U.S. government and demanded that President Wilson end the occupation of the Dominican Republic.

At the same time, leaders of the Dominican working classes influenced the American Federation of Labor to demand that President Wilson change his policy in Santo Domingo. Former President Henríquez y Carvajal and other nationalist leaders founded the Comisión Nacionalista Dominicana and began lobbiyng in Washington diplomatic circles to win the attention of the State Department. Since the war was over, the State Department eventually listened to Henríquez's demands that censorship and the military courts of justice be relaxed and that some Dominican courts that had been suppressed be restored. Henríquez also asked the U.S. government to name an advisory board to prepare the laws that would be needed to ensure the transition from the military government to a new civilian government managed exclusively by Dominicans.

This advisory board was named on November 3, 1919 and was comprised of prominent Dominicans who had collaborated with the military government. However, popular agitation in Santo Domingo coupled with the repressive actions of Snowden, who did not want to permit any manifestation against the military occupation, caused the board's members to resign at the beginning of January 1920. Two months laters, the leaders of the nationalist movement created a patriotic group called the Unión Nacionalista Dominicana presided over by the respected intellectual, Emiliano Tejera, with the aim of conducting a campaign of civil resistance against the military government to force the United States to withdraw from the Dominican Republic.

This nationalist campaign soon gained force outside the country and became a topic of discussion in the U.S. electoral campaign of 1920. In a speech given in August, one of the candidates for the presidency, Warren G. Harding, attacked Wilson's interventionist policy in the Caribbean and stated his intention to withdraw the U.S. troops from where they had been sent in violation of the rights of their Latin American neighbors. Thus, when Harding won the November elections, there was a favorable atmosphere for the termination of the intervention.

Renewed pressure from several Latin American countries that demanded a rapid U.S. withdrawal from the Dominican Republic led Wilson on December 24, 1920 to order Snowden to integrate a new commission to carry out the constitutional and legal reforms that the defunct advisory board should have accomplished. Furthermore, Wilson ordered the military government to liberalize the measures that restricted the freedom of the press and public meetings so as to permit Dominicans to campaign openly for withdrawal.

The Unión Nacionalista Dominicana then increased its campaign for a "pure and simple" withdrawal, but the U.S. government refused to leave the country unconditionally, since in the last four years many laws had been promulgated and many transactions had been made that created or involved the rights of third parties. The United States wanted to safeguard these rights with a guarantee that the Dominicans would accept a plan of withdrawal that would recognize the acts of the military government as good and valid. A few months after Harding took office he named a new military governor, Rear Admiral Samuel S. Robinson, to facilitate the work of withdrawal under these guarantees.

Robinson arrived in June, 1921, and published a proclamation prepared in Washington that contained a detailed step-by-step plan of evacuation. According to this plan, general elections supervised by the military government would be held to elect a president who would lead a constitutional government. Such a government would, in turn, recognize all the acts of the military government and would accept the direction of U.S. officials over the Dominican police force.

The plan was rejected unanimously in July 1921, in the meetings and public assemblies sponsored by the Unión Nacionalista Dominicana on the grounds that it tended toward the establishment of a government that would be merely a puppet of the United States. Because of this rejection, the U.S. government informed the Dominicans that the announced elections were suspended until the Dominican people were willing to collaborate with President Harding's plan for withdrawal under which the occupation would end before July 1, 1924.

Meanwhile, the "Dance of the Millions" was about to end. Due to the rise in sugar and cacao prices, money had been circulating in great quantities within the country and commerce was enjoying its most prosperous period yet. Predicting even higher prices than those of 1920, the merchants had planned huge business operations for the following year and had placed orders abroad, worth some $40 million. However, by that time beet sugar production had recovered in Europe, while other non-European countries had increased their sugar cane production hoping to take advantage of the high prices. Hence, when everyone was expecting great profits, world sugar production soared unexpectedly and the market was glutted, causing prices to fall from $22.50 a hundredweight in May 1921 to only $2.00 in September.

Merchants found themselves overstocked with goods that could not be sold. A great depression resulted causing a liquidity crisis for the sugar companies, the sugar workers, and the private cane producers, better known as *colonos*. In addition, the prices of cacao, tobacco, and coffee also fell for much the same reason. The country became involved in a major economic crisis in which hundreds of merchants were ruined as the buying power of the population collapsed. Many of the sugar companies were doubly harmed since Governor Snowden, before leaving office, forced the administrators to store some eight million pounds of sugar expecting even higher prices for the next year. But sugar had one-tenth the value it could have had in early 1920.

Merchants were forced to cancel many of their orders that had been placed, but more than half of them had already been delivered and had to be paid for. Many merchants had to seek arrangements with their creditors abroad, as well as local, in order to liquidate their debts in partial payments. The "Dance of the Millions" had ended. While some clever merchants took advantage of the overall economic crisis to avoid paying their debts altogether, many other merchants sacrificed their reserves and went into bankruptcy in order to save their prestige. Such bankruptcies became an everyday occurrence in towns and cities throughout the country.

The economic crisis also created a serious problem for the military government, which saw itself suddenly deprived of the revenues needed to continue its public works programs. At the beginning of 1922, the military government was forced to procure a new loan in order to continue the highway construction and to pay the salaries of public employees. This loan for some $6.7 million allowed the military government to survive economically during the following months, although it further compromised the financial position of the Dominican Republic.

ENDING THE OCCUPATION

While the economic crisis was plaguing the country, efforts to end the occupation continued. Since President Harding wanted to remove the troops from the Dominican Republic, Francisco J. Peynado, an important lawyer with connections to the sugar industry, went to Washington in May 1922 to seek an understanding that would harmonize the various positions and be acceptable to both parties. After several meetings with Secretary of State Charles Evans Hughes, Don "Pancho" Peynado, as he was called, arrived at a new agreement of evacuation to be submitted to Dominican political leaders.

This plan, known as the "Hughes-Peynado Plan," consisted of the following points: A provisional government would be installed whose president would be elected by the principal political leaders and the archbishop of Santo Domingo. This government would prepare the appropriate legislation to regulate the holding of elections, reorganize the municipal and provincial political structures, and modify the constitution so that the necessary reforms could be made. Later, the provisional government would organize elections, but in the meantime it would appoint plenipotentiaries to negotiate with the military government over the recognition of those legal acts which had created rights in favor of third parties. Among those acts, the issue or sale of bonds on the contracted loans, and the validity of the customs tariffs established by the military government in 1919 were of particular interest to the U.S. government. The Convention of 1907 would remain in effect until the Dominican Republic finished paying its foreign debts, now increased as a consequence of the new loans.

President Henríquez and the Unión Nacionalista Dominicana opposed the Hughes-Peynado Plan. They still called for a "pure and simple" withdrawal and the return of Henríquez to the presidency. But despite this opposition, the leaders of the most important political parties accepted the plan after discussing the arrangements with Peynado and the U.S. Secretary of State in Washington at the end of June 1922.

On September 23, 1922 a Dominican delegation comprised of Horacio Vásquez, Federico Velázquez, and Elías Brache, Jr., representing the Horacista, Velazquista and Jimenista parties respectively, along with Peynado and Monsignor Adolfo Nouel, signed the plan. Secretary of State Charles Evans Hughes and the diplomat Sumner Welles countersigned for the American government. Welles was named U.S. special commissioner in the Dominican Republic and was to work together with the other signatories in the execution of the plan.

On October 1, 1922, after several days of discussion about the candidates, the commission named as provisional president a merchant named Juan Bautista Vicini Burgos who was sworn in and began his term of office on the 21st of the same month. Commissioner Wells worked closely with the Dominican political leaders and managed to overcome the opposition of the navy which tried to prevent the early evacuation of U.S. troops.

Rear Admiral Robinson left the country, and his replacement was Brigadier General Harry Lee who had a purely military function and was to complete the training of the police force, which would be the only peace keeping force in operation after the withdrawal. Since command of the police was to be in Dominican hands, it was deemed urgent to complete the formation of its officers as this body should become a nonpolitical force at the service of the president of the Republic.

As soon as the government of Vicini Burgos began to work on the numerous legal reforms previously agreed on, the political parties reinitiated their activities and reorganization. During the years of occupation some changes had occurred. The Horacista party had changed its name and now called itself the Partido Nacional. The Velazquista party had also changed its name and was now called the Partido Progresista. The old party of Luis Felipe Vidal had lost force.

Juan Isidro Jimenes had died during the occupation, and his party had fallen under the influence of Desiderio Arias. But Arias's actions were of necessity very limited since during the occupation he had been forced to live in Santiago almost as a recluse making cigars for a living. During tenure of the Vicini Burgos's government, Arias left the direction of the Jimenista party in the hands of Elías Brache, a former leader of the Jimenista *pata blanca* faction.

As the military neared to its end, the old parties began to realign, and two new electoral forces emerged. The so-called Alianza Nacional Progresista grouped together the parties of Vásquez and Velázquez according to an agreement that gave Federico Velázquez the vice-presidency and his party 30 percent of the ministries and public offices if they won the elections. The other political force was called the Coalición Patriótica de Ciudadanos and grouped together the two old Jimenista factions according to an electoral formula that presented Francisco J. Peynado as a candidate for the presidency.

The elections to decide on the president and Congress were finally held on March 15, 1924, after an intense campaign that kept the whole country in suspense and revived the Dominicans' old partisan spirit. Vásquez won in a landslide victory because he still possessed a faithful political following and was surrounded by an aura of heroism due to his old revolutionary battle fights. These elections were orderly and free, and various control methods were used to avoid fraud. As soon as Peynado knew the results, he rushed forward to congratulate the winner and to offer his collaboration to the new constitutional government, which would begin on July 12, 1924.

Although the last group of U.S. troops did not leave until August, the military occupation officially ended on July 1, 1924. Thus, at the same time that preparations were being made for the inauguration of Vásquez's government, the foreign troops were breaking camp and preparing to leave. The military occupation had lasted eight years, and during that time the Dominican Republic had changed in many ways.

THE OCCUPATION'S IMPACT

The most influential change brought about by the military government was the new highway system that was completed shortly after the withdrawal of the troops. These roads linked the capital with the three major regions of the country, initiating the political unification of the country, a goal that had been impossible to achieve in the past. Transportation between the northern and southern coasts, which had previously taken the small ships devoted to coastal trade between two and three days, was now reduced to less than 12 hours. Cars and trucks became popular among the affluent, replacing the horse and donkey on long trips. These vehicles also caused the eventual demise of the railroads, the operations of which became too expensive and rigid for the country's needs.

Meanwhile, the mail service greatly improved due to the new highways, and traffic to and from the capital increased noticeably. For the first time the inhabitants of Santo Domingo had the opportunity to consume large quantities of fresh produce from the interior, thus stimulating both internal trade and agricultural production. Indeed, as soon as these highways were put in operation, a rapid migratory movement was noted among the previously isolated *campesinos* who now moved along the borders of these new roads. In later years, the highways would ease internal migration and contribute to the rapid growth of Santo Domingo, whose population had grown very slowly in the past.

While the number of schools and students greatly increased, the military government made education a permanent concern of public officials who had previously invested little in this area. Likewise, in the matter of sanitation, the occupation government established the bases to improve the health conditions of the population. These and other public works projects became a model for later governments. From then on, to govern became synonymous with construction so that a good government was measured in terms of the construction of public works that it accomplished.

The military government, nevertheless, left many weaknesses in the country's political and economic structure. Prior to the occupation, rebellion had been possible because of the isolation of the majority of the population and the abundance of arms in the hands of the people. Now that the population was disarmed, the National Police appeared adequately trained and strong enough to confront any intent of sedition. However, the military government had been a government of occupation and, as such, had taught the advantages of repressive methods, especially to the members of the police who were now in charge of maintaining order in the country. With the population disarmed, whoever controlled the National Police could easily exercise enormous power over the rest of the population.

The country's economic progress had been greatly affected by the military government, which had accelerated the growth of a plantation economy highly dependent on the world sugar market over which the country had little control. Attracted by the abundance of cheap land, foreign investors ended up by controlling all of the sugar industry, which thus remained largely outside the influence of the Dominican population. By the end of the military occupation, the sugar industry controlled some 438,000 acres of agricultural land which functioned as autonomous enclaves virtually independent from the government.

The U.S. military had openly favored the foreign-dominated sugar industry, and native industries were often discouraged. Although the new laws concerning production of alcoholic bev-

erages brought additional revenues to the state, they ruined
hundreds of family operations that had produced rum for the
national market or for export to Haiti. From the hundreds of
stills that had been in the country before the occupation and
which constituted an important sector of the national economic life, only a few dozen survived the occupation. This initiated
a rapid process of consolidation of rum production into a small
number of firms that would be reduced to less than a dozen in
the following decades.

Likewise, many small workshops and native industries were
ruined by the avalanche of U.S. goods that poured in after the
promulgation of the Tariff Act of 1919. Any incipient Dominican industrial development that could have been stimulated by
the high prices during the occupation was retarded by at least
20 years since competition was impossible against U.S. products that arrived in the country duty-free. Although this tariff
was eventually modified by Vásquez's government, industrial
investment was discouraged for a long time.

The U.S. occupation also left a marked taste for the consumption of U.S. goods. In the following years, Dominicans resumed
their use of European products, but more than half of the country's imports continued to come from the United States. A marked
Americanization of the language also took place during these
years with the dissemination of U.S. trade marks on almost all
the products consumed in the country. U.S. games and toys became popular, and baseball eventually replaced cockfighting
as the national sport. Among the urban elite U.S. music became
a sign of good taste, although the inverse phenomenon took
place among the mass of the population, which espoused the
merengue as a sign of protest against foreign domination.

The eight years of foreign rule left the Dominican Republic
with certain cultural ties to the United States. It also left the
country with an even heavier foreign debt. The loans that the
military governors had incurred to construct highways and other

public works increased the foreign debt. When the military government obtained the first loan in 1918, the debt of 1907 had already been reduced to less than $10 million. With new loans obtained to continue the public works program, the debt had risen to almost $15 million in 1922, despite the opposition of Dominican political leaders and businessmen who had argued that a foreign government did not have the right to contract debts for the Dominican Republic.

After the U.S. withdrawal in 1924, the Dominican Republic was once again under the administration of its own citizens. However, the country stayed in the juridical position of a protectorate, as established by the Dominican-American conventions of 1907 and 1924. The United States still reserved the rights to administer the customs houses, to intervene when it deemed necessary, and to authorize any increases in the public debt which the Dominican Republic wished to make. This protectorate could be exercised much more easily after the U.S. troops left because the Dominicans had learned that the center of political power in the Caribbean was in Washington and that the Dominican Republic was in the orbit of U.S. interests. From this time on, the exercise of sovereignty would be understood by Dominican leaders as always conditioned by U.S. foreign policy.

17.
Horacio Vásquez
and the rise
of Trujillo
(1924-1930)

UNDER THE U.S. PROTECTORATE

To some extent the government of President Horacio Vásquez was merely an extension of the U.S. military occupation.
All the occupation's programs were continued or terminated
during this regime, characterized by ample respect of civil liberties. The government paid close attention to public works
projects, sanitation services, education, and agriculture, and also
initiated new irrigation programs and the colonization of unused lands to make the country self-sufficient in certain basic
foodstuffs.

For some time, Dominicans had been dependent on imported rice, corn, beans, onions, garlic, potatoes, meat, and vegetables, although all of these could be produced in the country.
Likewise, a large amount of wood was imported each year in
spite of the existence of plentiful forests. The need to develop
agriculture and industry was clear, and the Vásquez government took it upon itself to foster it.

To promote agricultural development, Vásquez initiated several government-supported irrigation projects and encouraged
private landowners to irrigate their own lands, following the ex-

ample of a French immigrant, Mr. Bogaert, who had financed the construction of his own works in 1918. Vásquez also appointed Rafael Espaillat as minister of agriculture. Espaillat believed in the need of expanding technical education through agricultural schools and tried to attract European immigrants into model agricultural colonies created by the government.

To promote industrial development, Vásquez had to face more serious challenges. The Dominican-American Convention prevented the government from altering the Tariff Law of 1919. To circumvent it, Vásquez passed Law N° 190 in November 1925, creating several consumption taxes on imported items. Thus, with the passage of Law N° 190, the Dominican government tried to raise the price of imported merchandise to effectively protect local producers. Law N° 190 stimulated local production somewhat, though not decisively, and it actually served more to increase governmental internal revenues.

Over the years, Law N° 190 became a matter of serious contention between the U.S. government and the Dominican government. The United States claimed that the newly created internal taxes functioned as hidden customs duties and should therefore be collected by the Dominican Customs Receivership, not by Dominican officials. The issue was finally resolved in 1931 when the Dominican government accepted the U.S. position and allowed the Customs Receivership to collect those taxes. By then, the revenues produced by Law N° 190 had become the main source of income for the state.

In the first months of his administration, Vásquez desperately needed financial resources since funds from the 1922 loan contracted by the military government had already been depleted and fiscal revenues were not sufficient to continue the projects begun under the occupation. Vásquez sought to negotiate a new loan for $25 million in the United States in order to consolidate the debt left by the military government and to continue the development programs. Dominican congressmen from all parties objected to such a loan, and Vásquez had to drop the negotiations. Thus, during the second half of 1924 and all of 1925, the government could only work with the revenues provided by internal taxation and its share of the customs receipts. During this period, the public works projects were carried out without making any extraordinary advances.

Because the loans contracted by the military government had indebted the Republic without Dominican participation, both the United States and the Dominican Republic spent much of 1924 negotiating a new treaty. This second convention was signed on December 27, 1924 and was formally ratified at the end of April 1925. It slightly modified the 1907 convention and left the United States in control of the customs houses. Under its provisions, the Dominican Republic still could not increase its public debt without the prior consent of the United States, and the United States still reserved its right to intervene in the Dominican financial affairs. The U.S. officials of the Dominican Customs Receivership used this convention to support their claims against Law N° 190.

This new convention was harshly attacked by all members of Congress, especially those from the Partido Progresista led by Vice-President Federico Velázquez. Parliamentary debates over the convention seriously weakened the Alianza Nacional Progresista which had brought Vásquez and Velázquez to power the year before. The fierce attacks against President Vásquez by Velázquez's partisans during the debate were the result not only of antagonism against the convention, but of the growing displeasure of Velázquez and his men at being virtually left out of the government.

From the very beginning, the leaders of the Partido Nacional had sought to govern without giving the vice-president and his party any participation in the decision-making process. Moreover, Vásquez and Velázquez were old political enemies, and once the election was over, their old jealousies and antipa-

thies took little time to come to the fore. This antagonism between the two men was amply encouraged by the Horacistas
who feared that they would lose power if they allowed Velázquez to recover the power he held during the administration of
Ramón Cáceres.

The Alianza Nacional Progresista, which had acted as a capable election maneuver in Vásquez's rise to power, barely survived the elections. In the first two years of his government, the
relations between the two parties deteriorated to such a point
that Velázquez and his party soon left the government altogether. At this point, the Coalición Patriótica de Ciudadanos, previously in the opposition, joined the government. This new alliance between the former *bolos* and *coludos* noticeably strengthened Vásquez's regime after December 1926, when new provincial elections were held.

In September 1926, Vásquez again insisted before Congress
that the country needed to take out another loan in order to
undertake new development projects. Since the Velazquista
opposition was already debilitated and the Coalitionistas were
already supporting the government, Vásquez found it remarkably easy to obtain the necessary authorization from Congress
to issue two new series of bonds to undertake future public works
projects. Although Vásquez had originally only requested
$2,500,000, Congress said that this sum was insufficient and
raised the amount to $10,000,000.

By December 1926, Congress had approved the new loan
and the first bonds for $5 million were printed. These bonds
served to finance an impressive public works program that increased the circulation of money throughout 1927. This boom
in public expenditures coincided with a new period of favorable world prices for exports and gave the Republic another
short period of prosperity similar to the "Dance of the Millions."

The Vásquez government built an aqueduct for Santo Domingo, the population of which had been drinking water from

wells and cisterns for more than four centuries. It also dredged the ports of Santo Domingo, Puerto Plata, and San Pedro de Macorís, and improved the facilities of those harbors. It continued the irrigation and colonization projects in many parts of the country, especially in the northwest and along the border with Haiti. There, the government bought lands to establish new agricultural colonies. The government also constructed many school buildings, while it proceeded with opening new roads and building new bridges to link Santo Domingo with the most remote regions.

Some of these roads were not completed until several years later when the steel bridges constructed abroad were installed, but for practical purposes all were functional by 1930. From that time on, the country could count on the most complete highway network in the Caribbean area, and the most important population centers of the Republic were now connected. This occurred at a time when the population was little more than a million inhabitants and most of the country remained sparsely populated. With the transportation system so improved, automobiles use became increasingly popular throughout the country.

The year 1927 marked the peak of prosperity. Jobs and money were abundant. Peace and general well-being in the country allowed agriculture, commerce, and industry to flourish. In the capital, Santo Domingo, there were new modern structures, some of them several stories high. Modern chalets and homes were built, especially in the outskirts of the city. In the capital, the houses constructed of palm slats with thatched roofs that still existed on some important streets gave away to modern, showy structures of reinforced concrete.

The modernization of the Dominican Republic had begun. It had originated in the last quarter of the 19th century with the introduction of the modern sugar *centrales* with steam engines and railroads. These changes were complemented by the arrival of the telegraph and electricity, by the silent but continuous importation of thousands of modern products manufactured in Europe and North America, and by the construction of highways and the arrival of automobiles and trucks. New ideas accompanied these technological advances: positivism, for example, took hold during the establishment of the sugar industry and flourished in the first three decades of the 20th century.

Modernization was greatly accelerated by the U.S. military occupation. For the first time, the country was in direct contact with other lifestyles. U.S. organization methods greatly facilitated the administration of the state. The tariff act of 1919 allowed the introduction of large amounts of merchandise along with technological innovations. The growing Americanization of the urban elite meant the adoption of new lifestyles and consumption habits completely alien to traditional Dominican modes of behavior. Although the Dominican Republic still retained many of the characteristics of a rural, traditional, and backward society, by 1927 the urban classes had begun to experience changes much more profound than any since the arrival of the Spaniards in 1492.

RETURN TO CAUDILLO POLITICS

These changes came about through external influences as the Dominican Republic fell under the political and economic domination of foreign banks and corporations, mostly from the United States. Dominican leaders, however, in many instances failed to take into account the profound transformations taking place in their own society and kept intact their old caudillo mentality. Party politics continued to be viewed as the road to power to satisfy personal ambitions. Alliances and pacts based on personal interests were continually made to assure a greater participation in the spoils allotted to those in the government.

Thus, despite material advances made during Vásquez's government, old political habits again brought the country backwards by reviving *caudillismo*.

By the middle of 1926, the first signs of this return to the past began to appear in newspaper and magazine articles which discussed the presidential elections to be held in 1928. In those articles, various intellectuals and politicians suggesting that Vásquez and the members of Congress had been elected according to the Constitution of 1908 and therefore their terms should be extended to six years. They also suggested that since Vice-President Federico Velázquez had been elected after the proclamation of the Constitution of 1924, which established only a four-year term for the executive branch, he only had the right to stay in office until August 16, 1928. This meant that the presidential term was to be extended two more years, while that of the Vice-President was to be limited to only four years.

These opinions gained ground in the Partido Nacional and produced a movement called *La Prolongación*. The press devoted a great amount of space to the issue and debated whether or not the prolongation or extension of the term was constitutionally valid. Actually, it was invalid since Vásquez had not been elected according to the Constitution of 1908 but by virtue of the stipulations of the Evacuation Treaty which acted as a type of constitutional pact during the Vicini Burgos administration until the Constitution of 1924 was approved and proclaimed. Moreover, both Vásquez and Velázquez had sworn after its proclamation that they would respect and make others respect the new constitution. This meant that they both had accepted that their terms were limited to only four years.

But the official propaganda prevailed under the auspices of the Coalicionistas who hoped to occupy all the positions left by the Velazquistas who were to leave the government in 1928. By the beginning of 1927, everything was in readiness for Congress to pronounce its decision, although the president was receiving warnings from the American Legation that the United States would not look favorably on an unconstitutional extension of his powers. By September 1926, Vásquez had already stated that he was willing to accept the prolongation, and all that remained to be done was to discuss the procedures to legalize the extension because the existing constitution clearly established that the executive term was only for four years.

On April 7, 1927 several senators presented a bill to modify the constitution so as to extend the presidential term to August 16, 1930. This bill promptly passed in the Senate. Meanwhile, on the preceding April 1, elections had been held to elect deputies to the constituent assembly. This assembly met on June 9 and by the 17th had prepared a new constitution extending the terms of the president and vice-president as well as of the Deputies who were slated to end their terms in August 1928. Thus, the legal maneuvers to postpone the elections for another two years were quickly passed.

Although some deputies and officials of the Partido Progresista decided to join the government in the prolongation movement, the majority of the Velazquistas protested. Federico Velázquez himself went to Washington in an effort to seek U.S. support in preventing Vásquez from continuing in office until 1930, but he was totally unsuccessful. U.S. policy toward Latin American was then taking a new turn to avoid direct intervention so as not to become involved in such conflicts as had caused the military occupation of the Dominican Republic, Nicaragua, and Haiti. Thus, Vásquez's government found no obstacles in its path.

When the moment finally arrived for the prolongation, Velázquez was dropped as vice-president and on August 16, 1928 he was replaced by Dr. José Dolores Alfonseca, who also occupied the powerful position of president of the Junta Superior Directiva of the Partido Nacional. As early as 1924, Alfonseca had been the director of the Horacista party and had emerged as the presidential successor, especially since on more than one occasion Vásquez had announced his decision to leave Alfonseca in his place when his term expired. The rise of Alfonseca to the vice-presidency was therefore a personal triumph, and his succession to the presidency seemed even more likely.

Alfonseca had powerful enemies both inside and outside the party, and as soon as he was sworn in as vice-president a number of schemes began to prevent him from succeeding Vásquez in 1930. These intrigues took various forms. The most visible was planned by his enemies within his own Partido Nacional, who began a campaign to favor Vásquez's reelection in 1930. Alfonseca had to join this campaign in order not to be stigmatized as ambitious or as a traitor to the president. Thus, Alfonseca found himself trapped in the web spun by his own party to reelect Vásquez. At the same, time the president began to put forth his nephew, Martín de Moya, then secretary of finance, as another possible presidential candidate in order to balance Alfonseca's influence within the party.

Another important enemy of Alfonseca was Rafael Leonidas Trujillo, chief of the former Dominican National Police, which had its name changed to the National Army in May 1928. Martín de Moya and his followers took advantage of the antagonism between Trujillo and Alfonseca and the party was soon divided into the supporters of the vice-president and the supporters of the finance secretary and the chief of the army. This second group quickly became dominant as many saw more political potential in Moya, who was not only the nephew of the president, but also apparently enjoyed the decisive support of the Army. Nevertheless, as time passed, the campaign for reelection seemed more palpable. Vásquez favored this campaign by silently fostering both Moya and Alfonseca. In the end, many came to the conclusion that only Vásquez could continue in the presidency, because the other candidates were not capable of keeping the party united.

These political maneuvers were carried on in an environment of great prosperity and total freedom. The government continued its public works programs and its policy of colonization and agricultural development. Money circulated abundantly, and many new fortunes were made by various corrupt public officials. The press freely attacked and defended the government. There were progovernment newspapers such as the *Listín Diario* and opposition newspapers such as *La Opinión* in Santo Domingo and *La Información* in Santiago de los Caballeros. Debates in Congress were conducted openly, and no one was persecuted for their political views or ideas.

For the first time in Dominican history there appeared to be a government capable both of keeping order and of maintaining civil liberties. The novelty was clear to many Dominicans who could easily remember the former civil wars and the U.S. occupation with its political repression, press censorship, military courts, forced requisitions, and torture of political opponents. President Vásquez himself took special care to preserve civil liberties. On the few occasions that members of the opposition were detained, he had them quickly released, even when some stated their opposition to the government or publicly called for his assassination.

Nevertheless, the campaign for reelection and the divisions within the Partido Nacional gradually weakened the government. Both the Velazquistas and the Coalicionistas who held public offices in the administration were worried about the possibility that the Partido Nacional would continue in power after 1930. Although Vásquez had proven to be a man of great honor and honesty, his political sectarianism had proven to be a great obstacle for the Coalicionistas in the government. Some of the them therefore, approached the chief of the army, Rafael Trujillo, and cultivated him politically by exploiting his rivalry with Alfonseca and by making him consider his own presidential possibilities in case Vásquez died.

It was common knowledge at this time that Vásquez was in ill health and that he could die at any moment. Everyone also knew that in such a case Alfonseca would succeed Vásquez and that his first victim would be Trujillo. Both the Coalicionistas and Alfonseca's enemies within the Partido Nacional sought to prevent Alfonseca's ascension to the presidency and the only manner to do this was through Trujillo. Thus, the chief of the army became a key figure in the events of 1929, as the president's health deteriorated.

Vásquez lay prostrate on his bed, and on October 28 had to be taken on an urgent flight to Baltimore, for an emergency operation to remove a kidney at The Johns Hopkins University Hospital. For over one month the president lay on the verge of death, and it was not until January 5, 1930, that he finally returned to Santo Domingo with much of his strength gone forever. This prolonged illness gave ample opportunity for the designs of the chief of the army to take shape.

THE RISE OF TRUJILLO

Trujillo had risen rapidly in the military since his induction into the Dominican National Police during the U.S. occupation. During this ascent he had used his growing power to amass a personal fortune by undertaking shady business deals through the purchase of military food, clothing, and equipment. After becoming army chief he enriched himself even more and began to invest in land and urban properties, thus demonstrating a keen eye for business as well as an uncommon appetite for luxury. He enjoyed the unquestioning confidence of the president who had made him chief of the army in recognition of his strong support of the Horacista party.

Trujillo took advantage of this confidence to place his own followers in key army positions, although these followers appeared to be adherents of Horacio Vásquez. Little by little Trujillo began changing the army into both his own private business and a military machinery to serve his political ambitions. Trujillo's wealth was well known, as was the fact that the purchase and provisioning of army goods was the main source of his income. In 1927, there was a scandalous deficit in the army budget that Trujillo could not justify.

In 1929, an administrative-financial study made by a U.S. commission contracted by Vásquez to modernize various government departments discovered some of these irregularities in the army's budget. Despite the commission's recommendation that the situation be corrected and the Alfonsequistas's demands that Trujillo be removed from office, Vásquez continued to support the army chief. The President also refused to believe reports that Trujillo was conspiring with various Coalicionistas to overthrow the government. Vásquez's confidence in Trujillo also made the army chief an untouchable figure in the regime and a serious point of contention within the Partido Nacional.

During the ten weeks of Vásquez's absence, the reelection campaign continued as usual, but the political situation grew even more critical as rumors began circulating that Acting President Alfonseca would soon remove the chief of the army as a conspirator. Even more consternation arose when Trujillo arrived in Alfonseca's office with his bodyguards fully armed, in open defiance of the acting president.

From that moment, rumor spread that the army chief was conspiring with the Coalicionistas who realized that if Vásquez did not return alive, it was necessary to prevent Alfonseca from remaining in power. These rumors became so rife that on two separate occasions the U.S. minister invited Trujillo to come by his office and warned him that his government would not recognize any regime arising from force. On both opportunities Trujillo protested his innocence and declared his loyalty to

Vásquez, although preparations were clearly underway for a coup d'état.

Meanwhile, Rafael Estrella Ureña, a local politician from Santiago who had been secretary of foreign relations under Vásquez and who had left the government to oppose Vásquez's reelection, founded the Partido Republicano and was recruiting people to oppose the government. Estrella made a pact with leaders of other smaller parties opposed to Vásquez, such as the Partido Liberal and the Jimenista faction headed by Desiderio Arias. He made another agreement with the Progresistas, whereby opponents to the reelection would run Velázquez for president and Estrella Ureña for vice-president.

Behind these activities Trujillo was silently working with Estrella Ureña, and pulling together the opposition to support his own ends. By February, 1930, the two men had already agreed that Estrella Ureña and his men would start a "revolution" in Santiago de los Caballeros. Estrella Ureña would then take control of the San Luis Fortress and launch a so-called Movimiento Cívico. He would then march with men and arms to the capital to force Vásquez to resign while the Army, apparently wanting to avoid bloodshed, would abstain from any interference. Vásquez was receiving reports of the planned betrayal by Trujillo but rejected them and believed that they were mere rumors springing from the political antagonism between the army chief and Alfonseca.

The coup was planned for February 16, 1930, but could not be carried out at this time since it was the day on which the new U.S. minister was traveling to the Cibao. It was believed imprudent to initiate the movement with the U.S. diplomats so close. The coup was thus delayed until February 23, when Estrella Ureña and his followers along with Coalicionista leaders Desiderio Arias and Elías Brache, put the plan into action in Santiago.

Estrella Ureña's uncle, General José Estrella, "attacked" and took the San Luis Fortress, which put up no resistance. The march on the capital began, and three days later several hundred men partially armed with old rifles surreptitiously procured by Trujillo entered Santo Domingo. Then, and only then, Horacio Vásquez became finally convinced that the man whom he had raised to the highest military position in the country had betrayed him.

Vásquez quickly took asylum in the U.S. Legation despite the urgings of his friends to make a stand by firing Trujillo and gathering his own military forces. But the president was simply too old and sick to fight. In order not to disturb the constitutional order, Vásquez agreed to negotiate with the rebel leaders headed by Estrella Ureña, while Trujillo remained in the Ozama Fortress overseeing the plot.

An understanding was soon reached whereby Vásquez would name Estrella Ureña as secretary of the interior and the Police, a position third in line for the presidency after the President and the vice-president. On March 2, Vásquez and Alfonseca formally presented their resignations to Congress, and the next day Rafael Estrella Ureña was sworn in as president. Two days later Alfonseca and Vásquez left for exile to Puerto Rico.

Although the Vásquez reelection was now out of the question, there was still intense political excitement about the coming elections to be held on May 16. Thus, as soon as Vásquez and Alfonseca left the country, the various parties reinitiated their campaigns. The Progresistas and Coalicionistas who had supported Estrella Ureña were now hoping to win the elections as Estrella Ureña was now in a good position to promote his agreed candidacy with Velásquez. At this point there was not much fear of the chief of the army since the U.S. Legation had declared that it would not recognize any government presided over by Trujillo as a result of Vásquez's overthrow. All were sure that the elections would decide the outcome of the presidential race.

Such expectations soon proved wrong. Within a few days after Estrella Ureña took office, it became evident that the chief of the army was in command and that the new president was little more than his puppet. It was also clear that Trujillo himself wanted to be president and had no intention of ceding to either Estrella Ureña or Velázquez. The Coalicionistas supported these pretentions and reached an understanding with Trujillo and Estrella Ureña whereby they would drop Velásquez and run a new candidacy headed by Trujillo. A Confederación de Partidos was then formed that included the Coalicionistas Liberales of Arias, the Republicanos of Estrella Ureña and two small groups of little significance, the Partido Nacionalista and the recently created Partido Obrero.

Velázquez quickly understood his error in supporting Estrella Ureña and began new negotiations with the Partido Nacional to form another Alianza Nacional Progresista similar to that of 1924. The Alianza was formed and put forth as its candidates Velázquez for president and Angel Morales, a Horacista leader and the Dominican Minister in Washington, as vice-president.

Only a few days passed before the leaders of the Alianza discovered that their followers and partisans were being persecuted and jailed by members of the Army. Despite this persecution, Velázquez and Morales insisted on campaigning with the support of Martín de Moya and his partisans. On one occasion, Morales, Moya, and their companions were attacked by gunmen on the outskirts of Santiago where they had just attended several political meetings. Morales and Moya miraculously escaped alive with their pants and hats perforated with bullet holes.

Throughout April the campaign became increasingly violent with terrorist acts and police intimidation launched by Trujillo. Little by little, the Alianza Nacional Progresista suspended its activities, whereas the Confederación de Partidos enjoyed complete freedom in holding its meetings. Confronted with military violence, the Junta Central Electoral resigned on May 7, and it was soon replaced by members favoring the candidacy of Trujillo and Estrella Ureña. With no end to the violence and terrorism in sight, the Alianza Nacional Progresista finally announced on May 15, the eve of the election day, that it was withdrawing from the elections since there were no guarantees of a free vote.

The elections were held as planned the next day, but with the sole candidacy of Trujillo and Estrella Ureña who supposedly received 45 percent of the votes of the registered voters. Despite the protests of the Alianza Nacional Progresista and of the newspapers, the Junta Central Electoral recognized the validity of the elections on May 24, and proclaimed Trujillo and Estrella Ureña as President and vice-president of the Republic.

Terrorism continued in the following months. The most noticeable opponents of Trujillo were persecuted and jailed, while others were killed by paid assassins. One of the earliest victims was Virgilio Martínez Reyna, the Alfonsequista leader who had proposed the dismissal of Trujillo when Vásquez was ill in Baltimore, was cruelly assassinated along with his pregnant wife while they were sleeping in their country home in San José de las Matas.

Trujillo also organized a terrorist band, called *La 42*, to be in charge of persecuting and assassinating his opponents and to spread fear throughout the country. This band went by automobile throughout the country leaving a trail of corpses behind. The *Listín Diario*, which had campaigned in favor of the Alianza Nacional Progresista, was assaulted at the end of May and its directors forced to silence their attacks against Trujillo. After six years of political freedom, the Dominican people were again subjected to tyranny.

On August 16, 1930, Rafael Trujillo and Rafael Estrella Ureña officially took office as president and vice-president of the Republic to the consternation of the majority of the people. The Trujillo Era had begun.

18.
The Era
of Trujillo
(1930-1961)

TRUJILLO'S AMBITIONS

The rise of General Trujillo to power in 1930 made evident another of the consequences of the U.S. military occupation: the extremely influential role of the National Army in Dominican politics. With the population now totally disarmed, there was no group capable of taking a military stand against the soldiers and officers trained by the U.S. government. The United States had little room to maneuver in this process. Although U.S. diplomats in Santo Domingo tried to prevent the coup d'état, once confronted with the accomplished fact they accepted Trujillo, saying that they preferred him as a guarantor of political stability and as a better alternative to revolution.

Haiti was then still ruled by a U.S. military government, and the fact that Trujillo was a former officer trained by the U.S. Marine Corps guaranteed that both parts of the island would remain in peace for the time being. During the entire period that Trujillo governed the Dominican Republic, the United States always considered him a better option than his enemies from within or without. Thus, he enjoyed continuous U.S. support, except for a brief two-year period after the end of World War II when several liberal officials in the State Department objected to his regime and tried unsuccessfully to remove him from power.

Rafael Trujillo was an ambitious military man born in 1891 within a family of mixed Spanish, Creole, and Haitian blood from the lower classes of San Cristóbal, a village located about 30 kilometers west of the capital city of Santo Domingo. In 1918 he joined the Dominican National Police. There he learned new methods of military organization and discipline that had been imported by the U.S. military. Thanks to his own sense of discipline and his outstanding intelligence, he learned his job quickly and rose rapidly up the ladder of the organization that changed its name to the National Guard by the time the United States marines left the country. This name was changed again to National Army in 1927.

As he advanced in rank, Trujillo used his growing power as local commander to make a fortune arranging deals involving the purchase of food, clothing, and supplies for the soldiers. He was a ruthless commander who also plotted to have his main enemies removed from the army, so that when he became commander-in-chief in 1927, he was already both rich and extremely powerful. By 1928 his investments in urban lands and properties had become so publicized that Dominicans recognized him as having a decided entrepreneurial spirit and an unscrupulous zeal for wealth uncommon in a society where economic activity still focused on traditional possession of land and agriculture.

Trujillo took advantage of the excessive trust bestowed upon him by President Vásquez, who had promoted him to the uppermost rank of the army in recognition of his demonstrated personal loyalty, wanting to ensure that key positions in the army would be filled only by officers devoted to his person. Once in power, Trujillo used his army to impose his will on a disarmed population, using violence, terror, torture, and assassination.

From the beginning, Trujillo's government was a regime of plunder organized to furnish him with total control of every economic enterprise existing in the country. As he achieved control of those enterprises, Trujillo used the full power of the state to eliminate competition and establish monopolies. The business of purchasing supplies for the army was followed by a monopoly on the production and sale of salt.

Using his position as president, Trujillo was able to have a law approved prohibiting the traditional production of sea salt so the public would have to consume salt from the Barahona mines, whose production he controlled. Once the monopoly was established, the price of salt rose from $0.60 to $3 a hundred pounds, which according to contemporary reports, yielded profits for Trujillo of about $400,000 a year. The salt monopoly was followed by the meat monopoly. Control of the slaughterhouses in Santo Domingo added about $500,000 a year to his income. To this was added the rice monopoly, which Trujillo instituted by prohibiting the importation of rice and requiring Dominicans to buy creole rice distributed by his own company. That raised the price of a pound from about $0.06 to $0.12 or $0.15, according to the quality.

During his first four years in power, Trujillo moved rapidly in creating his network of monopolies. These included the sale and distribution of milk in the capital and the establishment of a bank for cashing government checks, managed by his wife, María Martínez. In this especialized bank, public employees could cash at a discount their payroll checks before their pay day.

In subsequent years, with the money that he rapidly accumulated from these initial enterprises, Trujillo bought stock in several already existing companies, eventually seizing them from their owners. In one case, for example, he forced the owners of an insurance company to sell out to him. From then on all insurance policies of the government had to be written with this company, which he had renamed Compañía San Rafael. In the case of the tobacco factory Compañía Anónima Tabacalera, the biggest in the country, the owners were forced to sell him shares only to find themselves later obliged to yield to him nearly all the stocks. The Tabacalera remained until the very end of his regime as the only cigarette producer in the country.

Trujillo's many other business ventures ranged from prostitution to fruit exports, and included commissions on concessions for public works contracts. He also imposed a 10 percent deduction from the salaries of the public employees that went to his political party, the Partido Dominicano, the accounts of which he managed personally. With these mechanisms, Trujillo managed to become the richest man in the country by the end of his first presidential term in August 1934.

For the rest of his life Trujillo would use political and military power to line his own pockets and to enrich members of his family and his closest supporters. The government, for him, was a means of personal aggrandizement rather than an instrument of public service, despite the efforts made by many of his followers to create an ideology based on the supposed reconstruction of the country.

That ideology was inspired in the notion that until 1930 the Dominican Republic had been a backward and stagnant country, politically divided by permanent strife between caudillos and humiliated by foreign diplomatic and military intervention. After he came to power, Trujillo started a process of national reconstruction based on the political unification of the territory and the development of the economic resources of the country. He was then acclaimed as "Father of the New Fatherland" and "Benefactor of the Fatherland." and hundreds of publications were printed and widely distributed in schools and offices to publicize it.

From early on, thousands of political meetings and rallies, where thousands of speeches were given, were organized every year to teach Dominicans of the providential miracle of having a God-sent ruler who would cure the Republic of all its historic maladies. Radio stations broadcast this message time and time again, every hour on the hour, and, as the Dictatorship aged, the message became more frequent, more elaborate, and more pervasive. Through that overwhelming propaganda apparatus, which pervaded all aspects of Dominican life, Trujillo managed to institutionalize a noncollectivist totalitarian political system without parallel in any other country in Latin America.

ECONOMIC POLICIES

In his zeal to increase his personal fortune, Trujillo faced the enormous task of developing the national wealth, because his own was necessarily contingent on it. This was the motivation behind his vigorous determination to pursue the policy of promoting agriculture and public works initiated by previous regimes. Throughout the 31 years of his regime, Trujillo's government carried out the most grandiose program of public works and construction ever realized in the Dominican Republic.

Because the country's economic situation after the crisis of 1929 was in a deplorable state due to the collapse of the prices of its principal exports, the Dominican Republic was left without enough foreign exchange to pay for the most essential imports or to amortize its public debt, much less to embark in a substantial program of public works. But as soon as the economy began to recover around 1938, the government resumed the previous projects of highways, bridges, irrigation canals, and agricultural settlement with unprecedented energy.

After a few years, the country's prosperity began to be evident, due to the opening of tens of thousands of hectares of land and the settling of thousands of peasant families on lands donated by the state in regions until then uncultivated. As a result of the colonization programs, agricultural production grew in every sector, making the country self-sufficient in rice, corn, beans, and other foodstuffs by 1950.

Trujillo made his deepest economic mark in fostering industrialization. His government was spurred by the scarcity of imports created by the Great Depression in the 30s. Trujillo was the main factor behind the establishment of new industrial plants for the production of shoes, beer, tobacco, alcohol, starch, pasta, and vegetable oil organized during the years before World War II. Born near the capital, the Dictator worked to transform the old city of Santo Domingo into the principal industrial center of the Dominican Republic by concentrating basic industrial complexes in the city to produce for the internal market during and after World War II. Trujillo took advantage of the economic crisis of 1929 to establish a program of austerity that froze salaries for many years and delayed his industrialization schemes. In 1936, he had the name of the capital changed into Ciudad Trujillo.

In 1942 he managed to modify the constitution to allow the executive power, which he controlled, to grant special incentives and tax holidays to new industrial enterprises created to substitute imports and saving foreign exchange. Using his well-organized system of monopolies, Trujillo managed to become the largest saver and investor in the Republic and finally became the first great captain of industry in the Dominican Republic, associating himself with national and foreign businessmen who either joined his companies or were forced to allow him to join their companies that had been established for years and had already demonstrated their profitability.

Several of Trujillo's first partners were Spanish, Syrian-Lebanese, or Dominican merchants and industrialists who had participated in the first phase of import substitution at the beginning of the century in the cities of Santo Domingo, Santiago, San Pedro de Macorís, and Puerto Plata. Trujillo's economic empire expanded due to the new scarcity of imported manufactured goods which was produced by the disruption of navigation and the restrictions of the war economy between 1939-45, a shortage that he set about satisfying rapidly, creating new industries by using his capital and that of his associates. After World War II these new enterprises profited from the boom in exports produced by the wake of worldwide demand for tropical products, particularly during the years of the Korean War.

At the end of World War II, the growth of Trujillo's industrial complex soared with the opening of new factories for cement, chocolate, alcohol, beverages, liquors, paper, cardboard, processed milk, flour, nails, bottles and glass, coffee, rice, marble, medicines, paint, sacks, cord and knitted goods, textiles, clothing, and sugar. Almost all the industries created during the postwar years, including those in which Trujillo was not a direct partner, were granted special concessions and tax exemptions and were protected by the government from labor unrest and trade union demands, as well as from foreign competition. On the other hand, most of the new modern plants were established in or around Ciudad Trujillo, thus converting, in less than 15 years, the old administrative capital into a thriving industrial and commercial center that attracted increasing waves of immigrants from the interior of the country.

One of the most impressive features of Dominican import substitution industrialization from 1938 to 1960 was the sustained secular growth of all its indicators. During that period the number of manufacturing establishments almost doubled; capital investment multiplied 9 times; the number of workers and employees grew almost 2.5 times; the amount of salaries paid by the industrial sector was 10 times more in 1960 than it was in 1938; the national raw materials used by the manufacturing sector also multiplied 14 times; fuel and lubricants expenditures increased 22 times; industrial sales also multiplied more than 12 times from $13.3 million to $164.4 million, an impressive growth in a 22 year period.

Sugar was one of Trujillo's biggest industrial ventures. With sugar prices depressed throughout the 30s, Trujillo never thought of taking charge of the sugar industry before World War II. But at the end of the war, he and his advisors could not fail to notice the enormous profits being reaped by the foreign owners of sugar mills that had been in existence for more than a century. He did not want to be left out of this business and in 1949 he began to build a midsize sugar mill, the Central Catarey, on a piece of land he owned on the outskirts of Villa Altagracia, 25 miles from Santo Domingo. But this mill was too small to satisfy his new aspirations, and by the following year he had already begun construction of the Central Río Haina, which he hoped would be the largest sugar mill in the country.

In the years that followed, Trujillo used state and personal funds filtered through a complex system of financial operations to buy most of the foreign mills operating in the country, thus establishing himself as the largest sugar producer in the Dominican Republic. To this end he launched a bitter nationalist campaign against the foreign domination of the sugar industry just as he was building his first two sugar mills.

To increase pressure against the foreign sugar companies Trujillo also imposed onerous export taxes, which convinced the owners that the best way out for them was to sell. The only mills remaining that he still had not bought by 1961 were those of the Casa Vicini and the Central Romana. The latter belonged to the South Puerto Rico Sugar Company, with whose proprietors Trujillo had been unable to come to an agreement about the selling price, but were about to sell when the Dictator was killed in May of that year.

Other foreign companies that Trujillo's government acquired during his campaign to control the economic life of the nation were the National City Bank, which he made into the Banco de Reservas in 1941, and the Compañía Eléctrica, today called the Corporación Dominicana de Electricidad. Besides those enterprises, Trujillo owned more traditional businesses: he was the biggest landowner in the country. His large latifundia included cattle ranches that produced meat and milk, as well as extensive forest reserves which he exploited through well-known figureheads by means of whom he monopolized the country's wood market.

Trujillo's economic and financial empire grew so large that at the end of his life in 1961 he controlled nearly 80 percent of the country's industrial production and his firms employed 45 percent of the country's active labor force. Combined with his absolute control of the state, which employed 15 percent of the labor force, this meant that nearly 60 percent of Dominican families depended on his will one way or another. All this was connected to a system of taxes and forced contributions to the Partido Dominicano's funds over which Trujillo had total control.

It was commonly said that during the Trujillo regime the situation reached such extremes that the Dominicans could not obtain food, shoes, clothing, or shelter without creating a profit in one way or another for Trujillo or his family. From the beginning, the Dominican government was a tool for his personal enrichment, and the reorganization of the state was a pretext for his own exaltation.

This could be clearly seen in his highly publicized accomplishment of being the liquidator of the external debt of the Dominican Republic. When Trujillo came to power in 1930, in the middle of a general economic crisis, an important part of the country's financial limitations could be traced back to its obligations under the Dominican-American Convention of 1924, which prevented the Dominican Republic from taking out new loans or raising customs tariffs without the consent of the U.S. government. At the same time, the Convention compelled the Dominican government to allow the distribution of customs revenues to be carried out by the United States through the General Customs Office, whereby 50 percent of customs revenues was deducted to pay the external debt.

In 1931 Trujillo's government began negotiating with the United States for a moratorium that would allow the Dominican Republic to pay interest on the debt only as long as the world economic crisis lasted. These negotiations yielded positive results and allowed Trujillo's government to count on larger resources than it would have enjoyed under the terms of the 1924 Convention.

The economic crisis also led the Dominican government to open negotiations with the United States in 1931 on the subject of restoring to the Republic the right to administer its own customs office, which had been under U.S. administration since 1905. This agreement was delayed for several years because negotiations were hampered by incidents on both sides and it was not easy to convince the bond holders that they would continue to enjoy the same guarantees for repayment of the debt. But finally, on September 24, 1940, Trujillo, who had already served two terms as president and now had been named extraordinary ambassador and minister plenipotentiary, and Cordell Hull, U.S. secretary of state, signed a treaty modifying the Convention of 1924 to the effect that from that moment on the Customs Office would no longer operate under the direction of the U.S. Government and that its offices and branches would become part of the Dominican public administration system.

This treaty, known as the "Trujillo-Hull Treaty" and ratified on February 15, 1941, was the object of an enormous government propaganda campaign to make Trujillo appear as the restorer of the country's financial independence. Government apologists exploited the scandalous and depressing financial history of the country to make Trujillo seem like a savior who had been able to restore the sovereignty of the Republic, which had been violated by the foreign administration of customs.

Although the administration of customs passed into Dominican hands after the Trujillo-Hull treaty, all the funds collected by the Dominican government in the customs houses still had to be deposited in the National City Bank of New York, which had a branch in Santo Domingo. Once these funds were deposited, one of the bank's officers, representing the bond holders, distributed the money between the Dominican government and the foreign creditors. This arrangement was the most Trujillo could get in 1940, and he continued searching for ways to amortize the Republic's foreign debt. Of the $16 million the country owed in 1930, only $9.4 million was still outstanding in July 1947.

Taking advantage of the country's improved financial situation which resulted from increased accumulation of reserves during World War II, the government paid off the creditors in full on July 21, 1947. The liquidation of the foreign debt was used by Trujillo as a pretext for launching a spectacular campaign to portrait him as the "father of national financial independence." To this end, the government unearthed and widely publicized the history of the Republic's financial troubles, and portraited Trujillo as a providencial ruler who had saved the country from financial chaos and political dependence.

THE HAITIAN QUESTION

Another issue inherited from the past that Trujillo sought to solve was that of the permanent Haitian settlement in Dominican territory. For more than a century Haitians had been peacefully penetrating the country and settling on agricultural lands abandoned by Dominicans during the Haitian-Dominican wars in the middle of the 19th century. In spite of Dominican efforts in the rest of the century to reach an agreement with Haiti, it had never been possible to clarify the problem of the border.

At the beginning of the 20th century the two nations tried to reach an agreement on the frontier line, and the issue was finally resolved in 1929 during Horacio Vásquez's tenure. But despite the fact that on January 21 of that year a treaty was signed fixing the frontier line, several tens of thousands of Haitians were still living as peasants near the border in the southwest and the northwest on the Dominican side, or working as laborers in the sugar industry in the southeast, or earning a living as domestic servants, farmers, or small businessmen in many towns of the interior.

The Haitians living near the border were completely marginal to Dominican society and the territory they occupied functioned as an extension of Haiti. Haitian currency circulated freely in the Cibao, the main agricultural region of the country, and in the south it circulated as far as Azua, only 120 kilometers from Santo Domingo. Trujillo did not want to accept that fact. He traveled to the frontier at the beginning of October 1937, and there gave a speech announcing that the occupation by Haitians of the frontier territories must not continue. Afterwards, he ordered that all Haitians remaining in the country be exterminated. In the days following October 4, 1937, the army assassinated all Haitians on sight. Eighteen thousand Haitians were killed. The only ones able to save their lives were those who managed to cross the border and those protected by the sugar mills, which did not want to lose their Haitian labor force.

The murder of the Haitians produced an international scandal and elicited a unanimous rebuke from all of Latin America and the United States. It also caused a gigantic shock among the Dominican people, who either witnessed with terror the massacre or heard the ominous rumors about it that circulated from household to household.

After a dramatic series of protests, investigations and diplomatic mediations, the case was closed in February 1939 when the Dominican government paid the Haitian government

$525,000 as compensation for damages and injuries occasioned by what officially was termed "frontier conflicts." Actually, the agreement was reached in January 31, 1938, and the compensation was fixed at $750,000 , of which Trujillo paid $250,000 in advance. He then sent a special envoy to Port-au-Prince who, after bribing some Haitian government politicians, managed to bring down the second and final payment to $275,000 in February, 1939, for a total compensation of $525,000.

Trujillo wanted to make the slaughter look like a simple frontier incident between Dominican peasants and Haitian livestock thieves which had occurred when the Dominicans, tired of being robbed, decided to attack the Haitians and managed to kill some of them. The truth is it was an act of genocide, but the government's apologists mounted an intense propaganda campaign defending Trujillo as the "savior of the nation."

In 1941, several years after the elimination of the Haitians from the frontier zone, the government launched a vast program of Dominicanization of the frontier consisting of the creation of towns all along the new line of demarcation, the Dominican identity of which would be assured by a series of military installations to prevent new Haitian penetrations.

In the following years, the Dominicanization of the frontier turned into a kind of crusade of national vindication to regain and bring once more under Dominican control those zones that had been lost more than a century before and that the Dominicans had been unable to win back, first because of the Haitian invasions during the wars of independence and later because of frontier commerce. These new towns and military outposts were furnished with every convenience.

The frontier was repopulated in a few years with Dominican families who were given lands in the many agrarian colonies created to settle a population which would revitalize these depopulated regions. The Catholic church was invited to join this campaign, and the Jesuit order sent its priests to the new towns along the frontier to bring into Christianity those people who had formerly been under the influence of voodoo.

The Dominicanization program definitely linked these territories to the Dominican Republic, organizing them into several provinces. Connected by many roads and crossed by irrigation canals, the frontier became a permanently populated zone integrated into the general production system of the country. This fact served to reinforce Trujillo's ideology that postulated that he was the true savior of the country's Hispanic and Catholic tradition. It became the central theme of the dictatorship's propaganda.

POLITICAL STABILITY

Politically, the Trujillo regime achieved stable continuity in spite of the many conspiracies against him and the invasions organized by exiled Dominicans in the years after World War II. Constitutionally, Trujillo was president of the Republic for four terms, the first of which ran from 1930 to 1934 and the second from 1934 to 1938. Although there were no legal provisions against the indefinite reelection of the president, he stepped out that year and sponsored the election of Jacinto B. Peynado, the man who until then had been his vice-president. When Peynado died in 1940 he was replaced by his vice-president Manuel de Jesús Troncoso de la Concha.

According to some sources, the reason why Peynado and Troncoso de la Concha were elected in 1938, although Trujillo continued to be the actual ruler, was that the United States opposed Trujillo's reelection because of the slaughter of the Haitians. Yet the diplomatic correspondence of the period does not substantiate this view and only points out at the existence of persistent rumors regarding the displeasure of the U.S. government toward the possible continuation of Trujillo's presidency.

In any case, after the program to Dominicanize the frontier had started, and after five years had elapsed to dim mem-
ories of the massacre the U.S. government did not object to
Trujillo's becoming president for a third term for five years,
from 1942 to 1947, nor to his reelection to another five-year
term between 1947 and 1952. In this latter year he imposed
his brother Héctor Bienvenido Trujillo as a new president, and
had him reelected in 1957.

In all elections after 1934, both Trujillo and his proxy candidates were elected virtually unanimously. Héctor Trujillo acted as president until August 1960, when he resigned because
of the international crisis facing the government over the economic sanctions imposed on it by the Organization of American States (OAS) after Rafael Trujillo tried to assassinate Rómulo Betancourt, president of Venezuela, in June 1960. Joaquín
Balaguer, who had been vice-president then became the new
puppet president.

THE COLLAPSE OF THE DICTATORSHIP

Of the two invasions carried out by Dominican exiles, (Luperón in June 1949 and Constanza, Maimón, and Estero Hondo in June 1959), the latter, despite its failure, created insoluble
problems for the regime, because afterwards many Dominicans
believed that they could enjoy the support of the Cuban government led by Fidel Castro, who had sponsored the last guerrilla
expedition.

Castro had come to power in January 1959 and was willing
to help Dominicans to overthrow Trujillo. His first international military endeavor was to arm and support a large military
expedition against Trujillo. The invading army was composed
mainly of Dominican exiles and some military commanders who
had accompanied Castro in Sierra Maestra. Once they arrived

at Dominican territory they were quickly defeated by Trujillo's imposing army in June 1959, and almost all the expeditionaries lost their lives.

From then on, Cuban radio stations continuously broadcasted messages encouraging the Dominican people to revolt against the dictator, supporting the idea of future actions against Trujillo. Stimulated by those messages, many people started to conspire. Conspiracies spread far and wide, but were promptly discovered, and by mid-1960 the jails were full of hundreds of political prisoners from every social class, while the government stepped up its old methods of open terror, threats, and spying on Dominican and foreign citizens.

Torturing and killing political prisoners and opponents became a daily practice. Many Dominicans were assassinated in 1960, among them three sisters from the respected Mirabal family, whose husbands had been jailed for participating in the conspiracy originating with the June 14 invasion of the previous year. The assassination of the Mirabal sisters on November 25, 1960 deeply touched the sensibility of decent people and definitely turned them against Trujillo, further charging the atmosphere with deep resentment against the government.

New conspiracies arose, even among Trujillo's own friends, government officials, and close associates. One of these conspiracies had the support of the U.S. government, whose leaders thought that the time had come to put an end to this long tyranny. It was the conviction of many policy makers in Washington that if Trujillo continued indefinitely in power, and the economic conditions of the country continued to deteriorate under the sanctions imposed by the OAS, the Dominican Republic risked the possibility of facing a Communist takeover similar to the recent Cuban Revolution. The Eisenhower administration had already been switching sides in regard to some of the Latin American dictators, and Trujillo was one of them. That policy was inherited in 1960 by the new Kennedy administration, which continued its contacts with high-ranking conspirators from within the regime itself.

Encouraged by this backing, a group of men led by former General Juan Tomás Díaz, a childhood friend of Trujillo who had lost his rank and had fallen from the dictator's grace because of his sister's political opposition, plotted to shoot Trujillo while he was on his way to his "Hacienda Fundación" in San Cristóbal. On the evening of May 30, 1961, after several frustrated attempts, the ploters finally killed Trujillo by shooting at him with machine-guns in a quick and dramatic car chase on the highway that connects San Cristóbal and Santo Domingo as he was going to meet one of his mistresses.

The assassination of the dictator took place while the regime was still in disarray as a result of the economic sanctions imposed the year before by the OAS, and while popular opposition was growing because of the attacks Trujillo had launched in recent months against the Catholic church after it had refused to grant him the title of "Benefactor of the Church," which he wanted to add to those of "Generalissimo," "Benefactor of the Fatherland," and "Father of the New Fatherland."

The economic sanctions had been only one last blow to the deep structural crisis that had been seriously affecting the Dominican economy since 1958 as a result of the fall of prices of its principal export commodities. The fall of foreign exchange revenues during those years worsened the Dominican Republic's balance of payments which had been experiencing significant capital drains after 1955 when Trujillo spent more than $30 million constructing an international fair to commemorate his 25 years in power. Following that, Trujillo critically drained the country's international reserves by paying cash to foreign investors for the purchase of several sugar mills and all the electricity plants in the country that were nationalized in the late 50s.

After enjoying an outstandingly strong balance of payment situation for almost 20 years, the government had to ask for aid to the International Monetary Fund (IMF), and in mid-1959 it signed a Stand-By Agreement for $11.5 million which provided for import restrictions and other monetary controls. But the guerrilla invasion of June 1959 scared many of Trujillo's relatives and associates, who suddenly began to transfer their savings to foreign banks. It also prompted Trujillo to spend more than $80 million in weapons and military supplies, with the consequent worsening of the balance of payments and disruption of the economy. It was in the middle of this financial crisis that Trujillo lost his life and his regime started to collapse after 31 years of dictatorship.

THE IMPACT OF TRUJILLO'S RULE

During his long absolute rule, Trujillo advanced the task of developing the national wealth that had begun at the turn of the century. But the predatory nature of his regime, which tended to exploit the country's riches for his own and his family's benefit, created a system of appropriation of national economic resources that eventually reverted his colonization policies of the 30s and 40s and, in the end, dispossessed thousands of peasants from their lands and forced them to emigrate to the cities during a period when demographic growth ran as high as 3.6 percent a year.

In the final analysis Trujillo created a government consisting of himself, his family, and his most intimate associates that limited participation by the majority in the exercise of power and reduced their potential to create wealth. The country grew economically during Trujillo's era, and although the state was well organized and the civil and military bureaucracies functioned with relative efficiency, they were only sustained on the basis of the fear inspired by the dictator and on their performance at the service of his personal interests. The monopolis-

tic nature of his enterprises left little room for private investment since no one felt safe from being stripped of their businesses once they proved profitable.

Trujillo's nationalization of a variety of foreign companies
was carried out for his own benefit, and although he normally
invested his profits in the creation of new companies, a substantial part of his fortune was deposited in foreign banks. When
he died in 1961 his family had about $300 million in accounts
outside the country. His companies functioned and made profits because they enjoyed every possible government protection.
Many paid no taxes, his workers earned very low wages, and
some of the companies used public employees, members of the
army, and convicts as workers. In those cases where a company
was showing a loss, he would sell it to the state at a profit. When
the company recuperated its losses, he would buy it back again
at a profit.

The notion that Trujillo made the Dominican state into a
private business is not far from the truth. Although it retained a
constitutional façade and had a National Congress, a Supreme
Court of Justice, and other public institutions, one should not
be misled by this semblance of constitutional separation of powers: all senators, deputies, judges, and public employees were
directly appointed by the dictator itself, although keeping external procedures as to simulate the formalities of a working
democracy. Thus, senators and deputies were "elected" by the
only political party that existed in the country, the Partido Dominicano, following the personal recommendation of the dictator. Before being appointed, senators and deputies signed a
resignation letter with no date that was delivered to the dictator to be used according to political convenience.

Many radio stations and the only television station, as well
as the two major daily newspapers, were directly owned by the
dictator and his relatives and were used to glorify the accom-
plishments of Trujillo and to spread the ideological catechism

of the regime. Within this framework, the educational system and student population were favorite targets of the massive propaganda machinery that kept the Dominican people almost totally brainwashed for 31 years. Textbooks were written to entirely reinterpret Dominican history and make Trujillo appear as the savior of the nation. Thousands of songs and poems exalting Trujillo were continuously written, published, and performed in schools to praise Trujillo and teach the students why he was the true "Benefactor of the Fatherland."

The industrialization that began during World War II and continued without interruption until 1960 altered the purely administrative character of Santo Domingo, converting it to a manufacturing center that attracted tens of thousands of Dominicans from the country and cities of the interior in search for jobs. This pattern of internal migration was echoed on different levels in the rest of the country's urban centers, so that by 1960 only 60 percent of the population lived in the countryside, in contrast to a rural population of 84 percent in 1920.

Health services and sanitation improved greatly during Trujillo's times and thus also contributed to making urban life more attractive than rural life to many peasants and laborers. Lured by the hope of finding work in one of the new industries being built, they began to form an ample urban labor market that would supply Dominican industry with a cheap labor force in the years to come. Construction of hospitals, improvement of medical services in the cities, training of hundreds of new doctors, implementation of intensive antiparasitic campaigns and introduction of antibiotics at the end of the 40s radically reduced the mortality rate and fostered greater fertility among Dominican women to such an extent that the years following World War II marked the beginning of rapid population growth.

As late as 1944, Dominican politicians still thought the country was underpopulated, and for more than 15 years encouraged childbearing by offering incentives to large families, an indication that the phenomenon of explosive population growth did not become apparent until the 1950 census, which counted three million inhabitants in contrast to the scarce one million of 1920. Many congratulated the government of Trujillo, thinking it responsible for the demographic growth that they believed was a sign of social maturity and development. Now, they thought, there would be enough workers for the Dominican economy, which for centuries had been limited by a permanent shortage of labor that made previous governments resort to policies encouraging immigration.

The population expansion required the government to enlarge its bureaucracy and extend public services at a time when the number of men employed in the armed forces was increasing to take care of the security needs of Trujillo's regime so that the number of jobs in the public sector increased. Even though the army of some 20,000 soldiers was a heavy burden for the Dominican economy, it was also an important source of employment for impoverished peasant youths. Together with the population employed in the many small industries and workshops and those who worked in the sugar industry, the employed population evolved into a variety of social sectors that received substantial impetus between 1948 and 1958 due to the extraordinary growth in the economy produced by favorable prices for Dominican export products.

Sugar, cacao, coffee, tobacco, and bananas produced the bulk of foreign exchange and provided the government with sizeable tax revenues that were used either to finance new industries or public works, or to keep the state apparatus running. During the 1950s the government began to harvest the fruits of its constant policy of agricultural colonization, which resulted in the opening of more than 125,000 hectares of land that had never been farmed. The opening of large numbers of irrigation canals in previously uncultivated areas helped to expand the cultivation of rice and plantains, whereas the extraordinary increase in livestock and the development of new crops like bananas, peanuts and vegetables broadened the rural horizon considerably during the 50s. Rapid population growth considerably increased the size of the internal market and stimulated agricultural production.

There was also an increase in school enrollments, and the number of university-educated professionals multiplied. It is noteworthy that the state-owned University of Santo Domingo, which had been reorganized in 1932 and had maintained a student enrollment of about 1,000 for many years, saw its enrollment grow to 3,000 students at the end of the 50s. The state university regularly graduated around 100 professionals each year, supplying the country, for the first time in its history, with a new middle stratum that could ultimately assume the social, political, and economic leadership once the Trujillo regime ended. Many of the professionals who graduated during the last ten years of Trujillo's era left the country to study abroad or to perform diplomatic duties and returned with new ideas. Many brought back modern technological innovations in various fields and specialities that were incorporated into the process of accelerated economic growth that would take place in the following two decades.

All these changes, nevertheless, were not enough to satisfy the basic needs of the population because the economic expansion and industrialization during those years rested on a system of family monopolies that, endorsed by a tyrannical political regime, took advantage of the development of Dominican wealth to amass enormous savings that were transferred outside the country. The result was a deformed economic growth, completely asymmetrical, in which only a tiny minority was able to take advantage of recent industrial development while the majority of the population enjoyed only marginal access to the nation's sources of wealth.

By 1960 it was already apparent that the hospitals constructed were inadequate; that the schools could not handle the population growth and that illiteracy had increased; that the cost of living had risen while real wages remained stagnant; that unemployment was growing in the cities while Trujillo's tiny family oligarchy drained the country of capital that should have been reinvested in the creation of new jobs; and that the countryside was becoming impoverished because several hundred thousand hectares of land had fallen into the hands of landlords who managed to increase their holdings at the expense of traditional peasant lands.

During the 50s, several urban groups, particularly merchants, professionals, and military personnel recently enriched, used their savings to buy rural properties as a means of acquiring economic security and social prestige. Many individuals, too, put their savings away in national or foreign banks waiting for new opportunities for investment as soon as the dictatorship came to an end.

At the same time, a rural proletariat appeared that grew larger and larger as a result of the government's profertility policies, and poorer and poorer as they continued to lose their land. The process of marginal urban settlements accelerated as an enormous mass of men and women who lacked education, health care, jobs, or land rushed to the main cities and settled in their peripheral zones. This marginalization process was noticeable by 1960 and it accelerated rapidly during the succeeding two decades, thus giving way to the formation of an extense urban proletariat composed of the unemployed and day laborers, called *chiriperos*, who came to constitute a ready market for cheap labor in the urban economy.

To be sure, many of those changes would have taken place, as they did in other parts of Latin America, even if Trujillo had not ruled the country between 1930 and 1961. In the end, Trujillo left the Dominican Republic with a dualist economy with a very poor, large working and peasant class, a very rich and very small upper class, and a total lack of democratic institutions. In 1930

Trujillo came to rule over a traditional two-class, provincial, peasant-based, backward, and poor society. When he died in 1961 he left a society in transition, but still underdeveloped, with a capitalist economy deformed by monopolistic industrial growth. By placing the control of the country's resources in the hands of an absolutely unscrupulous family, he deprived the nation of the opportunity of faster modernization and socioeconomic development. All of this left the country in a situation remarkably similar to that of many other Latin American societies, although on a different scale.

19.
Democracy vs. Neo-Trujilloism (1961-1978)

DEMOCRATIZATION AND CIVIL WAR

Trujillo's death on May 30, 1961 awakened the country's political and social energies and opened an intensive process of political democratization. Actors who had previously been on the sidelines of the dictatorship emerged: political exiles, political parties, trade unions, professional associations, student organizations, and a free press. In the following months, the Dominican political system underwent a rapid transformation as the nation was called on to shake off the dictatorship. As the months passed, political rallies and mass concentrations became the most effective means for exerting popular pressure against puppet President Joaquín Balaguer and the Trujillo family.

These rallies were organized by the new political movements and parties that came forward after June 1, 1961, and by the Movimiento Popular Dominicano (MPD), an extreme left party previously authorized by Trujillo in 1960. The main organizations founded in those days were: Unión Cívica Nacional (UCN), a strong popular movement headed by Dr. Viriato Fiallo, a man who never surrendered to the dictatorship; the Partido Revolucionario Dominicano (PRD) directed by the writer Juan Bosch and other political exiles who had returned to the country in July; Vanguardia Revolucionaria Dominicana (VRD), a small party ran by Horacio Julio Ornes, another exile who had participated in the Luperón invasion in 1949; and the Movimiento Revolucionario 14 de Junio (MR-1J4), a leftist revolutionary organization headed by Manuel Tavares Justo who wanted for his country a regime similar to the Cuban Revolution.

The new political groups worked to overthrow Balaguer, who represented the dictatorship, together with the sons and brothers of Trujillo who controlled the armed forces. On November 19, 1961, a group of military officers rebelled against the Trujillos and forced into exile the entire Trujillo family and its closest associates. They were supported by all the political organizations and by the U.S. Government. The Trujillos were expelled for life from the country, but the political crisis continued for two more months for Balaguer still maintained his grip on the presidency, helped by the new military leaders.

Balaguer tried to maneuver to stay in power and survive politically. He dissolved the Partido Dominicano, the dictatorship's official political party, and divided its funds among his friends in the bureaucracy, the armed forces, and the secret service. He also tried to win the support of the poor by lowering the prices of basic foodstuffs and abolishing import taxes on several consumer articles. Despite these measures, political agitation continued and a general strike that lasted 12 days shook the regime in December. Balaguer had to compromise and incorporated Unión Cívica Nacional and his opponents into the government. After long negotiations, he agreed to summon Congress to modify the constitution and create a Consejo de Estado of seven members to run the country under his presidency.

The Consejo de Estado was composed by members and supporters of Unión Cívica Nacional as the other political groups decided not to participate in the government. The Catholic church was also represented as well as the only two survivors of the plot that took Trujillo's life. The Consejo de Estado would exercise both legislative and executive powers until a new democratic constitution was drafted and free general elections were held one year later. On January 16, 1962, Balaguer overthrew the Consejo de Estado and replaced it with a five member civilian-military junta.

He was immediately confronted with a more violent general strike that completely paralyzed the country and overthrew the junta two days later, forcing him to resign and flee into exile. He was then replaced as president and head of the Consejo de Estado by Rafael F. Bonnelly, a long-time Trujillo bureaucrat that had lost the dictator's favor two years before when his son was arrested and sent to jail after joining a clandestine anti-Trujillo movement created in 1959.

The goals of the Consejo de Estado were essentially political. It was conceived as a transitional government, the main responsibility of which was to organize free elections within one year and to prepare the political climate for the installation of a new, democratic, constitutional government. Elections were held on December 20, 1962 and were won in a landslide by Juan Bosch, the candidate of the Partido Revolucionario Dominicano (PRD), founded in Cuba in 1939. Bosch had spent his adult life in exile during Trujillo's rule and had returned to the country in 1961 together with many other exiles.

The new government was inaugurated on February 27, 1963. His general ideas on economic development were reformist and populist. He had learned them in Costa Rica and Cuba in the 50s. For many in the Dominican Republic those ideas were too advanced, and Bosch was soon labeled Communist and pro-Communist by many businessmen, military officers, priests, and industrialists.

Notwithstanding the anti-Communist rhetoric of the extreme rightist groups, even those who did not trust Bosch gave him the benefit of the doubt. The political liberty and the climate of optimism offered by the new constitutional government opened up debate as to the best way to accelerate development. The Dominican economy had started to recover in 1962 due to an emergency plan put into operation by the Consejo de Estado with the help of the Alliance for Progress, a plan of economic aid designed by the United States in order to foster the development of Latin America.

The Consejo de Estado had been entirely responsive to industrial and commercial interests, but Bosch's new government was not so tractable, and two months after his innaugation, the Asociación de Industrias de la República Dominicana challenged him to define his economic policy and offer them firm guarantes for new investment. The Asociación de Industrias had been created in 1962 by the most important industrial entrepreneurs, some of whom had flourished during the 50s profiting from the extraordinary economic growth of the postwar years. Many of these industrialists had lacked the privileges enjoyed by Trujillo's enterprises. Many others, though, had been favorites of Trujillo and partners in some of his enterprises and had managed to survive the wave of confiscations that took place between 1961 and 1962 when Balaguer and the Consejo de Estado decided that Trujillo's monopolies became the property of the state.

Most businessmen had been protected by the Consejo de Estado and had participated in the electoral campaign against Bosch as they considered his behavior undependable and erratic. Some of them formed a political movement called Acción Dominicana Independiente (ADI) and established a common front within the Consejo Nacional de Hombres de Empresa (CNHE) against Bosch's government. They were joined by some members of the Catholic church and the extreme right. With this support, the ADI and several anti-Bosch clerics organized large concentrations of peasants called "meetings of Christian reaffirmation" to protest against Communist infiltration in Bosch's government and the Dominican Republic.

These were the days of an intensive continental propaganda campaign against the Cuban Revolution. The Dominican Republic had welcomed hundreds of Cuban exiles, especially businessmen, politicians, professionals and clerics, who were waging an active propaganda campaign against Fidel Castro, whom they erroneously associated with the Bosch government. They considered Bosch's reformist social-democratic philosophy as a threat to their interests. These Cuban exiles and clerics fueled the anti-Bosch movement and provided Dominican politicians with ideological support against Communism. Bosch was reluctant to move against the very few Dominican communists, whom he said should be tolerated. Bosch's attitude increasingly upset the members of the military mission at the U.S. Embassy who transmitted their discomfort to the Dominican military.

Day by day, opposition to Bosch grew. His lack of understanding of the Dominican reality after 25 years in exile led him into conflict with almost every social group, including his own party. Within a few months, Bosch found himself completely isolated, and most of his supporters deserted him. This became evident on September 20, 1963, when the business groups called a general strike that paralyzed the country for two days. This strike signaled to the military that the time was ripe for the coup d'état they had been planning with some important merchants, industrialists, landowners, and members of the minor political parties and the Catholic church. Five days later, on September 25, 1963, Bosch was deposed and replaced by a triumvirate composed of corporate executives and lawyers, and whose cabinet was made up of rightist entrepreneurs and lawyers with ties to the Dominican business community.

In December a guerrilla movement commanded by the leaders of the Revolutionary Movement 14 de Junio took to the mountains to fight against the triumvirate, but were quickly surrounded by army troops, and forced to surrender. Once taken prisoners, most of the guerrilleros were assassinated. When the triumvirate president, Emilio de los Santos, learned of the circumstances, he resigned his post declaring that he did not want to be an accomplice of the assassination of a group of youngsters. De los Santos was quickly replaced by Donald Reid Cabral, a car dealer related to Unión Cívica Nacional, who had been participating actively in the conspiracy against Bosch.

The triumvirate was only able to stay in power thanks to the support of the United States, the Catholic church and the Trujilloist generals in the armed forces, to whom Reid Cabral granted the most outrageous privileges. The most scandalous of those privileges was the permission to establish a commissariat to sell massive amounts of foreign manufactured goods smuggled into the country on Dominican Air Force planes. As a de facto regime created by a military coup, the triumvirate was extremely unpopular. In spite of Bosch's faults, the Dominican people enjoyed his democratic rule and had placed high hopes in his government. After all, Bosch had won the elections with the support of more than 60 per cent of the electorate.

Forced to operate in secrecy, the democratic political parties turned to conspiracy with Bosch, now exiled in Rio Piedras, Puerto Rico. A group of young military officers who wanted a return to a constitutional regime contacted Bosch and offered him support to overthrow the triumvirate and bring him back to power. At the same time, in New York Joaquín Balaguer formed the Partido Reformista with cadres from Trujillo's Partido Dominicano. When Bosch and Balaguer entered into an alliance, Reid Cabral's position became extremely weak. Constant strikes by workers in state enterprises and by taxi drivers, and equally frequent student demonstrations, obliged the triumvirate to keep the police in the streets to quell disturbances and arrest political and union leaders, workers, and students.

Despite the Bosch-Balaguer populist alliance, businessmen and landowners on the right organized a new party called the Partido Liberal Evolucionista (PLE), headed by Luis Amiama Tió, one of the survivors of Trujillo's assasination. It was an open secret that Reid Cabral had an understanding with them to run for president in the forthcoming elections set for September 1965. The elections were to be rigged and held without the participation of Bosch and Balaguer, the leaders of the two largest political forces in the country. To win, Reid Cabral was counting on the support of a faction of Bosch's PRD who believed the only way to move ahead and resolve the political crisis was to hold new elections.

Both Bosch and the Christian Democrats (organized into the Partido Revolucionario Social Cristiano -PRSC- early in 1962), had also signed a political pact in January 1965, called the Rio Piedras Pact, and agreed to denounce the illegality of the triunvirate and to mobilize public opinion in favour of a "return to constitutionality without elections." This formula meant nothing less than the overthrow of the triunvirate. This position was publicly supported by the small but strident Partido Socialista Popular (PSP), and by a good portion of the unions and student groups. To carry it out, Bosch secretly operated from Puerto Rico. There, he was able to orchestrate a conspiracy that reached the low ranks of the military, many of whom felt obliterated by the high rank officials that supported the triunvirate.

When the conspiracy was finally discovered on April 24, 1965, no one came forward to defend the triumvirate or Donald Reid Cabral. On the contrary, the mayority of the population poured into the streets to celebrate their downfall, which was mistakenly announced over radio and television ahead of time. This announcement gave rise to a serious crisis within the armed forces, which were divided into those who wanted Bosch's return to office without elections to finish his constitutional term and those who wanted to form a military junta to replace the triumvirate.

Reid Cabral vainly maneuvered in an effort to secure military support. Within 24 hours the military men who had backed him before made him a prisoner in the National Palace and began to negotiate with Constitutionalist military leaders. When both military groups could not reach a rapid agreement, the Constitutionalist military leaders distributed weapons to their civilian supporters. On April 25, 1965, civil war broke out in Santo Domingo. Leftist groups and Bosch's followers organized urban guerrillas to destroy the old Trujilloist army, which had been kept intact by the Consejo de Estado, Bosch, and the triumvirate.

After three days of intensive combat in the streets of Santo Domingo, the Constitutionalist forces managed to defeat the troops of the regular army and prepared to launch the final attack on the air base at San Isidro, which was the principal focus of resistance to the pro-Bosch movement. Meanwhile, the military posts in the interior watched and waited, under the control of their old military commanders.

The attack against San Isidro never materialized. In order to stop Bosch from returning to power and "to prevent the emergence of a second Cuba in Latin America," U.S. President Lyndon B. Johnson ordered 42,000 U.S. soldiers to the Dominican Republic, under the pretext of saving lives and protecting U.S. interests in the country. Hence, what began as a coup d'état ended as a civil war, and produced an international crisis linked to the U.S. policy against Cuba, the U.S. military escalation in Vietnam, and later, to the declared U.S. intention of saving democracy in the Dominican Republic.

The first U.S. marines landed on April 28, 1965 and sided with the Trujilloist army. Santo Domingo was rapidly divided into two zones occupied by the opposing armies. The Constitutionalist army was composed of several hundred officers and soldiers from the regular armed forces aided by several thousand men and women who had been given arms at the beginning of the revolt. They organized themselves into dozens of "Constitutionalist commando units" to defend their territory, the old colonial city and its surrounding neighborhoods built at the beginning of the century. On the other side were the Dominican army, navy, and air force assisted by troops from the United States, Brazil, Honduras, Paraguay and Costa Rica. After U.S. manipulation of the OAS, these countries formed a so-called Inter-American Peace Force to make the unilateral intervention of the United States appear legal, although the action was in violation of the OAS charter, as well as that of the United Nations.

Between May and September 1965 there were in fact two governments in the Dominican Republic: One was the "gobierno constitucionalista", presided over by the military leader of the revolt, Colonel Francisco Caamaño; the other was the "gobierno de reconstrucción nacional", headed by one of Trujillo's assassins, General Antonio Imbert Barreras, a declared enemy of Bosch and the Communists, whom the United States had picked and installed quickly so they could influence local politics.

In spite of the superiority of the foreign forces, the conflict could not be resolved through military action. The U.S. military actions served to distract the attention from the first military escalation of the United States in Vietnam. In April 1965, there were only 17,000 U.S. marines in Indochina while in December that number had risen to 245,000, a fact that went by unnoticed by the American people.

The civil war ended, after four months of intensive negotiations heavily influenced by the representative of the United States before the OAS. These negotiations alternated with bloody battles in the streets of Santo Domingo. As a result, an agreement was reached to end the Constitutionalist revolt. At the end of August 1965, both governments resigned and a new provisional civil government was installed on September 3 with a mandate to hold free elections in June 1966. This provisional

government was presided by Héctor García Godoy, a career diplomat and businessman, and one of the vice-presidents of Balaguer's Partido Reformista. In order to provide the new provisional government with some legality, the Constitucionalists
signed with the OAS an statute based on the Constitution of
1963, and also signed a pact of reconciliation.

A basic feature of the reconciliation pact signed on September 3, 1965, which put an end to the civil war, was that the
Constitutionalist military officers and soldiers were to be reintegrated into the barracks. Their leaders would also be able
to leave the country with the help of the provisional government if they wished to do so. Meanwhile, the occupation troops
would remain in the country until new elections were held
and a new constitutional government was in power. During
this period, the United States managed to reconstitute the
Dominican military as a force directly under their command
and entirely dependent on the U.S. government for the payment of salaries and the provision of clothing, food, munitions, and equipment.

García Godoy organized the elections. During the electoral
campaign, the two leading candidates were Joaquín Balaguer
and Juan Bosch, both of whom returned from exile and proceeded to reorganize their parties. Balaguer's Partido Reformista won the elections with the support of Trujilloist army officers, who sponsored a terrorist campaign against Bosch's PRD
in which more than 350 of its political activists were killed between January and May 1966. Bosch himself was not allowed
to go out of his house to campaign and had to address his constituency in daily speeches broadcasted through the radio. The
military made it publicly known that if Bosch ventured out of
his house he would be confronted with military force and prob-
ably killed. Immediately after his defeat, Bosch went into exile
to Spain and spent more than three years there.

TWELVE YEARS OF NEO-TRUJILLOISM

The electoral campaign simply extended the civil war. Only a few among the Constitutionalist military were accepted back by their old comrades in arms. Dozens were assassinated either during the transitional months of the provisional government or after Joaquín Balaguer was elected President of the Republic on June 1, 1966. It took many months for life in Santo Domingo to return to normal, as the open combat of the civil war was replaced by a long wave of anti-Communist and anti-Constitutionalist terrorism carried out by military patrols and paramilitary forces.

The leftist urban guerrilla groups made up of members of the old Constitutionalist commandos reacted to the right's terrorist campaigns by hitting back. Many former combatants were still in possession of weapons which were kept hidden in different places throughout the country. Some believed it possible to make the revolution from the streets, and during the following years violent confrontations took place in the major cities between the government's security forces and the leftist groups. Some of them took advantage of the confusion and used their weapons to rob banks and stores, while others attacked soldiers and policemen to take away their arms.

The Dominican Republic suffered for several years under the terror imposed by Balaguer's military and paramilitary forces. These groups systematically and randomly repressed the opposition parties at random without regard to whether they were leftists or not. The left wing of the PRD was severely persecuted and repressed between 1966 and 1970, as many of their members had tight links with the Movimiento Popular Dominicano (MPD), an extreme leftist group which endorsed the use of urban guerrillas to achieve a "revolutionary coup d'état".

In March, 1970, Juan Bosch returned from exile and dedicated himself to erase all traces of the MPD's influence over his party. At the same time, he influenced the PRD's decision to abstain from participating in the elections. Bosch maintained that the official violence and terrorism had turned the elections into "an electoral slaughterhouse" and that the PRD should not have a part in it. Persecuted and literally hunted down in the streets, the PRD leaders and the leftist parties did not offer a candidate in the 1970 elections and Balaguer ran almost unopposed. His only opponent was his dissident vice-president, Francisco Augusto Lora, who now headed a new party called Movimiento de Integración Democrática (MIDA).

In order to make the role of the regular armed forces less visible, Balaguer authorized the organization of a paramilitary group called La Banda made up of deserters from the leftist parties and professional assassins paid out of the military's intelligence budget. In order to separate himself from the actions of his paramilitary forces, and further terrorize the population, Balaguer referred to these rightist terrorists groups in his public speeches as "uncontrollable forces".

More than 3,000 Dominicans lost their lives in terrorist acts between 1966 and 1974. This situation only ended when the leadership of the leftist parties had been wiped out and the parties completely disorganized and when in 1972 the United States and other democratic countries demanded Balaguer, to put an end to terrorism and the violations of civil rights. These external pressures came as a result of an intense international campaign in Europe, Latin America, and the United States led by José Francisco Peña Gómez, leader of the PRD.

The PRD's campaign had converted Balaguer's terrorism and human rights violations into an electoral issue. In response to the international outcry demanding respect for human rights in the Dominican Republic, Balaguer reacted trying to convey the image of political normality. He dismantled La Banda and started to work toward his reelection as the presidential elections were scheduled for May 1974. There is also evidence that without the direct pressure of the U.S. State Department, Balaguer wouldn't have diminished political violence and repression as suddenly as he did. In terms of human lives, the cost of the political stability was extremely high, but Balaguer always presented the pacification of the country after the civil war as one of his great political achievements.

Colonel Francisco Caamaño was one of the many leftist leaders who lost their lives during this period. Following the civil war Caamaño had left the country for London designated by President García Godoy as military attaché in the Dominican Embassy. From there he had gone clandestinely to Cuba where he remained for several years indoctrinating and training himself for the day when he would return to the Dominican Republic to launch a socialist revolution. Bosch arranged Caamaño's departure to Cuba and planned his political reeducation there. During the following years, Bosch also maintained political contacts with Caamaño and with the Cuban government through personal emissaries who traveled to Havana.

Despite the opposition of Fidel Castro, who did not want to be involved in another guerrilla movement in the Caribbean after Ché Guevara's failure in Bolivia, Caamaño forced his way out of Cuba with a guerilla group and reached the Dominican mountains in February 1, 1973, eight years after the revolt of 1965. By then, the country had changed greatly. The army had been trained for guerrilla warfare, and the country itself had been transformed by economic recovery. A vigorous policy of industrial growth and accelerated urbanization had given rise to a middle class with a degree of affluence never before known in Dominican history.

Many of Caamaño's old comrades had also changed during these eight years. Some had seen their colleagues fall victim to the government's terrorism and were intimidated. Others joined the business world and inmersed themselves in their careers taking part in an expanding economy that between 1970 and 1974, achieved the highest growth rates of any Latin American country. Hence, Caamaño's guerrilla movement never received the popular backing he expected and remained completely isolated in the mountains, where it was quickly annihilated. In February 1973, Caamaño was taken prisoner and assassinated on Balaguer's orders in the mountains of Ocoa.

Meanwhile, Bosch had also gone through a profound personal and ideological transformation. Deeply embittered against the United States for the military intervention of 1965, he made contacts with the Chinese, the North Korean and the North Vietnamese governments, and began to study Marxism, quickly becoming a "Marxist-non-Leninist" adept. On his return to Santo Domingo, Bosch considered that the PRD had lost its mission and entered into serious personal and ideological conflicts with his followers. He rennounced his old faith in democracy and tried to no avail to impose on the PRD, a new political and radical line that proposed a "dictatorship with popular support."

Caamaño's death worsened Bosch's contradictions with his partisans, and bitter recriminations were constantly exchanged among the leaders of the PRD. Bosch thought that his party had shifted to the right and was no longer capable of carrying out the socialist revolution he was now promoting. Finally, in November 1973, Bosch resigned from the PRD, and created a new revolutionary organization called Partido de la Liberación Dominicana (PLD).

Shortly before Bosch's departure, the PRD had joined other parties in an alliance against Balaguer called Bloque de la Dignidad Nacional. Bosch and his new party became the leaders of this alliance with several letist parties. Meanwhile, the PRD, now headed by José Francisco Peña Gómez, managed to articulate a common opposition front with the Partido Revolucionario Social Cristiano (PRSC), the Movimiento Popular Dominicano (MPD), and the Partido Quisqueyano Demócrata (PQD). The PQD was founded by former General Elías Wessin y Wessin, who had been in exile since 1971 after found guilty of conspiracy to overthrow Balaguer. This opposition front, which comprised a radical left party (MPD) and an extreme right party (PQD), was called Acuerdo de Santiago. It carried out a powerful electoral campaign against Balaguer while simultaneously fighting Bosch's Bloque de la Dignidad Nacional.

Balaguer took advantage of this division within the opposition's ranks and ordered the army and the police to repress his adversaries. Political assasinations once again became the norm, and the political parties were persecuted and terrorized. During the last days of the electoral campaign, the army troops took out to the streets shouting political slogans for the president and his Partido Reformista, demanding Balaguer's reelection, and waving the Reformista red flags on their bayonets and military vehicles. The repression turned so violent that political activists from the opposition parties did not dare to go out fearing they would be killed or arrested. Terrorized by the armed forces, the Acuerdo de Santiago pulled out its candidates and abandoned the elections. Hence, Balaguer ran alone and unopposed for the second time enjoying the farcical opposition of a fake party led by a former Trujillo military henchman.

During his fourth administration, Balaguer felt quite safe. The most dangerous leftist leaders had been eliminated, and many survivors had been co-opted through various mechanisms: the engineers and kindred professionals received public works contracts from the state, while the intellectuals and professionals were mollified by their appointment as professors to the state university with total disregard for their professional qualifications. More than a thousand members of the minor leftist parties became professors or employees of the Universidad Autónoma de Santo Domingo. They eventually became politically conservative, although their discourse kept a strong revolutionary tone. Balaguer yielded the control of the state university to the revolutionary groups to keep them busy and under observation. The government's intelligence agencies kept the university under close surveillance and monitored most of the activities of the revolutionary parties there.

Many other militants of the left were offered jobs in the thousands of public projects under way, or in the many new companies which emerged during the economic boom of the seventies. Even the Communist party (PCD) was utilized by Balaguer in his agrarian reform program which after 1972 put an end to large landholdings in the country's rice districts. The leaders of the Communist party became the principal ideologues of the government's agrarian reform, and were used by Balaguer as communication channels between Fidel Castro and his government. They were allowed to freely leave and reenter the country, publish their newspapers and magazines, and hold their meetings publicly. In fact they were so affectively neutralized by Balaguer that, as an ultimate reward he legalized the Communist party in November 1977.

When Joaquín Balaguer assumed the presidency on June 1, 1966, the Dominican government was dominated by some 400 U.S. functionaries and advisors. The military were practically managed by a U.S. military team of 65 advisors. The Ministry of Agriculture was controlled by 45 U.S. technicians who made almost all the decisions. The National Police and security forces were advised by 15 experts on matters of public security, one-third of them members of the CIA. Other government departments, such as the Oficina de Desarrollo de la Comunidad and the Instituto Agrario Dominicano, operated under the supervision of U.S. advisers, as did the Ministry of Education.

When Balaguer took office, he inmediately annulled the influence of these foreign advisors and centralized the public administration under his personal control. These advisers had been putting considerable pressure on their Dominican counterparts to follow political or administrative policies emanating from the Agency for International Development (AID) or the U.S. Embassy. After 1966, the control of the government was again in Dominican hands, and Balaguer reinstated the Trujilloist centralist style of the presidency.

Yet for many months the continuity of the Dominican state had been in the hands of the foreign advisors. The civil war had created such a power vacuum that fiscal revenues practically disappeared because neither of the warring governments was capable of collecting taxes. If it had not been for the massive economic aid from the United States, and for the help of the AID and OAS advisors, the country would have been totally paralyzed.

The amount of money the United States poured into the Dominican Republic between 1966 and 1973 was enormous in proportion to the small size of the country's economy. Between April 1965 and June 1966 the republic received about $122 million, most of it in the form of donations granted with the purpose of staving off bankruptcy. In each of the following three years (that is, between 1967 and 1969), this aid increased to $133 million a year. Most of it was in the form of long-term low-interest loans for development programmes. These loans were negotiated through AID and on more than one occasion they came under the jurisdiction of Public Law 480, a special credit program for the acquisition of food.

From June 1969 to June 1973 the aid fell to $78 million a year. The country's economic dependence on foreign aid, especially during the period from 1966 to 1970, was truly remarkable. There is no doubt that without direct injections of cash and the sugar quota offered by Washington the country could have hardly survived under the policy of extreme austerity impossed by Balaguer in 1966. During this period, direct foreign aid from the United States and income from the sugar quota accounted for 32 percent of the country's revenues in foreign currency.

A large portion of the national budget in these years was used to cover salaries, while the bulk of investments was made with foreign-aid funds. This meant that the public investments program was effectively determined by the decisions of AID, the Inter-American Development Bank, and the World Bank. One condition of the aid was that the government assign resources of the national budget as matching elements for programs financed with U.S. aid. The Dominican government, however, was resistant to designating funds for these projects, finding it more politically useful to allocate its resources toward those investments that had a proven political impact, such as public works, where the outcome of the investment was visible and generated employment quickly.

AID's resources were generally oriented towards agricultural development, while the Dominican government made investments in the urban sector. The only interest the government had in AID's funds was the receipt of foreign currency, to assist the balance of payments. Before 1972, the year that marked a visible change in the government's agrarian policy, Balaguer's tendency to sacrifice rural development to the simple expedient of staying in power was noticeable and explains the slow growth in agricultural production during the 70s.

Although it gave low priority to social and economic development programs and squandered expenditures, which led to frequent friction with Washington, the Dominican government accepted what the U.S. government offered because Balaguer and his advisers knew they had little or no alternative. This became evident every time the Dominican government had to negotiate a favorable sugar quota in order to obtain foreign currency to pay for its imports.

For the Balaguer government, the sugar cuota was a top priority as it was the principal source of foreign currency. The quota was the object of intense lobbying in both Washington and Santo Domingo. In 1973, for example, when the U.S. Congress was debating cutting the quota, President Balaguer offered his resignation to President Nixon —not to the Dominican Congress- in case he constituted an obstacle to securing the sugar quota. Balaguer, of course, did not resign. The requested quota (700,000 tons) was obtained, and as a result he was able to reinforce his government's economic position and show that the United States was backing him politically.

The sugar quota was a matter of particular importance during 1966 and 1974 when the average price was much higher in the U.S. market than in the world market. In 1973 the Dominican Republic realized no advantage by exporting its sugar to the United States; rather, it was at a disadvantage in not having sold it at higher prices in the world market. In 1975 and 1976, as prices on the world market soared, the Dominican Republic received the highest export income in its history. The government accumulated enormous reserves of foreign currency, and was able to mask the profound contradictions of an economy that had been growing very rapidly but in an unbalanced fashion.

In 1966 U.S. aid and the sugar quota together represented 47 percent of all income in foreign currency; in 1972 they accounted for less than 9 percent. This reduction indicated both that the country had recovered from the civil war crisis and that the recovery had made foreign aid less necessary. Besides the aid, other factors central to the economic take-off included increase in foreign and domestic investment and Washington's continuing political support of the Dominican government. The U.S. government normally insured business ventures in the mining, industry, banking, and the service sectors, and guaranteed them against every type of political risk, particularly expropriation.

Capital formation in the Dominican Republic was quite impressive during those years considering the small size of the Dominican economy. Between 1966 and 1971 about $1 billion were invested in the country, a substantial part being directed to important sectors such as mining and energy. On the other hand, public investment was directed to infrastructure works as the physical plant of the country had considerably deteriorated after Trujillo's death. Besides, the development plans designed by the international development agencies required the government to build ports, highways, aqueducts, streets, and energy plants. The government also invested considerably in roads, schools, housing projects and service infraestructures for the future tourist industry that Balaguer planned to develop.

Hence, the most important cities as well as many villages in the rural zones underwent a process of physical renovation. Santo Domingo and Santiago received the bulk of the public expenditures, but La Vega, Moca, San Francisco de Macorís, San Juan de la Maguana, San Cristóbal, Haina, La Romana, Hato Mayor, Puerto Plata, Mao and Nagua also witnessed rapid growth and modernization during those years. In all of those urban centers, as in many other locations, the government built sport and educational facilities, new roads, and streets. At the same time, transportation increased and businesses flourished. The internal market expanded considerably. Thousands of small and medium entrepeneurs as well as young professionals created their own enterprises and business firms. Credit demand also increased, bringing about a great dynamism to the banking sector.

In the early 70s the economic growth of the Dominican Republic was one of the highest in Latin America due to foreign investment and to public and private domestic investment. In 1972, the gross national product grew at almost 12 percent. Optimism prevailed in the business community. Bankers, industrialists, merchants, and foreign investors were confident that the economy would maintain its rising trend. The conditions granted by the Dominican government to foreign investments were always extremely generous.

Falconbridge Dominicana, for example, a Canadian-American nickel-mining firm, invested about US$250 million and raised a substantial part of this capital in the national financial market. More modest, but also important, were the foreign investments of the U.S. owned gold mining company, Rosario

Dominicana, the Dominican Oil Refinery, jointly owned by Shell and the Dominican state, and a dairy products industry operated by Nestlé. Gulf & Western, owner of Central Romana, received substantial incentives for its sugar and tourist operations during Balaguer's presidency. Nestlé and Gulf & Western also raised part of their capital in the Dominican financial market and obtained substantial benefits when negotiating their installation contracts with the Dominican government. Other companies, like Philip Morris, also received presidential protection for their installation, even though they competed with public enterprises.

Balaguer frequently explained the need for foreign investment to finance Dominican development, and always offered generous concessions to foreign investors and adventurers. In 1972, for example, he leased the Saona island to a foreign firm for a ridiculous price and for a 99 year period. This contract had to be annulled when the Dominican people protested through various political organizations, as they remembered Buenaventura Báez's attempts to sell or lease the Samaná bay and peninsula in the 19th century.

During his 12 year regime, Balaguer confronted many times the Dominican media and politicians who constantly denounced numerous illegal operations carried out by high-ranking government officers, like enormous contrabands, payment of commissions to obtain government's contracts, or the practice of extorsion against businessmen by government officials. At the end of Balaguer's 12-year regime, national public opinion almost unanimously demanded from him to stop the constant violations of human rights committed under his protection by the high ranking military and the continuous political abuses committed by the top leaders of the Reformista party.

Public officials and high ranking military officers generously doled out contracts for public works among themselves, enjoyed exemptions for the tax-free import of all the consumer goods they desired, and became rich enough to play the roles of investor and entrepreneur in unfair competition with traditional commercial and industrial groups. Government corruption during Balaguer's regime expanded so much that even the Catholic church mentioned it in its pastoral letters. Balaguer sometimes denied it, but when the evidence was too overwhelming he admitted that his government was corrupt although he defended himself by stating that corruption stopped at his office door.

On the other hand, every time politicians from inside or outside the government raised their voices to ask that U.S. investment be limited, regulated, or expropriated, Balaguer responded by defending it, pointing to what he called the "geopolitical destiny" of the Caribbean. By this he meant that because of the sheer size of the United States, the Dominican Republic would always be its satellite in the region since the U.S. government would never permit another Cuba in the Caribbean. Balaguer's opinions were widely shared in the Dominican Republic. People remembered that the United States occupied the country in 1916 and governed it for eight years.

They also recalled that as a result of Trujillo's death Dominican policy was decisively influenced by the U.S. Department of State through its consular and diplomatic officers. They remembered that a triumphant civilian-military movement to reinstall the deposed President Bosch in office was frustrated by the massive use of U.S. military force in 1965. And they remembered that U.S. troops did not leave the country until they had helped to establish a dependable government that would protect and further U.S. interests.

These political convictions were confirmed in May 1978, when the President of the United States, Jimmy Carter, openly prevented Balaguer from fraudulently continuing in office –a move that would have challenged his human rights policy and would have prevented the democratization of the Dominican Republic. After 12 years of exercising all-encompassing power, Balaguer and his associates refused to accept the results of the elections held on May 16, 1978 in which Antonio Guzmán, running on the ticket of the PRD, emerged the victor by an overwhelming margin.

That night, while the population was watching on television the general count of votes, military officers and soldiers who supported the reelection of Balaguer entered the offices of the Junta Central Electoral and interrupted the count, which already showed Antonio Guzmán as the certain winner of the election. After beating many witnesses, they proceeded to confiscate and destroy the ballot boxes holding the votes, and jailed a large number of political representatives.

The indignation provoked by this act of force had no parallel in Dominican history. Immediately, hundreds of organizations throughout the country launched a campaign of peaceful protest and resistance, making it plain that the Dominican nation would not accept a fraudulent prolongation of Balaguer's government. Foreign observers who were in Santo Domingo representing the OAS, the U.S. Democratic party, the Partido Acción Democrática of Venezuela, and the Socialist International headed an international movement to repudiate the machinations of Balaguer and his political and military mafia.

On this occasion the United States stood firm in its position of not recognizing any government that had not won the majority of votes. The U.S. position was immediately endorsed by Venezuela and other governments friendly to the PRD. Balaguer finally had to give in. He handed over the government to Antonio Guzmán on August 16, 1978, after three months of profound political crisis, not without first forcing Antonio Guzmán to accept the falsification of the electoral results so that the Partido Reformista be granted a political majority in the Senate and an increased participation in the Chamber of Deputies. The falsification was made by members of the Junta Central Electoral who supported Balaguer, through a resolution called *fallo histórico*.

With this resolution, the Junta Central Electoral illegaly granted Balaguer's party the victory in four provinces, and was consequently granted the Reformistas four senators and an additional deputy. In order to assure the presidency, the winning candidate, Antonio Guzmán, made a pact with Balaguer accepting this resolution. He agreed to let the Partido Reformista keep an illegal majority in the Senate. In this manner Balaguer and his partisans could determine the election of the judges and could control the Justice Department. Thus, they couldn't be persecuted for their acts of corruption during the 12 year regime. Balaguer's reluctance to accept the results of the elections demonstrated that his government had been in more than one sense a prolongation of the Trujillo era. It also showed that he never had a democratic mentality.

20.
Social-democrats
in power
(1978-1986)

ANTONIO GUZMAN

Balaguer's attempt to stay in power illegaly was immediately repudiated by the Dominican people. It helped Antonio Guzmán to take office enjoying more political support than any previous politician in the Dominican Republic. After witnessing the various maneuvers Balaguer and the military officers had resorted to in their effort to strip the PRD of its electoral victory, the majority of the Dominican people turned their backs on him. Guzmán took advantage of the unpopularity of Balaguer and his military chiefs to dismantle the Trujilloist political and military oligarchy that Balaguer himself had restructured and nurtured since1966. This military oligarchy had become so powerful that it had even forced Balaguer to dismiss his candidate for vice-president during the last weeks of the 1978 electoral campaign.

The Dominicans had voted for change. Guzmán was the candidate of change and his whole electoral campaign was founded on this slogan. Until then, Guzmán had seemed like a man who was obedient to his party's bureaucracy and it was thought that after 15 years outside the government the party would govern in the manner attempted by Juan Bosch in 1963, that is, by accomplishing fundamental social reforms. But from the first day of his administration Guzmán made it clear that it was his government, not the PRD's. He appointed his own children, his children's friends, his nieces, brothers and cousins, and the children of his closest friends to very important government positions. Some of them governed to their own advantage and made use of their positions to enrich themselves. Corruption, which had reached scandalous levels in Balaguer's time because of the large number of people involved in it, was now concentrated among members of the President's inner circle.

As a result, the PRD split into two factions: Guzmán and his supporters, and those who remained outside the administration. Many members of the PRD became critical of the government and stated that Guzman and his family had betrayed the PRD. The rift became much deeper when Guzmán began to work towards his indefinite reelection in the style of Trujillo and Balaguer. Since this required a party machine and the PRD had always opposed presidential reelection, Guzmán tried to buy off the middle-level leaders and party activists by putting them on the government payroll. Guzmán appointed nearly 8,000 new public employees before the end of his first year in office. During his remaining period he augmented the state payroll from 129,161 to 201,301 public employees, many of them superfluous.

The government's administrative expenses soon swallowed up nearly 85 percent of the national revenues, leaving very little for investment. Public works programs came to a halt for need of investment funds, as did development projects financed with contributions from the Inter-American Development Bank, the AID, and the World Bank because the government lacked sufficient matching funds. To finance the unprecedented public sector deficit the government resorted to printing money without the necessary backing, and increased borrowing from internal and external sources.

At first, Guzmán's economists tried to justify their economic policy by saying that they were following a neo-Keynesian model of economic growth through the expansion of public spending and aggregate demand. The government's critics pointed out that the Dominican economy was extremely open and that the external sector would not be able to withstand an excessive increase in the money supply without incurring large deficits in the balance of payments. Not only were industry and agriculture incapable of supplying the country, but the government itself needed imports in order to assure itself of funds, since 43 percent of public revenues derived from import taxes. The economic debate was at times conducted with great vehemence, but Guzmán and his government continued to defend their policy of easy indebtedness and financial subsidies to the government agencies.

As the economic distortions became more evident it was recognized that many of them had originated in Balaguer's time, when the rapid growth of import-substitution industries was encouraged at the expense of agriculture, and a policy of freezing agricultural prices was pursued to the benefit of urban consumers. Guzmán vigorously supported a good number of rural development programs to favour agricultrural development, which had fallen behind during Balaguer's administration. But in order to finance his rural programs Guzmán also had to resort to printing money, so that the adjustments he made in favor of agricultural products, such as allowing prices to rise, were neutralized by inflation.

The rise in prices also seriously affected public enterprises. The Dominican Republic had one of the largest public enterprise sectors in Latin America because Trujillo's entire industrial, commercial, agricultural and livestock holdings were converted into state property in 1961 and 1962. The Dominican state found itself the proprietor of 60 percent of the country's sugar production, 100 percent of the electricity production, and nearly 50 commercial and industrial companies, which were consolidated in 1966 under the Corporación Dominicana de Empresas Estatales (CORDE).

During the Guzmán government, public enterprises were placed under the administration of Vice-President Jacobo Majluta, who had worked as CORDE's financial advisor during the Balaguer regime. In order to finance CORDE's financial and administrative plan, the Guzmán government obtained a $185 million loan from private sources in the United States. But the public enterprises, which had been generating great deficits under Balaguer, colapsed and became the main users of government subsidies.

Another deficit-producing government agency was the Instituto de Estabilización de Precios (INESPRE), created in 1968. Its purpose was to intervene in the marketing of agricultural and agroindustrial products with the aim of keeping stable prices. Over time, because of shortages in agricultural production, INESPRE was transformed into the largest commercial food importer in the country, with a budget larger than that of the Republic of Haiti. This process began under the Balaguer regime, and continued under Guzman's. Thus, INESPRE's main function became to subsidize urban consumers and save the cities from riots and social unrest.

With the increased dependence on imported food, which resulted from cheap financing under U.S. Public Law 480 and the U.S. Commodity Credit Corporation, Dominican agriculture encountered reduced demand for its products because it was unable to compete with the great merchants and commission agents that imported subsidized food products from the United States to be distributed at low price by INESPRE. With the new rise in oil prices in 1979, imported food prices began to increase as well. These increases began to be reflected in the prices of agricultural and industrial products, whether locally produced or imported.

With the rising deficit in the balance of payments, Domini-

can currency was losing its value. By 1982 a dollar was worth
1.35 Dominican pesos on the free market despite the government's attempts at maintaining the official parity of one U.S.
dollar to one Dominican peso. Under Balaguer, multiple exchange rates had been allowed by the government, keeping the
Dominican currency officially overvalued, even at the cost of
reducing exports. This monetary policy removed the possibility
of earning enough foreign currency to pay for imports. As the
balance of payments deteriorated, the government decided to
impose quotas and prohibit imports. Guzmán's economic policy forced the government into ever more frequent restrictive
measures, although eventually reality caught up with the desires of Guzmán and his economists. The growth of foreign debt
and the extraordinary rise in the price of oil left the government with very little foreign currency to pay for imports.

Guzmán tried in vain to subsidize the central government
with resources from the sale of gold from the mining company
Rosario Dominicana, which was nationalized at the end of 1979.
This did not amount to much, however, and by 1981 it was already evident that the entire public sector was on the edge of
bankruptcy. In constant deficit, both the central government
and the state enterprises increased their debt by negotiating
foreign loans at high interest rates. Yet the administration of
those funds was so deficient that more than $800 million in
foreign loans and grants readily available to finance the balance of payments deficit went unused by Guzmán because the
government did not provide the necessary matching funds.

In spite of the fact that sugar prices had reached their highest level in history between 1980 and 1981, the state sugar mills
were afflicted by the highest indebtedness in their history. The
Corporación Dominicana de Electricidad continued its policy
of selling cheap energy to the public in order to maintain the
government's political popularity. But, at the same time, it had
to purchase expensive foreign oil. The shortfall in the Corpo-

ración's cash flow was so severe that it frequently found itself unable to pay its suppliers on time, and the country was often left with barely a week's supply of oil reserves. In another effort to maintain his popularity, Guzmán tried to expand the role of INESPRE by bringing subsidized food to ever larger numbers of people in the urban areas, further aggravating the public sector's deficit.

Despite all his efforts, Guzmán's popularity began to evaporate. His government was widely seen by his critics as a great political fraud in which the president had exploited the PRD to enrich his family and friends and to keep himself in power indefinitely. Disenchantment became universal. Merchants and industrialists, antagonized from the first day by Guzmán's functionaries, constantly complained about unfair competition from public enterprises and INESPRE. Landholders protested about the continuous threats levied against them by the government's agrarian officials who wanted to implement agrarian reform without complying with the law and without offering adequate compensation to the owners of confiscated land. Labor unions and the poor protested against the rise in the cost of living.

As Guzmán's popularity declined, the political rehabilitation of Balaguer advanced. The massive public investments that Balaguer had realized to stimulate the economy were favorably compared with Guzman's unproductive spending in government salaries. People remembered that under Balaguer's 12 year regime the internal market had expanded considerably and that many social groups had become richer, particularly the urban middle class and the business class. Guzmán's most visible achievement had been political: he had dismantled the top of Balaguer's military mafia, he had respected freedom of speech, and he had also allowed freedom of action on the part of the National Congress, which in Balaguer's time had been a mere extension of the executive branch.

Meanwhile, the PRD had become divided into two irreconcilable factions. One functioned as an opposition party, and reorganized itself under the leadership of its secretary-general, José Francisco Peña Gómez, and the senator for the National District, Salvador Jorge Blanco, a well-known lawyer who had run against Guzmán during the first party primaries in 1977. When Guzmán realized that it would no longer be possible to get his party to nominate him for a new term, he tried to impose his vice-president, Jacobo Majluta, as the PRD's presidential candidate. But it was already too late. The party had emancipated itself from the government, and had chosen Salvador Jorge Blanco as its presidential candidate for 1982. Jorge Blanco promised to establish a government of the party and for the party, and projected an image of irreproachable integrity that was then recognized even by his enemies.

Guzmán and his family maneuvered to prevent Jorge Blanco from being elected president. They approached and wooed Balaguer, and some high-level functionaries even went so far as to suggest to the military to prevent the holding of the elections, or see to it that Jorge Blanco not live to take office if he won the election. But the military refused. The composition and mentality of the armed forces had been changing as a result of the depoliticization that Guzmán himself had introduced during the first two years of his government and the insistence of the United States that the Dominican armed forces be a force sustaining democracy, not a hindrance to it, in order to avoid a cataclysm like the civil war of 1965.

Salvador Jorge Blanco was elected on May 16, 1982, defeating Joaquín Balaguer after an impressive electoral campaign in which the most modern marketing techniques were utilized. Guzmán and his family found themselves isolated and disgraced, and some government officials took advantage of the last few months of their term to amass more wealth. The money transfers to banks in Miami, Brazil, New York, Switzerland, and

London, as well as the huge quantities of dollars bought in the exchange houses of Santo Domingo by some of Guzman's relatives and government officials, became an open secret in the national banking community. Some of these transactions were detected and reported by the foreign press.

Guzmán became acutely depressed. More than once, he and some important members of his family had privately assured the military that Jorge Blanco would only become President over Guzman's dead body. Ashamed for not having fullfilled his promise to stop Jorge Blanco, and fearing the growing daily accusations of corruption branded against the top officials of his government, Guzmán shot himself in the head on the night of July 3, 1982.

Vice-President Jacobo Majluta was immediately sworn in as president and worked to get the military officers who had supported Guzmán to accept Jorge Blanco. This was an important move, for some high-ranking officers had been influenced by Guzmán and distrusted Jorge Blanco. After 43 hectic, transition days, Jorge Blanco was finally inaugurated on August 16, 1982, in the middle of a financial crisis which threatened the Dominican Republic with bankruptcy.

SALVADOR JORGE BLANCO

The economic policy of the Jorge Blanco government was designed several months before his election and was prefigured in numerous public discussions in which most of the organized groups of the country participated. During his electoral campaign Jorge Blanco promised to perfect political democracy with an "economic democracy." Yet his management of the crisis, and the adjustment plan his government had to carry out with the International Monetary Fund (IMF), buried the dream of building such an economic democracy and led to an intensive process of income concentration. This took place just as the living standard of the middle class was dramatically falling and as the lower classes were burdened by inflation.

When he began his term in August 1982, Jorge Blanco announced that his government was going to correct the distortions that affected the Dominican economy. It was not possible, he said, in a country afflicted by serious problems in the balance of payments, for imports to be protected by an overvalued exchange rate that had nothing to do with the reality of a depreciated currency. Nor was it appropriate, in his view, for the public sector to continue indebting itself in order to subsidize other economic sectors. He also said that it was unhealthy for the national economy that internal prices did not reflect the structure of prices in the world economy, including interest rates. Due to the widespread state subisidies to to private sector and to the state enterprises, the internal price structure was too low when compared to that of the United States, the Republic's main trade partner.

If in August 1982 there was any consensus about the Dominican crisis, it was that the economy needed to be readjusted. Agriculture was at a standstill for lack of incentives. Industry was inefficient due to exaggerated protection and the immense subsidies and incentives offered by the state. Public enterprises were on the edge of bankruptcy and the government could no longer afford to subsidize them. The fiscal system had lost its capacity to collect resources to finance the public sector adequately. The deficit in the balance of payments exceeded the $400 million, and the net international reserves had a deficit of more than $700 million.

For a small country with a population of 5.6 million whose exports did not exceed one billion dollars yearly, and whose budget was only one billion Dominican pesos, the situation was serious. Jorge Blanco said that without an extraordinary austerity effort, limitation of spending and public credit, as well as a substantial increase in foreign aid to attack the problem of the balance of payments, the country would not be able to move forward.

In August 1982, just as Jorge Blanco took office, Mexico declared a moratorium over its foreign debt and stopped paying its creditors altogether. From then on, the foreign banks that had so gladly loaned money to Guzman's government, now refused to extend credit to the Dominican Republic unless it came to an agreement with the IMF. The new monetary authorities had prepared themselves to negotiate with the IMF before the government's innauguration, and after intensive negotiations succesfully arranged for three-year extended facilities agreement with the IMF which was signed on January 21, 1983. This agreement was quickly objected by some important public officers and ministers of the Jorge Blanco team.

Eventually, this division would cost dearly to the government. From the beginning, the negotiations with the IMF were exceedingly stormy because the government claimed that the fiscal austerity, contraction of credit, reduction of salaries, rise of prices, and new restrictions on imports were impositions of the IMF. Thus, by publicly rejecting what it was privately negotiating, the Jorge Blanco government ended up eroding the necessary public support for its own program of economic adjustments. The monetary authorities were then trapped between government anti-IMF rethoric and their official economic adjustment measures.

In their determination to reduce the type of exchange with the U.S. dollar to reach a parity lost long ago, the government used police and army troops to close the exchange houses so that people would have to buy and sell dollars at the commercial banks. The immediate and predictable result of this measure was an extraordinary financial turmoil, a dizzy flight of capital, and a wave of speculation which devalued the peso by more than 100 percent. The government soon recognized that these measures had been ill conceived, and chose to legalize the exchange houses in an effort to restore financial equilibrium. But the exchange rate remained at three pesos to the dollar, and prices did not stop rising because importers immediately adjusted their domestic prices to reflect the new rate of exchange.

The government continued to publicly denounce the conditions imposed by the IMF agreement which were fundamentally to halt the issue of all unbacked money, to freeze public spending, to control deficits in state enterprises and the public deficit, to raise direct taxes so as to increase fiscal revenue, to impose greater control of imports, and to raise interest rates. All these measures were contained in Jorge Blanco's economic program, but the government found in the IMF a villain whom it could blame for the adjustment program. The government's strategists justified this attitude by arguing that a program of this nature meant adjusting domestic prices to the real rate of exchange, and the result would be an increase in prices that would be intolerable for the population. They preferred a policy of gradual adjustments which could maintain the government's popularity.

This policy failed because the IMF was constantly attacked by public officials while the government tried to execute the IMF recommendations. Consequently, the government ended up discrediting its own adjustments policy. This became evident at the end of April 1984 when the government policy makers attempted to take advantage of the Holy Week vacation to raise prices of all essential products while the urban middle class was away from the cities. The isolation of the government officials prevented them from realizing that protests would come from the poor who had gone neither to the mountains nor to the beaches. On the following Monday, April 24th, the country woke up to a popular uprising that was only quelled three days later after the army had killed more than 70 people who protested against the government's economic policy.

By this time, the PRD had become badly divided and con-

fused. Its secretary general, José Francisco Peña Gómez sometimes attacked the government's economic policy, while at other times he supported it. Peña Gómez's support had a price. He
needed political and financial assistance to play a good role as
mayor of Santo Domingo and to become presidential candidate in 1986. On the other hand, Jacobo Majluta had become
president of the Senate and used his congressional platform to
promote his candidacy antagonizing Jorge Blanco's policies both
within Congress and the party.

Majluta systematically opposed all of Jorge Blanco's legislative initiatives and prevented passage of the legislation
needed to implement the government economic program. As
a result of the congressional boycott led by Majluta, many
development projects designed to reactivate the economy and
match the IMF program could not be implemented. This dispute, aired daily in the press, radio, and television, confirmed
that the government and the party were incapable of managing the nation efficiently. The lack of congressional support
put a lock on the government and prevented it from reacti-
vating the economy.

The government continued its policy of conflict with the
IMF until November 1984, when it became apparent that the
Dominican Republic could not avoid renegotiating its debt with
foreign governments and commercial banks, not to mention
without signing a new agreement with the IMF. Only then did
Jorge Blanco and his advisors proceed to soften the government's position in order to stave off a total collapse in the balance of payments which would have meant the cessation of all
foreign credit, the paralyzation of the country due to lack of oil,
and the cancellation of most imported industrial supplies. This
policy change permitted the government to sign a stand-by
agreement with the IMF in April, 1985.

This agreement was designed to completely overhaul the
Dominican financial system and boost the economy. In January

1985, before the signature of the agreement, the government allowed the dollar to float freely in the market and set a new unified exchange rate for all the financial operations in the country. Interest rates and prices were also adjusted according to the new exchange rate which devalued the peso against the dollar by almost 30 percent. These measures created an immediate demand for U.S. currency and pushed the Dominican economy into a process of de facto dollarization similar to the previous experiences of other Latin American countries.

The effects of the new IMF agreement were at once noticeable. It stimulated Dominican agriculture and offered new incentives to agroindustrial producers as prices, previously subject to control, were allowed to float. The limitation of credit to the public sector helped to ease the pressure on the money supply, while the government was again able to increase its tax revenue by holding its hand on import duties and some export duties. The restrictions imposed over the printing of paper money, and the new austerity measures, helped to keep inflation under control. IMF resources and income generated by tourism and the free zones, as well as remittances from Dominicans abroad, increased the foreign reserves. Thus, between 1985 and 1986 the Dominican peso appreciated again from 3.35 pesos to 2.80 per dollar.

Besides the IMF adjustment program, Jorge Blanco introduced one very important political reform. In his effort to eliminate all traces of Trujilloism within the armed forces, Jorge Blanco promoted a very strong sense of institutionalization and professionalism within the armed forces, thus continuing the efforts initiated by Guzmán. During his first two years in office, he spent a great deal of time preaching to the military on the need to become professional and obedient to civilian democratic rule. He fired hundreds of older officers and replaced them with young ones recently promoted from the military academy or from the lower ranks.

Initially, the military were very enthusiastic about Jorge Blanco, as he had finally removed the obstacles to promotion that the Balaguerista top commanders had endeavored to preserve even under Guzmán. Thus, Jorge Blanco managed to build his own military base in a short time and became quite popular among both soldiers and officers. Military equipment and supplies were modernized or renewed, and training became a serious concern of the recently promoted officers. For the first time, the regulations and procedures for military promotion were fully operational.

Surprisingly, however, Jorge Blanco did not know when or how to stop. During his last two years in office he was led into a frantic wave of promotions and dismissals that greatly upset the military establishment and opened a serious rift with the U.S. government, which had spent many years training a pro-U.S. Dominican military corps. To make matters worse, Jorge Blanco continued firing many military officers suspected of being too loyal to the United States, or who had more than 20 years of service. Jorge Blanco fired more than 4,000 military officers at a time when the armed forces had less than 22,000 members. By early 1986, there remained only two high-ranking officers of those who had joined the armed forces before the death of Trujillo in 1961.

The political effects of this policy were clearly visible during the last year of Jorge Blanco's rule, as his own supporters within the military became increasingly fearful of being suddenly fired. Jorge Blanco quickly lost the support of many of his earlier friends within the armed forces as they became convinced that they too would be fired. By the end of his government Jorge Blanco had lost all his previous military support.

Jorge Blanco's military policy convinced his adversaries, that he was preparing the armed forces to remain loyal to him after he stepped out of power in August 1986. Jorge Blanco reinforced those suspicions as he bestowed upon the military and many civilian supporters lavish gifts, using his constitutional right to lift custom duties or to redistribute unused funds of the presidency's budget. He conceded import privileges to almost everyone, supporter or not, who requested permission for importing automobiles duty-free. Many merchants and industrialists took advantage of their close relation with the president and imported huge quantities of raw materials and merchandise duty-free.

He also allowed some friends to enter the business of supplying the military significant quantities of food, clothing, weapons, munitions, and so on. By allowing these newcomers to break into the tightly closed circle of suppliers to the military who had been linked with Balaguer and the Reformistas for more than 15 years, Jorge Blanco touched a sensitive political fiber. As a result, during Jorge Blanco's last year, Balaguer's agents orchestrated a well-articulated campaign to show that Jorge Blanco's military policy was tainted with corruption. As the campaign mounted and he did nothing to dispel it, Jorge Blanco only helped to reduce even more his falling popularity. His prestige as an honest president was also seriously eroded when it was rumored that certain important members of his government were doing fabulous business deals in various public agencies and state enterprises.

Jorge Blanco and several of his high-ranking officers frequently showed their intolerance towards the government's critics. Their relations with the media and other interest groups were usually tense. Very soon, Balaguer and his followers accused the government of being "arrogant and abusive". These adjectives were widely used to describe government's deeds and were promptly adopted by the populace. This negative image followed some of these functionaries until the very last days of Jorge Blanco's government, and hurt their candidacies when they tried to get elected as senators or deputies in the 1986 elections.

Although widely respected for his democratic values and his intention of not seeking reelection, Jorge Blanco approached the end of his administration extremely debilitated by his military policy. Not only had he frightened the remaining officers, but he also offended the U.S. government by trying to declare persona non grata the chief military attaché when this officer tried to block the policy of military dismissals and promotions. In addition, Jorge Blanco repeatedly expressed his intent of staying active in politics with an eye in the 1990 elections. This frightened his adversaries who expected to find a hostile environment within the military establishment if they won the elections.

Meanwhile, the parties began to prepare for the general elections to be held on May 16, 1986. The main candidates were Joaquín Balaguer, Jacobo Majluta, and Juan Bosch. President Jorge Blanco worked hard to make the elections free and clean. He appointed a special commission to supervise them when the Junta Central Electoral showed signs that it was unable to run the elections without problems. This Comisión de Asesores Electorales was composed of nine prestigious nonpartisan citizens who took over the whole electoral process and guaranteed what has been the cleanest vote counting in Dominican history. Jorge Blanco supported the Comisión's task even though the PRD, his own party, lost the elections and some PRD's politicians tried to alter the electoral results.

The elections were extremely contentious. Joaquín Balaguer of the Partido Reformista won by a narrow margin of 40,000 votes over Jacobo Majluta, candidate for the PRD. The return of the 80-year old former president to power for the fifth time in 25 years was quite an exceptional event, in view of the fact that he lost the presidency in 1978 in the midst of the greatest discredit possible and when glaucoma had made him lose his vision. Although blind and ill, Balaguer was able to unify and reorganize his party, assimilating along the way the old Christian Social Revolutionary Party, and changing its name to Partido Reformista Social Cristiano (PRSC).

This change was intended to formally give the Reformistas an acceptable ideology and a structure of international relations similar to the Social Democratic network of contacts of the PRD, which had been associated for years with the Socialist International. The international support of the Christian Democrats helped Balaguer to modernize his party and run a modern campaign in which propaganda, speeches, and political marketing were based on extensive surveys measuring public opinion. Balaguer's return to power was also aided by the PRD's management of the economic crisis during its eight-year rule. Balaguer appeared as the only one capable of imposing political authority and reorganizing the economy.

Balaguer was also aided by the leaders of the PRD as they kept alive their internal strifes, which were widely aired in the media. These conflicts discredited and disorganized the PRD, and contributed to Balaguer's electoral triumph, particularly after the PRD's convention to nominate presidential candidates ended in major confusion, with gunshots and mutual accussations of fraud. Many experts observed that the PRD would not have lost those elections, had it not been for the enmities and the systematic smearing that its leaders threw upon each other.

Third place in the presidential elections of 1986 went to former president Juan Bosch, who in the previous years had managed to organize his Partido de la Liberación Dominicana (PLD) as a large ideological party made up of revolutionary cadres. This party captured 18 percent of the votes in 1986, doubling its performance in the 1982 elections, and signaling the rapid growth of a radical left that proposed to come to power through elections in the Dominican Republic.

21.
Balaguer's
return
(1986-1990)

THE DESTRUCTION OF JORGE BLANCO

Balaguer returned to the presidency in 1986 with the decision to remain in power for as long as he lived. He was convinced that Jorge Blanco had created a powerful and rich political group that would finance his presidential campaign in 1990 and that the former president would be the natural candidate for the PRD in 1990. To prevent Jorge Blanco's return to power, Balaguer spent most of his first year as president working to destroy whatever prestige and influence Jorge Blanco could have preserved.

As soon as Jorge Blanco returned to his home he was accused, alongside two dozen other charges, of conspiring to overthrow the government, ordering the assassination of a banker, embezzling funds, smuggling, and using the president's office to enrich himself as well as his friends and protégés. The focus of the accusations was the sale of supplies to the armed forces, which had simply followed the same pattern of overpriced sales and commissions practiced by the Balaguer and Guzmán administrations in previous years.

Balaguer recruited several lawyers, journalists, and television commentators to fabricate accusations against Jorge Blanco and his closest collaborators, and gave them copies of documents from the presidential and armed forces archives that they used to support the accusations. These accusations against Jorge Blanco were continuously broadcasted on radio and television programs during several months.

When coming to power in 1986, Balaguer feared Jorge Blanco's influence within the armed forces. To protect himself from the new military organization created by Jorge Blanco, Balaguer brought back into the military a group of officers that had been dismissed by the PRD governments, and placed them in key command posts. These appointments violated the organic law of the armed forces which forbid the reappointment of any dismissed officer or soldier. Yet, the depoliticization of the military now worked to Balaguer's advantage as the armed forces had been taught to unconditionally obey civilian rule.

Balaguer appointed General Antonio Imbert Barreras as chief of the armed forces. Imbert Barreras had commanded the military against the PRD during the 1965 civil war. Balaguer also recruited several right wing politicians associated with the triumvirate and appointed them in key positions. The most visible of these appointments were the former triumvirate president Donald Reid Cabral as minister of foreign relations. Another triumvirate's member, Ramón Tapia Espinal, was appointed by Balaguer as the government's lawyer in charge of prosecuting Salvador Jorge Blanco. Retired General Elías Wessin y Wessin, military leader of the coup against Juan Bosch and the PRD in 1963, and chief of the armed forces that fought the PRD during the civil war, was appointed secretary of interior representing his right-wing party, the Partido Quisqueyano Demócrata (PQD). In 1988 Wessin opened up the campaign to reelect Balaguer. Immediately, Balaguer reinstated him illegally in the army as a Mayor General, and designated him secretary and chief of the armed forces in 1988.

For ten months, every Monday evening, Balaguer presided over a weekly television broadcast in which his ministers and heads of government agencies poured out long litanies of charges against Jorge Blanco's ministers and functionaries, accusing them of the worst crimes against the state. Jorge Blanco did not help his own cause when he decided to remain silent. People interpreted his silence as a sign of guilt, and his popularity dropped to zero while his prestige and political support crumbled under the avalanche of accusations. When he tried to counterattack with a series of speeches on television in November 1986, it was already too late.

Between October and December Jorge Blanco's political enemies formally accused him of 31 legal, criminal and constitutional charges. If the former president was found guilty, he would loose his political and civil rights and would never be able to run for office. He was abandoned by many of his former friends and collaborators while some prominent members of the PRD joined his accusers trying to disengage themselves from the corruption charges branded against Jorge Blanco's government. Thus, the PRD division once again helped Balaguer against the PRD itself for eventually the whole campaign was directed to demonstrate that the PRD was the most corrupt party in Dominican history.

On April 29, 1987, Jorge Blanco went to court for a preliminary interrogation by a *Juez de Instrucción*. This judge had to decide if the charges against him were valid. The judge aggressively questionned him for more than ten hours, assuming that most of the accusations were valid. At the end of the session, the judge ordered him immediately to prison. At that moment, Jorge Blanco suddenly became ill with high blood pressure and coronary spasms. His friends took this opportunity to take him home for medical treatment. The next day, the former president took refuge in the Venezuelan Embassy and sought political asylum.

The Venezuelan president, Jaime Lusinchi, rejected Jorge Blanco's petition. The Venezuelan government's position reflected Lusinchi's personal efforts at escaping himself from the corruption charges already raised against his government and his party, Acción Democrática, wished to preserve intact the candidacy of ex-President Carlos Andrés Pérez, who in previous years had also had to face the Venezuelan Senate on corruption charges. When asked about the merit of Jorge Blanco's arguments for political asylum by the leaders of the official Venezuelan party, the PRD's main leaders dismissed Jorge Blanco's claims of political persecution. Thinking along the same lines, the Venezuelan ambassador in Santo Domingo recommended against the granting of political asylum.

That sealed Jorge Blanco's fate. When news arrived at the embassy that the Venezuelan government would not grant the asylum, Jorge Blanco's heart and coronary condition quickly deteriorated. Jorge Blanco finally collapsed within the Venezuelan Embassy and was urgently taken to a private hospital. But neither Lusinchi nor Balaguer were moved. The government pressed to take him out of the hospital and send him to jail. A great deal of bargaining was necessary to convince Balaguer that he should allow Jorge Blanco to be taken to a hospital in the United States to save his life. Balaguer agreed to release Jorge Blanco on the condition that his representatives sign a document agreeing that he was technically in prison and should return to jail as soon as he recuperated.

This drama lasted for almost nine months during which the government spent most of its energies in the political persecution of Jorge Blanco. Meanwhile, some of his closest collaborators were sent to prison without trial, or managed to flee into exile. The government accused them of different crimes. None of these people were never duly tried, and all were eventually released at Balaguer's convenience, while the government upheld the accusations.

By the end of his first year in power, Balaguer had already inflicted enormous damage on the PRD and had politically destroyed his most feared adversary. Balaguer considered that it would be easier to defeat Bosch, Majluta, and Peña Gómez than Jorge Blanco in the 1990 elections. On several occassions Balaguer told his closest associates that Dominican history had taught him that anyone who had ruled the country, sooner or later would rule it again.

With Jorge Blanco out of the way, the road for reelection was clear, though for the moment the government had to pay attention to the deteriorating economic condition. By the middle of 1987, the focus of public opinion was gradually turning to the increasing social and economic problems created by Balaguer's new economic policy. This policy was designed to reverse everything that had been accomplished under the IMF adjustment program, which Balaguer and his advisers blamed for being the immediate cause of slow economic growth.

AN ECONOMIC DICTATORSHIP

Once in power, Balaguer abandoned all his electoral promises of privatizing and reorganizing the economy and ran the country against all free-market principles. First was the total disorganization of the monetary system by arbitrarily manipulating the Central Bank and adopting numerous authoritarian measures to force exporters to surrender their dollars to the government at an undervalued exchange rate. In his first 13 months in office, Balaguer's newly appointed governor of the Central Bank and the members of its monetary board passed 84 ordinances designed to expand government control over the economy, and to reverse everything that had been accomplished under the IMF adjustment program during Jorge Blanco's administration.

During the first year, while credit to the public sector quickly expanded to finance an ambitious public works program. Balaguer tried to reactivate the economy by expanding public expenditure and printing money without backing. When he took office in August 1986, the money supply was 1.4 billion pesos, but at the end of his first year in office it had doubled to 2.7 billion. An inmediate result of the increased money supply was the increased demand for foreign currency and the devaluation of the Dominican peso, which fell from 2.70 pesos per dollar in August 1986, to 4.75 pesos per dollar by mid-1987.

The simultaneous consequences of this policy were sudden inflation and monetary chaos. The Dominican Republic reverted again to a system of multiple exchange rates designed by the government to subtract a substantial proportion of the dollar earnings from the export sector. Balaguer expanded his political power by arbitrarily allocating foreign exchange to the industrialists and importers. Thus, when the dollar was still floating at 4.75 pesos in the free market, the government legislated to oblige exporters to surrender their earnings to the Central Bank at 3.50 pesos each dollar.

The exporters' reaction was, of course, to hide their dollar earnings by undervaluing exports, or by simply refusing to comply with the government's regulations. The government reacted by exerting political pressure on them, and threatening with prosecuting them, or by sending some to jail. Additionally, the government put pressure on the banks and the tourist operators to coerce them into surrendering their dollar revenues to the Central Bank. When these groups reacted by delivering less than the government expected, they were forbidden to receive foreign exchange from their debtors at the floating rate and were forced to surrender their dollars to the government at the official devaluated rate.

The dollar and other foreign currencies were withdrawn from circulation, and a black market very quickly took shape.

The government used the military to close the exchange banks and intervened in the monetary market by using the secret police to enforce the Central Bank's regulations. Some bankers, industrialists, and merchants were detained and sent to prison without trial, accused of illegally retaining dollars, while many others were forced to open their books to special inspectors from the Central Bank supported by squads of the secret police.

The government called this new system of exchange controls, imposed in August 1988, "Sistema de Reintegro de Divisas." Balaguer and his ministers justified it as the only possible instrument capable of ending speculation and checking inflation. Since the government could not collect enough dollars, the most important operations in foreign currencies moved to the United States. As a result, the government's foreign reserves decreased and the Central Bank again fell in arrears with its international creditors. By December 1987, the exchange rate had deteriorated to five pesos to one dollar.

Balaguer continued printing money. In his second year in office, he increased the money supply to 3.1 billion pesos. He based his macroeconomic policies on the assumption that the economy could only be boosted by means of heavy public investment in urban works personally directed by him. His monetary policy contributed to the expansion of the internal market and to high rates of economic growth in 1987 and 1988, but also produced inflation and devaluation.

Initially, the business community felt optimistic about the economic growth resulting from the increase in public expenditure. The investments made in the construction sector accounted for the 8 percent growth rate of the economy in 1987. With the money supply increasing more than 50 percent yearly, the economic cycle accelerated and business enjoyed a visible boom. Between 1987 and 1989, Dominican industries operated at full capacity. Importers of consumer articles experienced the same kind of bonanza. This explains why the business leaders did not question Balaguer's unfullfilled electoral promises to privatize the economy and institutionalize the Dominican state.

But some economists, professionals, and business leaders finally realized the damage being done to the economy and asked Balaguer to gradually reduce the money supply. Balaguer refused. In an effort to keep up with the parallel market rates, the government devaluated the official exchange rate to 6.35 pesos per dollar in August 1988, but as foreign reserves declined, devaluation accelerated. Inflation, which had been high the previous year, reached almost 60 percent in 1988. By the end of March 1989, the money supply had reached the record level of 4.7 billion pesos, more than three times the level of 1986. Consumer prices went up five times, while the peso continued its decline. In April 1989, Dominicans had to pay 6.63 pesos for 1 dollar in the parallel market.

Although the printing of money by the government slowed down for a few months, in July 1989 the peso had fallen to 7 pesos to a dollar. By December, it reached the record level of 8.40 pesos to 1 dollar. Yet the government kept the official exchange rate at 6.35 pesos per dollar, despite protests from the exporters, tourists, and tourist operators. These groups were the greater generators of foreign exchange, but were forced to surrender all their dollars earned to the Central Bank.

Without foreign reserves, the government was forced to delay payment for short-term debts to international creditors, particularly those for oil, medicines, and food imports. In May 1989, the government suspended servicing most of its foreign debt and did not pay $23 million due to foreign commercial banks. In August, the government failed to pay other $12 million, and in September the governor of the Central Bank announced the total suspension of payments of its commercial bank debt reaching $800 million. As other arrears increased in 1989, many suppliers cut off their credits to the Dominican Republic.

In September 1989, Venezuela stopped delivering oil and the population suffered the scarcity of oil, food, and medicines. The same thing happened when other suppliers cancelled their deliveries of food, medicines and raw materials to Dominican importers and industrialists. Balaguer tried to discourage oil consumption by raising gasoline prices by 67 percent in October 1989, thus provoking a wave of popular protests. Yet the government had a limited capacity for buying oil to supply the national refinery and the thermoelectric plants. The Central Bank simply did not have enough foreign reserves to pay strategic imports. Thus, the fuel and energy scarcity continued.

Blackouts, which had been a daily occurrence since 1986, now became a national nightmare. At the beginning of his government, Balaguer had declared that the Compañía Dominicana de Electricidad (CDE) would be under his personal control. By the third year, the CDE could not produce half of the demand, and no person, household or business, could receive more than three hours of electricity per day. To make matters worse, the government arbitrarily increased the price of electricity by more than 20 percent based on global consumption averages, thus making the population pay more for a service that they were not receiving. In December 1989, only 7 thermoelectric plants were producing electricity. The other 12 had been shut down for repairs, or were simply idle for lack of fuel.

Devaluation continued, and by April 1990 it reached 11 pesos to 1 dollar. Facing a resentful business class which resisted yielding their dollars to the government, Balaguer agreed to devaluate the official exchange rate from 6.35 pesos to 7.30 to the dollar in April 1990. Again, this devaluation was insufficient to compensate for the gap in the parallel market price. Even though it was necessary to change the course of the economy, Balaguer remained defiant, and continued accusing some business groups of speculation, blaming them for the current inflation and devaluation.

The tour operators and exporters were not willing to give in their dollars at the new official rate of 7.30 pesos per dollar. Realizing that repression was not enough to convince them, the government further devalued the peso to 11.50 per dollar in October 1990. When this decision was made, the parallel market rate was reaching almost 15 pesos per dollar. In October 1990, the money supply reached the record figure of 6,573 million pesos. Meanwhile, the net foreign reserves, had also reached a record low of $106 million, while the balance of payments deficit for the year was more than $1.1 billion. Never before, since the days of Ulises Heureaux, had the Dominican people witnessed such a monetary chaos.

Importers in need of foreign exchange quickly learned that they could solve their problems by visiting the National Palace. There they could negotiate the rapid approval of their letters of credit or pay bribes to Central Bank officers to expedite their approvals. Since most imports were subject to control, any decision to lift them had to be sought at the National Palace. Therefore, an extended market of political influence quickly developed. Interviews with Balaguer became a valued commodity, and those responsible for his agenda profited by selling appointments with the president. Cabinet ministers soon revived the old practice, so popular during the 12 years regime, of purposely delaying decisions so as to give time to their agents to collect payoffs.

Corruption was back in the government, stronger than ever. Again, it became common practice to overvalue everything sold to the government. Bribes and commissions became the golden rule when doing business with the administration. At the beginning, Balaguer authorized the bribing of public employees, including those wearing a military uniform, and justified bribing them as a help for supplementing their meager salaries. As a result, even the simplest transactions made in the bureaucracy, like getting a driver's license or a passport, were subject to the paying of bribes.

These practices helped to create a new breed of millionaires, and fostered a new wave of income concentration that widened the gap between the rich and the poor. Most of the new fortunes made during this period sought the security offered by foreign banks. Not only the new millionaires, but also investors and small savers preferred to keep their dollars abroad for fear of having them confiscated by the government. Consequently, the private deposits of Dominican citizens in U.S. banks jumped from $936 million to $1,098 million during Balaguer's first year in this new administration.

These were only a few of the most visible consequences of Balaguer's new economic policy. During the 1986 electoral campaign, Balaguer and his advisors promised to privatize the economy and to decentralize the state. This political platform helped him to assemble a wide coalition of voters who believed he was the only candidate capable of accelerating the the country's institutionalization, given the PRD's strife and internal division. But once in power, Balaguer abandoned all his electoral promises and returned to his old personalistic practices. In open contradiction to their writings, as soon as his economists and technocrats were appointed in different ministries and high government posts they became the most radical defenders of political centralism and state interventionism. Under Balaguer's influence, these functionaries quickly changed their minds and frequently attacked the private sector while defending the government's neo-Trujilloist style.

As Balaguer entered the third year of his administration, the failure of his policies had become evident in the clear stagnation of the economy. The growth rate for 1988 was only 0.7 percent. Inflation was running around 60 percent. Food shortages were more serious than ever, and capital flight was already taking its toll on the economy. Most businessmen quickly learned that to cope with this phenomenon they had to adjust their prices in advance to compensate for future inventory restocking. Thus, price speculation became a visible feature of this whole process. Disclaiming responsability, Balaguer accused the businessmen of speculation and blamed them for inflation.

Yet Balaguer's policies worsened the situation of the poor and the middle class and promoted the deterioration of income among most of the population. While in 1984 there were one million Dominicans below the poverty line, in 1989 this figure had duplicated to more than two million. In 1989, 57 percent of the Dominican households lived under the line of poverty. If income concentration had been high in Jorge Blanco years, it reached the highest possible levels under the new Balaguer administration.

In reaction, popular protests were evident everywhere. Labor strikes organized by unions and professional organizations demanding higher salaries became a daily occurrence. At first, Balaguer tried to woo the strikers by stating his support for their demands, but as the political situation deteriorated in towns and villages, the government made increasing use of the police to repress the strikes and impose order. Once again, Balaguer showed his dislike of organized labor. He tried to break apart the most important unions by bribing their leaders or by simply sending them to prison each time they organized a strike.

In February 1988, 5 people were killed and more than 20 were seriously injured by the police in different riots organized to protest against the deterioration of living standards, and to denounce the government's and private sector's resistance to an increase of the minimum salary from 300 to 400 pesos ($60) a month. At the end of the month, Balaguer sent the army into the poorest neighborhoods of Santo Domingo to crush the protests. Two more strikes took place in March and April. The latter was called by the doctors working in the state hospitals because their real income was quickly dwindling, and their nominal salary was less than $140 a month.

On June 19 and 20, 1988, the most important labor unions called for a general strike to protest against the economic policies, and to demand new salary increases and improvement of public services. Once again, Balaguer sent the army to the streets to reinforce the police. More than 20,000 soldiers and policemen were mobilized to patrol the streets of Santo Domingo. Four people were killed and more than 3,000 were arrested. In August, new demonstrations for higher salaries took place in Santo Domingo. Again, their leaders were persecuted or jailed. When the government raised the gasoline prices, in October of that same year, the labor unions and the popular organizations arranged new riots.

In February 1989, more than 100 peasants and agricultural workers in Cotuí were jailed after clashing with the army. They were also protesting about their shrinking income caused by inflation. During the first two weeks of March, the population of San Francisco de Macorís and several other neighboring towns went on a general strike to protest the deterioration of basic social services. The strikers clashed with the police. One person was killed and many were injured. On May 15, the labor unions called for a national general strike. Another person was killed in the clashes with the government's forces.

CAUDILLISM, ELECTIONS, AND CRISIS

By 1990, the Dominican people as a whole had been so rapidly impoverished by inflation and devaluation that consumers could not keep up with the new prices. Widespread poverty accelerated migration to the United States and Venezuela. Illegal migration to Puerto Rico by boat became one of the most popular ways to leave the island, despite the enormous risks involved in crossing the Mona Canal. An indicator of the magnitude of this problem is the fact that in 1989 and 1990, immigration authorities in Puerto Rico deported an average of 300 Dominicans per month. In 1987 immigration authorities in Puerto Rico estimated in 160,000 the number of Dominican illegal immigrants. In 1990, New York contained close to 900,000 Dominicans, or 12 percent of the entire Dominican population.

A paradoxical feature of Dominican political life has been the increasing internationalization of party politics, while the Dominican political culture continues to be dominated by caudillism and personalism. Political parties have allied themselves with Social-Democrat and Christian-Democrat international networks based in Europe, as well as with the Communists. But these alliances have not altered the caudillistic essence of Dominican political culture. Parties have sought and received support from their foreign allies, but their leaders still control the party machineries in a personalistic manner. Thus, political campaigns, although quite modern in their techniques of communication, are not based on programs or platforms but on the personal appeal of their political caciques.

More paradoxical still is the fact that caudillism in the Dominican Republic flourishes within the formal context of a dynamic institutional pluralism. Since 1961, after Trujillo's death, Dominicans have created thousands of trade unions, political parties, entrepreneurial organizations, newspapers, journals and magazines, schools, universities, foundations and not-for-profit organizations, churches, sports associations, radio and television stations, and publishing houses that have contributed to the pluralization of Dominican society. Yet caudillism still prevails, pervading and corrupting most aspects of institutional life. In this sense, it can be asserted that the Dominican Republic has evolved from a ruthless totalitarian dictatorship into an imperfect democracy.

For many years, the Dominican Republic was mentioned as a successful "capitalist revolution" in the Caribbean at a time when Cuba was offering an alternative socialist model. Yet, the limits to this "revolution" have already become apparent in the deterioration of all economic and social indicators, as well as in the perpetuation of a caudillistic and authoritarian political culture that has hampered most of the efforts made to modernize and democratize the political system. To mention just an example: in the presidential election held in May 1990, the major contending candidates were Bosch and Balaguer, two octogenarian caudillos who became presidents of the Republic for the first time in 1960 and 1963, and have dominated Dominican political life since then.

The growth of Bosch's Partido de la Liberación Dominicana (PLD) can be largely explained by the difference in political style it brought to the country. While the other large traditional parties had maintained a discourse that expressed their internal strife or the interests of their leaders, Bosch's party, in contrast, consistently maintained a political line of defending the poorest groups in the nation. On April 1989, a public opinion survey showed that Bosch was leading over Balaguer 37 to 19 per cent, although Peña Gómez also got 19 percent and Majluta 15 percent. It then became clear that if elections were held in that month, and the PRD remained divided, Juan Bosch could easily be chosen as president. Wishing to consolidate its advantageous political position, the PLD selected Bosch early as its presidential candidate for the 1990 elections.

Gradually, but visibly, Bosch changed his former radical leftist political discourse for a more conservative one that appealed to wider segments of the middle class and even to the business class, to whom he promised an economic policy based on privatization of the state firms and industrial development. Clearly aware of Balaguer's political ruthlessness, Bosch opted for not confronting the government in the open. He mildly criticized Balaguer's economic policy from a businesslike perspective, but silently and effectively supported the popular protests and strikes that challenged the government all over the country. Moreover,

Bosch approached many social groups that had formerly supported the PRD, and thus was able to built a sizable political constituency throughout 1989. A substantial part of this new constituency was composed of disenchanted PRD followers and disappointed Reformista voters.

To Bosch's advantage was the fact that the PRD was seriously divided between the followers of José Francisco Peña Gómez, Salvador Jorge Blanco, and Jacobo Majluta, and had become an ineffective opposition instrument. Bosch also profited from the internal division of Balaguer's Partido Reformista Social Cristiano. Many Reformista leaders had become convinced that Balaguer's unpopularity was a sure ticket to electoral defeat in 1990 and joined forces with Fernando Alvarez Bogaert to offer an alternative candidacy. Alvarez Bogaert had been Balaguer's vice-presidential candidate in 1978 and had been able to build his own political base within the Reformista party. Yet Alvarez Bogaert could not win over Balaguer's political machinery, and eventually was left out of the race when Balaguer outmaneuvered him by bribing and terrorizing his followers at an irregular convention of the Partido Reformista.

As the country's economic and financial situation worsened, so did Bosch's popularity increase, despite the strong campaign for Balaguer reelection. The PRD could not resolve its internal disputes, and thus could not offer a plausible alternative to Balaguer. The rift between these different factions whithin the PRD was projected daily in the media and badly discredited its leaders. They accused each other of the worst possible actions, thus adding more mud to their already tarnished reputations. Peña Gómez and Jorge Blanco joined forces against Majluta, but were not strong enough to take full control of the party until early 1990. Then the PRD became definitively divided as Majluta formed his own organization called Partido Revolucionario Institucional (PRI). On several occasions Majluta tried unsuccessfully to negotiate an electoral agreement with Balaguer and the PRSC.

The divisions within the PRD worked against them, for they were unable to present a common front against Balaguer and Bosch. That gave the two old caudillos and edge over the two younger candidates. Thus, as the elections approached, the electorate became polarized between Bosch and Balaguer. By the end of April 1990, Bosch was still leading public opinion polls with 36 percent, while Balaguer remained at 26 percent. Peña Gómez was a distant third with 15 per cent, and Majluta had dropped to the fourth place with only 9 percent.

Faced with the eventual victory of Bosch, the Reformista leaders became depressed and convinced that they would lose the elections. But Balaguer's strategists devised a new tactic to stop Bosch. Knowing that most of Bosch's constituency was composed of nonparty members who had formerly voted for the PRSC and the PRD, they decided to buy them back with money. The Partido Reformista set up a national network for buying electoral ID cards of all those known for their new sympathies for Bosch, but who were willing to receive between 100 to 500 pesos for it. Given the desperate situation of the poor, particularly in the rural areas, thousands of people sold their cards, thus depriving Bosch of their votes.

In addition, the secretary of the armed forces, General Elías Wessin y Wessin, who had been one of the strongest advocates for Balaguer's reelection, instructed several thousand of the military and veterans to vote for Balaguer and for Wessin's own party, the PQD. Close to 8,000 active members of the armed forces and the national police were given illegal electoral ID cards to allow them to illegally cast their votes for Balaguer. A great number of Reformistas were also illegally registered with duplicate and triplicate ID cards and were able to vote up to three times.

A virulent negative campaign against Bosch was unleashed by the government in the three weeks before the election. This campaign completely destabilized Bosch, who engaged in two violent public disputes with the Catholic archbishop, who had been publicly supporting Balaguer for years, and with the chief of the armed forces and leader of the PQD, who was openly supporting Balaguer's reelection. The government took advantage of Bosch's verbal violence, and immediately portrayed him on television and the press as a potentially dangerous and unstable president.

Bosch himself did not help his own cause. As the pressure of the campaing mounted, he started to show public signs of his age. Arteriosclerosis was crippling his former brilliant oratory faculties, and his public appearances became dull performances dotted with logical hesitations, crude contradictory statements, and long periods of conceptual vacuum. Moreover, he frequently erupted in verbal, emotional violence on simple issues and personally offended the members of the press as well as his political critics.

Additionally, the government spread the rumor that the armed forces would not accept Bosch as president, and a coup would take place plunging the country again into a military dictatorship or a civil war. On the other hand, the Catholic church did not conceal its distaste toward Bosch's candidacy and advised voters against a candidate with his qualities. This strategy worked out quite effectively. During the last days of the campaign, many who had considered the idea of voting for Bosch started to retract.

Unwilling to vote for the existing parties, 40 percent of the electorate abstained from participating in the presidential elections held on May 16, 1990. The Partido de la Liberación Dominicana (PLD) obtained 653,278 votes while the Partido Reformista Social Cristiano (PRSC) obtained 647,616 votes. Yet, Balaguer turned out to be the winner as the votes of Wessin's Partido Quiqueyano Demócrata (PQD), the Partido Nacional de Veteranos Civiles (PNVC), and the Partido La Estructura were also cast for him. The latter was initially supporting Majluta but, at the last moment, its leader went for Balaguer. In the end, Balaguer totalled 678,055 votes, and with them the blind president of the Republic defeated his adversaries once more.

Balaguer received 35.06 percent of the votes, while Bosch obtained 33.81 percent. At the last minute, Peña Gómez gained many of Bosch's previous followers and increased his participation to 23.23 percent, while Majluta collapsed to 6.99 percent. The margin between Balaguer and Bosch was only 24,460 votes, most of them supplied by the paramilitary party of Elías Wessin y Wessin, the chief of the armed forces. Given the high rate of abstention, Balaguer only received 21 percent of the registered votes.

As the votes were being counted at the Junta Central Electoral, Bosch and his most radical partisans cried fraud, and a serious political crisis ensued in the following weeks. This crisis was partially defused with the intervention of former U.S. president Jimmy Carter and OAS secretary-general Adolfo Baena Soares who were in Santo Domingo acting as international observers to the election. Meanwhile, Balaguer sent the army out to patrol the streets, and imposed de facto martial rule all over the country, thus preventing Bosch from launching the popular revolt he had promised if he were deprived of the triumph. Two months later, the Junta Central Electoral proclaimed Balaguer reelected for a sixth term in his long presidential career.

Bosch and his followers declared that they would not recognize the government, denouncing it as illegitimate and fraudulent. Despite these allegations, Balaguer was inaugurated again as president in August 16, 1990, after two days of violent demonstrations that left 12 people killed and more than 5,000 arrested. Six weeks later, on September 26, a three-day general strike was staged by the major labor unions demanding salary increases. Again, 23 people were killed and more than 400 arrested.

With the peso devalued to 15 units per dollar, prices had become simply unbearable for most of the population. Again, the government failed to pay its debt with the oil suppliers and oil deliveries were suspended. For almost three months, between September and November, the Dominican Republic was virtually paralyzed without fuel, electricity, running water, or transport.

For several weeks, many groups, including political parties, labor unions, business groups, and professional organizations publicly demanded Balaguer's resignation as the only way to avoid a military coup or a social explosion. In a speech on October 18, 1990, Balaguer rejected the idea, but as a new general strike was being organized to force him to resign, he tried to prevent it by promising to allow free elections in 1992 to select a new government. His party, of course, rejected the idea, but the confusion he created among the opposition parties gave him enough time to recover politically as his announcement of a possible resignation divided the opposition. Balaguer averted the strike by threatening and bribing different union leaders and stayed in power for the rest of his term.

Once he evaded the possibility of a strike, the secret police started again to harass businessmen to whom the Central Bank accused of trafficking in dollars. In the following months the government continued intimidating those businessmen by sending them secret police agents who would threaten them with violence and jail if they failed to open their safety boxes and accounting books to prove that they were not hiding dollars.

This intense wave of persecution against the dollar holders in October 1990 was used by the government to hide a more serious financial problem than the control of the exchange rate. After four weeks of police brutality against selected targets in the business sector, the government could not longer conceal that six commercial banks had to be closed and intervened. These institutions were unable to cope with the chaotic monetary policies and restrictions imposed by the Central Bank. Two other banks had also closed the year before for similar reasons. Some of the banks that failed were badly mismanaged by their owners and directors. These bankers and businessmen publicly enjoyed the political protection of Balaguer and his closest relatives and were never prosecuted nor indicted by the monetary authorities.

September, October, and November 1990 were three months of financial panic as well as generalized economic and moral depression. Inflation hit a record 100 percent in 1990, the highest rate throughout the 20th century. A frantic flight of capital and foreign exchange took place as thousands of Dominican migrants who had returned to their country packed their belongings and headed back to the United States, thus reversing the traditional trend of returning home for the Christmas holidays. Without gasoline, electricity, running water, flour, sugar, milk, or basic foodstuffs; with no transportation, police protection, schools or hospitals, the Dominican people lived the most depressing crisis in modern history.

Never since the end of the Trujillo dictatorship, had the Dominican Republic experienced such a dismal economic and spiritual state. As these lines are being written in January 1991, most Dominicans are convinced that Balaguer will rule the country until he dies, in total disregard for legal and constitutional principles, oblivious to the consequences of his economic policies. As the middle class succumbs to poverty, its members strive to migrate to the United States, Venezuela, Spain, or Europe. The brain drain is now seriously affecting some key professions, and is depleting the country of its thin intellectual elite that cost more than 20 years and much needed resources to create. Disenchantment and disappointment have become the prevalent attitude of the Dominicans towards the future, contrary to the optimism of the past two decades.

A crumbling economy and strong international pressure forced Balaguer, in August and September 1990, to promise fundamental reforms to ease the crisis, but the final result of those promises is yet to be seen. At the beginning of 1991, the Dominican Republic is still a country without social security,

without adequate schools and hospitals, with an ailing and un-
dernourished population, and with an authoritarian and corrupt political system. If Joaquín Balaguer were to step down
today, his legacy would be seriously questioned considering that
he has been President of the Republic for six times and for 17
of the 25 years elapsed since the civil war.

Maps

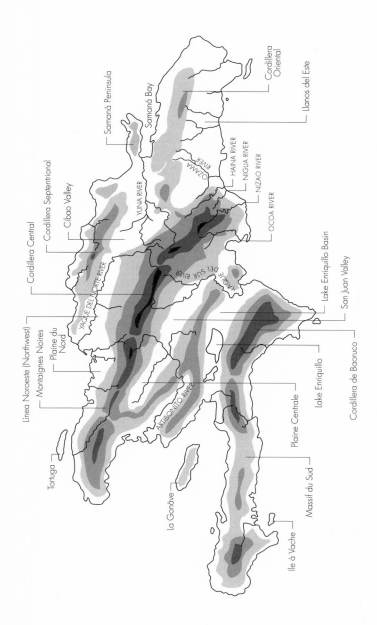

Map No. 1: *Hispaniola mountains, valleys and rivers.*

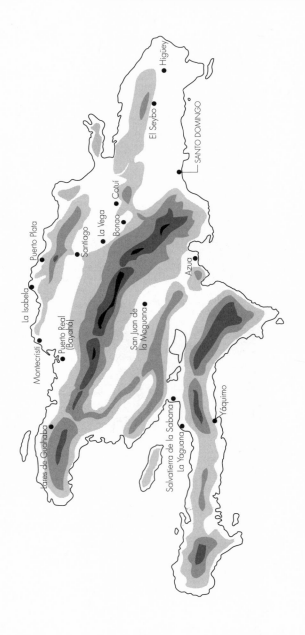

Map No. 2: *First Spanish towns.*

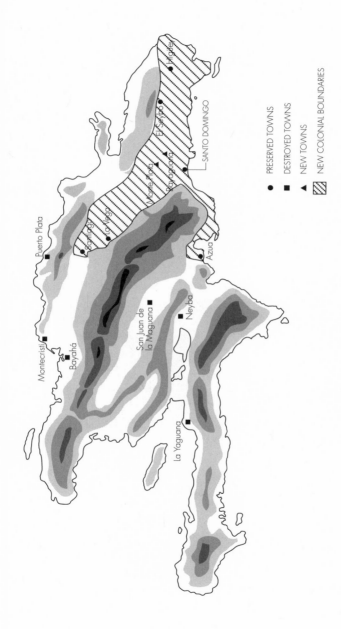

Map No. 3: *Devastation of the northern and western towns.*

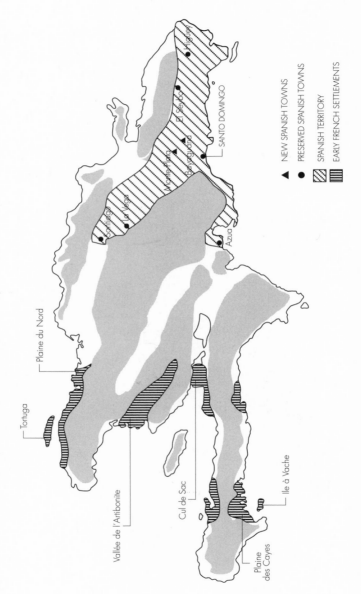

Map No. 4: *Early French settlements in the west.*

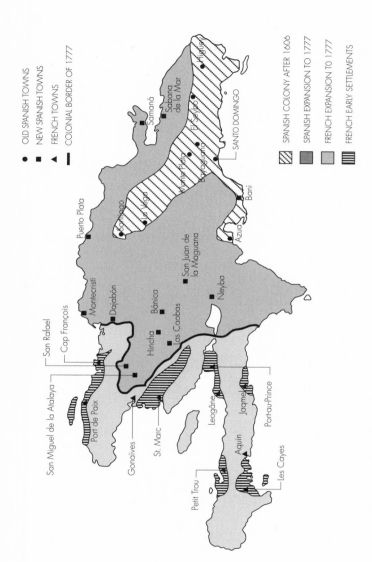

Map No. 5: *French expansion to the east and Spanish repopulation of the western lands.*

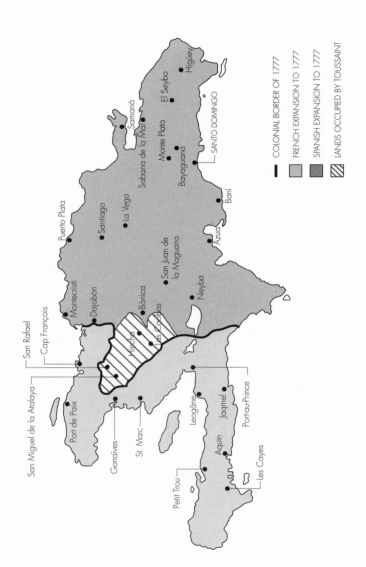

Map No. 6: *Western lands occupied by Toussaint L'Ouverture in 1794.*

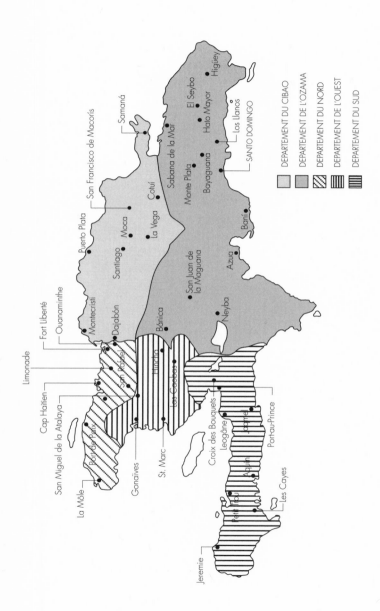

Map No. 7: *Political division during the Haitian domination (1822-1844).*

DEPARTEMENT DU CIBAO
DEPARTEMENT DE L'OZAMA
DEPARTEMENT DU NORD
DEPARTEMENT DE L'OUEST
DEPARTEMENT DU SUD

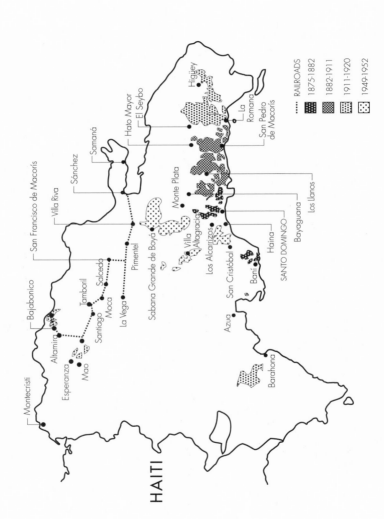

Map No. 8: *Expansion of the sugar cane plantations, and construction of railroads.*

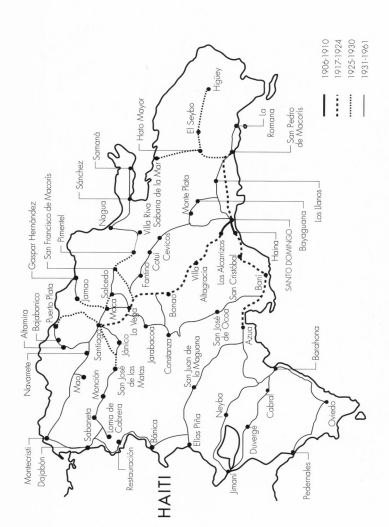

Map No. 9: *Highways and roads built between 1906 and 1961.*

Bibliography

1. THE ABORIGINAL POPULATION

Most of the information in this chapter about the aboriginal population of Española derives from the early Spanish chroniclers. The most important are Bartolomé de las Casas, *Apologética Historia Sumaria* (Mexico, 1958), and H*istoria de las Indias* (Mexico, 1965); and Gonzalo Fernández de Oviedo, *Historia General y Natural de las Indias* (Madrid, 1959). Other contemporary accounts include Cristóbal Colón, *Carta a Luis de Santángel Anunciando el Descubrimiento del Nuevo Mundo* (Madrid, 1961); Fernando Colón, *The Life of the Admiral Christopher Columbus by his son Ferdinand* (New Brunswick, N.J., 1959); Hernán Pérez de Oliva, *Historia de la Inuención de las Indias* (Bogotá, 1965); Ramón Pané, *Relación Acerca de las Antigüedades de los Indios* (Mexico, 1974); and Pedro Mártir de Anglería, *Décadas de Nuevo Mundo* (Mexico, 1964).

Early modern works which are still useful are Hy Ling Roth, "The Aborigines of Hispaniola," in the *Journal of the Anthropological Institute of Great Britain and Ireland* (1887), 16: 247-286; Svén Lovén, *The Origins of the Tainian Culture* (Göteburg, 1932); Felipe Pichardo Moya, *Los Aborígenes de las Antillas* (México, 1956); and Irving Rouse, "The West Indies-The Arawak-The Carib," in the *Handbook of the South American Indians* (1963) 4: 481-565.

More recent works are Irving Rouse, *The Taínos, Rise and Decline of the People Who Greeted Columbus* (New Haven, Conn., 1990); Jacobs

Francine, *The Taínos. The People Who Welcomed Columbus* (New York, 1992); Samuel Wilson, *Hispaniola. Caribbean Chiefdoms in the Age of Columbus* (Tuscaloosa, Ala., 1990); John Weeks and Peter Ferbel, *Ancient Caribbean* (New York, 1994); Antonio Stevens Arroyo, *Cave of the Jagua. The Mythological World of the Taínos* (Albuquerque, 1988); Marcio Veloz Maggiolo, *Panorama Histórico del Caribe Precolombino* (Santo Domingo, 1991), *Arqueología Prehistórica de Santo Domingo* (Singapore, 1972), *Las Sociedades Arcaicas de Santo Domingo* (Santo Domingo, 1980), and *Vida y Cultura en la Prehistoria de Santo Domingo* (San Pedro de Macorís, 1980); Francisco Moscoso, *Tribu y Clases en el Caribe Antiguo* (San Pedro de Macorís, 1986); and Roberto Cassá, *Los Taínos de La Española* (Santo Domingo, 1974). A general bibliography is Jalil Sued Badillo, *Bibliografía Antropológica para el Estudio de los Pueblos Indígenas en el Caribe* (Santo Domingo, 1977). A general introduction is Frank Moya Pons, "The Taínos," in *Caribbean Review*, 13 (Fall 1984), 4: 20-22,47-48.

On the Caribe indians, Jalil Sued Badillo, *Los Caribes, Realidad o Fábula: Ensayo de Rectificación Histórica* (Río Piedras, 1978), is a controversial essay aimed at denying the cannibalism of the Caribe indians. Late accounts of the Caribes published in the 17th and 18th centuries include Charles de Rochefort, *Histoire Naturelle et Morale des Iles Antilles de l'Amerique, Enrichie d'un Grand Nombre de Belles Figures en Taille Douce...Avec un Vocabulaire Caraïbe* (Rotterdam, 1681); Jean Baptiste Du Tertre, *Histoire Générale des Antilles Habitées par les François* (Paris, 1667-1671); and Jean Baptiste Labat, *Nouveau Voyage aux Isles de l'Amerique* (La Haye, 1722). A general description based on earlier chroniclers is Ricardo Alegría, *Las Primeras Noticias sobre los Indios Caribes* (San Juan, 1981).

2. THE EARLY SPANISH RULE (1492-1606)

Besides the chronicles of Las Casas and Oviedo, the main sources for the study of the *encomienda* period are the documents contained in the *Colección de Documentos Inéditos Relativos al Descubrimiento, Conquista y Colonización de las Posesiones Españolas en América y Oceanía, Sacados en su Mayor Parte del Real Archivo de Indias* (Madrid,

1864-1889), and the *Colección de Documentos Inéditos Relativos al Descubrimiento, Conquista y Organización de las Antiguas Posesiones Españolas en Ultramar* (Madrid, 1883-1932).

On the implantation and collapse of the *factoría* system, see Juan Pérez de Tudela Bueso, "Castilla ante los Comienzos de la Colonización de las Indias," in *Revista de Indias* (Jan-Mar, 1955), 59: 11-88; "La Quiebra de la Factoría y el Nuevo Poblamiento de la Española," in *Revista de Indias* (Apr-Jun, 1955), 60: 197-252, and "Política de Poblamiento y Política de Contratación de las Indias (1502-1505)," in *Revista de Indias* (Jul-Dec, 1955), 61-62: 311-420.

The social, economic, and political problems derived from the exploitation of gold and Indian labor under the *encomienda* system have been studied by Lesley Byrd Simpson, *The Encomienda in New Spain. Forced Labor in the Spanish Colonies, 1492-1559* (Berkeley, 1929); Carl Ortwin Sauer, *The Early Spanish Main* (Berkeley, 1966); Frank Moya Pons, *Después de Colón. Trabajo, Sociedad y Política en la Economía del Oro* (Madrid, 1987); Lewis Hanke, *The Spanish Struggle for Justice in the Conquest of America* (Boston, 1967), and *The First Social Experiments in America* (Cambridge, Mass., 1935); Manuel Giménez Fernández, *Bartolomé de las Casas. Política Inicial de Carlos I en Indias* (Sevilla, 1950); Ursula Lamb, *Frey Nicolás de Ovando. Gobernador de Indias (1501-1509)*, (Madrid, 1956); Troy S. Floyd, *The Columbus Dynasty in the Caribbean, 1492-1526* (Albuquerque, 1973); Luis Arranz Márquez, *Don Diego Colón, Almirante, Virrey y Gobernador de las Indias* (Madrid, 1982); and Manuel Serrano Sanz, *Orígenes de la Dominación Española en América* (Madrid, 1918).

On the origins of sugar cane cultivation and the early plantations in Española, see the documents published by Irene Wright, "The Commencement of Cane Sugar Industry in America, 1519-1538," in the *American Historical Review* (July, 1916), 21: 755-780; Mervin Ratekin, "The Early Sugar Industry in Española," in the *Hispanic American Historical Review* (February, 1954), 34: 1-19; and Frank Moya Pons, Azúcar, Negros y Sociedad en la Española en el Siglo XVI," in *Eme-Eme Estudios Dominicanos* 1 (Jan-Feb, 1973), 4: 3-18. Justo L. del Río Moreno, *Los Inicios de la Agricultura Europea en el Nuevo Mundo (1492-1542)*, (Sevilla, 1991) is a recent scholarly work based on original research at the Archivo General de Indias, in Seville.

Other documents related to sugar, as well as to cattle ranching and smuggling in the 16th century appear in J. Marino Incháustegui, *Reales Cédulas y Correspondencia de Gobernadores de Santo Domingo* (Madrid, 1958), vols. I-II. Export statistics for hides and sugar in the 16th century have been collected by Pierre and Huguette Chaunu, *Seville et l'Atlantique* (Paris, 1955-58). Américo Lugo, *Historia de Santo Domingo, 1556-1608* (Ciudad Trujillo, 1952), also published some relevant data on the same products based on Emilio Rodríguez Demorizi, *Relaciones Históricas de Santo Domingo*, vol. II (Ciudad Trujillo, 1945), which contains 16th-century documents regarding the contraband trade and the "Devastaciones."

For information on the the early penetration of English smugglers and corsairs into the Caribbean, see Irene Wright (ed.), *Spanish Documents Concerning English Voyages to the Caribbean, 1527-1568* (London, 1928). On the role of the Dutch during the years before the "Devastaciones," see Engel Sluiter, "Dutch-Spanish Rivalry in the Caribbean Area, 1594-1609, in the *Hispanic American Historical Review* (February, 1948), 28: 165-196; and Cornelis Goslinga, *The Dutch in the Caribbean and on the Wild Coast 1580-1680* (Gainesville, Fl., 1971).

3. THE ISLAND DIVIDED (1607-1697)

Some modern interpretations about the causes and consequences of the "Devastaciones" are Manuel Arturo Peña Batlle, *Las Devastaciones de 1605 y 1606 (Contribución al Estudio de la Realidad Dominicana)* (Ciudad Trujillo: 1938); Frank Moya Pons, *Historia Colonial de Santo Domingo* (Santiago, 1973), chaps. 4-10; and Juana Gil-Bermejo García, *La Española. Anotaciones Históricas (1600-1650)* (Sevilla, 1983). Less scholarly are Pedro Mir, *El Gran Incendio* (Santo Domingo, 1974); and Frank Peña Pérez, *Cien Años de Miseria en Santo Domingo 1600-1700* (Santo Domingo, n.d.). Carlos Esteban Deive, *Las Devastaciones* (Santo Domingo, 1979) is a novel about this important event.

Emilio Rodríguez Demorizi, *Apuntes y Documentos* (Ciudad Trujillo, 1957), and *Relaciones Históricas de Santo Domingo*, vols. I, III (Ciudad Trujillo, 1957), contain many important documents concerning the social conditions of Santo Domingo in the 17th century. Some social aspects are presented by Frank Moya Pons (ed.), in *La Vida Escandalosa en Santo Domingo en los Siglos XVII y XVIII* (Santiago, 1977), and by Carlos Esteban Deive, *La Mala Vida en Santo Domingo* (Santo Domingo, 1989). Fray Cipriano de Utrera, *Historia Militar de Santo Domingo* (Ciudad Trujillo, 1950), deals with the process of militarization of Santo Domingo in the 16th and 17th centuries. Carlos Esteban Deive, *Los Cimarrones del Maniel de Neiba. Historia y Geografía* (Santo Domingo, 1985), is a recent monograph on the runaway slaves during the 17th century. See also, "Campaña Militar contra los Negros Alzados en el Maniel en 1665," *Eme Eme Estudios Dominicanos* 2 (Aug-Sep 1972), 2: 113-117.

The role of pirates, corsairs, bucaneers, and filibusters was described in the 17th century by the pirate-surgeon Alexandre Olivier Exquemelin, *The Buccaneers of America* (London, 1951), and early in the 20th century by Clarence H. Haring, *The Buccaneers in the West Indies in the 17th Century* (London, 1910), and Violet Barbour, "Privateers and Pirates of the West Indies," *American Historical Review* XVI (April 1911), 3: 529-566. A pro-Spanish narrative is Manuel Arturo Peña Batlle, *La Isla de la Tortuga* (Madrid, 1951). See also, Roland D. Hussey, "Spanish Reaction to Foreign Aggression in the Caribbean to about 1680," *Hispanic American Historical Review* IX (August, 1929), 286-302.

On the English invasion of Santo Domingo in 1655, see Irene A. Wright (ed.), *Spanish Narratives of the English Attack on Santo Domingo 1655* (London, 1926); Arthur Watts, *Une Histoire des Colonies Anglaises aux Antilles (de 1649 à 1660)* (Paris, 1924); J. Marino Incháustegui, *La Gran Expedición Inglesa contra las Antillas Mayores* (Mexico, 1953); Emilio Rodríguez Demorizi, *Invasión Inglesa de 1655* (Ciudad Trujillo, 1956); and Stanley Arthur Goodwin Taylor, *The Western Design: An Account of Cromwell's Expedition to the Caribbean* (Kingston,1965).

On the role of tobacco in the origins of the French colony in the western lands of Española, see Jacob M. Price, "Colonial Supplies and the Crisis of St. Domingue," in *France and the Chesapeake. A History of the French Tabacco Monopoly, 1674-1791, and of its Relationship to the British and the American Tobacco Trades* (Ann Arbor, 1973), 1: 73-115. See also Gabriel Debien, "Le Peuplement des Antilles Francaises au XVII siècle," *Notes d'Histoire Coloniale* (Dakar, 1942), *Les Engagés pour les Antilles (1634-1715)* (Paris, 1952). Additional documentation on the origins of the intercolonial trade appears in Gobierno Dominicano, *Recopilación Diplomática Relativa a las Colonias Francesa y Española de la Isla de Santo Domingo, 1640-1701* (Ciudad Trujillo, 1944).

4. THE FRONTIER (1697-1789)

Contemporary sources are Pierre François Xavier de Charlevoix, *Histoire de l'Ile Espagnole ou de S. Domingue* (Paris, 1731), recently published in Spanish as *Historia de la Isla Española o de Santo Domingo: Escrita Particularmente sobre las Memorias Manuscritas del Padre Jean Baptiste Le Pers, Jesuita, Misionero en Santo Domingo, y sobre los Documentos Originales que se Conservan en el Depósito de la Marina* (Santo Domingo, 1977); Médéric-Louis-Elie Moreau de Saint-Méry, *A Topographical and Political Description of the Spanish Part of Saint-Domingue* (Philadelphia, 1796), also published as *Descripción de la Parte Española de la Isla de Santo Domingo* (Santo Domingo, 1944); Antonio Sánchez Valverde, *Idea del Valor de la Isla Española* (Santo Domingo, 1947), initially published as *Idea del Valor de la Isla Española, y Utilidades, que de Ella Puede Sacar su Monarquía* (Madrid, 1785); and the documents collected by Américo Lugo in the Archivo General de Indias, published as Colección Lugo, "Recopilación Diplomática Relativa a las Colonias Española y Francesa de la Isla de Santo Domingo," *Boletín del Archivo General de la Nación*, vols. 79-98 (Oct 1953-Dec 1959). Another contemporary source with some information related to the cattle trade is Luis Joseph Peguero, *Historia de la Conquista de la Isla Española de Santo Domingo Trasumptada el Año de 1762* (Santo Domingo, 1975). For the French side of the island, an important source is Médéric-Louis-Elie Moreau de Saint-Méry, *Description Topographique, Physique, Civile, Politique et Historique de la Partie Française de l'Ile Saint-Domingue* (Paris, 1797-98; 1958).

The economic reactivation of Santo Domingo, the formation of the frontier, and the repopulation of the borderlands during the 18th century are studied in María Rosario Sevilla Soler, *Santo Domingo Tierra de Frontera (1750-1800)*, (Sevilla, 1971); Frank Moya Pons, *Historia Colonial de Santo Domingo* (Santiago, 1973); and Antonio Gutiérrez Escudero, *Población y Economía en Santo Domingo (1700-1746)*

(Sevilla, 1985). Two earlier studies on the border between Santo Domingo and Saint Domingue are Manuel Arturo Peña Batlle, *Historia de la Cuestión Fronteriza Domínico-Haitiana* (Ciudad Trujillo, 1946); James J. McLean and T. Pina Chevalier, *Datos Históricos sobre la Frontera Domínico-Haitiana* (Santo Domingo, 1921). See also Antonio Gutiérrez Escudero, "Cuestión de Límites en la Isla Española, 1690-1777," *Temas Americanistas* (Sevilla, 1982), 1: 22-24, and "Contrabando en el Caribe: Comercio Ilícito entre Españoles y Franceses en Santo Domingo," *Estudios de Historia Social y Económica de América* (Madrid, 1985), 1: 71-91.

On the immigration of families from the Canary Islands and the repopulation of the borderlands, see Emilio Rodríguez Demorizi, *Fundacion de Baní* (Santo Domingo, 1974); *Noticias de Puerto Plata* (Santo Domingo, 1975); *Nueva Fundación de Puerto Plata (22 de julio de 1736)* (Santo Domingo, 1975); *Samaná, Pasado y Porvenir* (Ciudad Trujillo, 1945); and Carlos Esteban Deive, *Las Inmigraciones Canarias a Santo Domingo (siglos XVII y XVIII)*, Santo Domingo, 1991).

5. THE FRENCH REVOLUTION IN SANTO DOMINGO (1789-1809)

Hundreds of works have been written about the French colony of Saint Domingue and the Haitian Revolution. Some of the most relevant to the narrative of this book are: Médéric-Louis-Elie Moreau de Saint-Méry, *Description Topographique, Physique, Civile, Politique et Historique de la Partie Francaise de l'Ile Saint-Domingue* (Paris, 1797-98); Brian Edwards, *An Historical Survey of the French Colony in the Island of St. Domingo* (London, 1797); François Alexandre Stanislaus, Baron de Wimpffen, *A Voyage to Saint-Domingo, In the Years 1788, 1789, and 1790* (London, 1797); Pierre De Vaisièrre, *Saint Domingue. La Societé et la Vie Créoles* (Paris, 1909); François Girod, *La Vie Quotidienne de la Societé Creole. Saint-Domingue au XVIIIe siècle* (Paris,1972); and Charles Frostin, *Les Révoltes Blanches à Saint-Domingue aux XVIIe et XVIIIe siècles (Haiti avant 1789)* (Paris, 1975). There is a very abridged English translation and edition of Saint-Méry's work by Ivor D. Spencer, *A Civilization that Perished. The Last Years of White Colonial Rule in Haiti* (Lanham, 1985).

On the colonists, slaves, and mulattos in the French colony, see the works by Gabriel Debien, "La Nourriture des Esclaves sur les Plantations des Antilles Francais aux XVIIe et XVIIIe Siècles," *Caribbean Studies* 4 (1964), 3: 3-27; *La Question des Vivres pour les Esclaves des Antilles Françaises aux XVIe siècle* (Caracas, 1972); "Le Marronage aux Antilles Francaises aux XVIIIe siècle." *Caribbean Studies* 6 (October 1966), 3: 1-43; "Les Affranchissements aux Antilles Françaises aux XVIIe et XVIIIe siècles," *Anuario de Estudios Americanos* 23 (1966): 1177-1203; "Les Colons des Antilles et leur Main-d'Oeuvre a la fin du XVIIIe Siècle," *Annales Historiques de la Révolution* 3 (Juillet-Septembre, 1955); *Les Esclaves aux Antilles Françaises (XVIIe-XVIIIe siècles)* (Basse-Terre, 1974); "Les Grand'Cases des Plantations a Saint-Domingue aux XVIIe et XVIIIe siècles," *Annales des Antilles, Bulletin de la Societé d'Histoire de la Martinique* 15 (1970): 1-39; "Nouvelles de Saint-Domingue." *Notes d'Histoire Coloniale* 59; "Plantations et Esclaves a Saint-Domingue: la Sucrerie Cottineau." *Notes d'Histoire Coloniale. Dakar* 66 (1962); "Sur la Sucrerie Bréda du Haut-du-Cap," *Révue de la Faculté d"Ethnologie* 10 (1965): 18-27; "A Saint-Domingue avec deus Jeunes Economes de Plantation (1774-1788)," *Révue de la Societé d'Histoire et de Geographie d'Haiti* (July, 1945): 64-86.

The Haitian Revolution has been dramatically depicted by C. L. R. James, *The Black Jacobins. Toussaint L'Ouverture and the San Domingo Revolution* (New York, 1963). An good summary is Thomas O. Ott, *The Haitian Revolution, 1789-1804* (Knoxville, Tennessee, 1972). An outdated but still useful summary is J. Lothrop Stoddard, *The French Revolution in San Domingo* (Boston, 1914). A modern biography of Toussaint Louverture is Ralph Korngold, *Citizen Toussaint* (New York, 1965). Two modern accounts of the disastrous British Expedition are David P. Geggus, *Slavery, War, and Revolution: the British Occupation of Saint Domingue, 1793-1798* (New York, 1982); and Charles Frostin, L'Intervention Britannique à Saint Domingue en 1793," *Révue Francaise d'Histoire d'Outre-Mer* 46 (1962). See also Phillip D. Curtin, "The Declaration of the Rights of Man in Saint-Domingue, *Hispanic American Historical Review* 30 (May 1950): 157-175. Another recent history of the Haitian Revolution is also Carolyn Fick, *The Making of Haiti. The Saint Domingue Revolution from Below*, (Knoxville,Tennessee, 1990).

On the French colonists during the revolution, see Gabriel Debien

"Esprit Colon et Esprit d'Autonomie a Saint-Domingue," *Notes d'Historie Coloniale* 25 (1954); "Gouverneurs, Magistrats et Colons. L'Opposition Parlamentaire a Saint-Domingue, 1763-1769," *Révue d'Histoire d'Haiti* (1946); "L'Esprit d'Independence chez les Colons de Saint Domingue au XVIIIe siècle," *Notes d'Histoire Coloniale* 13 (1947); *Les Colons de Saint-Domingue et la Revolution. Essai sur le Club Massiac* (Paris, 1953); "Les Colons de Saint-Domingue Refugiés à Cuba," *Révista de Indias* 14 (1954): 559-605 (1955): 13-26; "Refugiés de Saint-Domingue aux Etats-Unis," *Révue de la Societé d'Histoire et de Géographie d'Haïti* (1948-1950); "Les Colons de Saint-Domingue passés à la Jamaïque (1792-1835)," *Bulletin de la Societé d'Histoire de la Guadeloupe* 26 (1975).

The impact of the Haitian Revolution on the Spanish part of the island has been documented by Antonio del Monte y Tejada, *Historia de Santo Domingo*, vols. 3-4 (Santo Domingo, 1892); Ramón Lugo Lovatón, "El Tratado de Basilea," *Boletín del Archivo General de la Nación* 68 (Jan-Mar, 1951): 86-119; Wendell Schaeffer, "The Delayed Cession of Spanish Santo Domingo to France, 1795-1801," *Hispanic American Historical Review* 29 (February 1949): 46-68; Manuel Arturo Peña Batlle, *El Tratado de Basilea* (Ciudad Trujillo, 1952); J. Marino Incháustegui Cabral (ed.), *Documentos para Estudio: Marco de la Epoca y Problemas del Tratado de Basilea de 1795 en la Parte Española de Santo Domingo* (Buenos Aires, 1957); Emilio Rodríguez Demorizi (ed.), *Cesión de Santo Domingo a Francia. Correspondencia de Godoy, García, Roume, Hedouville, Louverture, Rigaud y Otros, 1795-1802* (Ciudad Trujillo, 1958); Carlos Esteban Deive, *Los Refugiados Franceses en Santo Domingo, 1789-1801* (Santo Domingo, 1984), and *Las Emigraciones Dominicanas a Cuba (1795-1808)* (Santo Domingo, 1989); and Frank Moya Pons, "The Haitian Revolution in Santo Domingo (1789-1809)," *Jahrbuch fur Geschichte von Staat, Wirschaft und Gesellschaft Lateinamerikas* 28 (1991), 125-162. On the abolition of slavery on the Spanish colony, see also Frank Moya Pons, "La Primera Abolición de la Esclavitud en Santo Domingo," *La Torre. Revista General de la Universidad de Puerto Rico* 21 (Jul-Dec 1973), 81-82: 229-255.

The Haitian invasions commanded by Toussaint Louverture and Jean Jacques Dessalines against the Spanish part of Santo Domingo are documented by Emilio Rodríguez Demorizi (ed.), *Invasiones Haitianas de 1801, 1805 y 1822* (Ciudad Trujillo, 1955) and *La Era de Francia en*

Santo Domingo (Ciudad Trujillo, 1958). Toussaint Louverture's decrees in Santo Domingo have been published as "Decretos y Proclamas," *Eme-Eme Estudios Dominicanos* 2 (May-June, 1974), 12: 146-162.

Two very important French narratives on the War of Reconquest are Gilbert Guillermin, *Journal Historique de la Revolution de la Partie de l'Est de Saint-Domingue Commencée le 10 Aout 1808, avec des Notes Statistiques sur Cette Partie* (Philadelphia, 1810); and M. Lemonier Delafosse, *Seconde Campagne de Saint Domingue du 1er. Decembre 1803 au 15 Juillet 1809; Précedée de Souvenirs Historiques & Succints de la Première Campagne. Expedition du Général en Chef Leclerc, du 14 Décembre 1803* (Havre, 1846).

A Dominican counterpart to these narratives is Juan Sánchez Ramírez, *Diario de la Reconquista* (Ciudad Trujillo, 1957). An article on the expulsion of the French from Santo Domingo is Miguel Artola, "La Guerra de la Reconquista de Santo Domingo, 1808-1809," *Revista de Indias* 11 (1951), 447-484. An English description of Santo Domingo during this period is William Walton, *Present State of the Spanish Colonies; Including a Particular Report of Hispaniola, or the Spanish Part of Santo Domingo* (London, 1810).

6. THE HAITIAN DOMINATION (1809-1843)

Among the contemporary sources written by foreign observers, see Jonathan Brown, *The History and Present Condition of St. Domingo* (Philadelphia, 1837); John Candler, *Brief Notices of Hayti, with its Conditions, Resources, and Prospects* (London, 1842); James Franklyn, *The Present State of Hayti (Saint Domingo)* (London, 1828); Charles Mackenzie, *Notes on Haiti, Made during a Residence in that Republic* (London, 1830); and Romuald Lepelletier de Saint-Rémy, *Saint-Domingue, Etude et Solution Nouvelle de la Question Haitienne*, (Paris, 1846).

Haitian narratives of this period are fewer, but important. An outstanding source is Beaubrun Ardouin, *Etudes sur l'Histoire d'Haiti*, 11 vols. (Paris, 1853-60). Other relevant works are Thomas Madiou, *Histoire d'Haiti: Annés 1843-1846*, 4 vols. (Port-au-Prince, 1847-48 and 1904); H. Pauléus Sannon, *Essai Historique sur la Révolution de 1843* (Les Cayes, 1905); and Pierre-Eugene De Lespinasse, *Gens d'Autrefois...*

Vieus Souvenirs... (Paris, 1961). Besides Ardouin, the other indispensable Haitian source for this period is Listant Pradine, *Recueil de Lois et Actes du Gouvernement Haitienne*, vols. III-V (Paris, 1860-66)

On the negotiations for France's recognition of Haiti's independence in 1825, see M. Wallez, *Précis Historique des Negotiations entre la France et Saint Domingue suivi des Pieces Justificatives* (Paris, 1826); Benoit Joachim, "La Reconnaisssance d'Haiti par la France (1825): Naissance d'un Nouveau Type de Rapports Internationaux," *Révue d'Histoire Moderne et Contemporaine* 11 (1975): 369-396; and "L'Indemnité Colonial de Saint-Domingue et la Question des Repatriés," *Révue Historique* 246 (1971): 359-376; and "Commerce et Decolonization: L'Experience Franco-Haitienne au XIXe siècle," *Annales: Economies, Societés, Civilizations* 27 (1972): 1497-1525.

Other modern works dealing with this period include James C. Leyburn, *The Haitian People* (New Haven, 1941); Robert K, Lacerte, "The Evolution of Land and Labor in the Haitian Revolution, 1791-1820," *The Americas* 34 (1978): 449-454; David Nicholls, "Rural Protest and Peasant Revolt in Haiti (1804-1869), in Malcom Cross and A. Marks (ed.), *Peasants, Plantations, and Rural Communities in the Caribbean* (Guilford and Leiden, 1979); Leslie F. Manigat, *La Politique Agraire du Gouvernement d'Alexandre Petion, 1807-1818* (Port-au-Prince, 1967); Hubert Cole, *Christophe, King of Haiti* (New York, 1967); Paul Verna, *Petión y Bolívar. Cuarenta Años (1790-1830) de Relaciones Haitianovenezolanas y su Aporte a la Emancipación de Hispanoamérica* (Caracas, 1969); Frank Moya Pons, "The Land Question in Haiti and Santo Domingo: The Sociopolitical Context of the Transition from Slavery to Free Labor, 1801-1843," in Manuel Moreno Fraginals, Frank Moya Pons, and Stanley L. Engerman, *Between Slavery and Free Labor. The Spanish Speaking Caribbean in the Nineteenth Century* (Baltimore, 1985); and Frank Moya Pons, "Haiti and Santo Domingo, 1790-c.1870," in Leslie Bethel (ed.), *The Cambridge History of Latin America. From Independence to c. 1870* (Cambridge, 1985), 3: 237-275.

On the Dominican side, there are several sources which should be consulted. Foremost among them is José Gabriel García, *Compendio de la Historia de Santo Domingo*, vols. 2-3 (Santo Domingo, 1893-1906). See also Emilio Rodríguez Demorizi, *La Imprenta y los Primeros Periódicos en Santo Domingo* (Ciudad Trujillo, 1944), *Santo Domingo y la Gran Colombia. Bolívar y Núñez de Cáceres* (Santo Domingo, 1971), and "La Revolución de 1843. Apuntes y Documentos para su Estudio," *Boletín del Archivo General de la Nación* 25-26 (January-April, 1943):28:109; Gustavo A. Mejía Ricart, *El Estado Independiente del Haití Español* (Santiago, 1938); José Luciano Franco, *Revoluciones y Conflictos Internacionales en el Caribe, 1789-1854* (La Habana, 1965); Víctor Garrido, *Antecedentes de la Invasión Haitiana de 1822* (Santo Domingo, 1972); Emiliano Jos, *Un Capítulo Inacabado de Historia de la Isla Española en 1819-1820* (Sevilla, 1952); Felipe Fernández de Castro, "Memorial Acerca de la Reclamación de la Parte Española de la Isla. Independencia de 1821. Documentos," *Boletín del Archivo General de la Nación* 44-45 (Jan-Apr, 1946): 65-83; Carlos Larrazábal Blanco, "Felipe Fernández de Castro y la Dominación Haitiana," *Clío* 91 (Sept-Dec, 1951): 135-136; José María Serra, "Apuntes para la Historia de los Trinitarios, Fundadores de la República Dominicana," *Boletín del Archivo General de la Nación* 32-33 (January-April, 1944):49-69. A modern monograph on the Haitian domination is Frank Moya Pons, *La Dominación Haitiana, 1822-1844* (Santiago, 1973). An interpretation reflecting the old Dominican resentment against Haiti is Manuel de Jesús Troncoso de la Concha, *La Ocupación de Santo Domingo por Haití* (Ciudad Trujillo, 1942). A study on the mercantile economy of Haiti under Boyer based on the books of James Franklin, Jonathan Brown, and John Candler is Roberto Marte, "Estudio Preliminar," *Estadísticas y Documentos Históricos sobre Santo Domingo (1850-1890)* (Santo Domingo, 1984), pp. 1-50.

7. SEPARATION FROM HAITI AND INDEPENDENCE (1843-1844)

There are no monographs in English about the Dominican separation from Haiti in 1844. Yet, the first chapters of Sumner Welles, *The Naboth's Vineyard. The Dominican Republic, 1844-1924,* (New York, 1928), can be used as an introduction. The same can be said of the corresponding chapters of Charles Callan Tansill, *The United States and Santo Domingo, 1798-1873. A Chapter in Caribbean Diplomacy* (Baltimore, 1938), and David Dixon Porter, *Diario de una Misión Secreta a Santo Domingo (1846)* (Santo Domingo, 1978). Relevant articles are

Emilio Rodríguez Demorizi, "El Acta de la Separación Dominicana y el Acta de Independencia de los Estados Unidos de América," *Cuadernos Dominicanos de Cultura* 1 (September, 1943): 25-46; Guido Despradel Batista, "La Municipalidad de Santo Domingo ante el Golpe Libertador del 27 de Febrero," *Boletín del Archivo General de la Nación* 26-27 (Jan-Apr, 1943): 3-21; and Max Henríquez Ureña, "Un Proyecto Anglófilo en 1843 frente al Plan Levasseur," *La Nación* 610 (October 23, 1941).

The military aspects of the war have been researched by Ramiro Matos González, *Historia Militar Dominicana* (Santo Domingo, 1984) and Rhadamés Hungría Morell, *Calendas Históricas y Militares Dominicanas* (Santo Domingo, 1985). See also Ramiro Matos José and Miguel Soto Jiménez, *Historia Militar Dominicana: Cronología* (Santo Domingo, 1984). Two Haitian perspectives are Jean Price Mars, *La République d'Haiti et la République Dominicaine: Les Aspects Divers d'un Problème d'Histoire, de Geographie et d'Ethnologie* (Port-au-Prince, 1953); and Thomas Madiou, *Histoire d'Haiti: Années 1843-1846* (Port-au-Prince, 1904). The first campaign of the Haitian-Dominican war has been described by Frank Moya Pons, "Guerra y Política en 1844: La Batalla del 30 de Marzo en el Contexto Histórico de la Independencia," *Eme-Eme Estudios Dominicanos* 7 (March-April, 1979): 41: 3-18.

Most of the documentation regarding Dominican independence has been collected and published in numerous independent volumes. The most important are Emilio Rodríguez Demorizi, *Correspondencia de Levasseur y de Otros Agentes de Francia Relativa a la Proclamación de la República Dominicana, 1843-1844* (Ciudad Trujillo, 1944); *Correspondencia del Cónsul de Francia en Santo Domingo*, 2 vols. (Ciudad Trujillo, 1944, 1947); *Documentos para la Historia de la República Dominicana*, 3 vols. (Ciudad Trujillo, 1944-47); *La Marina de Guerra Dominicana* (Ciudad Trujillo, 1959); and *Guerra Domínico-Haitiana* (Ciudad Trujillo, 1957). The latter is an enhanced edition of the earlier works of José Gabriel García, *Partes Oficiales de las Operaciones Militares Realizadas durante la Guerra Domínico-Haitiana, Recopilados y Ampliados con Notas* (Santo Domingo, 1888), and *Guerra de la Separación Dominicana: Documentos para su Historia Coleccionados y Ampliados con Notas* (Santo Domingo, 1890). Additional documents have been published in Emilio Rodríguez Demorizi, *En Torno a Duarte* (Santo Domingo 1976); *Acerca de Francisco del Rosario*

Sánchez (Santo Domingo, 1976); and *Homenaje a Mella. Centenario de la Muerte de Mella, 1864-1964* (Santo Domingo, 1964).

Monographs and secondary sources include Vetilio Alfau Durán, *Contribución de Higüey a la Independencia Nacional* (Ciudad Trujillo, 1944); Emilio Rodríguez Demorizi, *Juan Isidro Pérez, el Ilustre Loco* (Ciudad Trujillo, 1944); Ramón Lugo Lovatón, *Sánchez* (Ciudad Trujillo, 1947); Francisco Elpidio Beras, *Nuevas Perspectivas del Procesamiento de María Trinidad Sánchez* (Ciudad Trujillo, 1957); Víctor Garrido, *Los Puello* (Ciudad Trujillo, 1959); *Política de Francia en Santo Domingo, 1844-1846* (Santo Domingo, 1962); Leonidas García Lluberes, *Crítica Histórica* (Santo Domingo, 1964); Alcides García Lluberes, *Duarte y Otros Temas* (Santo Domingo: 1971); and José Aníbal Sánchez Fernández, *El Golpe del 9 de Junio de 1844* (Santo Domingo, 1974).

8. THE FIRST CAUDILLOS: SANTANA AND BAEZ (1844-1856)

Many of the personal papers of Santana and Báez, and most of the contemporary literature both in favor and against these two caudillos have been collected and edited by Emilio Rodríguez Demorizi, *Papeles de Santana* (Roma, 1952); *Santana y los Poetas de su Tiempo* (Santo Domingo, 1969); *Papeles de Buenaventura Báez* (Santo Domingo, 1969). Some contemporary pamphlets deal with the political discords between Santana and Báez. They are Buenaventura Báez, *A sus Conciudadanos* (Santomás, 1853); Manuel María Gautier, *Escrita por un Dominicano. La Gran Traición del General Pedro Santana, Actual Presidente de la República* (s.l., 1853); and Varios Dominicanos, *Publícanla Varios Dominicanos Amantes de su País. Vida Política de Pedro Santana Actual Presidente de la República* (Nueva York, 1856). See also, Vetilio Alfau Durán (ed.), *Controversia Histórica. La Polémica de Santana* (Santo Domingo, 1968); and César Herrera, *Batalla de las Carreras* (Ciudad Trujillo, 1949). José Gabriel García, *Compendio de la Historia de Santo Domingo* (Santo Domingo, 1893) still remains a basic source for this period.

Many of the most important documents concerning the diplomatic relations with the United States during this period have been published in William Ray Manning (ed.) *Diplomatic Correspondence of the United States Concerning Independence of the Latin-American Nations* (New York, 1925). These documents, plus some additions, have been recently translated and published in Spanish by Alfonso Lockward (ed.), *Documentos para la Historia de las Relaciones Domínico-Americanas* (Santo Domingo, 1987). Other important contemporary accounts are Gustave D'Alaux, "L'Empereur Soulouque et Son Empire" *Révue des Deux Mondes*, Paris (April 15-May 1,1851); and Britannicus, *The Dominican Republic and the Emperor Soulouque: Being Remarks and Strictures on the Misstatements, and a Refutation of the Calumnies, of M. D'Alaux, in the Article under the Above Title in the Révue Des Deux Mondes: Preceded by a Concise Account of the Historical Events of the Dominican Republic, and a Glance at the Peninsula of Samana* (Philadelphia 1852). Britannicus was the pseudonym of Theodore Stanley Heneken, a British merchant who resided in Santiago. A modern appraisal is Murdo J. Macleod, "The Soulouque Regime in Haiti, 1847-1859: A Reevaluation," *Caribbean Studies*, 10 (October 1970), 3: 39-55. Fundamental diplomatic histories of this period are Sumner Welles, *The Naboth's Vineyard* (New York, 1928), and Charles Callan Tansill, *The United States and Santo Domingo, 1798-1873* (Baltimore, 1938). On the economic conditions immediately after independence, see Frank Moya Pons, "Datos sobre la Economía Dominicana durante la Primera República," *Eme-Eme Estudios Dominicanos* 4 (May-June, 1976), 24: 21-44.

Both Santana and Báez had to confront the issue of the properties of the Catholic church confiscated by the Haitians. The debate on this issue was opened by José María Bobadilla, *Opinión sobre el Derecho de las Iglesias y Dominicanos Emigrados, en los Bienes de que Fueron Despojados por el Gobierno Haitiano durante su Ocupación en la Parte del Este de la Isla de Santo Domingo* (Santo Domingo, 1845). Bobadilla signed his piece with the pseudonym "Un Dominicano," and was immediately rebuked by a former officer during the Haitian occupation, Manuel María Valencia, in his pamphlet *Homenaje a la Razón* (Santo Domingo, 1845). Valencia used the pen name "Un Aprendiz." This debate continued over the years and provoked the well known conflict between Pedro Santana and the Archbishop Tomás de Portes e Infante in 1853. Details about this confrontation were published by Carlos Nouel, *Historia Eclesiástica de la Arquidiócesis de Santo Domingo* (Santo Domingo, 1914). Nouel's book is still the only history of the Catholic church in the 19th century. Báez also tried to negotiate a Concordat with the Vatican. Details on this issue are given by Vetilio Alfau Durán, *El Derecho de Patronato en la República Dominicana* (Santo Domingo, 1975).

9. THE REVOLUTION OF 1857

This political event still lacks a solid monographic treatment. Details on the financial and political causes and consequences have to be sought in the more general works of José Gabriel García, *Compendio de Historia Dominicana*, Sumner Welles, *Naboth's Vineyard*, and Frank Moya Pons, "La Economía Dominicana en la Primera República," already quoted. The justification for the revolution was published in the *Manifiesto de los Pueblos del Cibao y de las Causas que los Han Impulsado a Reasumir sus Derechos* (Santiago, 1857). A controversial discussion of the role of Buenaventura Báez and Francisco del Rosario Sánchez during the revolution are the mimeographed papers by José Aníbal Sánchez Fernández, *Historia Política de la Independencia y Prejuicio Racial en Análisis Documental* (Santo Domingo, 1975), and *Sánchez y la Problemática Dominicana de su Epoca* (Santo Domingo, 1976). The constitutional problem during and after the revolution is studied by Frank Moya Pons in "Acerca de las Luchas Constitucionales Dominicanas en el siglo XIX," *Eme-Eme Estudios Dominicanos* 5 (May-June, 1977),30, 3-15. A contemporary explanation is Manuel Lavastida, *Memoria Acerca de las Circunstancias y Principales Causas que Provocaron los Sucesos Políticos Ocurridos en la República Desde el Año de 1856 Hasta el Alzamiento Nacional de Julio de 1857, Dirigida por el Secretario Encargado de las Relaciones Exteriores al Excelentísimo Señor Don Pedro Santana* (Santo Domingo, 1859). On the return of Santana, see P. Evanson, "The Third Dominican-Haitian War and the Return of Pedro Santana: Part of a Long Story," *Caribbean Studies*, 4 (April 1964), 1: 13-27. The monetary and financial questions are discussed by Manuel Arturo Peña Batlle, "Historia de la Deuda Pública Dominicana en la Primera República," *Boletín del Archivo General de la Nación* 3 (1940): 393-411, and 4 (1941): 10-24, 188-200; Luis A. Canela B. "Administración Pública y Deuda Nacional 1844-1861," *Eme-Eme Estudios Domini-canos* 1 (Oct-Nov 1972), 3: 3-32; and Luis Armando Guzmán-Taveras, "El Peso de los Gastos Militares en la Economía de la Primera Repú-blica," *Eme-Eme Estudios Dominicanos* 1 (Oct-Nov 1972), 3: 33-57.

10. ANNEXATION TO SPAIN AND REPUBLICAN RESTORATION (1859-1865)

The literature on the Spanish annexation of Santo Domingo and the national war to restore the Dominican Republic is extensive. The background of the annexation is to be found in Emilio Rodríguez Demo-rizi, *Antecedentes de la Anexión a España* (Ciudad Trujillo, 1955), and *Relaciones Domínico-Españolas (1844-1859)* (Santo Domingo, 1955); Dexter Perkins, *La Cuestión de Santo Domingo, 1849-1865* (Ciudad Truji-llo, 1956); and Mariano Torrente, *Política Ultramarina, Que Abraza To-dos los Puntos Referentes a las Relaciones de España con los Estados Uni-dos, con la Inglaterra y las Antillas, y Señaladamente con la Isla de Santo Domingo* (Madrid, 1854). See also, Federico García Godoy, "La Anexión a España," *Estudios Históricos* 37 (1921): 25-40; and David G. Yuengling, *The Spanish Annexation of the Dominican Republic* (Pottsville, 1940).

The most important Spanish contemporary accounts of the annex-ation and the Restoration War are José de la Gándara, *Anexión y Guerra de Santo Domingo* (Madrid, 1884), by the Spanish governor in charge of ending the war; Ramón González Tablas, *Historia de la Dominación y Ultima Guerra de España en Santo Domingo* (Madrid, 1870), written by a perceptive Spanish captain; and Adriano López Morillo, *Segunda Rein-corporación de Santo Domingo a España* (Santo Domingo, 1983), a mon-umental narrative prepared as the memoirs of a young lieutenant who later became a General of the Spanish army. Emilio Rodríguez Demorizi, *Diarios de la Guerra Domínico-Española de 1863-1865* (Santo Domingo, 1963), compiled several narratives of other Spanish army officers and military doctors. More recently, María Magdalena Guerrero Canó has edited the "Memoria Médico-Topográfica de Santo Domingo (1864) por el Médico Andrés Alegret y Mesa," in *Acta Hispanica ad Medicinae Scientiarumque Historiam Illustrandam* 7-8 (1987-88), 367-412.

Other contemporary sources include *Bando de Política y Gober-nación Mandando Observar en la Parte Española de Santo Domingo el*

19 de Enero de 1863 (Santo Domingo, 1862); *Discurso que en el Solemne Acto de Apertura de la Real Audiencia Chancillería de Santo Domingo Pronunció el Día 2 de Enero de 1864 su Regente Don José Bárbara Mato* (Santo Domingo, 1864); F. de Bona. *Cuba, Santo Domingo y Puerto Rico. Historia y Estado Actual de Santo Domingo, su Reincorporación y Ventajas o Inconvenientes Según se Adopte o No una Política Liberal Para su Gobierno, Para el Desarrollo de las Demás Antillas y Para Nuestras Relaciones Internacionales; Estado Actual Político y Económico de Cuba y Puerto Rico. Urgente Necesidad y Conveniencia de Liberarizar su Administración* (Madrid, 1861); J. Ferrer de Couto, *Reincorporación de Santo Domingo a España. Breves Consideraciones Sobre Este Acontecimiento* (Madrid, 1861); *Les Interets Français et Europeéns a Santo Domingo* (Paris, 1861); República Dominicana, *Respuesta a la Protesta que Hace el Gobierno Haitiano del Uso que el Pueblo Dominicano ha hecho a su Soberanía Reincorporándose a la Madre Patria* (Santo Domingo, 1861); *Proclamación de S.M. la Reina Doña Isabel II, Como Reina Soberana de la Española de Santo Domingo* (Santo Domingo, 1861); *Reincorporación de Santo Domingo a España* (Madrid, 1861); *Código Civil de la Provincia Española de Santo Domingo* (Santo Domingo, 1862); J. M. Muzquiz y Callejas. *Una Idea Sobre la Cuestión de Santo Domingo* (Madrid, 1864); J. F. Campuzano, *Santo Domingo. Remedio Radical para su Situación, la de Cuba y Puerto Rico* (Madrid, 1864); J. Ferré de Couto, *La Cuestión de Santo Domingo* (La Habana, 1864); C. Martín y Oñate, *España y Santo Domingo. Observaciones de Simple y Racional Criterio Acerca de lo que Interesa a la Nación Española, la Posesión de Dicha Isla, y Sobre los Beneficios que han de Recibir en Consecuencia los Mismos Dominicanos, Seguida de una Descripción Histórica y Geográfica de tan Vasta y Rica Antilla* (Toledo, 1864); Gaspar Núñez de Arce, *Santo Domingo* (Madrid, 1865); S. Bermúdez de Castro Díaz, *Cuestión de Santo Domingo. Discurso Pronunciado en el Senado por el Excmo. Sr. Marqués de Lema* (Madrid, 1865); and José de la Gándara, *Contestaciones y Documentos Publicados en la Gaceta de Santo Domingo sobre las Negociaciones de Paz Celebradas entre el Excmo. Señor Capitán General José de Gándara y Navarro y el Gobierno de Santiago Pedro Antonio Pimentel* (Santo Domingo, 1865).

The debates in the Spanish Cortes were published in *Documentos Relativos a la Cuestión de Santo Domingo Remitidos al Congreso de los*

Diputados por el Ministerio de Estado (Madrid, 1864), and the *Diario de la Sesión de Cortes. Senado. Legislatura de 1864 a 1865* (Madrid, 1865). A version in English of those debates is David G. Yuengling, *Highlights in the Debates in the Spanish Chamber of Deputies Relative to the Abandonment of Santo Domingo* (Washington, D. C., 1941). Three pieces written by the controversial Spanish archbishop are Bienvenido Monzón y Martín, *Carta Pastoral que el Excmo,. e Ilmo Sr. D. Bienvenido Monzón, Arzobispo de Santo Domingo, Dirigió al Clero y Pueblo Dominicano con Motivo de los Sucesos de Monte Christi y de San Lorenzo de Guayubín desde la Santa Visita de Hato Mayor, en 7 de Marzo de 1863* (Santo Domingo, 1863); *Los dos Principados, o sea, Instrucción Sobre la Soberanía Espiritual y Temporal de la Santa Sede* (Santo Domingo, 1864); *Carta Pastoral que el Excmo. Señor Don Bienvenido Monzón y Martín Arzobispo de Santo Domingo Dirigió al Clero y al Pueblo Dominicano, Anunciándoles su Viaje a la Corte Para Asuntos y Negocios Esclesiásticos, y Haciéndoles Algunas Reflexiones Sobre los Actuales Acontecimientos de la Isla, el 5 de Mayo de 1864* (Santo Domingo, 1864).

Relevant official documents and papers of the Dominican government-in-arms during the Restoration War have been edited by Emilio Rodríguez Demorizi, *Actos y Doctrina del Gobierno de la Restauración* (Santo Domingo, 1963); *Próceres de la Restauración. Noticias Biográficas* (Santo Domingo, 1963); and *Cancionero de la Restauración* (Santo Domingo, 1963). The most important Dominican contemporary accounts are Manuel Rodríguez Objío, *Relaciones* (Ciudad Trujillo, 1951); and *Gregorio Luperón e Historia de la Restauración* (Santiago, 1939); Gregorio Luperón, *Notas Autobiográficas y Apuntes Históricos* (Santiago de los Caballeros, 1895-96); and the short but revealing narrative of Benito Monción, "De Capotillo a Santiago," *Clío* 16 (1948), 33-39, originally published as Benito Monción, *De Capotillo a Santiago. Relación Histórica Concerniente a la Restauración Dominicana Dictada en Turks Islands en 1887* (Santo Domingo, 1902).

The first general history of the war written in the 20th century is Pedro M. Archambault, *Historia de la Restauración* (Paris, 1938). Other accounts include Vetilio Alfau Durán, "El Bloqueo Marítimo durante la Restauración," *Clío* (1960), 28: 331-341; Ramón Lugo Lovatón, *Manuel Rodríguez Objío, Poeta, Restaurador, Historiador, Mártir* (Ciudad Trujillo, 1951); J. Marino Incháustegui, "Relaciones entre España, Santo

Domingo y Haití," *Revista de Indias* 99-100 (1965): 11-25. Eugenio J. Senior, *La Restauración en Puerto Plata. Relato de un Restaurador* (Santo Domingo, 1963). More recent interpretations are Jaime de Jesús Domínguez, *La Anexión de Santo Domingo a España, 1861-1863* (Santo Domingo, 1979); Luis M. Alvarez, *Dominación Colonial y Guerra Popular, 1861-1865. La Anexión y la Restauración en la Historia Dominicana* (Santo Domingo, 1986); and Juan Bosch, *La Guerra de la Restauración* (Santo Domingo, 1982). See also, Charles C. Hauch, "Attitudes of Foreign Governments Towards the Spanish Reoccupation of the Dominican Republic," *Hispanic American Historical Review* 27 (May 1947), 2: 247-268.

Some recent pro-Spanish interpretations include Cristóbal Robles Muñoz, *Paz en Santo Domingo (1854-1865). El Fracaso de la Anexión a España* (Madrid, 1987); J. Castel, *Anexión y Abandono de Santo Domingo (1810-1865)* (Madrid, 1954); and Magdalena Guerrero Canó, *Disciplina y Laxitud: La Iglesia Dominicana en Tiempos de la Anexión* (Cádiz, 1984). Guerrero Canó has also published "La Ciudad de Santo Domingo a Raíz de la Anexión a España," in *Andalucía y América: Urbanismo* (Sevilla, 1990): 71-117; and "Las Obras Públicas en el Santo Domingo de la Anexión," in *Anales de la Universidad de Cádiz* 7-8 (1990-91): 249-265.

11. CAUDILLO POLITICS AND POLITICAL INSTABILITY (1865-1879)

Dominican political affairs after the War of Restoration are extensively covered by José Gabriel García, *Historia Moderna de la República Dominicana* (Santo Domingo, 1906); Casimiro Nemesio de Moya, *Bosquejo Histórico de la Isla de Santo Domingo* (Santo Domingo, 1976); and Manuel Ubaldo Gómez Moya, *Resumen de la Historia Dominicana* (Santo Domingo, 1923). Both De Moya and Gómez Moya balance García's account with details of events in the interior of the country. Some fundamental sources are Gregorio Luperón, *Notas Autobiográficas y Apuntes Históricos* (Santiago 1939); Ulises Francisco Espaillat, *Escritos* (Santo Domingo, 1962); Emilio Rodríguez Demorizi, *Papeles de Pedro Francisco Bonó* (Santo Domingo, 1964); and *Papeles de Espaillat. Para las Ideas Políticas de Santo Domingo* (Santo Domingo, 1963).

Modern studies include Jaime de Jesús Domínguez, *Notas Económicas y Políticas Dominicanas sobre el Período Julio 1865-Julio 1886,*

2 vols. (Santo Domingo, 1983-84); Gregorio Lanz, "El Caudillismo Dominicano a Mediados del Siglo XIX," *Eme-Eme Estudios Dominicanos* 2 (Nov-Dec 1973), 9: 15-42; Rafael A. Brugal P., "Puerto Plata y los Levantamientos Armados," *Eme-Eme Estudios Dominicanos* 8 (Nov-Dec 1979), 45: 45-94; Carlos Fernández Rocha, "Génesis e Ideología del Partido Azul," *Eme-Eme Estudios Dominicanos* 1 (Jun-Jul 1972), 1: 40-63; Adriano Miguel Tejada, "El Partido Rojo, el Partido Azul y el Partido Verde," *Eme-Eme Estudios Dominicanos* 3 (Jan-Feb 1975), 16: 21-42; and Peng Kiam Miguel Sang, "Finanzas y Economía en el Gobierno de Ulises Francisco Espaillat," *Eme-Eme Estudios Dominicanos* (1 (Oct-Nov 1972), 3: 89-102.

The efforts of the United States to annex the Dominican Republic are studied in Sumner Welles, *Naboth's Vineyard* (New York, 1928), and Charles Callan Tansill, *The United States and Santo Domingo, 1789-1873. A Chapter in Caribbean Diplomacy* (Baltimore, 1938). Recent studies include William Javier Nelson, *Almost a Territory. America's Attempt to Annex the Dominican Republic* (Newark, 1990); and Luis Fernández Martínez, "Caudillos, Annexation, and the Rivalry between Empires in the Dominican Republic, 1844-1874," *Diplomatic History*, 17 (Fall 1993), 4: 571-597. The proponents of annexation produced also some reports on the natural resources and social conditions of the island, like W. S. Courtney. *The Gold Fields of St. Domingo with a Description of the Agricultural, Commercial and Other Advantages of Dominica, and Containing Some Account of Its Climate, Seasons, Soil, Mountains and Its Principal Cities, Rivers, Bays and Harbors* (New York, 1860); Joseph Warren Fabens, *Facts about Santo Domingo, Applicable to the Present Crisis. Address Delivered before the American Geographical and Statistical Society at New York, April 3, 1862* (New York, 1862); *In the Tropics. By a Settler in Santo Domingo* (New York, 1873), also published by Jane Maria McManus Cazneau as *Life in Santo Domingo* (New York, 1873); Fabens also published *Resources of Santo Domingo. From a Paper Read Before the American Geograpical and Statistical Society of New York, 1862* (Washington, D.C., 1869); American West-India Company, *Santo Domingo, A Paper from the Knickerbocker Magazine, for March 1863, Giving Much Useful Information About the Climate, Soil and Productions of the Island* (New York, 1863); William Leslie Cazneau, *To the American Press: The Dominican Negotiations. I. Samana as a Naval*

Station, II. Samana as a Free Port, III. Samana and Annexation (Santo Domingo, 1870); and

The text of the annexation treaty and some newspapers articles were published as *Annexario of San Domingo* (New York, 1870). Opposition in the U.S. Senate was led by Senator Charles Sumner, *Naboth's Vineyard: Speech of Hon. Charles Sumner, of Massachusetts, on the Proposed Annexation of the "Island of San Domingo", Delivered in the Senate of the United States December 21, 1870* (Washington, 1870). The investigation of the U.S. Senate commission sent to Santo Domingo was published as United States Senate. Commissioners B. F. Wade, A. D. White, S. G. Howe. Commission of Inquiry to Santo Domingo, *Report of the Commission of Inquiry to Santo Domingo, With the Introductory Message of the President, Special Reports Made to the Commission State Papers Furnished by the Dominican Government, and the Statements of Over Seventy Witnesses* (Washington, D. C., 1871). The commission's report has been published in Spanish as Emilio Rodríguez Demorizi (ed.), *Informe de la Comisión de Investigación de los Estados Unidos de América en Santo Domingo en 1871* (Santo Domingo, 1960). Other documents related to the commission's work and the annexation project were published in Emilio Rodríguez Demorizi (ed.), *Proyecto de Incorporación de Santo Domingo a Norteamérica. Apuntes y Documentos* (Santo Domingo, 1963) A response of one of the commisioners to some public accusations by the American press is Samuel Gridley Howe, *Letters on the Proposed Annexation of Santo Domingo in Answer to Certain Charges in the Newspapers* (Boston, 1871).

Other relevant pieces are: Godlove S. Orth, *The Island Republics of St. Domingo. Speech of Hon. Godlove S. Orth, of Indiana, in the House of Representatives, April 5, 1869* (Washington, 1869); United States Department of the Navy, *Message of the President of the United States Communicating Copies of Correspondence With and Orders Issued to the Commander of Our Naval Squadron in the Waters of the Island of San Domingo Since the Commencement of the Late Negotiations* (Washington, D.C., 1871); United States Senate, *San Domingo. Debate in the United States Senate on the Resolutions of Hon. O. P. Morten, Authorizing the Appointment of a Commission to Examine Into and Report Upon the Condition of the Island* (Washington, D. C.,1871); James Harlan, *The President and San Domingo. Speech of Hon. James Harlan, of Iowa,*

Delivered in the Senate of the United States, March 29, 1871 (Washington, D. C., 1871); Justin Smith Morill, *Annexation of Santo Domingo. Speech of Hon. Justin S. Morril, of Vermont, Delivered in the Senate of the United States, April 7, 1871* Washington, D. C.,1871); Carl Shurz, *Annexation of San Domingo. Speech of Hon. Carl Schurz, of Missouri Delivered in the Senate of the United States, January 11, 1871.* (Washington, D. C., 1871); and Charles Sumner, *Violations of International Law and Usurpations of War Powers: Speech of Hon. Charles Sumner, of Massachusetts, on his St. Domingo Resolutions, Delivered in the Senate of the United States, March 27, 1871* (Washington, D. C., 1871).

The report of the U.S. Senate's Commision of Inquiry supporting annexation was refuted by José Gabriel García on behalf of the Dominican exiles. See Varios Dominicanos, *A Brief Refutal of the Report of the St. Domingo Commissioners Addressed to the People of the United States* (New York, 1871); Varios Dominicanos, *Breve Refutación del Informe de los Comisionados de Santo Domingo Dedicada al Pueblo de los Estados Unidos* (Curazao, 1871); Varios Dominicanos, *A Critical Review of the Report of the St. Domingo Commissioners, Addressed to the People of the United States* (New York, 1871); and Varios Dominicanos. *Examen Crítico del Informe de los Comisionados de Santo Domingo Dedicado al Pueblo de los Estados Unidos* (Curacao, 1871).

After the failure of the annexation project, its proponents tried to lease the Samana Bay and Peninsula. See, for example, Samana Bay Company of Santo Domingo, *Report of the Commissioners Who Negotiated the Convention with the Dominican Republic* (New York, 1873). Some documents concerning these efforts were published in *Convenio para el Arrendamiento de la Península y Bahía de Samaná, y Otros Documentos Importantes Publicados en la Gaceta Oficial de Santo Domingo* (Santo Domingo, 1873). A curious document is Samuel Samuels, *Demandante. Memorial of Stockholders of the Samana Bay of Santo Domingo Against the Dominican Government* (Washington, D.C., 1873). Two interesting travel books resulted from the U.S. annexation efforts: D. B. Randolph Keim, *San Domingo. Pen Pictures and Leaves of Travel, Romance and History, from the Portfolio of a Correspondent in the American Tropics* (Philadelphia, 1870), and Samuel Hazard, *Santo Domingo, Past and Present, With a Glance at Hayti* (New York, 1873). Hazard accompanied the U.S. Senate commision on its trip to the Dominican Republic in 1871.

12. THE LIBERALS IN POWER (1879-1886)

For the political history of this period, the basic sources are Gregorio Luperón, *Notas Autobiográficas y Apuntes Históricos* (Ciudad Trujillo, 1939); *Escritos de Luperón* (Ciudad Trujillo, 1941); and the third volume of Casimiro Nemesio de Moya, *Bosquejo Histórico del Descubrimiento y Conquista de la Isla de Santo Domingo* (Santo Domingo, 1976). Both Luperón and Moya were relevant actors and witnesses. See also "Memorias de Casimiro N. de Moya sobre la Revolución que Encabezó en el 1886," *Eme-Eme Estudios Dominicanos* 1 (May-June 1973), 124-140. Jaime de Jesús Domínguez, *Notas Económicas y Políticas Dominicanas sobre el Período Julio 1865-Julio 1886* (Santo Domingo, 1984); Sumner Welles, *Naboth's Vineyard*; and Manuel Ubaldo Gómez Moya, *Resumen de Historia de Santo Domingo*, are important sources.

Two excellent books on the structural changes during this period are Harry Hoetink, *The Dominican People 1850-1900. Notes for a Historical Sociology* (Baltimore, 1982), and Jacqueline Boin and José Serulle Ramia, *El Proceso del Desarrollo del Capitalismo en la República Dominicana. El Desarrollo del Capitalismo en la Agricultura (1875-1930)* (Santo Domingo, 1981). Emilio Rodríguez Demorizi, *Hostos en Santo Domingo*, 2 vols. (Ciudad Trujillo, 1939); Eugenio María de Hostos, *Páginas Dominicanas* (Santo Domingo, 1963); and *Papeles Dominicanos de Máximo Gómez* (Ciudad Trujillo, 1954), are also very useful.

On the development of the sugar industry, see Juan José Sánchez, *La Caña en Santo Domingo* (Santo Domingo, 1972); Patrick Bryan, "The Transition to Plantation Agriculture in the Dominican Republic, 1870-1884," *Journal of Caribbean History* (1978), 10-11: 82-105; and "The Question of Labor in the Sugar Industry of the Dominican Republic in the Late Nineteenth and Early Twentieth Centuries," in Manuel Moreno Fraginals, Frank Moya Pons, and Stanley L. Engerman (eds.), *From Slavery to Free Labor. The Spanish Caribbean in the Nineteenth Century* (Baltimore, 1985), 235-251. See also José del Castillo, "The Formation of the Dominican Sugar Industry: From Competition to Monopoly, from National Semiproletariat to Foreign Proletariat," in Moreno Fraginals et al. (eds.), *From Slavery to Free Labor*, 215-234; and Michiel Baud, "The Origins of Capitalist Agriculture in the Dominican Republic, *Latin American Research Review* 22 (1987), 2: 135-

153. A recent book which closely follows Hoetink's and Moya Pons' writings is Julio A. Cross Beras, *Sociedad y Desarrollo en la República Dominicana, 1844-1899* (Santo Domingo, 262). See also, Antonio Lluberes, "La Economía del Tabaco en el Cibao en la Segunda Mitad del siglo XIX," *Eme-Eme Estudios Dominicanos* 1 (Jan-Feb 1973), 4: 35-60; Freddy Peralta, "La Sociedad Dominicana vista por Pedro Francisco Bonó," *Eme-Eme Estudios Dominicanos* 5 (Mar-Apr 1977), 29: 13-54; and Harry Hoetink, "The Dominican Republic c.1870-1930," in Leslie Bethell (ed.), *The Cambridge History of Latin America* 5 (Cambridge, 1986): 287-305.

13. ULISES HEUREAUX (1886-1899)

The standard study on the social, cultural, and political changes in the Dominican Republic under Heureaux is Harry Hoetink, *The Dominican People 1850-1900. Notes for a Historical Sociology* (Baltimore, 1982). Two recent monographs on Ulises Heureaux are Jaime de Jesús Domínguez, *La Dictadura de Heureaux* (Santo Domingo, 1986), and Mu-Kien A. Sang, *Ulises Heureaux. Biografía de un Dictador* (Santo Domingo, 1987). A traditional treatment is Rufino Martínez, *Hombres Dominicanos. Deschamps, Heureaux, Luperón* (Ciudad Trujillo, 1939). Two general descriptions of the country in those years stand out; they are José Ramón Abad, *La República Dominicana. Reseña General Geográfico-Estadística* (Santo Domingo, 1888) and Bureau of the American Republics, *Hand Book of Santo Domingo* (Washington, D. C., 1895). The financial question is well described by Antonio de la Rosa, *Las Finanzas de Santo Domingo y el Control Americano* (Santo Domingo, 1969); and César Herrera, *De Hartmont a Trujillo* (Ciudad Trujillo, 1953), and *Las Finanzas de la República Dominicana* (Ciudad Trujillo, 1955). Sumner Welles, *The Naboth Vineyard*, describes the diplomatic and political crisis created by the treaty of reciprocity signed with the United States in 1892. This treaty has been studied by Thomas J. Dodd, "Un Tratado Inconcluso entre los Estados Unidos y la República Dominicana en 1892," *Eme-Eme Estudios Dominicanos* 3 (Jul-Aug 1974), 13: 26-46. See also Donna Marie Wolf, "Double Diplomacy: Ulises Heureaux and the Cuban Independence Movement," *Caribbean Studies* 14 (April 1974),

1: 75-104. On the assassination of Heureaux, see Emilio Rodríguez Demo-rizi, *La Muerte de Lilís. Versos y Documentos* (Santo Domingo, 1983). On the dictator's personal fortune, the *Resumen General del Activo y Pasivo de la Sucesion Heureaux, Hecho por el Notario Miguel Joaquín Alfau a Requerimiento de la Comisión Judicial Designada para la Formación del Inventario* (Santo Domingo, 1900), contains the inventory of the dicta-tor estate. The division of the estate is told by Américo Lugo, *Partición de los Créditos a Favor de la Sucesión Heureaux a Cargo del Estado entre los Acreedores de la Misma Sucesión Hecha por el Notario Miguel Joaquín Alfau* (Santo Domingo, 1901). An example of the anti-Heureaux litera-ture after his death is J. V. Flores, *Lilí, El Sanguinario Machetero Domini-cano, Titulado "Pacificador" de la República, en Vez de "Sacrificador" y "Verdugo" de sus Conciudadanos* (Curazao, 1901). Some pictoresque accounts of Heureaux's anecdotes include Víctor M. Castro, *Cosas de Lilís* (Santo Domingo, 1919); Gustavo E. Bergés Bordas, *Otras Cosas de Lilís* (Santo Domingo, 1921); Vigil Díaz, *Lilís y Alejandrito* (Ciudad Trujillo, 1956); José Ulises Franco, *Semblanza de la Vida y Muerte del Presidente Ulises Heureaux (Lilís)* (Santiago de los Caballeros, 1987); and Emilio Rodríguez Demorizi, *Cancionero de Lilís* (Santo Domingo, 1962).

14. TOWARD A U.S. PROTECTORATE (1899-1911)

The literature of this period is dominated by the country's finan-cial problems. Some early sources on the political and financial prob-lems immediately after the death of Heureaux are Cayacoa y Cotu-banamá, *Artículos Publicados en "La Lucha" y en "El Liberal"* (Santo Domingo, 1900); *Santo Domingo Improvement. Contrato con la Im-provement y Demás Compañías Americanas. Dos Artículos de Cayacoa Relativos al Mismo Contrato* (Santo Domingo, 1901); *Actualidad de la Deuda Flotante Interior* (Santo Domingo, 1902); and Horacio Vásquez. *Aspecto Final de la Deuda Flotante Interior, Junio 23 de 1902* (Santo Domingo, 1902). Cayacoa and Cotubanamá were the pen names of Vásquez's Finance Minister Francisco Henríquez y Carvajal. The best accounts of the dire economic situation of the Dominican Republic immediately after the death of Heureaux are Jacob Hollander, *Debt of Santo Domingo. Report on the Debt of Santo Domingo Submitted to the*

President of the United States (Washington, D. C., 1905); Jacob Hollander, "The Readjustment of San Domingo's Finances," *Quarterly Journal of Economics* 21 (May 1906): 405-426; and Antonio de la Rosa. *Las Finanzas de Santo Domingo y el Control Americano* (Santo Domingo, 1969). Hollander was a consultant appointed by the U.S. government to study and report on the Dominican external debt, so as to allow President Theodore Roosevelt to take a decision on the Dominican situation. Antonio de la Rosa is the pseudonym of the Haitian influencial writer Alexander Pujol. He finished the manuscript in 1915 and predicted the U.S. military occupation of the Dominican Republic.

On the arbitration problems, see *Dominican Republic Arbitration. San Domingo Improvement Company. Argument of the Dominican Republic Under the Provisions of the Protocol of January 31, 1903* (New York, 1904). The modus vivendi of 1905 and the Dominican-American Convention of 1907 are discussed in Fred J. Rippy, "The Initiation of the Customs Receivership in the Dominican Republic," *Hispanic American Historical Review* 17 (November, 1937), 419-457; Emily S. Rosenberg and Norman L. Rosenberg, "From Colonialism to Professionalism. The Public-Private Dynamic in United States Foreign Financial Advising, 1898-1929," *Journal of American History* 74 (June 1987), 1: 59-82; and Manuel de Jesús Troncoso de la Concha, *La Génesis de la Convención Domínico-Americana* (Santiago, 1946). On the juridical consequences of the Dominican-American Convention, see Tulio Franco-Franco, *La Situation Internationale de la Republique Dominicaine à partir du 8 Février, 1907* (Paris, 1923). Manuel Arturo Peña Batlle (ed.), *Emiliano Tejera: Antología* (Ciudad Trujillo, 1951), collects some texts written by the one of the principal negotiators of the Convention. A political account of the problem is Rafael Abreu Licairac, *La Cuestión Palpitante* (Santo Domingo, 1906). A bitter attack against the United States is Elpidéforo Bercedo y García, *Los Yankees en Calzoncillos (Escenas Hipócritas)* (Santo Domingo, 1905).

On the government of Ramón Cáceres the standard text is Pedro Troncoso Sánchez, *Ramón Cáceres* (Santo Domingo, 1964). The economic and social situation of the country is described by the Secretaría de Estado de Fomento y Obras Públicas, *La República Dominicana* (Santo Domingo, 1906), also published as Department of Promotion and Public Works, *The Dominican Republic* (Jamestown, 1907); and by Enrique Deschamps, *La República Dominicana: Directorio y Guía General* (Barcelona, 1907). Some important reports on the economic recuperation of the country under Cáceres appear in yearly *Report of Dominican Customs Receivership* (Washington, D. C., 1908-1911).

Economic change during this period and in subsequent years is studied by Paul Muto, "La Economía de Exportación de la República Dominicana, 1900-1930," *Eme-Eme Estudios Dominicanos* 3 (Nov-Dec, 1974), 15: 67-110; and "Las Importaciones y el Impacto del Cambio Económico en la República Dominicana," *Eme-Eme Estudios Dominicanos* 4 (Sep-Oct 1975), 20: 15-36; José del Castillo and Walter Cordero, *La Economía Dominicana durante el Primer Cuarto del Siglo XX* (Santo Domingo, 1980); and Jaime de Jesús Domínguez, *La Sociedad Dominicana a principios del Siglo Veinte* (Santo Domingo, 1994). See also Patrick Bryan, "The United States and the Economic Penetration of the Dominican Republic 1900-1916," in K. O. Laurence (ed.), *A Selection of Papers Presented at the Twelfth Conference of the Association of Caribbean Historians (1980)* (Barbados, 1985); and "Staple Exports and Mercantile Sector in the Dominican Republic, 1900-1916," in Barry W. Higman (ed.) *Trade, Government and Society in Caribbean History 1700-1920. Essays Presented to Douglas Hall* (London, 1983).

15. THE COLLAPSE OF SOVEREIGNTY (1911-1916)

Some of the chapters of Luis Felipe Mejía, *De Lilís a Trujillo* (Caracas, 1944), contain revealing information about the causes of political instability after the death of President Cáceres. Similarly, Graham H. Stuart, *Latin America and the United States* (New York, 1922); Dana Gardner Munro, *Intervention and Dollar Diplomacy in the Caribbean, 1900-1921* (Princeton, 1964), are essential for the understanding of the role of the United States during this turbulent period. The standard interpretation for this period is still the second volume of Sumner Welles, *The Naboth's Vineyard* (New York, 1928). A contemporary pamphlet crying for political stability is Francisco José Peynado, *Por el Establecimiento de un Gobierno Civil en la República Dominicana* (Santo Domingo, 1912). An interesting description of the social conditions is to be found in A. Hyatt Verril, *Porto Rico, Past and Present, and Santo Domingo of To-*

day (New York, 1914). Antonio de la Rosa, *Las Finanzas de Santo Domingo y el Control Americano*, already quoted, contains also very important political and financial information. Some political details appear in Bernardo Pichardo, *Resumen de Historia Patria* (Santo Domingo, 1921), and Antonio Hoepelman, *Páginas Dominicanas de Historia Contemporánea* (Ciudad Trujillo, 1951). On the country's economic conditions, two useful references are C. H. Albrecht and Fran Anderson Henry, *Development of the Dominican Republic* (Washington, D. C., 1914), and Archibald Joseph Dunn, *Santo Domingo. Its Resources and its Future* (London, 1911).

16. THE U.S. MILITARY OCCUPATION (1916-1924)

The best monograph on the occupation is Bruce Calder, *Some Aspects of the U.S. Occupation of the Dominican Republic, 1916-1924* (Austin, Texas, 1983). A classic critical account of the occupation is Melvin Knight, *The Americans in Santo Domingo* (New York, 1928). A pro-American interpretation is Marlin D. Clausner, *Rural Santo Domingo. Settled, Unsettled, and Resettled* (Philadelphia, 1973). See also, R. G. Adams, *Santo Domingo. A Study in Benevolent Imperialism* (Durham, N.C., 1921). On the withdrawal of the marines, see Kenneth J. Grieb, "Warren H. Harding and the Dominican Republic U. S. Withdrawal, 1921-1923," *Journal of Inter-American Studies* 11 (July 1969): 425-440; and Joseph Robert Suárez, "United States Withdrawal from Santo Domingo, *Hispanic American Historical Review* 42 (March 1962), 2: 152-190. See also Luis Felipe Mejía, *De Lilís a Trujillo* (Caracas, 1944). Many important political and diplomatic aspects are covered in the second volume of Sumner Welles, *Naboth's Vineyard*. Welles actively participated in the negotiations to put and end to the occupation, and he uses his memoirs as history.

Some works on the resistance to the occupation are Marvin Goldwert, *The Constabulary in the Dominican Republic: Progeny and Legacy of United States Intervention* (Gainesville, Florida, 1962); Bruce Calder, "*Caudillos* and *Gavilleros* versus the United States Marines: Guerrilla Insurgency during the Dominican Intervention, 1916-1924," *Hispanic American Historical Review* 58 (Nov 1978), 4: 649-675; and

"Varieties of Resistance to the United States Occupation of the Dominican Republic 1916-1924," *Secolas Annals* 11 (March 1980): 103-
136; Stephen M. Fuller, *Marines in the Dominican Republic 1916-1924*
(Washington, D. C., 1974); Gregorio Urbano Gilbert, *Mi Lucha contra
el Invasor Yanqui de 1916* (Santo Domingo, 1975); Felix Servio
Ducoudray, *Los "Gavilleros" del Este. Una Epopeya Calumniada* (Santo
Domingo, 1976); John Blassingame, "The Press and the American Intervention in Haiti and the Dominican Republic, 1904-1920," *Caribbean Studies*, 9 (July 1969), 2: 27-43; and Nancie L. González, "Desiderio
Arias. Caudillo, Bandit and Culture Hero," *Journal of American Folk-
lore/America Folklore Society* 85 (Jan-Mar 1972), 335: 42-50;

Contemporary descriptions written by the U.S. military government and its officers, travelers, journalists, and scholars are also abundant. See, for example, "Wards of the United States. Notes on What
Our Country is Doing for Santo Domingo, Nicaragua, and Haiti," *National Geographic Magazine* 30 (Aug 1916), 2: 143-177; George Marvin,
"Watchful Acting in Santo Domingo." *World's Work* 34 (June 1917):
205-218; Theorore H. N. de Booys, "Eastern Part of the Dominican
Republic," *Pan American Union Bulletin* 40 (September, 1917), 3: 315-
321; Fred R. Fairchild, "The Public Finance of Santo Domingo," *Political Science Quarterly* 33 (December, 1918): 461-481; Otto Schoenrich,
Santo Domingo, A Country with a Future (New York, 1918); Samuel
Guy Inman, *Through Santo Domingo and Haiti, a Cruise with the Marines* (New York, 1919); Alvin B. Kemp, "Private Kemp Reports on our
War in Santo Domingo," *Literary Digest* 60 (22 February 1919): 105-
108; Harry Alverson, *Roaming Through the West Indies* (New York,
1920), and "Santo Domingo, the Land of Bullet-Holes", *Century Magazine*, 100 (July, 1920): 300-311; Arthur H. Mayo, *Report on Economic
and Financial Conditions of the Dominican Republic* (Santo Domingo,
1920); Otto Schoenrich, "The Present American Intervention in Santo
Domingo and Haiti" in Blakeslee and George Hubbard, eds., *México
and the Caribbean* (New York, 1920); George C. Thorpe, "American
Achievements in Santo Domingo, Haiti and the Virgin Islands," *Journal of International Relations* 11 (1920), 1: 63-86; Military Government
of Santo Domingo, *Santo Domingo; its Past and its Present Condition*
(Santo Domingo, 1920); Libro Azul de Santo Domingo, *Dominican Blue
Book, 1920* (New York, 1920); Pan American Federation of Labor, *Re-

port of the Proceedings of the Second Congress of the Pan-American Federation of Labor held at New York City, N. Y. July 7th to 10th, inclusive, 1919. (Washington, D. C., n. d.); American Federation of Labor, Report of Proceedings of the 40th Annual Convention of the American Federation of Labor held at Montreal, Quebec, Canada, June 7 to 19, inclusive, 1920 (Washington, D. C., 1920); United States Department of the Navy, Information on Living Conditions in Santo Domingo and Haiti (Washington, 1921); Edwin N. McClellan, "Operations Ashore in the Dominican Republic," United States Naval Institute Proceedings 47 (February 1921), 216: 235-245; E. H. Gruening, Conquest of Haiti and Santo Domingo: A Documented Narrative of the United States Government's Seizure of Political and Military Control in the Two Island Republics (New York, 1922); United States Senate, Inquiry into Occupation and Administration of Haiti and Santo Domingo. Hearings Before a Select Committee on Haiti and Santo Domingo 67th Congress., 1st and 2nd Sessions., (Washington, D. C., 1922); Rufus H. Lane, "Civil Government in Santo Domingo in the Early Days of the Military Occupation," Marine Corps Gazette 7 (June 1922): 127-146; and Trailing the Conquistadores (New York, 1930); Carl Kelsey, "The American Intervention in Haiti and the Dominican Republic," The Annals of the American Academy of Political and Social Science 100 (March 1922), 189: 110-202; William E.Pulliam, "The Chocolate Age: Dominican Cacao," Pan American Union Bulletin, 57 (September 1923): 245-252; C. C. Baughmann, "United States Occupation of the Dominican Republic", United States Naval Institute Proceedings 51 (December 1925), 274: 2306-2327; and Arthur J. Burks, Land of Checkerboard Families (New York, 1932). See also the legislation and regulations passed by the military government in Colección de Ordenes Ejecutivas, 6 vols. (Santo Domingo, 1917-1922).

The wave of nationalist denounciations against the occupation was initiated by Américo Lugo, La Intervención Americana (Cartas al Listín) (Santo Domingo, 1916), and Federico García Godoy, El Derrumbe (Santo Domingo, 1916). Garcia Godoy's book was immediately confiscated and burned by the U.S. military censors. One single copy survived until its re-publication in 1975. The nationalist reactions are registered in the following books and pamphlets: Academia Colombina, Memorial de Protesta Contra la Arbitraria Ocupación Militar de la

República Dominicana por Tropas de los Estados Unidos de Norte-América (Santo Domingo, 1916); Carlos Pereyra, *El Crimen de Woodrow Wilson. Su Contubernio con Villa - Sus Atentados en Santo Domingo - Su Régimen en Nicaragua - Los dos Polos de la Diplomacia Yanqui: La Hipocresía y el Miedo* (Madrid, 1917); Emilio Roig de Leuchenring, *La Ocupación de la República Dominicana por los Estados Unidos y el Derecho de las Pequeñas Nacionalidades de América* (La Habana, 1919); Fabio Fiallo, *Plan de Acción y Liberación del Pueblo Dominicano. Mensaje a las Asociaciones Independientes de Jóvenes de la República Dominicana* (Santo Domingo, 1922); Américo Lugo, *Lo que Significaría para el Pueblo Dominicano la Ratificación de los Actos del Gobierno Militar Norteamericano* (Santo Domingo, 1922); Federico García Godoy, *Al Margen del Plan Peynado* (La Vega, 1922); Américo Lugo, *El Plan de Validación Hughes-Peynado* (Santo Domingo, 1922); D. A. Regalado. *De Mi Vía-Crucis (A Través de la Ocupación Militar Norteamericana)* (Santiago, 1922); Francisco J. Peynado, *Informe sobre la Situación Económica y Financiera de la República Dominicana y el Modo de Solucionar sus Problemas, Presentado por el Lic. Francisco J. Peynado a la Comisión Especial del Senado de los E.E.U.U. para Investigar los Asuntos de la República Dominicana* (Santo Domingo, 1922); Federico Henríquez y Carvajal, *Nacionalismo* (Santo Domingo, 1925); Horacio Blanco Fombona, *Crímenes del Imperialismo Norteamericano* (México, 1927); Tulio M Cestero Burgos, *Entre las Garras del Aguila* (Santo Domingo, 1922), and *El problema Dominicano.* (New York, 1919); Luis C. Del Castillo *Medios Adecuados para Conservar i Desarrollar el Nacionalismo en la República.* (Santo Domingo, 1920); Fabio Fiallo, *La Comisión Nacionalista en Washington, 1920-1921* (Ciudad Trujillo, 1939); Max Henríquez Ureña, *Los Estados Unidos y la República Dominicana. La Verdad de los Hechos Comprobada por Datos y Documentos Oficiales* (Havana, 1919); and *Los Yanquis en Santo Domingo. La Verdad de los Hechos Comprobada por Datos y Documentos Oficiales* (Madrid, 1929); Federico Henríquez y Carvajal, *Nacionalismo. Tópicos Jurídicos é Internacionales* (Santo Domingo, 1925); Antonio Hoepelman and Juan A. Senior, *Documentos Históricos que se Refieren a la Intervención Armada de los Estados Unidos de Norte-América y la Implantación de un Gobierno Militar en la República Dominicana* (Santo Domingo, 1922); Enrique Apolinar Henríquez, *Episodios Imperialistas*

(Ciudad Trujillo, 1959); Enriquillo Henríquez García (ed.), *Cartas del Presidente Francisco Henríquez y Carvajal* (Santo Domingo, 1970); Américo Lugo, *El Nacionalismo Dominicano* (Santiago, 1923); Logia "La Fe N° 7, *El Caso de la Respetable Logia "La Fe" N.° 7 con el Gobierno Militar. Relación Documentada.* Santo Domingo, 1926); Félix Evaristo Mejía, *Alrededor y en contra del plan Hughes-Peynado* (Santo Domingo, 1922); Gustavo Adolfo Mejía Ricart, *Acuso a Roma. Yo Contra el Invasor* (La Habana, 1920); Misión Nacionalista Dominicana. *Memorándum del Entendido de Evacuación de la República Dominicana por las Fuerzas Militares de los Estados Unidos de América* (Santo Domingo, 1922); Julio V. Arzeno, *Sumario Explicativo de los Actos del Gobierno Militar que Valida el Plan Hughes-Peynado* (San Pedro de Macorís, 1923); J. R. Bordas, *Frente al Imperialismo.* Santo Domingo, 1923); P. J. Rosa, *Crímenes del Imperialismo* (Paris, 1924); O. Helena Guzmán, *Al Margen de la Actual Situación Política del País con Motivo de la Próxima Deso-cupación del Territorio por las Fuerzas Estadounidenses* (Santiago, 1924); *Protesta Contra la Sentencia que Condena al Patriota Domi-nicano Dr. Federico Ellis Cambiaso.* (Santo Domingo, 1925); D. A. Regalado, *Historia de mi Martirio en la Torre del Homenaje A Través de la Ocupación Militar Norteamericana* (Santo Domingo, 1925); R. Vargas López Méndez, *El Pueblo Dominicano Frente a la Intervención Norteamericana: Artículos Editoriales* (Santo Domingo, 1928); L. Araquistain, *La Agonía Antillana, el Imperialismo Yanqui en el Mar Caribe. Impresiones de un Viaje a Puerto Rico, Santo Domingo, Haití y Cuba* (Madrid, 1928); Federico García Godoy, *Al Margen del Plan Peynado* (La Vega, 1929), and Fabio Fiallo, *The Crime of Wilson in Santo Domingo* (La Habana, 1940). The only defense of the interven-tion was the pamphlet written by Pelegrín Castillo, *La Intervención Americana* (Santo Domingo, 1916). Later, after Castillo discovered the impopularity of his views, he changed sides and supported the nation-alist movement. Three novels on the occupation are Horacio Read, *Los Civilizadores* (Santo Domingo, 1924); Rafael Damirón, *¡Ay de los Vencidos!* (Santo Domingo, 1925); and J. A. Osorio Gómez. *Silvana. O, Una Página de la Intervención* (Moca, 1929).

17. HORACIO VASQUEZ AND THE RISE OF TRUJILLO (1924-1930)

The standard monographs on this period are Víctor Medina Benet, *Los Responsables. Fracaso de la Tercera República. Narraciones de Historia Dominicana, 1924-1930* (Santo Domingo, 1976), and Luis Felipe Mejía, *De Lilís a Trujillo* (Caracas, 1930). Both are written by two intelligent and well positioned witnesses. Other than those books, the literature on Horacio Vásquez is very scarce. Writing or speaking about Vásquez was dangerous under the Trujillo dictatorship, and very few people dared to spell his name with sympathy. A contemporary pamphlet opposing Vásquez's reelection is Tomás Hernández Franco, *La Más Bella Revolución de América* (Santo Domingo, 1930). Three recent monographs on the overthrow of Vásquez and the rise of Trujillo are Bernardo Vega, *El 23 de Febrero o la Más Anunciada Revolución de América* (Santo Domingo, 1989), *Los Estados Unidos y Trujillo 1930* (Santo Domingo, 1986), and *Trujillo y las Fuerzas Armadas Norteamericanas* (Santo Domingo, 1993).

On the U.S. policy toward the Dominican Republic during the Vásquez and early Trujillo regimes, see Earl R. Curry, "The United States and the Dominican Republic, 1924-1933. Dilemma in the Caribbean" unpublished Ph.D. dissertation, University of Minnesota (Minneapolis, 1966), and the corresponding chapters of Dana G. Munro, *The United States and the Caribbean Republics, 1921-1933* (Princeton, 1974). A description of the economic conditions and tariffs is W. M. St. Elmo, *Santo Domingo-Dominican Republic, in the West Indies, 1905 to 1925: Its Commerce, Shipping, Customs Procedure...* (Santo Domingo, 1926). The financial and administrative condition of the Dominican government in 1929 is described in the *Report of Dominican Economic Commission* (Chicago, 1929). This commission was invited by President Vásquez and was presided by ex-U.S. vice-president Charles G. Dawes.

On politics, see *El Período Presidencial de 6 Años del General Don Horacio Vásquez* (Santo Domingo, 1928), and O. Delanoy. *La Política del Momento (Combatiendo la Prórroga de Poderes y la Reelección del Presidente General Horacio Vásquez* (Santo Domingo, 1928). See also Federico C. Alvarez. *Ideología Política del Pueblo Dominicano* (Santiago,1929. On the border with Haiti, several publications were issued before the treaty in 1929: Moisés García Mella, *La Cuestión Límites* (Santo Domingo, 1923); Federico Velázquez Hernández, *La Frontera de la República Dominicana* (Santo Domingo, 1929); Cayetano Armando Rodríguez, *La Frontera Domínico-Haitiana. Estudio Geográfico, Jurídico, Histórico* (Santo Domingo, 1929).

On the creation of agricultural colonies in the border region, see República Dominicana. Comisión para el Establecimiento de Colonias de Inmigrantes, *Informe que Presenta al Poder Ejecutivo la Comisión Creada por la Ley no. 77 para Estudiar las Tierras de la Frontera y Señalar los Sitios en que se han de Establecer las Colonias de Inmigrantes* (Santo Domingo, 1925); Luis Felipe Vidal. *Apuntes sobre Inmigración* (Santo Domingo, 1926); and the publications of the Secretaría de Estado de Agricultura e Inmigración, *Plan que se Propone Seguir en Sus Trabajos el Departamento de Agricultura e Inmigración* (Santo Domingo, 1924); *Ley No. 670, sobre Colonización* (Santo Domingo, 1927); *Instrucciones sobre Colonización* (Santo Domingo, 1927); and *Resumen de la Actividad del Departamento de Agricultura en sus Puntos Más Importantes* (Santo Domingo, 1927).

18. THE ERA OF TRUJILLO (1930-1961)

The literature on Trujillo is overwhelming. Most of it is either apologetic or derogatory. An exhaustive bibliography of the pro-Trujillo literature and propaganda was published by Emilio Rodríguez Demorizi, *Bibliografía de Trujillo* (Ciudad Trujillo, 1955). It contains more than 5,000 items. There is no comparable list of the anti-Trujillo production. For the chronology of the regime, see also Emilio Rodríguez Demorizi, *Cronología de Trujillo* (Ciudad Trujillo, 1955), and Rafael Leonidas Trujillo Molina, *Discursos, Mensajes y Proclamas*, 11 vols. (Santiago, 1946-1953).

The best critical biography of Trujillo, which is also a political history of the regime, is Robert D. Crassweller, *Trujillo: The Life and Times of a Caribbean Dictator* (New York, 1966). The classic study of the dictatorship is Jesús de Galíndez, *La Era de Trujillo. Un Estudio Casuístico de Dictadura Hispanoamericana* (Santiago de Chile, 1956). This is a version in Spanish of the author's doctoral dissertation at

Columbia University. Galíndez was a Basque exile who resided in Santo Domingo before moving to the United States. Once published, this work cost Galíndez his life after being kidnapped by Trujillo's agents in New York. An English edition is Jesús de Galíndez, *The Era of Trujillo: Dominican Dictator* (Tucson, Arizona, 1973). Rarely mentioned, but useful, is Jesús de Galíndez, "Un Reportaje sobre Santo Domingo," *Cuadernos Americanos* 80 (Mar-Apr 1955): 37-56. Trujillo's conspiracy to kidnap and assassinate Galíndez, as well as the dictator cover-up, is thouroughly investigated by Manuel de Dios Unanue, *El Caso Galíndez. Los Vascos en los Servicios de Inteligencia de los EEUU* (New York, 1988). Unanue uses documents from the FBI and other U.S. government sources. Another revealing book that Galíndez used as a source is Gregorio Bustamante, *Una Satrapía en el Caribe* (Mexico, 1950). Bustamante is the pseudonym of José Almoina, another Spanish exile who had previously been a private secretary of Trujillo. To conceal his identity, Almoina published almost simultaneously the apologetic book *Yo Fui Secretario de Trujillo* (Buenos Aires, 1950), but the dictator discovered Almoina's plot and had him assassinated in Mexico.

Critical narratives of the Trujillo regime include Albert Hicks, *Blood in the Streets. The Life and Rule of Trujillo* (New York, 1946); Luis Felipe Mejía, *De Lilís a Trujillo* (Caracas, 1944); and the pioneer article by C. A. Thompson, "Dictatorship in the Dominican Republic," *Foreign Policy Reports* 12 (April 15, 1936). Based on these and other sources, three Dominican exiles wrote the following useful interpretations: Germán E. Ornes, *Trujillo: Little Caesar of the Caribbean* (New York, 1958); Juan Bosch, *Trujillo: Causas de una Tiranía sin Ejemplo* (Caracas, 1959); and José Cordero Michel, *Informe sobre la República Dominicana, 1959* (Santo Domingo, 1970).

Other sources written by Dominican political exiles include Angel Miolán, *La Revolución Social Frente a la Tiranía de Trujillo* (México, 1938); Juan Isidro Jimenes Grullón, *La República Dominicana. Análisis de su Pasado y su Presente* (La Habana, 1942); and *Una Gestapo en América* (La Habana, 1946); Unión Democrática Antinazista Dominicana, *Trujillo. A Nazi: (Exhibits)* (Mayagüez, 1944); Pericles Franco Ornes, *La Tragedia Dominicana* (Santiago de Chile, 1946); Dato Pagán Perdomo, *Por Qué Lucha el Pueblo Dominicano. Análisis del Fenómeno Dictatorial en América Latina* (Caracas, 1959); Ramón Grullón, *Repúbli-*

ca Dominicana. Una Dictadura al Servicio del Imperialismo (Mexico, 1954); Juan Enrique Puigsubirá Miniño, *Pensamientos en la Lucha contra la Tiranía* (Santo Domingo, 1963); Nicolás Silfa, *Guerra, Traición y Exilio*, 3 vols. (Barcelona, 1980); Tulio H. Arvelo, *Cayo Confites y Luperón. Memorias de un Revolucionario* (Santo Domingo, 1982); Justino José del Orbe, *Del Exilio Político Dominicano Anti-Trujillista en Cuba* (Santo Domingo, 1983) A historical novel based on the failed expedition of Cayo Confites written by one of the actors is Angel Miolán, *Los Hombres de Cayo Confites* (Santo Domingo, 1993).

Modern studies in English include Howard J. Wiarda, *Dictatorship and Development: The Methods of Control in Trujillo's Dominican Republic*. (Gainesville, Florida, 1968); Pope Atkins and Larman Wilson, *The United States and the Trujillo Regime* (New Brunswick, N. J., 1972); Hardy Osgood, "Rafael Leónidas Trujillo Molina," *Pacific Historical Review* 15 (1946), 4: 409-416; Enrique V. Corominas, *In the Caribbean Political Areas* (Cambridge, 1954); and Raymond Pulley, "The United States and the Trujillo Dictatorship, 1933-1940: The High Price of Caribbean Stability," *Caribbean Studies* 5 (Oct. 1965), 3: 22-31. Several chapters of Dana G. Munro, *The United States and the Caribbean Republics 1921-1933* (Princeton, 1974), and Marlin D. Clausner, *The Dominican Republic: Settled, Unsettled, and Resettled* (Philadelphia, 1973), are useful.

The Venezuelan government exposed the assassination attempt against President Betancourt in *El Atentado contra el Señor Presidente de la República de Venezuela Rómulo Betancourt* (Caracas, 1960). Trujillo's conspiracy to kill Betancourt is described by Miguel Guerrero, *La Ira del Tirano* (Santo Domingo, 1994). The impact of the sanctions imposed by the Organization of the American States on the Trujillo regime has been studied by C. Lloyd Brown-John, "Economic Sanctions: The Case of the O.A.S. and the Dominican Republic, 1960-1962," *Caribbean Studie*s 15 (July 1975), 2: 73-105. On the invasions of 1959, see Juan Deláncer, *Primavera 1959. Constanza, Maimón y Estero Hondo* (Santo Domingo, 1979); Anselmo Brache B. *Constanza, Maimón y Estero Hondo: Testimonio e Investigación sobre los Acontecimientos* (Santo Domingo, 1985); and Dominican Republic, Caribbean Anti-Communist Research and Intelligence Bureau, *Constanza, Maimón, Estero Hondo. Communist Aggression against the Dominican Republic* (Ciudad Trujillo, 1959).

On the collapse of the dictatorship see Arturo Espaillat, *Trujillo: The Last Caesar* (Chicago, 1964); Rafael Valera Benítez, *Complot Develado (Génesis y Evolución del Movimiento Conspirativo-Celular "14 de Junio" contra el Gobierno Dominicano Descubierto por el "SIM" en enero de 1960)* (Ciudad Trujillo, 1960); Bernard Diederich, *Trujillo: The Death of the Goat* (Boston, 1978); Frank Moya Pons, "La Muerte de Trujillo entre dos Crisis Económicas," *Investigación y Ciencia* 1 (Jan-Apr 1986): 69-82; Teodoro Tejeda, *Yo Investigué la Muerte de Trujillo* (Barcelona, 1963); Víctor Grimaldi, *Los Estados Unidos en el Derrocamiento de Trujillo* (Santo Domingo, 1985); and Miguel Guerrero, *Los Ultimos Días de la Era de Trujillo* (Santo Domingo, 1991). Two recent scholarly articles are Frank Moya Pons, "The Dominican Republic since 1930," in Leslie Bethell (ed.), *The Cambridge History of Latin America* (Cambridge, 1990), 7: 509-543; and "Import-Substitution Industrialization Policies in the Dominican Republic, 1925-1961," *Hispanic American Historical Review* 70 (November 1990), 4: 539-577.

A recent series of volumes containing documents concerning the Trujillo regime is Bernardo Vega, *Los Estados Unidos y Trujillo. Año 1945. Colección de Documentos del Departamento de Estado y de las Fuerzas Armadas Norteamericanas* (Santo Domingo, 1982). There are volumes for the years 1946 (1982) and 1947 (1984). Other recent titles by the same author are *La Migración Española de 1939 y los Inicios del Marxismo-Leninismo en la República Dominicana* (Santo Domingo, 1984); *Nazismo, Fascismo y Falangismo en la República Dominicana* (Santo Domingo, 1985); *La Vida Cotidiana Dominicana a Través del Archivo Particular del Generalísimo* (Santo Domingo, 1986); *Unos Desafectos y Otros en Desgracia. Sufrimientos bajo la Dictadura Trujillista* (Santo Domingo, 1986); *Control y Represión en la Dictadura Trujillista* (Santo Domingo 1986); *Los Trujillo se Escriben* (Santo Domingo, 1987); *Un Interludio de Tolerancia (El Acuerdo de Trujillo con los Comunistas en 1946)* (Santo Domingo, 1987); *Trujillo y el Control Financiero Norteamericano* (Santo Domingo, 1990); *Kennedy y los Trujillo* (Santo Domingo, 1991); and *Trujillo y las Fuerzas Armadas Norteamericanas* (Santo Domingo, 1992). Vega's documentation rests on the diplomatic correspondence of the U.S. embassy in Santo Domingo and the archives of the National Palace and the Ministry of Foreign Relations of the Dominican Republic.

Other studies are Pablo Maríñez, *Agroindustria, Estado y Clases Sociales en la Era de Trujillo (1935-1960)* (Santo Domingo, 1993); Roberto Cassá, *Capitalismo y Dictadura* (Santo Domingo, 1982); Rafael Mencía Lister, *Trujillo y su Epoca* (Santo Domingo, 1992); Franklin Franco, *La Era de Trujillo* (Santo Domingo, 1992); Jacinto Gimbernard, *Trujillo* (Santo Domingo, 1976), and Orlando Inoa, *Estado y Campesinos al Inicio de la Era de Trujillo* (Santo Domingo, 1994). Other titles containing anecdotic and political narratives are Ramón Alberto Ferreras, *Cuando la Era era Era*, 4 vols. (Santo Domingo, 1980); *Preso 1960: La Cárcel bajo Trujillo* (Santo Domingo, 1980); and *Trujillo y sus Mujeres* (Santo Domingo, 1984). See also Ramón Alberto Ferreras et al., *Trujillo 20 Años Después* (Santo Domingo, 1981); Manuel de Jesús Javier García, *Mis 20 Años en el Palacio Nacional Junto a Trujillo y Otros Gobernantes Dominicanos* (Santo Domingo, 1985); Gilberto de la Rosa, *Petán. Un Cacique de la Era de Trujillo* (Santiago, 1987); Flor de Oro Trujillo, "My Tormented Life as Trujillo's Daughter," *Look* 29 (June 15, 1976), 12: 44-66; and "My Life as Trujillo's Prisoner," *Look* 29 (June 29, 1965), 13: 52-71.

On the Haitian massacre of 1937, see, Juan Manuel García, *La Matanza de los Haitianos. Genocidio de Trujillo, 1937* (Santo Domingo, 1983); José Israel Cuello, (ed.), *Documentos del Conflicto Domínico-Haitiano de 1937* (Santo Domingo, 1985); Bernardo Vega, *Trujillo y Haití* (Santo Domingo, 1988); Robin L. Derby and Richard Turits, "Historias de Terror y los Terrores de la Historia: La Masacre Haitiana de 1937 en la República Dominicana", in *Estudios Sociales* 16 (April-June, 1993): 65-76; and R. Michael Malek, "Dominican Republic's General Rafael L. Trujillo M. and the Haitian Massacre of 1937: A Case of Subversion in Inter-Caribbean Relations," *Secolas Annals* 11 (March 1980): 137-155. A revealing novel about the massacre is Freddy Prestol Castillo, *El Masacre se Pasa a Pie* (Santo Domingo, 1974). A recent, penetrating analysis of the role of the intellectuals is Andrés L. Mateo, *Mito y Cultura en la Era de Trujillo* (Santo Domingo, 1993).

Many apologetic books on Trujillo contain some facts and figures about the country's material progress. The problem with those sources is that the information is mixed with a great deal of propaganda and some blatant falsifications of the country's history. Some of these books include Sander Ariza, *Trujillo: The Man and His Country* (New York,

1939); the racist analysis of Joaquín Balaguer, *La Realidad Dominicana. Semblanza de un País y de un Régimen* (Buenos Aires, 1947); the revealing books by Zenón Castillo de Aza, *Trujillo: Benefactor de la Iglesia* (Ciudad Trujillo, 1955), and *Trujillo y otros Benefactores de la Iglesia* (Ciudad Trujillo, 1961); Gerardo Gallegos, *Trujillo en la Historia: Veinticinco Años en la Ruta de un Glorioso Destino* (Ciudad Trujillo, 1956); Ismael Herraiz, *Trujillo Dentro de la Historia* (Madrid, 1957); Juan Ulises García Bonnelly, *Las Obras Públicas en la Era de Trujillo* (Ciudad Trujillo, 1955); Pedro González Blanco, *Algunas Observaciones sobre la Política del Generalísimo Trujillo* (Madrid, 1936), and *La Era de Trujillo* (Ciudad Trujillo, 1955); César Herrera, *Las Finanzas de la República Dominicana* (Ciudad Trujillo, 1955); Rafael L. Trujillo, *Reajuste de la Deuda Externa* (Ciudad Trujillo, 1937 and 1959); Jesús María Troncoso, *La Política Económica de Trujillo* (Ciudad Trujillo, 1953); Pedro González Blanco, *Decadencia y liberación de la Economía Dominicana* (Mexico, 1946); Emilio Rodríguez Demorizi, *Trujillo y las Aspiraciones Dominicanas: Discurso en Santiago* (Ciudad Trujillo, 1957); Gilberto Sánchez Lustrino, *Trujillo. El Constructor de una Nacionalidad* (La Habana, 1938); R. Abelardo Nanita, *La Era de Trujillo* (Ciudad Trujillo, 1955); J. A. Osorio Lizarazo, *The Illumined Island* (Mexico, 1947); Armando Oscar Pacheco, *La Obra Educativa de Trujillo* (Ciudad Trujillo, 1955); Ernesto Vega Pagán, *Síntesis Histórica de la Guardia Nacional Dominicana* (Ciudad Trujillo, 1953), and *Historia de las Fuerzas Armadas* (Ciudad Trujillo, 1955); Ramón Marrero Aristy, *La República Dominicana: Origen y Destino del Pueblo Cristiano más Antiguo de América* (Ciudad Trujillo, 1958); Joaquín Balaguer, *El Pensamiento Vivo de Trujillo* (Ciudad Trujillo, 1955), and Rafael Leonidas Trujillo, *Fundamentos y Política de un Régimen* (Ciudad Trujillo, 1959). As a self-justification, Balaguer has recently published two other books on Trujillo and himself. They are *La Palabra Encadenada* (Mexico, 1975) and *Memorias de un Cortesano de la Era de Trujillo* (Santo Domingo, 1988). Three of the few reliable sources published under the Trujillo regime are Joaquín Marino Incháustegui, *La República Dominicana de Hoy* (Ciudad Trujillo, 1938); *21 Años de Estadísticas Dominicanas* (Ciudad Trujillo, 1957); and the *Anuario Estadístico de la República Dominicana* (Ciudad Trujillo, 1936-1956).

19. DEMOCRACY VS. NEO-TRUJILLOISM (1961-1978)

The transition from the Trujillo dictatorship to a pluralistic political system is studied by Howard J. Wiarda, Dictatorship, *Development and Disintegration: Politics and Social Changes in the Dominican Republic* (Ann Arbor, Michigan, 1975). Other works dealing with the same process as well as with the origins of the 1965 civil war and the subsequent U.S. military intervention are: Juan Bosch, *The Unfinished Experiment. Democracy in the Dominican Republic* (New York, 1964); and *Crisis de la Democracia de América en la República Dominicana* (Mexico, 1964); John Bartlow Martin, *Overtaken by Events. The Dominican Republic from the Fall of Trujillo to the Civil War* (Garden City, New Jersey, 1966); Tad Szulc, *Dominican Diary* (New York, 1966); Piero Gleijeses, *The Dominican Crisis. The 1965 Constitutionalist Revolt and the American Intervention* (Baltimore, 1978); Abraham Lowenthal, *The Dominican Intervention* (Cambridge, Mass., 1971), and "The United States and the Dominican Republic to 1965. Background to Intervention," *Caribbean Studies* 10 (July 1970), 2: 30-55; Jerome Slater, *Intervention and Negotiation. The United States and the Dominican Revolution* (New York, 1970); Eduardo Latorre, *Política Dominicana Contemporánea* (Santo Domingo, 1975); José A. Moreno, *Barrios in Arms* (Pittsburgh, 1970); Fidelio Despradel, *Manolo Tavares en su Justa Perspectiva Histórica* (Santo Domingo, 1983); Toni Raful, *Movimiento 14 de Junio. Historia y Documentos* (Santo Domingo, 1983); Danilo Brugal Alfau, *Tragedia en Santo Domingo* (Santo Domingo, 1966); John Carey (ed.), *The Dominican Republic Crisis 1965. Background Paper and Proceedings of the Ninth Hammarskjöld Forum* (New York, 1967); Eugenio Chang Rodríguez, *The Lingering Crisis. A Case Study of the Dominican Republic* (New York, 1969); Margarita Cordero, *Mujeres de Abril* (Santo Domingo, 1985); Abraham F. Lowenthal, "The United States and the Dominican Republic to 1965: Background to Intervention," *Caribean Studies*, 10 (July 1970), 2: 30-55; José Israel Cuello and Narciso Isa Conde, "Revolutionary Struggle in the Dominican Republic and its Lessons," *World Marxist Review* 8 (December 1965), 12: 71-81, and "Part II," *World Marxist Review* 9 (January 1966), 1: 53-56; Center for Strategic Studies, Georgetown University, *Dominican Action - 1965. Intervention or Cooperation?* (Washington, D.C., 1966); Theodore Draper,

The Dominican Revolt. A Case Study in American Policy (New York, 1968); William J. Fulbright, "The Situation in the Dominican Republic," *Congressional Record* 3 (September 15, 1965): 23, 855-861; Víctor Grimaldi, *El Diario Secreto de la Intervención Americana de 1965* (Santo Domingo, 1985); Dan Kurzman, *Santo Domingo. The Revolt of the Damned* (New York, 1965); Carlos Newton, *Santo Domingo. La Guerra de América Latina* (Buenos Aires, 1965); Luis Homero Lajara Burgos, *¿Por Qué se Produjo la Revolución del 24 de Abril del Año 1965?* (Santo Domingo, 1987); Leslie F. Manigat, "La Crise Dominicaine," *Révue Française de Science Politique* 15 (December 1965), 6: 1170-87; Thomas C. Mann, "The Dominican Crisis: Correcting some Misconceptions," *Department of State Bulletin* 53 (November 8, 1965), 1376: 730-738; Marcel Niedergang, *La Révolution de Saint-Domingo* (Paris, 1966); Howard Wiarda, "The United States and the Dominican Republic: Intervention, Dependency, and Tyrannicide," *Journal of InterAmerican Studies* 22 (May 1980), 2: 247-260; and Charles H. Weston, Jr., *The Failure of the Democratic Left in the Dominican Republic: A Case Study of the Overthrow of the Juan Bosch Government*. Milwaukee: The University of Wisconsin. Center for Latin America. Discussion Paper No. 65, June 1, 1975. Other recents accounts are Bruce Palmer, *Intervention in the Caribbean. The Dominican Crisis of 1965* (Lexington, KY, 1989), by the U.S. general commander of the intervention army in 1965; Bernardo Vega, *Kennedy y Bosch*, (Santo Domingo, 1993); Miguel Guerrero, *El Golpe de Estado: Historia del Derrocamiento de Juan Bosch* (Santo Domingo, 1993); *Enero de 1962: El Despertar Dominicano* (Santo Domingo, 1988); and José Rafael Lantigua, *La Conjura del Tiempo. Memorias del Hombre Dominicano* (Santo Domingo, 1994).

On Balaguer's 12-year regime, the list of books and scholarly articles is very short. A political critique is José Israel Cuello, *Siete Años de Reformismo* (Santo Domingo, 1973). Scholarly works include Pope Atkins, *Arms and Politics in the Dominican Republic* (Boulder, Colorado, 1981); Roberto Cassá, *Los Doce Años* (Santo Domingo, 1978); Wilfredo Lozano, *El Reformismo Dependiente* (Santo Domingo, 1985); Howard J. Wiarda, *The Dominican Republic. A Nation in Transition* (New York, 1969); Howard J. Wiarda and Michael Kryzanek, *The Dominican Republic. A Caribbean Crucible* (Boulder, Colorado, 1982). See also the article by the same authors, "Dominican Dictatorship Revisited: The Caudillo Tradition and the Regimes of Trujillo and Balaguer," *Revista Interamericana* (7 (1977), 3: 417-435. Other articles are James Petras, "The Dominican Republic: Revolution and Restoration, *New World Quarterly* 3 (1967), 4: 1-11; Frank Moya Pons, "Quid Pro Quo: Dominican-American Economic Relations 1966-1974." *SAIS Review* 19 (January 1975), 1: 3-19; Michael Kryzanek, "Diversion, Subversion and Repression: The Strategies of Anti-opposition Politics in Balaguer's Dominican Republic," *Caribbean Studies* 17 (Apr-Jul 1977), 1-2: 83-104; "Political Party Decline and the Failure of Liberal Democracy: The PRD in Dominican Politics," *Journal of Latin American Studies* 9 (May 1977), 1: 115-143; "The 1978 Election in the Dominican Republic: Opposition Politics, Intervention and the Carter Administration," *Caribbean Studies* 19 (Apr-Jul 1979), 1-2: 51-74; Rosario Espinal, *Torn Between Authoritarianism and Crisis-Prone Democracy: The Dominican Labor Movement*, Kellog Working Paper #116, University of Notre Dame (December 1988); and José A. Moreno, "Intervention and Economic Penetration: The Case of the Dominican Republic," *Summation* 5 (Summer-Fall 1975), 1-2: 65-85, also published as No. 13 of the Occassional Papers of the Center for Latin American Studies of the University of Pittsburgh (Jan 1976). On the government-sponsored terrorism, see *La Banda. An Episode of Terror* (Toronto, 1972). On Caamaño's failed guerrilla expedition, see Hamlet Hermann, *Caracoles: La Guerrilla de Caamaño* (Santo Domingo, 1993). Economic policies and the process of import substitution industrialization have been studied by Frank Moya Pons, *Empresarios en Conflicto: Políticas de Industrialización y Sustitución de Importaciones en la República Dominicana* (Santo Domingo, 1992). On the evolution of banking and the financial sector, see also Frank Moya Pons, *Pioneros de la Banca en la República Dominicana. Una Historia Institucional del Banco Popular Dominicano y del Grupo Financiero Popular* (Santo Domingo, 1989).

20. SOCIAL-DEMOCRATS IN POWER (1978-1986)

On the administrations of Antonio Guzmán and Salvador Jorge Blanco, scholarly publications are very scarce.[1] Some useful titles are Claudio Vedovato, *Politics, Foreign Trade, and Economic Development:*

A Study of the Dominican Republic (New York, 1986); Miguel Ceara Hatton, *Tendencias Estructurales de la Economía Dominicana 1968-1983* (Santo Domingo, 1985), and Eduardo J. Tejera, *Diagnóstico de la Economía Dominicana, 1979-1981* (Santo Domingo, 1981); Bernardo Vega, *La Coyuntura Económica Dominicana, 1980-1981* (Santo Domingo, 1981), and *Crisis del Sector Externo y Política Cambiaria* (Santo Domingo, 1987); Eddy Enrique Leyba, *El Sector Privado y la Economía Dominicana* (Santo Domingo, 1985); Hugo Guiliani Cury, *Políticas de Estabilización y Discursos* (Santo Domingo, 1985); and Milton Messina, *Memorias del Ajuste de una Economía en Crisis* (Santo Domingo, 1988).

Frank Moya Pons has edited a series of 32 volumes containing 150 papers discussing the most important political, economic, and social issues between 1981 and 1988. The titles are: *Los Problemas del Sector Externo en la República Dominicana* (Santo Domingo, 1982); *Implicaciones de la Nueva Política Económica.* (Santo Domingo, 1982); *Los Grandes Problemas Nacionales* (Santo Domingo, 1982); *Los Déficit del Sector Público en la República Dominicana* (Santo Domingo, 1982); *El Régimen de Incentivos en la República Dominicana* (Santo Domingo, 1983); *La Situación Cambiaria en la República Dominicana* (Santo Domingo, 1984); *Causas y Manejo de la Crisis Económica Dominicana* (Santo Domingo, 1986); *Los Problemas de la Inflación en la República Dominicana.* (Santo Domingo, 1986); *La Situación y los Problemas del Sistema Financiero Nacional* (Santo Domingo, 1986), *Posibilidades de Privatización Económica en la República Dominicana* (Santo Domingo, 1987); *El Impacto Económico del Gasto Público en la República Dominicana* (Santo Domingo, 1988). This series also include *Los Problemas de la Institucionalización y Preservación de la Democracia en la República Dominicana* (Santo Domingo, 1982); *Los Problemas del Sector Rural en la República Dominicana* (Santo Domingo, 1982); *La Situación Laboral en la República Dominicana* (Santo Domingo, 1983); *Reformas a la Constitución* (Santo Domingo, 1983); *Prensa y Política en la República Dominicana* (Santo Domingo, 1984); *Población y Pobreza en la República Dominicana* (Santo Domingo, 1984); *Anomalías y Contradicciones de la Legislación Económica Dominicana* (Santo Domingo, 1984); *Presente y Futuro de la Reforma Agraria en la República Dominicana* (Santo Domingo, 1985); *Situación y Perspectivas de la Educación en la República Dominicana* (Santo Domingo, 1985); *Situación de la Vivienda en la República Dominicana* (Santo Domingo, 1985); *Impacto Económico del Turismo en la República Dominicana*. (Santo Domingo, 1986); *Condiciones Socioeconómicas de la Mujer Trabajadora en la República Dominicana* (Santo Domingo, 1986); and *El Régimen de Partidos y el Sistema Electoral en la República Dominicana* (Santo Domingo, 1986).

21. BALAGUER'S RETURN (1986-1990)

The last administration of Joaquín Balaguer is too recent to have elicited much literature. Thus, the reader should look into current publications like magazines and newspapers. Some useful articles have been published in yearbooks and quarterly reports. See, for example, the section "The Dominican Republic," published in the *Latin American and Caribbean Contemporary Record* (New York, 1983-1990). See also The Economist Intelligence Unit, *Country Report, Cuba, Dominican Republic, Haiti, Puerto Rico* (London, 1986-1990). The Dominican newspapers *Listín Diario, El Caribe, Hoy, Ultima Hora, El Siglo, El Nuevo Diario, La Información, El Nacional, La Noticia,* and *El Sol* are important sources of political and economic news which contain abundant material. Three essential volumes are Andrés Dauhajre hijo (ed.), *Sábado Económico, Números 1-52* (Santo Domingo, 1989), and *Sábado Económico, Números 53-104* (Santo Domingo, 1990); and *Sábado Económico, Números 105-157* (Santo Domingo, 1991). These three books contain a series of important papers published in a special weekly section of *Listín Diario*. James Ferguson, *Dominican Republic. Beyond the Lighthouse,* (London, 1992) is a recent introduction to the Dominican Republic which describes the country's situation under Balaguer's rule.

GENERAL WORKS

In addition to the sources listed for each of the chapters of this book, there are other books which cover wider periods and should be mentioned separately. Recent general histories of the country include Frank Moya Pons, *Manual de Historia Dominicana* (Santiago, 1977), updated in 1992 for its ninth edition; and *Historia Colonial de Santo Domingo* (Santiago, 1973); Jacinto Gimbernard, *Historia de Santo Domingo*, (Santo Domingo, 1978); Ian Bell, *The Dominican Republic* (Boulder, Colorado, 1981); Roberto Cassá, *Historia Económica y Social de la República Dominicana* (Santo Domingo, 1989); Valentina Peguero and Danilo de los Santos, *Visión General de la Historia Dominicana* (Santiago, 1978); Juan Bosch, *Composición Social Dominicana* (Santo Domingo 1970); Franklin Franco, *Historia del Pueblo Dominicano* (Santo Domingo 1992); Juan Francisco García, *Manual de Historia Crítica Dominicana* (Santo Domingo, 1991); Juan Isidro Jiménez Grullón, *La República Dominicana: Una Ficción* (Santo Domingo, 1966); and Ramón Marrero Aristi, *La República Dominicana: Origen del Pueblo Cristiano Más Antiguo de América* (Ciudad Trujillo, 1957-58). The quality of these works varies widely.

Other general introductions are the U.S. Government Area Handbook Series, *Dominican Republic and Haiti: Country Studies* (Washington, D. C., 1991); Howard Wiarda and Michael Kryzanek, *The Dominican Republic. A Caribbean Crucible* (Boulder, Colorado, 1982); Howard Wiarda, *The Dominican Republic. A Nation in Transition* (New York, 1968); Robert Weyl (ed.), *The Dominican Republic. A Country Study* (Washington, D. C., 1973); Julio G. Campillo, *Historia Electoral Dominicana 1848-1986.* (Santo Domingo, 1986); and Wenceslao Vega, *Historia del Derecho Dominicano* (Santo Domingo, 1994). Other titles dealing with contemporary issues are: Martin F. Murphy, *Dominican Sugar Plantations: Production and Foreign Labor Integration* (New York, 1991); Jan Knippers Black, *The Dominican Republic. Politics and Development in An Unsovereign State* (London, 1986); Michael J. Kryzanek, *The Politics of External Influence in the Dominican Republic* (New York, 1988); Roger Plant, *Sugar and Modern Slavery. A Tale of Two Countries* (London, 1987); and William Louis Wipfler, *The Churches of the Dominican Republic in the Light of History. A Study of the Root Causes of Current Problems* (Cuernavaca, 1967). A recent general bibliography of the Dominican Republic which includes numerous historical works is Kai P. Schoenhals, *Dominican Republic* (Oxford, 1990).

Two periodical publications stand out as very useful tools for the serious researcher. They are the *Boletín del Archivo General de la Nación*; and *Clío*. The latter is the journal of the Academia Dominicana de la

Historia. Both contain a wealth of documents and scholarly articles written by well known traditional historians. Several journals specializing in the social sciences occasionally publish historical articles based on original research. These are: *Estudios Sociales,* published by the Centro de Investigación y Acción Social de la Compañía de Jesús; *Eme-Eme Estudios Dominicanos,* published by the Centro de Estudios Dominicanos of the Universidad Católica Madre y Maestra; *Ciencia y Sociedad* published by the Instituto Tecnológico de Santo Domingo; *Ciencia,* published by Departamento de Investigaciones of the Universidad Autónoma de Santo Domingo; *Aula,* published by the Universidad Nacional Pedro Henríquez Ureña; *Investigación y Ciencia,* published by the Universidad Apec; and *Ecos,* published by the Instituto de Historia of the Universidad Autónoma de Santo Domingo. A historical dictionary is Rufino Martínez, *Diccionario Biográfico-Histórico, 1821-1930* (Santo Domingo, 1971).

Index